True Faith and Allegiance

True Faith and Allegiance

IMMIGRATION AND AMERICAN CIVIC NATIONALISM

Noah Pickus

PRINCETON UNIVERSITY PRESS

PRINCETON AND OXFORD

Copyright © 2005 by Princeton University Press
Published by Princeton University Press, 41 William Street, Princeton, New Jersey 08540
In the United Kingdom: Princeton University Press, 3 Market Place, Woodstock, Oxfordshire
OX20 1SY

Library of Congress Cataloging-in-Publication Data

Pickus, Noah M. Jedidiah, date.
True faith and allegiance : immigration and American civic nationalism / Noah Pickus.
    p.   cm.
Includes bibliographical references and index.
ISBN-13: 978-0-691-12172-7 (acid-free paper)
ISBN-10: 0-691-12172-9 (acid-free paper)
    1. Citizenship—United States—History.   2. United States—Emigration and
immigration—History.   3. Americanization—History.   I. Title.

JK1759.P44 2005
323.6'0973—dc22   2004059989

British Library Cataloging-in-Publication Data is available

This book has been composed in Minion Typeface
Printed on acid-free paper.
pup.princeton.edu

Printed in the United States of America

10   9   8   7   6   5   4   3   2   1

For my parents, Robert and Sara Pickus, and
for Trudi, Micah, and Mira

Contents

Preface

In June 2000, when this book was midway through its gestation, I participated in an immigration conference at Cantigny, Colonel Robert McCormick's former estate near Chicago. McCormick, the editor and publisher of the *Chicago Tribune* for many years, was an officer in World War I and an ardent proponent in the 1930s and 1940s of the isolationist cause America First. His estate includes a museum that highlights the carnage of the Great War and honors the patriotic courage of those who fought in it. That war also spurred a nationwide effort to "Americanize" immigrants and to pass legislation that discriminated against new arrivals from southern and eastern Europe. This potent reminder of the relation between immigration and nationalism made Cantigny the appropriate setting for the conference, "Citizenship in Conflict in the 21st Century." That relation, specifically the difficult dialectic between maintaining the bonds of nationhood and allowing them to be flexible enough to include newcomers, constitutes the essence of this book. In the pages that follow I advance three substantial claims about the incorporation of immigrants, the nature of American nationalism, and the primacy of politics over economics and culture in forging citizenship policy for the twenty-first century.

First, for some time now the United States has neglected the rituals of allegiance and strategies of incorporation that turn immigrants into citizens and full members of the American nation. Advocates instead wage pitched battles over partisan proposals that fail to meet the needs of immigrants or citizens. This policy of neglect emerged in the second half of the twentieth century as Americans became increasingly unsure of the meaning of their national identity and the value of U.S citizenship. The left promoted global rights and group representation and demanded special treatment for immigrants rather than casting them as future citizens and members of the American people. The right staked the future of the United States on a distinct definition of American nationhood (though proponents disagreed as to its cultural or civic character) and argued that all that was necessary for qualified immigrants to join the mainstream was to embrace that definition. Since the terrorist attacks of September 11, 2001, the global conflict over terrorism and religious fundamentalism has heightened these differences between left and right, but it has not produced a more serious effort to attend to both the profound and the programmatic dimensions of integrating newcomers.

Second, these views of rights, representation, and nationhood have obscured a more complex and, in my view, constructive tradition of citizenship that offers a better approach to the incorporation of immigrants. This tradition of what I call civic nationalism held sway at the Founding and in the Progressive Era, and I concentrate on these periods in this book. From James Madison to Teddy Roosevelt, proponents of civic nationalism sought to combine liberal principles and communal solidarity, to meld a rational commitment to a common creed and a reverential attachment to the bonds of nationhood. In balancing reason and reverence, civic nationalism allowed violations of America's political principles. But in the midst of fierce conflicts over belief and belonging it more often succeeded in strengthening a common citizenship and expanding the definition of who belonged to the American nation. Today, a renewed civic nationalism offers the best chance to bolster institutional capacities for incorporating immigrants in ways that foster a shared sense of peoplehood and that generate attachment to common political principles. This civic nationalism can vigorously combat more exclusionary claims of communal solidarity while protecting individual rights and liberties.

Third, I propose that such a civic nationalism is uniquely suited to manage this difficult feat because of its pragmatic sensibility. In contrast to the schemes of proponents further to the left and the right who proffer fixed and often simplistic notions of creed or culture, civic nationalism points to the constant political work that must be done to meld ideals and allegiance. It emphasizes the need to account for actual practice in spurring attachment and engagement, rather than relying only on core values, universal rights, cultural cohesion, or racial identity. A contemporary civic nationalism seeks to bridge the gap between immigrants' needs and interests, on the one hand, and the values, rituals, and practices of American life, on the other. It looks for ways to press home the vital link between the experiences of immigrant families and communities and the principles and functions of American public institutions. This supple and versatile civic nationalism is best able to confront the challenges posed by immigration, by declining civic commitment among citizens, and by the twin dangers of a too assertive or too timid nation.

In the long period it has taken me to disentangle the complex and fraught relations between immigration and nationalism I sometimes forgot why I began in the first place. Family, friends, and colleagues spurred me to complete the task, and I owe them enormous debts of gratitude. A colleague who became a friend, Peter Skerry, pressed me to think boldly and clearly. His unsparing criticism sharpened my analysis, and his belief in my work bolstered my spirits. Suzanne Shanahan's combination of original thinking and common sense helped me overcome innumerable obstacles. Yossi Shain's unwavering support was critical to finishing the first draft of this book, and Amitai Etzioni's interest and engagement spurred its completion. I have depended as well on the advice and counsel of friends around the world, from Berkeley to Cape Town to Durham, especially Susan Bailey, Jonathan Klaaren, Avi Bernstein, Mark Grinstaff, Fabienne Meyers, Max Wallace, and Carol Tadeusik.

Although I am critical of the direction taken by many advocates for immigration, I have learned a great deal from the experience, commitment, and thinking of the best among them. At various junctures, I have been pressed to distinguish between real and illusory problems by Rick Swartz, founder of the National Immigration Forum; Frank Sharry, president of the National Immigration Forum; and Juan Jose Guttierez, director of the One Stop Immigration Center in Los Angeles. I especially learned from Gary Rubin, a leading voice at the New York Association for New Americans in the mid-1990s. His death in 2003 robbed us of a passionate advocate for immigrants and for America. I did not know Gary well, but our conversations and his letters and emails served as a powerful reminder not to let lofty notions of citizenship impose undue hardships on our most vulnerable populations.

A number of different institutions have been my home over the course of writing this book. At Princeton, Jennifer Hochschild was an ideal reader whose careful criticisms improved every draft and whose interest in linking American political thought and practice helped spur my own. Will Harris set a demanding intellectual agenda that pressed me to think creatively about the meaning of citizenship in a constitutional order. Walter Murphy gave shape and direction to my work and offered sage advice. John DiIulio Jr., introduced me to the study of American politics and the mysteries of teaching about it. Other faculty provided a wide-ranging education in American political thought; I am particularly appreciative of Alan Ryan for his seminar on the subject.

At Duke I have been fortunate to be surrounded by generous colleagues and a remarkable set of graduate students. Tom Merrill made significant contributions to the chapters on the Founding and the early Republic. His research and analysis convinced me to expand my treatment of this period and, especially, to think more deeply about the origins and implications of the initial exclusion of blacks from U.S. citizenship. Scott Kirkhuff informed my understanding of the Progressive Era and its leading thinkers. Troy Dostert helped shape my understanding of citizenship itself and the combination of history and theory that is required to account for the contentiousness that surrounds debates over it. On immigration and citizenship at the end of the twentieth century, I benefitted significantly from the contributions of John Griffin, Johnnie Goldfinger, and Elizabeth Zechmeister.

The time I spent teaching in the Political Science Department at Middlebury College was also valuable to me, and I am grateful for the hospitality and friendship I encountered there, especially from Russ and Cilla Leng and David and Jean Rosenberg. It was a special pleasure to work with Murray Dry, whose commitment to providing a truly liberal education I found invigorating. My debt also extends to Wesleyan University, and especially the tutors in the College of Social Studies. The college is a remarkable institution, and to Rich Adelstein and his fellow teachers I owe my introduction to disciplined academic study.

The subject of immigration cannot be contained in any single field. It requires insights from a range of disciplines including law, sociology, history, public policy, and political theory. Writers and scholars from these disciplines have graciously helped me understand the scope of my project. For helpful readings, I am grateful to Linda Bosniak, Miriam Feldblum, David Jacobson, Robert Lieberman, Stanley Renshon, Jim Sleeper, and Peter Spiro. I learned a lot from conversations with Chuck Bahmueller, Joseph Carens, Rom Coles, Paul Donnelly, Toby Ewing, Michael Fix, John Fonte, Lawrence Fuchs, Gary Gerstle, Ed Grant, Ruth Grant, Gary Jacobsohn, Tamar Jacoby, Robert Keohane, Charles Kesler, Desmond King, Elizabeth Kiss, Susan Martin, John Miller, Martin Schain, Peter Schuck, Rogers Smith, Dan Tichenor, and K. Scott Wong.

At the Immigration and Naturalization Service and the Bureau of Citizenship and Immigration Services, David Rosenberg, Gerry Ratliff, David Howell, and Marian Smith have tutored me in the nuances of policy implementation. Under difficult circumstances they have sought to improve this country's citizenship practices. I am grateful to Suzanne Harris, Tab Lewis, and Aloha South at the National Archives and to Ann Miller at Duke's Perkins Library for helping me penetrate the thickets of bureaucratic history.

Over the course of this project I have benefitted from the experience and expertise of two extraordinary editors: Maura High and Lauren Osborne. Their sharp pencils and keen eyes have made this book more manageable and more interesting. Chuck Myers at Princeton University Press remained committed to this project even when I had to step away from it for a time, and he provided sound advice throughout the process of publication.

For financial support, I am especially appreciative of the H. B. Earhart Foundation, as well as Betsy Shirley and the Jockey Hollow Foundation, the Kathleen Price Bryan Family Fund, and the North American Studies Program at Duke University.

Earlier versions of some of the material in this book have appeared elsewhere including parts of chapter 1 ("'Hearken Not to the Unnatural Voice': Publius and the Artifice of Attachment," in *Diversity and Citizenship: Rediscovering American Nationhood*, ed. Gary J. Jacobsohn and Susan Dunn [Rowman and Littlefield, 1996]); chapter 7 ("Does Immigration Threaten Democracy? Rights, Restriction, and the Meaning of Membership," in *Democracy: The Challenges Ahead*, ed. Yossi Shain and Aharon Klieman [St. Martin's Press, 1997], and "To Make Natural: Creating Citizens for the Twenty-First Century," *Immigration and Citizenship in the 21st Century*, ed. Noah Pickus [Rowman and Littlefield, 1998]); chapter 8 ("Which America? Nationalism among the Nationalists," in *One America? Leadership, National Identity, and the Dilemmas of Diversity*, ed. Stanley Renshon [Georgetown University Press, 2001], and "Citizenship and Commitment," *The Responsive Community* 11, no. 3 [summer 2001]: 93–95; and the epilogue (*Diversity within Unity: A Communitarian Position Paper* [The Communitarian Network, 2001]).

Like most books on immigration, this one has personal has well as intellectual roots. These roots have less to do with the fact of being a grandchild of immigrants—I never knew my grandparents and so can only honor their sacrifice at a distance—and more to do with my parents' engagement with American public life. My father, Robert Pickus, participated in the conference at Cantigny, and it has been one of my deepest pleasures to join forces with him when we agreed and to argue over our differences when we did not. Although this is not the book he would have written, it reflects much of what he taught me about the value of America, the necessity of civil society, and the role both can play in managing the perennial tension between universalism and particularity. The wellsprings of my interest in the tensions between belief and belonging are also found in the example of my mother, Sara Pickus. In the 1950s, she lost her job teaching in the Chicago public schools because she refused on principle to sign a loyalty oath. Her willingness to put conscience over country has served as a constant reminder that nations can ask too much of their citizens and that oaths of allegiance can serve base as well as virtuous purposes. In writing this book, my parents and my brother, Josh Pickus, offered unstinting support, helpful criticism, and common sense. My brother, in particular, wisely counseled that prudence is a virtue only in moderation.

To my wife, Trudi Abel, I owe my deepest experience of the bonds of belonging and of the sacrifices that all true unions require. She has been my steadfast partner on this and many other projects. Our children, Micah and Mira, learned to read while I worked on this book, and their joyfulness and forbearance have made its completion possible. Dad's finally done. Let's go play.

Introduction

IN THE United States of America, naturalizing citizens must declare an oath of "true faith and allegiance" to the Constitution.[1] What does this oath mean? If it is a blanket promise to obey the law then it may exclude people who would make excellent American citizens—those who have deep moral convictions about right and wrong and the limits of legitimate political authority. Perhaps this oath merely requires a willingness to abide by a new political system, although the invocation of faith and allegiance seems to suggest something deeper, a change in one's sense of self and belonging akin to religious conversion.[2] Native-born citizens are not required to profess their allegiance—what, then, must newcomers give up in order to abide by their declaration of "true faith"?[3] What does it mean to become an American?

These questions have come to the fore with great force since the events of September 11, 2001, but they had already generated increased attention and concern over a decade before. Some observers argued that the notion of immigrants becoming citizens of an American nation was outdated and should be replaced by an emphasis on group representation, cultural rights, and membership in multiple political communities. In their view, the United States was on the verge of developing new forms of citizenship and community, ones that could successfully weave together plural allegiances from the local to the universal. Others contended that these new forms of transnational and multicultural citizenship threatened basic principles of American democracy. They worried that the shared national identity that makes both self-governance and the protection of rights possible would erode if these changes came to pass.

These arguments took place in the context of an increasingly fragile sense of public commitment to the commonweal and the weakening of institutional capacities for incorporating newcomers. A slew of changes including the dislocation caused by global markets, the rise of a rights-oriented culture, the dissolution of common military service, and the attenuation of local government created greater uncertainty as to whether new arrivals and American citizens would regard one another as equals bearing mutual obligations. The decline of traditional civic associations made "bowling alone" a national metaphor for the loss of social bonds and institutional sinews that made a diverse democracy function.

Changes in immigration patterns also raised thorny questions about the meaning of citizenship and national identity in the United States. Traditional models of migration assume migrants settle in one place and take on a new, singular political identity. But a more closely interconnected world means that links between countries are no longer severed and can even be strengthened by migration. As one indication of this change, dual citizenship is increasingly prevalent in the United States. "At a time when so much of the American public is disengaged from civic life," muses the sociologist Alejandro Portes, "what does it mean to have so many citizens who are, in a very real sense, neither here nor there?"[4] A different but equally important set of issues was raised after September 11 by the growing cultural conflict between Islam and the West, political friction in the United States among Muslim, Arab, and other Americans, and the link between immigration and terrorism—not, as the political scientist Robert Leiken notes, "because all immigrants are terrorists but because all, or nearly all, terrorists in the West have been immigrants."[5] Immigration policy, previously focused on Latin America and the Caribbean, now had to wrestle with the racial profiling of Arabs, the mandatory registration of men from Muslim countries, and the broader relation between assimilation and national security in the case of migrants from the Middle East.

The incorporation of new or previously excluded groups into American life and politics is a place where conflicts over citizenship and nationhood erupt with special ferocity. In this book, I examine those conflicts in one key aspect of the process by which immigrants become part of the United States: naturalization. Over the last half-century few paid attention to naturalization's role in the creation of new citizens, though recently concerns have been raised in Congress and in many regions of the country over the integrity of the naturalization process and the value of American citizenship.[6] (These concerns have contributed to a major effort to revise the naturalization examination by the federal government.) But naturalization has been a critical focus at other times in U.S. history, and understanding how concerns over naturalization played out in those periods illuminates deeper conflicts over belief and belonging then and today. Naturalization policy is integrally linked to *immigrant* policy—policies that regulate immigrants who reside in the United States. The distinction between citizens and aliens, dual citizenship, and broader forms of assimilation and incorporation are all aspects of immigrant policy, and I analyze naturalization in relation to them. Naturalization is a particularly good primary focus because it so explicitly invokes the formative aspects of citizenship. It suggests the rather odd, if not oxymoronic, notion that a person can be "made natural." What this phrase means (now and in the past) opens into the broader question of what it means to be and to become an American.

Throughout U.S. history Americans have given different answers to those questions. In 1915, President Woodrow Wilson told a group of newly naturalized citizens in Philadelphia that they had just sworn allegiance "to no one," only to "a great ideal, to a great body of principles, to a great hope of the human race."[7] Six years later, a district court in the state of Washington expressed a far more restrictive view. Not every immigrant was capable of becoming an American. Asians, one judge concluded, were properly excluded from citizenship because the "yellow or brown racial color is the hallmark of Oriental despotisms," and the subjects of these despotisms "were not fitted and suited to make for the success of a republican form of Government."[8]

The views of Wilson and the district judge represent two traditions in the history of American citizenship. In the inclusive view, national identity is defined by consent to a set of shared principles—the "American Creed." This civic tradition forms the basis for rights and political structures that advance personal freedom, protect minority groups, and encourage civic involvement. America, in this view, is the first truly "universal nation" because immigrants from the entire world have become citizens by accepting universal principles of individual liberty, equal opportunity, democracy, and constitutionalism. Proponents of this civic tradition interpret laws and policies that exclude or coerce newcomers as running contrary to a basically welcoming American citizenship. They reject the equation of American citizenship with any single cultural heritage. "American symbols and ceremonies are culturally anonymous," writes the political philosopher Michael Walzer, "invented rather than inherited, voluntaristic in style, narrowly political in content: the flag, the Pledge, the Fourth, the Constitution."[9]

This traditional interpretation of American citizenship has been countered in recent years by one that focuses on a racial ideology of nationalism. This latter view sees a strong illiberal trend operating from the beginning, in which for most of U.S. history Americans have failed to adhere to universal principles. Rather than an heroic struggle to put its principles into practice, American history is the story of discrimination against minorities. In fact, these commentators observe, citizenship has always had a differential status based on one's race or ethnicity. This revisionist approach to citizenship has called attention not only to restrictionist immigration policies based on race but to the laws governing American citizenship itself. Revisionists especially emphasize the crucial role played by the first naturalization act of 1790, which limited citizenship to "free white persons" and which is, in their view, an unequivocally white supremacist law. "The law's wording denotes an unconflicted view of the presumed character and unambiguous boundaries of whiteness," declares the historian Matthew Frye Jacobson.[10]

This view has challenged the story of a gradually unfolding and expanding American citizenship. The free white clause was not abolished until 1952, and it had significant long-term consequences in determining the subordinate status of minority groups and in generating crises in American citizenship. Nonetheless, this perspective is also fundamentally misleading. Its proponents are wrong to say that restrictive definitions of nationhood have predominated. Instead, American definitions of citizenship have blended civic principles and national belonging. The meaning of America has not been static or uncontested. Treating it as if it has been, notes the historian David Hollinger, has especially deflected energy "from the analysis of what kinds of nationalism have actually existed and what kinds are now defensible in what contexts."[11] In America, nationalism has changed its shape depending on who is invoking it and for what reasons.

Some political leaders have seen a communal sense of belonging derived from a specific cultural, racial, ethnic, or religious background: to be American is to possess one or more of these particular characteristics. This sense of belonging is not treated as an unthinking or irrational allegiance or quality; it is backed by scientific claims and enjoys widespread support as an intellectually respectable position.[12] Other supporters of the notion that the nation is a community have emphasized the importance of scale. Democratic rule, they contend, is difficult to maintain when individuals become more distant from one another, unable to maintain the ties of social solidarity that come from shared experience and interaction. Hence, characteristics like language and custom, as well as, to varying degrees, ethnicity and religion, are necessary.[13] A third variant of the nation-as-community approach has urged the creation of a common sensibility rather than depending on it as natural and preexisting. This approach regards political, legal, and educational institutions, as well as language and literature, as essential in forging a sense of communal obligation and responsibility. It often includes civic education and patriotic ceremonies, a narrative stressing a shared history and experience, and an emphasis on the sacrifices made to achieve the community's present state. This approach claims not that the nation is an organic community but that it has progressively become one.[14]

These various definitions of the national community have had both exclusionary and inclusionary consequences. Appeals to ascriptive categories of belonging have served diametrically opposed positions, such as when defenders of slavery appealed to the "natural order of things" and critics invoked God's punishment for slavery. At times, national identity has been inclusionary, while more liberal, rights-oriented persuasions have been exclusionary. In the eighteenth century, for example, the Federalists secured individual rights partly by rooting a new national identity in assertions of shared blood and religious mission, while Republicans, who upheld religious freedom and more open immigration, justified slavery. In the post–Civil War era, a strong sense of national identity had both inclusionary and exclusionary consequences: Republicans advocated using national power to safeguard former slaves, but they also supported using severe measures against Indians and Chinese immigrants.[15] In the twentieth century, defenders of national authority and communal identity countered exclusionary appeals to democratic principles of states' rights and local control, as well as to the primacy of smaller, homogeneous identities. Nationalist movements to limit corporate power, provide economic security, and protect civil rights recast and broadened the definition of full membership in the American community.[16]

This complex history of inclusion and exclusion poses a difficult dilemma for political leaders: how to meld the national and civic dimensions of citizenship in ways that honor rather than undermine the moral commitments and political dynamics that underlie each. Nationalism, which is commonly construed as an emotional or organic bond, sits uneasily with civic-mindedness, which implies rational commitment to a common creed based on abstract ideals and values. Nationalism values tradition, inherited opinion, and a set of obligations that flow from sharing a distinctive history and culture. By contrast, the civic tradition favors individual liberty, critical judgment, and chosen obligations. Where nationalism prizes reverence, the civic tradition treasures reason. Where nationalism venerates peoplehood, the civic tradition cherishes principles. "If the United States strives to rest American citizenship solely on adherence to liberal principles, as many liberal theorists and policy analysts still advocate, it may fail to respond to the desires, and indeed, moral claims for community solidarity that have always been potent in American politics," observes the political theorist Rogers Smith. "Yet if America departs from liberal principles and instead takes its bearing from its more communitarian traditions, it risks encouraging impulses that have led to some of the nation's ugliest abuses."[17]

Finding ways to combine liberal principles and communal solidarity is paramount today when reason and reverence are regarded as enemies and the civic and national dimensions of citizenship are pitted against each other, a division especially apparent in contemporary debates over immigration and citizenship. Advocates in these debates appeal to civic ideals or national belonging in ways that avoid rather than address the perennial tensions between the two. They traffic in one-dimensional notions of culture or creed: on the left, nationalism is vilified and democratic civic principles are reduced to immigrant and minority rights; on the right, nationalism is heralded and debate over civic ideals is circumscribed. These one-dimensional views have marginalized more complex and constructive traditions of dealing with the relation between culture and creed, especially the tradition of civic nationalism. That tradition has taken different and often radically divergent forms and gone by different names. Despite these differences, its proponents shared the conviction that America's civic principles, its commitment to individual rights and democratic deliberation, could best be realized if they were rooted in a robust sense of national identity. Civic nationalists in our history—especially James Madison and John Marshall at the Founding and Theodore Roosevelt and Randolph Bourne in the Progressive Era—regarded America as a remarkable nation and were deeply attached to its history, institutions, and people. They defended that nation against the cultural, political, and economic forces they believed threatened to undermine its great promise. At the same time, these leading figures aimed to treat the nation as an instrument in the service of individual liberty and communal self-governance, not as an object in itself. In their mind, civic principles and American nationalism reinforced each other.

Civic nationalism has, nonetheless, been fraught with tensions. Its proponents have had to negotiate continually between the particularistic demands of communal solidarity and the universalistic thrust of individual freedom. They have not always found a workable balance between the two. At times, the nationalist dimension has been unable to forestall more repressive measures; at other times, it has facilitated or tolerated significant violations of America's civic principles. For its part, the civic dimension has struggled to secure a common identity based on abstract principles, and its efforts to establish loyalty have also sometimes become coercive and exclusionary. These are significant drawbacks and I explore them in this book. I probe the complexities of the civic nationalist tradition, examining both its limitations and strengths.

In the end, I find in civic nationalism a capacity to strengthen civic resources and foster common aims, which is much needed today. It can be a powerful bulwark against more exclusionary forms of nationalism while offering a sense of belonging more robust than one based on principles alone. It offers our best chance to incorporate immigrants, sustain a robust American nationalism, and foster a meaningful, democratic form of citizenship. The history of civic nationalism shows that there is no single balance between principles and peoplehood that is good for all time. Instead, policies and institutions must be modified and adapted to meet contemporary challenges. Civic nationalism emphasizes the art of politics and illuminates the constant work that must be done to fuse the civic and national traditions.

NATURALIZATION AND NATIONHOOD IN THREE ERAS

In debates over naturalization, the difficult but necessary task of combining principles and peoplehood is particularly evident during the Founding and in the Progressive Era, when leading figures engaged in a family argument over the relation between the civic and the national dimensions of citizenship and the consequences of that relation for immigration and naturalization. The terms of that argument continue to inform the incorporation of immigrants and the treatment of aliens today, and I concentrate on them (as well as touch on developments shaped by other periods in American history). They demonstrate in particular the enormous promise of civic nationalism as well as the risks that must be guarded against in reviving it today.

At the Founding and in the early Republic, restrictions on naturalization and the rights of aliens developed as logical extensions of mainstream nationalism. Proponents of these restrictions advocated extensive residency requirements for owning land, becoming a citizen, and holding office; they flirted with the idea that only native-born citizens could be eligible for election to the House and Senate, demanded character references before immigrants could qualify for citizenship, and rejected claims based on aliens' rights. In their view, multiethnic societies were too discordant, and peace and prosperity depended on citizens' possessing an instinctive sense of attachment to the nation. Critics of these policies regarded immigrants as part of the broader project of creating a national identity. This inclusive approach set the dominant tone for the rules regulating naturalization, officeholding, and the rights of aliens, though the more exclusionary side made its mark as well.

The Founding also provides a cautionary example of how quickly nationalist concerns can be pressed to extreme ends in unsettled times. The Alien and Sedition Acts and the Naturalization Act of 1798 show how exclusionary and inclusionary impulses developed into competing visions of national identity. The same set of concerns about community and creed that aroused the civic nationalism championed by James Madison and John Marshall also provoked a far more narrow, exclusionary nationalism. And while Madison and Marshall's more moderate civic nationalism resisted the most extreme claims of its opponents, it, too, placed significant limits on citizenship when it came to issues of racial difference. The attention devoted to the civic and the national dimensions of citizenship thus had both exclusionary and inclusionary origins and in practice produced policies that combined both impulses.

By the end of the nineteenth century, new doctrines of social Darwinism and eugenics had begun to strengthen the beliefs of legislators, opinion leaders, and the public that immigrants from Asia and from southern and eastern Europe were racially deficient. Such views contributed heavily to the exclusion of Asians from citizenship and the establishment in 1924 of immigration quotas that discriminated against southern and eastern Europeans. In contrast to those who wanted to restrict immigration, a disparate group of moderate civic nationalists continued to believe that a shared national identity could be constructed. They worried primarily that civic processes of incorporation were not functioning adequately and proceeded to formalize the rules governing naturalization and to consciously mold immigrants into citizens.

A wide variety of these "Americanizers," from cosmopolitan pluralists such as the philosopher John Dewey, the journalist Randolph Bourne (a critic of formal Americanization programs), and the social reformer Jane Addams, to the new nationalists led by Theodore Roosevelt, the writer Herbert Croly, and the civic activist Frances Kellor, offered alternatives to the most coercive and exclusionary forms of nationalism. The Americanizers who followed Roosevelt believed that immigrants had an obligation to identify completely with America, and their nationalism excluded the possibility that non-whites could assimilate. Pluralists and social reformers treated immigrants' ethnic heritage with greater respect and envisioned a dynamic exchange between immigrant and American cultures that would provide both stability and vitality. Both strands of the Americanization movement wanted immigrants to participate in the public life of their new country and, in doing so, help revitalize citizenship. By the 1920s, Americanization had shifted in a more coercive and exclusionary direction, in part because of the country's entry into World War I and in part for reasons internal to the movement. The Americanization movement exemplifies the difficulty of sustaining a moderate, middle ground, even as its Rooseveltian proponents offered a realistic alternative to racial supremacists and successfully expanded who was included in the American nation.

The pragmatic, flexible, and ultimately political sensibility that characterized civic nationalism at the Founding and during the Progressive Era contrasts sharply with modern conceptions of citizenship. From the 1960s through the early 1990s, the moderate civic nationalism represented by Madison and Marshall at the Founding and Roosevelt and Bourne in the Progressive Era was displaced by a range of views, each of which separated rather than blended the civic and national dimensions of citizenship. One position contended that democratic civic principles required the United States to protect the rights of all human beings who are physically present in the country, whether nationals or not. This view was articulated by leading political theorists, law professors, and sociologists, such as Joseph Carens, Jamin Raskin, and Robert Bach, and was embodied in immigrant and ethnic rights organizations and philanthropic foundations. This position had much in common with a second position, which emphasized political and legal strategies as the best way to protect the rights of immigrants and to strengthen the standing of minority groups. Advocates for this position included political scientists who were deeply involved in Latino empowerment strategies, such as Louis DeSipio and Harry Pachon, and advocacy groups like the National Association of Latino Elected Officials.

In the 1980s and early 1990s, as these claims to greater global rights and group representation became more firmly rooted (especially among ethnic advocates and academics), a significantly different set of views became prominent in popular political discourse. Voters and legislators grappled over a series of policies that sought to restrict immigration, strengthen citizenship, and limit the rights of aliens. Two nationalist versions of a robustly American citizenship were particularly visible in these debates. The first staked the future of the United States on its capacity to maintain a European culture and a homogeneous definition of American identity. Its proponents included conservative journalists like Peter Brimelow and Lawrence Auster and the presidential aspirant Patrick Buchanan, as well as conservative advocacy organizations like the Federation for American Immigration Reform and the American Immigration Control Foundation. This group of American cultural nationalists was censured by a second brand of nationalism, one that saw U.S. nationhood stemming from a distinctly American commitment to universal political principles. This latter view emerged most clearly in neoconservative journals and think tanks and was expressed by writers like John J. Miller at the Center for Equal Opportunity, John Fonte at the American Enterprise Institute and the Hudson Institute, and Peter Salins at the Manhattan Institute, as well as by nationally syndicated columnists like Georgie Anne Geyer and *U.S. News and World Report* commentator Michael Barone.

These competing conceptions of citizenship each drew on ideas and formulations that emerged from earlier debates at the Founding and in the Progressive Era. The modern debate differed from those periods in the significantly reduced attention participants paid to finding a workable balance between civic ideals and national allegiance.[18] Advocates of immigrant rights and proponents of cultural nationalism both disdained this task because, despite their radical differences, they shared the view that prepolitical social identities take precedence over politically forged affiliations. For rights advocates, personhood and social membership sufficed for receiving the rights and benefits of citizenship. For cultural nationalists, cultural affinity, not attachment to civic ideals or the exercise of self-governance, formed the basis for membership.

Proponents of increased minority group representation and advocates for a distinctly American definition of universal nationalism paid greater attention to the effect of political institutions on immigrants and citizenship. But they, too, evaded the challenge of combining the civic and national dimensions of citizenship in ways that are responsive to the challenges posed by global markets, clashing cultures, and weakened political institutions. These two approaches especially limited the search for ways to recognize the critical role played by group identity while avoiding the problems caused by group rights. The proponents of minority representation schemes reduced citizenship to electoral and organizational arrangements that are designed to reinforce subnational group identity. For their part, universal nationalists tended to deify individual liberty, neglecting to account for the role of group identity in fostering assimilation and downplaying the extent to which individualism can be at odds with nationalism.

All these approaches are antipolitical in their intent to circumscribe radically the issues, institutions, and identities that a democratic people can rethink and restructure. Serious difference of opinion is restricted to marginal issues, as answers to core questions about the rights and benefits of citizenship, the meaning of U.S. ideals, and the nature of American nationhood have been predetermined by fixed and often simplistic notions of culture and creed. As a result, it has become increasingly difficult to address a range of issues relating to immigration and citizenship. Immigrant and minority group advocates often limit opportunities to generate trust and forge alliances by casting newcomers largely as supplicants who demand special rights rather than engaged citizens or dedicated Americans. Proponents of cultural and universal forms of American nationalism, meanwhile, stoke social fragmentation and increase civic alienation by seeking to suppress rather than to engage and, where possible, to mediate conflicts among contending allegiances and among divergent views of America's civic principles. These antipolitical approaches have contributed to a climate characterized by extreme proposals—deport all illegal aliens or offer them amnesty; slash social benefits for immigrants or increase them substantially; raise naturalization standards or junk them entirely—which generate enormous controversy but rarely result in sustained or systemic change. This climate means that public and private efforts are less likely to focus on forging new approaches and strengthening the institutions that can incorporate newcomers while building a common citizenship. It means that both the realities of immigrant life and the demands of a civic nation are disregarded.

To turn away from this policy of neglect requires reclaiming a political sensibility that melds the civic and national dimensions of citizenship. The tradition of civic nationalism that held sway at the Founding and in the Progressive Era exemplifies that sensibility. It offers the best chance today to foster a common sense of peoplehood and generate attachment to civic ideals in ways that strengthen social and civic capacities for incorporating immigrants. In the mid-1990s, a new approach to citizenship emerged that draws explicitly on that tradition.[19] This new civic nationalism rejects a narrow definition of citizenship even as it insists that American identity requires more than a commitment to democratic political principles. Although it must address longstanding questions about the relation between its civic and nationalist dimensions, this new civic nationalism promises to revalue American identity in a manner that turns aliens into allies and forges the broadest possible political commitments.[20]

Modern civic nationalists include conservatives and liberals who draw extensively on Roosevelt and Bourne in formulating their proposals for America in the twenty-first century. I argue that contemporary civic nationalism should draw on James Madison as well. A Madisonian civic nationalism would focus on social and political practices at the subnational and supranational level that develop civic capacities. At the same time, it would understand that those practices will not flourish if they are too readily detached from a shared sense of national citizenship. Madison's flexible and adaptive nationalism is especially appropriate for confronting the problems posed by both too forceful and too feeble a sense of American nationhood. This versatility is necessary today to overcome the general neglect of programs to incorporate newcomers effectively into the nation. It can take advantage of significant domestic and global changes that have made the time ripe for reshaping the public debate over immigration, assimilation, and citizenship and for building a civic nationalist approach that invests more in immigrants and expects more of them and native-born citizens.

In this book, I analyze civic nationalism in essentially chronological fashion. The main part of the book, chapters 1–6, focuses on the Founding (1787–1802) and the Progressive Era (1903–24). These chapters are followed by a more selective account of the modern period (1965–97) in chapters 7 and 8, and an epilogue. In chapter 1 I show how law and policy governing immigration and citizenship emerged from competing ideas about the meaning of American nationhood at the Founding. Chapter 2 concentrates on the Alien and Sedition Acts and the Naturalization Act of 1798. In chapter 3 I return to the Naturalization Act of 1790 to consider the origins and implications of the "free white clause," which denied citizenship to non-whites. In doing so I replicate the

Founders' own approach to the issue of citizenship, which considered the profoundly disruptive question of membership for non-whites separately from the more everyday problems of immigration and membership.

In chapter 4 I analyze the rise of the Americanization movement, particularly its culturally pluralist and social reformist wing. Chapter 5 explores the new nationalism of Teddy Roosevelt and its influence on the Bureau of Naturalization and the Bureau of Education. Chapter 6 describes the turn to a more coercive approach to Americanization and analyzes the dynamics that brought about this change. In chapter 7 I discuss the evolution of a shared American citizenship from the 1930s to the 1960s, and the subsequent domestic and global challenges to that citizenship; this chapter sets the framework for assessing the revival of civic nationalism at the end of the millennium. In chapter 8 I characterize and assess the dominant conceptions of civic nationalism, compare them to the models of citizenship described in the previous chapter, and advance my own version of civic nationalism. The epilogue sketches the policy implications of this vision.

CITIZENSHIP IN THEORY AND PRACTICE

My analysis focuses on controversies in public policy while pressing us to recognize the ways in which our politics is itself structured by deeper and more constitutive issues. Efforts to fix immigrant policy without careful attention to competing conceptions of citizenship will result in bad theory and bad policy. Thinking about citizenship does not, however, mean concentrating solely on policy; nor does it entail trying to find the most pristine theory and then apply it to the raw material of social and political life. Instead, it uses history and politics as guides. This kind of analysis examines public debates that involve a range of institutions and actors. It teases normative claims out of political practices as well as applying them to policy.

Those who believe we should concentrate on policy alone suggest that the way questions about immigration and citizenship will get answered is a matter of economic interests.[21] This hard-nosed approach offers an important corrective to what is often unqualifiedly praised as America's "immigrant tradition" of accepting newcomers. Economic interests have played a significant role in regulating the admission and incorporation of immigrants. Economic interests do not, however, fully explain America's treatment of newcomers. Waves of restriction have not followed the turns of the economy. Neither the Naturalization Act of 1790 nor the National Origins Act of 1924 was passed in a period of extensive economic turmoil.[22] Nor, as Rogers Smith has noted, have important political actors always "play[ed] the role dictated by class interests."[23] Industrial leaders, for example, have supported policies that restrict the flow of inexpensive labor. Moreover, it is far from clear what policy toward immigrants serves whose economic interest. As the sociologist Nathan Glazer remarks, the economic data on immigration are "contradictory and ambiguous."[24] Studies vary widely, for instance, over whether immigrants' contributions to the general welfare outweigh the social costs they impose. Even if we agreed on the data, the political scientist Peter Skerry observes, determining what level of competition is too much still requires interpretation of those data.[25]

The political process shapes how immigration issues are interpreted, but those interpretations are not simply conditioned by economic or narrow political interests. Jews, for example, whose political and economic standing might be threatened by newcomers, nonetheless support high levels of immigration, as do conservatives who worry about multiculturalism but see America as a universal nation open to all. A significant part of political life involves ideas about group and national identity, as well as aspirations based on civic principles of freedom and equality. These views are rarely separable from the self-interest of political leaders and groups, but they are also not reducible to those interests. Thus, how Americans perceive their identity will help determine a series of pressing issues of public policy: how many immigrants become citizens and under what conditions; what those newcomers learn—and teach—about the meaning of citizenship; what benefits are available to immigrants; and whether Americans regard newcomers as intruders or as partners with whom they share a common fate. We need to account for these competing conceptions of citizenship because they lie at the root of our deepest disagreements and play such a crucial role in shaping public policy.

The other prevailing method of analyzing citizenship uses moral and political philosophy to focus on the normative dimensions of public policy. Many practitioners of this approach employ abstract analysis to construct theories of justice or equality and then judge policies by those values. This method of analysis can help clarify murky discussions by pressing arguments to their first principles. At its best, it shows where tradition is defended entirely on the ground that it is a tradition, rather than on the reasons for supporting that tradition. The theoretical approach, however, can be misleading as philosophy and a poor guide to practice.[26] It often invokes hypothetical cases that leave out precisely what is at stake in public debate. For example, some arguments for preferential hiring, as the political theorist Robert Goodin points out, avoid analyzing whether "affirmative action means hiring less-qualified candidates and what *less-qualified* might mean."[27] Other examples include arguments for welfare that avoid claims about moral responsibility, or arguments for open borders that treat the relation between sovereignty and security as a regrettable necessity.[28]

The abstract approach is also insufficiently realistic in refusing to account for considerations of human nature—pride, envy, lust, dominion, cruelty, and passion, as well as the need to belong and share commitments.[29] By considering these aspects of social life as unfortunate impediments to elegant philosophical solutions, theory does not take seriously the social resources necessary to engage fellow human beings in common projects. It fails to assess policies in the context of whether they are necessary to make the system function.[30] It therefore judges as wanting a system that may have the best practical chance of achieving its aspirations. Despite its focus on the normative dimension of public policy, the theoretical approach for a long time largely ignored questions regarding what kinds of citizens are necessary to support a political system and how political institutions might form such citizens. Eager to avoid the coercive aspects of such a project, it has instead concentrated on assessing whether basic institutional arrangements fulfill abstract theories of justice.[31] The policy approach is no better in this regard; it also has disregarded the formative nature of political institutions, emphasizing instead strategic considerations of what can be done within established parameters.[32]

In recent years it has become clear that, as the political philosophers Will Kymlicka and Wayne Norman point out, the "health and stability of modern democracy depends on the qualities and attitudes of its citizens."[33] Increasing voter apathy, long-term welfare dependency, and renewed racial and religious conflict are among the trends that have recently focused attention on citizens' "sense of identity and how they view potentially competing forms of national, regional, ethnic and religious identities; their ability to tolerate and work with others who are different; to participate in and promote the public good; to show self-restraint."[34] We cannot, it seems, take for granted that democratic citizens will simply sprout of their own accord; they must be fashioned actively.

My approach picks up on precisely these issues and concerns. It emphasizes that conceptions of citizenship matter in designing institutions and formulating policies. This approach recognizes, however, that we do not begin thinking about citizenship in a vacuum. To understand American citizenship we must examine actual practices. Hence, I pay attention to public policies such as naturalization as concrete expressions of principles, as well as to a wide range of institutions and actors that play an indispensable role in shaping citizens. I also recognize that our traditions of citizenship are not simply the product of what academics or intellectuals have conjured up over the years but are actual historical attempts to carve out workable understandings of citizenship. I do not expect to find a single coherent tradition; instead, I make room for the contentiousness that surrounds debates over citizenship.

The practice of citizenship—testing what works and is feasible and adapting our approach "as we go"—becomes a part of our tradition when the concepts are actually applied and affirmed by the people themselves. By identifying the traditions that characterize the history of American citizenship we can develop a good sense of the normative constraints and possibilities that shape our political life. Understanding those constraints and possibilities can then help us better negotiate future crises. This understanding is especially important in managing the tensions between belief and belonging that shape what it means to be and to become an American citizen.

CHAPTER ONE

Immigration, Citizenship, and the Nation's Founding

AT AMERICA'S FOUNDING and in the nation's early years, almost all of the leading political figures believed that civic freedom depended on a shared sense of belonging, but they disagreed over its meaning. Competing views of citizenship appealing variously to nationalist conceptions of history, culture, and experience, as well as civic notions of individual consent and mutual deliberation, emerged initially in the debates over the proposed constitution as a distinction between Anti-Federalists and Federalists. The former contended that liberty could only be preserved in small, homogeneous republics, while the latter argued for a system that embedded civic principles in a broadly defined national identity. The positions were not set in stone, however. Some Federalists, like Gouverneur Morris, articulated Anti-Federalist-like views in calling for restrictive immigration and citizenship laws. Other Federalists, like James Madison, continued to emphasize a more liberal approach, even as in the 1790s he joined the Jeffersonian Republicans against the Federalist Party.

As with the broader discussion of citizenship during the ratification debates, no one who argued about naturalization, aliens' rights, or eligibility for office-holding disputed that attachment to America, knowledge of the rights and principles of self-governance, and adoption of the individual habits necessary for engagement in public life were the essential ingredients in forming new citizens. Despite this level of agreement, the framers of the new constitution and early legislators disagreed significantly as to how to turn newcomers into the proper kind of citizens. What kind of requirements for officeholders or immigrants wishing to naturalize would best ensure their loyalty and their ability to understand America's civic principles and participate in its public life? Was the simple fact that the immigrant chose to come to the United States sufficient, or should there be a required amount of time before naturalization, variously set between three and fourteen years? Or could newcomers never be trusted fully and be barred for life from holding elective office?

As the broader views of citizenship intersected with partisan politics, threats of war and insurrection, and nascent ideological divides from 1787 to 1802, two broadly different answers to these questions emerged. Proponents of longer waiting periods and more restrictive policies argued that only deeply ingrained habits of emotional attachment could support a free government that preserved liberties and protected rights. Critics of this view also worried about emotional bonds in pluralistic societies. They were, however, more confident that basic social and educational processes could generate a shared sense of national identity among new and native-born citizens. They were also concerned that severely limiting the rights of aliens would harm America's civic character. Most policies regarding naturalization and officeholding followed this moderate civic nationalism, though a more extreme nationalist side exerted influence in important ways.

DIVERSITY AND NATIONHOOD

The Declaration of Independence rooted the legitimacy of the American Revolution in two civic principles: human equality and consent of the governed. According to the first principle, all men are created equal and therefore possess the same natural rights to life and liberty. These rights are insecure outside of government, so, according to the second principle, humans form governments to protect their rights. An individual's consent to a social contract therefore forms the basis of political obligation. Individual rights are universal, but they are protected only when a specific group succeeds in establishing its own political system. The Declaration sought to reconcile the universality of rights and the particularity of independent polities by emphasizing the primacy of choice. This resolution of the tension between the universal and the particular engendered other tensions. A government based on consent may not always secure individual rights. The majority, as Madison wrote in *Federalist* 10, may become a faction and violate minority rights. Too popular a form of democratic governance would enable a majority to "sacrifice to its ruling passion or interest, both the public good and the rights of other citizens."[1]

The primary solution offered by the proponents of the new constitution to the tension between consent and rights was structural. Madison, Alexander Hamilton, and John Jay, writing under the Roman pen name "Publius," proposed (following Montesquieu) allowing a multitude of interests to clash over an extended republic so as to limit the authority of any one interest. Madison, in particular, rejected a homogeneous society as unnatural. In a large, more diverse society, people with unpopular views would find it easier to secure allies. By constructing a system that "let ambition counteract ambition," Madison and his compatriots sought to limit the extent to which the republic depended solely on the existing character and spirit of its people.[2]

Madison's opponents believed that the new system would fail because it sought to do the impossible: to outfox human nature by turning self-interest into good government.[3] Yet Madison clearly believed in a conception of the public good (factions are "adverse to the rights of other citizens, or to the permanent and aggregate interests of the community") and in the importance of virtue in attaining that good ("To suppose that any form of government will secure liberty or happiness without any virtue in the people, is a chimerical idea").[4] Proponents of the new constitution further agreed with their critics that self-government required cultivating citizens who could control their desires and moderate their passions. Civic institutions, in this widely shared view, were instruments essential to the formation of such self-governing citizens.[5]

Self-governance would ensure that citizens respected the rights of others and sought to do what was right rather than simply what they wanted. Such citizens especially needed to understand the political principles that undergirded free government. Citizens, as George Washington observed in his First Annual Address to Congress, had "to know and to value their own rights, to discern and provide against invasions of them; to distinguish between oppression and the necessary exercise of lawful authority."[6] The tension between consent and rights could be managed if the majority would be considerate of minority rights. "[B]ear in mind this sacred principle," Thomas Jefferson said in his First Inaugural Address, "that though the will of the majority is in all cases to prevail, that will, to be rightful, must be reasonable."[7] To ensure this reasonableness, many framers and early legislators focused on the importance of moral and religious education in teaching vital habits and promoting civic virtue.[8]

Proponents and opponents of the Constitution thus both believed that citizens needed to possess moderate character habits and civic knowledge. The primary purpose of cultivating the proper temperament of moderation, of subordinating individual interests to the common good, and of actively engaging in public life was to preserve the larger political community that makes individual liberty possible. That liberty could be threatened by politics, but it was also a result of engagement in communal self-government. To be free required the capacity to shape one's future, and that capacity depended crucially on being part of a larger community that was free to control its destiny.[9]

The relation of the national community to individual rights posed a second, more vexing problem for the Founding generation. In their view, free government depended on a shared sense of commonality and belonging. The consent argument might seem to resolve the tension between universal and particular in the abstract, but the framers worried that it would not prove robust enough in practice. The diversity of groups within society especially strained the capacity of a political system based on abstract civic principles to secure itself against tyranny. Differences between debtors and creditors, between landed and commercial interests, and between northerners and southerners were thought to pose the greatest challenges to forming a united country. "It was true as had been observed we had not among us those hereditary distinctions of rank which were a great source of the contests in the ancient governments as well as the modern States of Europe, nor those extremes of wealth or poverty which characterize the latter," Madison wrote. "We cannot, however, be regarded even at this time, as one homogeneous mass, in which every thing that affects a part will affect in the same manner the whole."[10] The extent of national consciousness was itself at issue during the debates over ratifying the proposed constitution and in the early Republic. In response, the Founding generation offered competing answers to the question of how much and what kind of national identity was necessary to sustain their experiment in free government.

Opponents of the proposed constitution argued that a public-spirited citizenry depended on a small republic. Only there could natural homogeneity reduce corruption and conflict. Small republics, in which rulers were physically close and closely checked by the ruled, made it possible for the people to control the government. Their size made it possible for citizens to engage in the actual practice of democratic governance, which was the best means for gaining knowledge of public affairs and for protecting individual rights. Publius's scheme of representation could not ensure that citizens would feel connected to the government. A strong national government would be distant from the people and would abuse its power to annihilate or absorb the functions that properly belonged to the states. Such a government was required only when society was so heterogeneous as to present significant opportunities for conflict.

Yet the colonies were already too diverse to be tightly joined in political union. Prior to the Massachusetts ratification debate, "Agrippa" (most likely James Winthrop, the librarian at Harvard) worried that a strong national government would undermine the cultural and racial integrity of individual states by threatening their capacity to "keep their blood pure." Pennsylvania, he contended, had been the most receptive to newcomers, and this had diluted its moral purity. It had bought its increase in population and size "at the expense of religion and good morals." By contrast, "the eastern states have, by keeping separate from foreign mixtures, preserved their religions and morals. They have also reserved the manly virtue which is equally fitted for rendering them respectable in war, and industrious in peace."[11]

Publius's critics more often discussed homogeneity in terms of their praise for small republics. They did not argue that one culture was superior to another. Rather, they made a structural argument that a free society could not work if there were too many conflicting interests at play. They emphasized that there were significant differences among the thirteen states with regard to economics, law, customs, character, and climate. Writing in the *Massachusetts Gazette,* Agrippa offered an extended comparison of the northern and southern states, pointing especially to the differences based on slavery and a wealthy upper class in the South. The North, in his view, was much more likely to preserve its form of government. The greater attention to education, the smaller and more equal distribution of land, the absence of slavery and the inequality of rights it produced, and even the colder weather all combined to make Northerners "active, industrious, and sober." In contrast, the great differences in land ownership, slavery, widespread poverty and lack of education, warmer weather, and a general "dissoluteness of manners" made Southerners less well suited for the rigors of free government.[12]

The difference between commercial and landed interests loomed especially large. "So different are many species of property," the "Impartial Examiner" pointed out in the *Virginia Independent Chronicle*,

> so various the productions, so unequal the profits arising, even from the same species of property, in different states, that no general mode of contribution can well be adopted in such a manner as at one to affect all in an equitable degree. Hence may arise disagreeable objects of contention. A diversity of interests will produce a diversity of schemes. Thus, each state, as it is natural, will endeavor to raise a revenue by such means, as may appear least injurious to its own interest.[13]

The critics of the proposed constitution thought it impossible that Georgia and Massachusetts could be governed under the same set of laws. If such a government did manage to maintain order, it would accomplish this only by curtailing liberty and crushing diversity. A legislature formed of representatives from all parts of the country would, "Brutus" wrote in the *New York Journal*, "be composed of such heterogenous and discordant principles as would constantly be contending with each other."[14] These conflicts could best be avoided by limiting public rule to small societies where "the manners, sentiments and interests of the people" were similar.

Free government not only required citizens with the proper temperament of moderation but also had to be moderate itself. Rights could not be properly protected in a society that featured significant differences based on property, income, education, and character, as well as ethnicity and religion. Societies in which citizens shared a rough degree of equality across a range of categories would compel citizens to look out for the common good, sensing that public life reflected their own values and identity. Disagreement would be sufficiently muted so as to avoid the heavy hand of the state, which would, inevitably, curtail rights as it expanded to prevent discord.

This understanding of the nature and necessity of homogeneity was rooted in a well-developed theory of the relation between rights and culture. In this view, law is found rather than created. It memorializes settled practices and codifies existing rules; it does not consciously make new rules. The Pennsylvania father-son team of Judge George Bryan and Samuel Bryan, writing as "Centinel," proclaimed that "it is the genius of the common law to resist innovation."[15] In their view, a constitutional text should reflect rather than shape a people's culture.[16] The bond among citizens is preconstitutional, rooted in the importance of shared customs and manners, in laws and forms of labor and ownership, and in religious belief and cultural heritage. The opponents of the proposed constitution favored religious toleration, for instance, but they assumed that this meant toleration for a plurality of Protestantisms. As the political theorist Herbert Storing notes, "They saw no conflict between religious liberty and public support for a religious and generally Protestant community."[17]

Jay, Hamilton, and Madison's concern for a national identity took a different form. Their embrace of the extended republic posed particularly vexing problems for ensuring a shared sense of belonging and patriotism. To moderate the effects of difference and diversity, an extended republic would have to generate a collective sensibility. As the political theorist Charles Kesler observes, "Living together in society is not an easy task, and the republican insistence that societies must be able to govern themselves by 'common consent' makes that task harder still." The framers were "therefore not embarrassed to try to find ways to make the enterprise easier and happier. . . . [Their] chief concern was to 'cement' the Union, to overcome the centrifugal forces that had almost shattered the Union during the war and again in the 1780s, and to bolster and deepen the young country's sense of nationhood."[18]

Jay sought to generate this identity by claiming that Americans already shared a sufficiently homogeneous culture. In *Federalist* 2, he evokes the cultural foundation of American nationhood. "Providence," he asserts, "has been pleased to give this one connected country to one united people—a people descended from the same ancestors, speaking the same language, professing the same religion, attached to the same principles of government, very similar in manners and customs."[19] Jay's claim was rooted, to some degree, in social fact. Eighty percent of the new nation's white population in 1790 was of British derivation and shared the Christian religion and English language, as well as customs and manners.[20] Immigrants to New York, the historian Thomas Archdeacon writes, "entered an English-based culture and they were expected to operate within it. Members of foreign ethnic groups were entitled to citizenship and the full range of civic privileges, but English political forms and economic practices remained the norm, and success fell to those best able to conform to them."[21]

Jay's invocation of a natural unity among Americans was, nonetheless, strained, and he must have known it was overstated. There were significant differences among the German Pietists in Pennsylvania, the Catholics in Maryland, the Quakers in Pennsylvania and New Jersey, and the Scotch-Irish Presbyterians scattered throughout several states.[22] "Even in relatively homogeneous, Puritan New England towns," Archdeacon points out, "there had been tension between colonists from different regions of England over matters of agricultural technique and religious enthusiasm."[23] Antipathy toward Dutch and German speakers was especially common. Benjamin Franklin undercut any pretensions to homogeneity when he asked, "Why should *Pennsylvania*, founded by the *English*, become a colony of *Aliens*, who will shortly be so numerous as to Germanize us instead of Anglifying them, and will never adopt our Language or Customs, any more than they can acquire our Complexion?"[24]

Jay's claim was not a description of actual social life but rather, as Willi Paul Adams notes, "an incantation."[25] He invoked the natural unity of the Americans as a strategic effort to increase support for the new constitution. In doing so, he suggested the importance many colonists attached to their Anglo-Saxon heritage.

They believed it made them especially suited for the rigors of free government. Once committed to the break with Britain, Americans could conceive of themselves as the lone hope for fulfilling the Anglo-Saxon commission to create a free society. References such as Jay's to cultural commonality as a basis for American peoplehood were, however, infrequent, suggesting that Jay and other proponents of the proposed constitution regarded these claims as less important than others.

Hamilton, for example, offered a robustly formative vision of nationhood. In his first draft of Washington's speech to Congress, he wrote, "To render the people of this country as homogenous as possible, must tend as much as any other circumstance to the permanency of their union and posterity."[26] To this end, he sought to foster a national sentiment that supported the Constitution, and less strongly the government in power, more than he worried about ensuring that civic virtue flourished among the people. For Hamilton, the success of the government depended on its capacity to work its way into the daily sensibilities of the citizenry. "[T]he more the citizens are accustomed to meet with [national authority] in the common occurrences of their political life," he wrote in *Federalist* 27, "the more it is familiarized to their sight and to their feelings."[27] Hamilton looked suspiciously on citizens' attachments to their localities, regarding them as evidence of a parochialism that needed to be overcome. His position was also markedly different from those who held traditional fears of corruption, with regard to both strong executives and capitalist markets. He treated public finance as an especially appropriate method of solidifying support for the new nation. By taking on the debts of individual states, Hamilton aimed to enlist the more well-off in the success of the new political institutions.[28]

Madison aimed for a greater balance between federal and state authority and identity than did Hamilton, especially following the ratification debates. He nonetheless believed that it was crucial to forge a broad sense of national identity. During the ratification debates, Madison utilized a great jumble of principles, culture, and experience to portray subnational identities as less real than the colonists' shared identity. "Hearken not to the unnatural voice," he warns in *Federalist* 14,

> which tells you that the people of America, knit together as they are by so many cords of affection, . . . can no longer be fellow-citizens of one great, respectable, and flourishing empire. The kindred blood which flows in the veins of American citizens, the mingled blood which they have shed in defense of their sacred rights, consecrate their Union and excite horror at the idea of their becoming aliens, rivals, enemies.[29]

Madison looks inward into the Revolution's principles, backward into shared ancestry, and outward into recent history to invoke a people who possess a specific genius. "It is evident that no other form [than the form proposed in the Constitution] would be reconcilable with the genius of the people of America;

with the fundamental principles of the Revolution; or with that honorable determination which animates every votary of freedom to rest all our political experiments on the capacity of mankind for self-government."[30] What they believe ("the capacity of mankind for self-government"), as well as who they were and what crucible they have passed through (the "kindred blood" which has become "mingled blood") suggest who they have already become.

Madison, Hamilton, and Jay offered divergent accounts of the people's shared ancestry and experiences and the civic ideals in which they believed. They did so in a common effort to legitimize the new constitution by referring to political principles set within a wider context of social and cultural nationhood. Indeed, they wanted that people's understanding of itself to derive in part from the Constitution and the arguments they advanced in favor of it.

The Federalists' account also linked American national identity to a document that projected itself onto the future, rather than memorialized the past. The Constitution established political institutions and formal processes by which changes could be made in its own values and structure. Significant change would not depend on external revolution because that process had been built into the system. This internalization of change meant that the meaning of American identity would rely on what Hamilton called in *Federalist* 1 "reflection and choice." It would be intertwined with citizens' understanding of constitutional principles and their interpretation of those principles in changing conditions. Changes in the Constitution and the political order it established were not merely structural adjustments; they had implications for the meaning of American national identity as well.[31]

Madison, Hamilton, and Jay saw the American nation as a political creation based on a combination of principles, culture, experience, and fellow feeling, and as linked to a constitutional process that required ongoing public deliberation. Their account contrasts with those of Agrippa, Brutus, and Centinel, in which free and independent persons formed a society and became a people who then established a government.[32] For them, community was rooted in the functional importance of shared customs and manners, in laws and forms of labor and ownership, and in religious belief and cultural heritage, and could serve its purpose only on a small scale. The entire Founding generation saw civic principles as dependent on a shared sense of nationhood, but they differed deeply as to the meaning of that nation and whether it could change.

IMMIGRATION AND CITIZENSHIP

In keeping with the competing views of citizenship during the ratification debates, the Constitution of 1787 did not formally define this status. It refers to citizenship only three times: Article I, Section 8 authorizes Congress "[t]o establish a uniform Rule of Naturalization"; Article I, Section 2 restricts eligibility for the House of Representatives to persons who have been citizens for seven years and eligibility for the Senate to persons who have been citizens for nine years; and Article II, Section 1 restricts the presidency to "natural born Citizens, or a Citizen of the United States, at the time of the Adoption of the Constitution."

The absence of any formal definition of citizenship in the Constitution in large part reflected the unresolved dispute over whether Americans were to be understood first as citizens of the nation as a whole or of the individual states. Congress had the authority to establish a uniform naturalization code, but the Constitution did not specify whether this authority was an exclusive power of the federal government or a concurrent power shared with the states. Restricting the presidency to native-born citizens reflected an assumption (shared by many of the framers) of birthright citizenship and further enabled the framers to postpone deciding the primacy of state or federal citizenship. Birthright citizenship was also as an incentive for immigrants who expected to have children, and thus served to help populate the new nation.[33]

For those not born on American soil, citizenship could be gained through a naturalization process that emphasized the civic principle of consent. This emphasis reflected new ideas about membership as well as practical experience with immigration in the colonial era. In seventeenth-century England, citizenship had been defined as "natural, personal, and perpetual," writes the historian James Kettner. "Once a man became a subject—by birth or otherwise—he remained a subject forever, owing a lasting obedience to his natural superior the king." But the Declaration of Independence asserted that "Governments are instituted among Men, deriving their just powers from the Consent of the Governed." Under this principle, naturalization law in the colonies and the new nation became largely "volitional and contractual." The naturalization process "involved a form of contract between an alien who chose a new allegiance and a community that consented to adopt him as a subject."[34]

The shift to a more consensual form of citizenship also reflected the framers' view that control over immigration and membership policies was beneficial to their struggle for independence. In 1773 the British crown ruled that colonial assemblies could not naturalize immigrants because they lacked the constitutional authority to grant British citizenship.[35] Colonists objected to the crown's actions on the grounds of self-governance as well as out of practical concerns: "Emigrants of property will not choose to come to a country whose form of government hangs but by a thread," said Tom Paine, "and who is everyday tottering on the brink of commotion and disturbance; and numbers of the present inhabitants would lay hold of the interval to dispose of their effects and quit the continent."[36]

The civic dimension of citizenship shaped the boundaries of membership in other parts of the Constitution as well. In particular, it did not require cultural, religious, or linguistic tests for citizenship. Article VI explicitly replaces religious test oaths for officeholders with an oath (or affirmation) to support the Constitution. This policy repudiated state policies, such as that in Massachusetts, which required church membership for political membership. It also rejected policies, such as that in Virginia, that refused to offer membership to indentured servants of different religious backgrounds and those that limited the right of Jews to vote. This approach further contrasted with England's policy; the historian Lawrence Fuchs notes that "only Protestants who took sacraments in the Church of England were eligible for naturalization."[37] America, declared George Washington, was "open to receive not only the opulent and respectable stranger, but the oppressed and persecuted of all nations and religions."[38]

While the civic dimension of citizenship's inclusive aspects was readily apparent in the Constitution, almost all of the major political leaders rejected any universal right to entry or membership in a specific political community, basing their rejection on the distinction between natural and political rights. In their view, all humans possessed the same rights to life, liberty, and the pursuit of happiness. But the only way to protect those rights was for men to form a particular government by mutual consent. That government would then be responsible for securing the rights of its members. It had no obligation to admit as an immigrant or offer citizenship to those who did not partake of the original act of consent.[39]

Many framers and leaders in the early Republic expressed significant concerns about the effects of immigration. Washington, in affirming openness to immigrants of all nations and religions, modified that statement by saying, "We shall welcome [them] to a participation of all our rights and privileges, if by decency and propriety of conduct they appear to merit the enjoyment."[40] Some, like Franklin, emphasized the work ethic as the crucial character trait immigrants needed to succeed in America. "Industry and constant Employment," he wanted potential immigrants to know, "are great Preservatives of the Morals and Virtue of a Nation."[41]

Thomas Jefferson was even more concerned about immigrants' political ideologies:

> Every species of government has its specific principles. Ours perhaps are more peculiar than those of any other in the universe. . . . To these nothing can be more opposed than the maxims of absolute monarchies. Yet from such we are to expect the greatest number of emigrants. They will bring with them the principles of the governments they leave, imbibed in their early youth; or, if able to throw them off, it will be in exchange for an unbounded licentiousness, passing, as is usual, from one extreme to another. It would be a miracle were they to stop precisely at the point of temperate liberty.[42]

Hamilton, an immigrant and Jefferson's ideological and political nemesis, supported immigration as a means of populating the country and building a great nation. Nonetheless, he found common ground with Jefferson:

The safety of a republic depends essentially on the energy of a common national sentiment. . . . [F]oreigners will . . . entertain opinions on government congenial with those under which they have lived; or if they should be led hither from a preference to ours, how extremely unlikely is it they will bring with them that *temperate love of liberty* so essential to real republicanism?

He worried as well that immigrants would lack the intuitive "love of country which will almost invariably be found to be closely connected with birth, education, and family."[43]

The debates over immigration and citizenship at the Founding and during the early Republic focused on these questions of political ideology, civic capacity, and national belonging. The task of sorting out the framers' positions on these issues is complicated by the fact that the residency requirement for officeholding was also thought by some as necessary to ensure that representatives knew their own districts and constituencies well enough to do a good job. And at the Constitutional Convention the debate was not only over the prudence or rightness of these specific provisions, but also over whether those topics needed to be dealt with in the text of the Constitution itself or could be left to the discretion of the legislature.

Still, by analyzing the debates during the Constitutional Convention and in the Naturalization Acts of 1790 and 1795, we can distill two broad approaches that strike significantly different balances between nationhood and civic principles. These positions did not change radically in this period and hence can be considered thematically rather than chronologically. One position stressed instinctive attachment as the basis of national identity and the importance of early education in developing the necessary civic virtues. The competing position emphasized the relatively easy acquisition of citizenship and the civic character of the political system.

"Men Who Can Shake Off Their Attachments to Their Own Country"

At the Constitutional Convention, the debate on immigration and citizenship focused on residency requirements for officeholders. The Committee on Detail recommended a three-year citizenship requirement for representatives and a four-year requirement for senators. Some delegates proposed seven years for representatives and fourteen for senators. The convention ultimately settled on seven and nine years, respectively. The convention also adopted, without debate, the requirement that the president be a native-born citizen. In 1790, the first naturalization law required two years' residency for "free white persons," a demonstration of good character, and the swearing of an oath or affirmation to support the Constitution. The Naturalization Act of 1795 extended the residency requirement to five years, required that an immigrant declare his intent to naturalize three years prior to being admitted to citizenship, and added renunciation of former allegiances to the affirmative oath in support of the Constitution. This act also required applicants for citizenship to renounce hereditary titles or orders of nobility and to satisfy a court of admission as to their good moral character and of their attachment to the principles of the Constitution.

Proponents of longer waiting periods and more restrictive rules had a strong sense of the kind of individuals and the type of society that could ensure a government that was responsive to its citizens. On issues of citizenship, those who favored stiff requirements expressed four interrelated concerns: 1) the economic effect of immigration on individual character and class differences; 2) the instinctive nature of national attachment and the problem of community in multiethnic societies; 3) the early acquisition of habits of self-governance; and 4) the dangers of radical ideologies. These concerns expressed traditional anxieties about the rigors of citizenship in a free society more than doubts about the suitability of certain groups for citizenship. Unsettled America, the leading Massachusetts Federalist Theodore Sedgwick argued, was to be kept as "the best capital stock of the future enjoyment of Americans; as an antidote against the poison of luxury; as the nursery of robust and manly virtue, and as a preventative of a numerous class of citizens becoming indigent, and therefore dependent."[44]

Sedgwick also expressed deep reservations about attracting immigrants by offering easy access to land and promising the rapid accumulation of wealth. Such claims were likely to undermine the moderation and homogeneity necessary for free government. "Property was in some sense power; and the possession of immense property generated daring passions which scorned equality, and with impatience endured the restraints of equal laws. . . . The ardent ambition inspired by the possession of great wealth, and the power of gratifying it, which it conferred, had in many instances disturbed the public peace, and in not a few destroyed liberty."[45]

Specific concerns about the level of attachment expected of newcomers were also expressed separately from doubts about immigration. A number of delegates to the Constitutional Convention thought that too easy access to naturalization and eligibility for office would make it more likely that new citizens would destabilize the new regime. George Mason, an ardent opponent of slavery who framed the Virginia Declaration of Rights in 1776, proposed to extend the requirement of residency prior to officeholding from three to seven years. "[A] rich foreign Nation, for example Great Britain," he speculated, "might send over her TOOLS who might bribe their way into the Legislature for insidious purposes." Mason further worried that no residency requirement, or a very short one, would open the door to the corrupting influence of wealth by allowing "[r]ich men of neighboring States" to buy their way into public office. This, he said, is the practice in England. Other delegates focused on the "peculiar dangers" of allowing immigrants to wield senatorial authority over foreign affairs after too brief a residency in the country. Charles Pinkney from South Carolina invoked "the jealousy of the Athenians on this subject who made it death for any stranger to intrude his voice into their legislative proceedings."[46]

These specific concerns over subversion were placed in the context of a broader argument about the nature of nationhood. In advocating extending the Senate requirement from four to fourteen years, Gouverneur Morris argued that those who opposed stricter requirements were being entirely too "rational and cosmopolitan": "What is the language of Reason on this subject? That we should not be polite at the expence of prudence. There was a moderation in all things. . . . It is said that some tribes of Indians, carried their hospitality so far as to offer to strangers their wives & daughters. Was this a proper model for us?" In his notes on the debates, Madison reports Morris's distaste for his opponents, whom he called "those philosophical gentlemen, those Citizens of the World. . . . I do not wish to see any of them in our public Councils. I would not trust them. The men who can shake off their attachments to their own Country can never love any other. These attachments are the wholesome prejudices which uphold all Governments."[47]

For Morris, the United States was obligated to allow only its own citizens to participate in public life. (Among U.S. citizens, he had advocated limiting suffrage to freeholders.) These citizens had a high degree of attachment to the place they were born and raised. This sense of instinctive patriotism was, for Morris, a well-founded assumption, not simply American chauvinism. America, England, and France all needed the kind of instinctive attachment that leads citizens to trust each other and their leaders. Sedgwick expressed similar views in the debate over the 1790 naturalization law, worrying that since Europeans' "sensations" had been dulled by their upbringing, they were not sufficiently able to express true passion and gratitude for republican government. He supported longer terms of probation before citizenship to enable newcomers "to feel and be sensible of the blessing[s]" of republican government.[48]

During the debate in 1794 over extending the residency requirement to five years, Sedgwick further pointed to the problems of multiethnic societies. If people of different backgrounds are put together in close proximity, he argued, they have a tendency to fight with one another. This rule is not confined to groups from widely different backgrounds, like whites and blacks, but between Angles and Saxons as well. He asked his colleagues if they could "recollect the rage of ages, which existed in the country from which we came, between the Saxon, the Danish, and Norman emigrants and the natives of that country? The cruelties, the oppressions, the assassinations, in a word the miseries to which this gave birth?"[49]

In addition to attachment to the nation, it was crucial that new citizens have the requisite habits of self-governance. Sedgwick contended that the singular achievement of American politics was that every man could participate in the common deliberations of local communities. This civic participation, however, depended heavily on one's having developed the proper character traits and habits, ones instilled by "early education."

> In that part of the country with which he was best acquainted, the education, manners, habits, and institutions, religious and civil, were Republican. The community was divided into corporations, in many respects resembling independent republics, of which almost every man, the qualifications were so small, was a member. They had many interesting and important concerns to transact. They appointed their executive, enacted bye laws, raised money for many purposes of use and ornament. Here, then, the citizens early acquired the habits of temperate discussion, patient reasoning, and a capacity for enduring contradiction.[50]

This education, in his view, could not be the product of one or two years' residence in America. "The Republican character," he said, "was no way to be formed but by early education. . . . Shall we alone adopt the rash theory, that the subjects of all Governments, Despotic, Monarchical, and Aristocratical, are, as soon as they set foot on American ground, qualified to participate in administering the sovereignty of our country?"[51]

Proponents of longer waiting periods and more restrictive rules were also worried about the ideological beliefs of newcomers. At the convention Pierce Butler, an immigrant from Ireland to South Carolina who authored the fugitive slave clause in the Constitution, urged that the requirement for eligibility for the Senate be extended from four to fourteen years. Immigrants, he fretted, would bring "not only attachments to other Countries; but ideas of government so distinct from ours in every point that they are dangerous." Butler spoke from personal experience—he claimed that he would have been unsuitable for public office if he had been elected soon after his arrival. This concern over foreign ideologies heightened in the immediate years after ratification of the new constitution, especially during the turmoil in France. Sedgwick described the current situation as "the most inauspicious time for the indiscriminate admission of aliens to the rights of citizenship. A war, the most cruel and dreadful which had been known for centuries, was raging in all those countries from which emigrants were to be expected. The most fierce and unrelenting passions were engaged in a conflict, which shook to their foundations all the ancient political structures in Europe."[52] In arguing during the debates preceding the ratification of the 1795 naturalization act for extending the residency period from two to five years and for requiring character references for applicants for citizenship, Sedgwick observed that the French Revolution "was supported on the one hand by men who believed personal political distinctions were necessary to the great purpose of security, and on the other by those who thought that society could be protected and individuals secured by a Government with departments, and without checks; neither embracing the principles established here."[53]

America's Civic Character

Opponents of longer waiting periods and more restrictive rules thought that some constraints on eligibility for office were appropriate. Most agreed that some period of residency should be required prior to naturalization, but they argued that only minimal or moderate restrictions were sufficient. Their views reflected a basic confidence in existing processes of nationhood formation. They also evinced greater concern about the effect of more restrictive requirements on America's capacity to attract the most suitable immigrants—as well as the illiberal cast such restrictions would give to the civic character of the new regime—than about threats posed by newcomers.

At the convention, Madison's most strenuous defense of immigration came during the eligibility debates for representatives. He "wished to invite foreigners of merit & republican principles among us. America was indebted to emigration for her settlement & Prosperity. That part of America which had encouraged them most had advanced most rapidly in population, agriculture & the arts." Expressing a concern seconded by many at the convention, Madison worried that the proposed restrictions would make immigrants feel "the mortification of being marked with suspicious incapacitations." He did qualify his views by emphasizing practical considerations. "[M]en with foreign predilections" could gain authority in the government, Madison acknowledged, but he doubted that Americans would elect them. "For the same reason that they would be attached to their native Country, our own people would prefer natives of this Country," he sought to reassure his opponents.[54]

Pennsylvania's James Wilson more forthrightly criticized Morris's proposal to require fourteen years' residency as a qualification of senators. He called such a requirement "degrading discrimination" and feared it would discourage "meritorious strangers." Wilson explained that he had suffered the indignity of being ineligible for office when he first moved to Maryland. His ineligibility troubled him less because he desired to hold office immediately than because it suggested that he did not belong in or to his new community. "To be appointed to a place may be a matter of indifference," he attested. "To be incapable of being appointed, is a circumstance grating and mortifying."[55]

Opponents of more severe residency and eligibility proposals doubted that new immigrants would subvert the government. Madison argued that it was unlikely "any dangerous number of strangers would be appointed by the State legislatures" or that foreign governments would try to use immigrants to infiltrate American politics. It was more likely, he felt, that they would bribe a native-born American, as that would arouse less suspicion.[56] Opponents did, however, appear to agree with proponents when it came to the highest office in the land. There is no recorded debate over limiting this office to native-born citizens and it is not discussed in the *Federalist Papers* or elsewhere. Even moderate nationalists like Jay believed that post should not be held by any "but a natural-born citizen." This position was not an argument that the presidency should be reserved for those with pure Anglo-Saxon blood. Rather, Jay's view reflected the assumption that, when it came to the nation's most powerful office, it was prudent to rely on birth and education in the country as an extra safeguard of allegiance to the nation.[57]

In the debate over eligibility issues that related to the Senate and House, opponents of longer residency requirements expressed much less concern about officeholders' attachment to the country. In some cases, they offered significantly different standards for judging loyalty and commitment. Despite his concerns about assimilating Germans in Pennsylvania, Franklin suggested that residence or citizenship itself revealed nothing about the nature or strength of an individual's patriotism. "[S]trangers served us faithfully" during the Revolutionary War, he reminded his colleagues, while "natives took part against their country." Rather than residency, he suggested that moving to the United States was sufficient to demonstrate an immigrant's commitment to the new nation. "When foreigners after looking about for some other Country in which they can obtain more happiness, give a preference to ours, it is a proof of attachment which ought to excite our confidence & affection."[58]

Aedanus Burke, an immigrant from Ireland to South Carolina, where he staunchly supported slavery and opposed the Constitution, suggested a standard of attachment similar to Franklin's. Service on the revolutionaries' side in the war with Britain, he said, counted for more than having been educated under a monarchical government: "[F]oreigners made as good citizens of Republics as the natives themselves. Frenchmen, brought up under an absolute Monarchy, evinced their love of liberty in the late arduous struggle; many of them are now worthy citizens, who esteem and venerate the principles of our Revolution."[59] James Wilson underscored the link between liberty and immigration. He pointed out that three members of the Pennsylvania delegation to the Constitutional Convention had been born abroad, including himself. Most of the general officers of the Pennsylvania line, he noted, had been foreigners and "no complaint had ever been made against their fidelity or merit."[60] Wilson also noted the incongruity of the fact that he might not be able to hold office under the constitution he helped write.[61] During the 1790 debate, Wilson's fellow Pennsylvanian William Maclay wrote privately:

We Pennsylvanians act as if we believed that God made of one blood all the families of the earth; but the Eastern people seem to think he had made none but New England folk. It is strange that men born and educated under republican forms of government should be so contracted on the subject of general philanthropy. . . . They really have the worst characters of any people who offer themselves for citizens. Yet these are the men who affect the greatest fear of being contaminated with foreign manners, customs, and vices.[62]

Opponents of the more restrictive requirements frequently raised broad concerns about the nature and effect of such proposals on the civic character of the new government. They objected that these proposals would undermine the liberal, rights-oriented claims of the new nation. At the convention, Edmund Randolph, a Virginian who would refuse to sign the Constitution because it was insufficiently republican, objected strenuously to Morris's proposal to require fourteen years' residency for senators. He acknowledged that immigration might not be useful to the United States but contended that this ought to have nothing to do with participation in public life. He "reminded the Convention of the language held by our patriots during the Revolution, and the principles laid down in all our American Constitutions. Many foreigners may have fixed their fortunes among us under the faith of these invitations."[63] In the debate over the 1790 naturalization act, the Federalist John Lawrence, who had emigrated from England to New York in 1767, invoked the principles of the Revolution for an even more radical cause: immediate citizenship upon entry. He extended the principle of no taxation without representation to the treatment of aliens: "It has been said, that we ought not to admit [immigrants] to vote at our election. Will they not have to pay taxes from the time they settle amongst us? And is it not a principle that taxation without representation ought go hand in hand? Shall we restrain a man from having an agency in the disposal of his own money?"[64]

John Page, a Virginia Republican and close friend of Jefferson, also argued in the 1790 debate against any residency requirement whatsoever as a prerequisite for citizenship. Such requirements, he asserted, were a holdover from European ways of doing things and were no longer necessary in this new kind of country:

> [T]he policy of European nations and States respecting naturalization, did not apply to the situation of the United States Bigotry and superstition, or a deep-rooted prejudice against the Government, laws, religion, or manners of neighboring nations had a weight in that policy, which cannot exist here, where a more liberal system ought to prevail. . . . It is nothing to us, whether Jews or Roman Catholics settle amongst us; whether subjects of Kings, or citizens of free States wish to reside in the United States, they will find it their interest to be good citizens, and neither their religious nor political opinions can injure us, if we have good laws, well executed.

He further argued against requiring character references for applicants for citizenship. Such references were, he said, one step toward government control of speech and morals. If the law required a grand jury to judge references provided by applicants for citizenship, Page claimed, it would mean expelling those found unworthy. This process would become an "inquisition, and as it will not be sufficient for our views of having immaculate citizens, we should add censors, and banish the immoral from amongst us. Indeed, sir, I fear if we go on as is proposed now, in the infancy of our republic, we shall, in time, require a test of faith and politics, of every person who shall come into these States."[65]

Representatives who stressed the civic dimension of citizenship did so within a robust vision of national identity and citizen virtue. They were civic nationalists, defenders of the reverential dimensions of citizenship who believed deeply that America's commitment to the "temperate love of liberty" would also secure the allegiance of new citizens. In the 1795 debate, Page noted that "he thought nothing more desirable than to see good order, public virtue, and true morality, constituting the character of citizens of the United States, for, without morality, and indeed a general sense of religion, a Republican Government cannot flourish, nay, cannot long exist."[66] He thought it difficult to sort out "good men and bad men" in the immigration process; instead "he trusted that a Constitution much admired and with such wholesome laws, will be an inducement to many good men to become citizens, and that, should bad men come amongst us, they will be discountenanced by the more virtuous class of citizens, and if necessary be punished by the laws." In addition, a proper educational system will inculcate "good sense and virtue" in newcomers and native-born citizens alike.[67]

Madison and Wilson joined Page and Lawrence in objecting to lengthy residency requirements.[68] But they counseled moderation: "When we are considering the advantages that may result from an easy mode of naturalization," Madison said, "we ought also to consider the cautions necessary to guard against abuses. . . . And what is proposed by the amendment is that they shall take nothing more than an oath of fidelity, and declare their intention to reside in the United States." These minimal requirements would enable immigrants to gain the rights of citizenship without ensuring that they were committed to their new nation and that they remained long enough to fulfill the duties of citizenship. "I should be exceedingly sorry, sir, that our rule of naturalization excluded a single person of good fame that really meant to incorporate himself into our society; on the other hand, I do not wish that any man should acquire the privilege, but such as would be a real addition to the wealth or strength of the United States. It may be a question of some nicety, how far we can make our law to admit an alien to the right of citizenship, step by step; but there is no doubt we may, and ought to require residence as an essential."[69]

In the debates during the Constitutional Convention and over the Naturalization Acts of 1790 and 1795 a moderate civic nationalist approach emerged in much of the policy and law governing naturalization, officeholding, and aliens' rights. The residency period stayed at five years and eligibility for House and Senate settled at seven and nine years, respectively. The native-born citizenship requirement for the presidency fit within the concerns of both civic nationalists and their opponents, as did the obligation for immigrants to renounce any hereditary titles.

These policies did not, however, resolve the broader tensions between the civic and the national dimensions of citizenship, between a rational commitment to abstract ideals and an organic bond. By the mid-1790s, two broad approaches to managing those tensions emerged, approaches that strike significantly different balances. Proponents of longer residency periods and more restrictive policies argued that the kind of natural affection that flows from birth and extensive early education in a country provides the commitment and skills necessary to sustain a free society. Knowledge of civic principles is important, but only within the boundaries of a sense of belonging to the nation. When reason faltered, reverence for tradition, customs, and culture would hold the people together.

Critics of longer waiting periods and more restrictive policies also worried about attachment and affection in pluralistic societies. But they were more concerned that restrictive requirements were themselves illiberal and compromised the new nation's civic commitment to protecting rights and expanding liberty. They emphasized the task of generating a shared sense of national identity and the habits of self-governance, and regarded immigrants as part of the central nation-building task of Americanizing the Americans. Belonging to the nation and reverence for its traditions mattered, but these would grow over time and in no small part because of an individual's appreciation of the country's commitment to advancing the universal cause of liberty.

At the time, these differences were more or less crosscutting issues that did not excite the passions of organized parties. (In fact, there were no organized parties.) All that changed with the increasingly heated atmosphere of the middle to late 1790s, as we see in the next chapter. As the eighteenth century wound to an end, the contending positions became more explicit and hardened into political ideologies and parties, and the combatants did battle just this side of actual fighting.

CHAPTER TWO

Alienage and Nationalism in the Early Republic

THE SIGNIFICANT ideological differences that emerged at the Constitutional Convention and became firmly established in the 1795 naturalization act were even easier to see during the debates over the Alien, Sedition, and Naturalization Acts of 1798. The Alien and Sedition Acts were designed to give the president greater power to move against enemies and potential enemies within the country, and the Naturalization Act made it more difficult for immigrants to become citizens. The disputes over these acts were fierce and roughly along partisan divisions between the two major postratification groupings, the Federalists and Republicans. These disputes lend themselves to an interpretation of history in which the forces of civic freedom do battle with the nationalist forces of reaction and repression. Federalists, proponents of closer ties with the monarchy of Britain, passed measures designed to hamstring the Jeffersonian Republicans, advocates of revolutionary France, self-styled friends of the people, and defenders of liberty.

As with other national myths, this story captures a truth and obscures the complexity of what did happen. Americans still associated political parties with factions and conspiracies, and adherents of contending ideologies shared an overarching sensibility to different degrees. Both Federalists and Republicans thought they were acting to protect what was best in the American experiment, and both, in their different ways, saw themselves as protecting America's core civic principles. The conflicts over the Alien and Sedition Acts and the Naturalization Act of 1798 were not simply political ploys by elites or expressions of nativism, as they have often been portrayed. Nor were they simply a contest between an exclusionary nationalism and an inclusionary civic orientation. Rather, these conflicts pitted two visions of a free American nation against one another, visions that were being filtered through a particularly anxious period in U.S. foreign affairs.

Although Jefferson and Madison, the leaders of the Republicans, had both supported the new constitution in 1787, by 1798 the Republicans envisioned a decentralized political system and a broadly defined sense of national identity.[1] They believed that civic principles would flourish if arbitrary authority was clearly limited, state prerogatives respected, and the rights of aliens and citizens protected. Their Federalist opponents, by contrast, believed that civic principles depended on a robust and narrowly defined sense of nationhood, one that was best preserved by limiting immigration, access to naturalization, and the rights of aliens—and doing so through unlimited federal authority.

Because these two understandings of citizenship both sprang from ideas about the proper relation between the civic and the national dimensions of American citizenship, they had some ideals in common. These ideals can be seen joined in the figures of the Federalist John Marshall and the Republican James Madison. Madison's moderate civic nationalism in particular combined the best aspects of the other, more extreme positions. At the same time, the attempts by both men to balance individual freedom and national community gave concrete expression to the conflict between the two that is at the core of civic nationalism.

Partisan and Ideological Divisions

The Sedition Act made it possible for the president to prosecute critics of the government on the grounds that there was such a thing as a seditious libel. The Alien Enemies Act enabled the president to detain and deport aliens who were citizens of countries with whom America was at war; it was much less controversial than the other parts of the legislation and remains in effect today. The Alien Friends Act said the same thing but with regard to countries with whom America was not in a declared war. The alien acts gave the president unlimited power to expel any alien "whom he shall judge dangerous to the peace and safety of the United States."[2] The Naturalization Act of 1798 required an alien to register with federal officials, file a declaration of intention to become a citizen at least five years before becoming a citizen, and wait fourteen rather than five years before becoming eligible for naturalization.

The differences between the proponents of the Alien, Sedition, and Naturalization Acts and their critics stemmed in part from the battle between Jefferson and Hamilton in the early 1790s when they were both in George Washington's cabinet (Jefferson as secretary of state and Hamilton as secretary of the treasury). There they had clashed over the national bank, the interpretation of the Constitution, and the character of the American nation. Hamilton wanted to create a national bank and a near permanent national debt. These measures would allow the United States to create a solid public credit that would come in handy if the United States ever needed to go to war. They would also put the country on a path of industrialization by supporting American manufacturers. These goals aligned America's interests in international relations with Great Britain. Hamilton believed that Jefferson, by contrast, "drank freely of the French Philosophy, in Religion, in Science, in politics. He came from France in the moment of a fermentation which he had had a share in exciting, & in the passions and feelings of which he shared both from temperament and situation."[3]

From Jefferson's perspective, each one of Hamilton's ideas was wrong. He believed that America's interests as well as its philosophy led it naturally to align with revolutionary France. In his view, Hamilton's plans for American manufacturers would create a monied, corrupt class that would wrest power from the honest producers and the small farmers, and his strong central government would be extremely distant from the people. All of the traditional republican worries that Jefferson had inherited from the radical Whigs in England were excited by this vision that Hamilton and his friends meant to establish a monarchy or hereditary aristocracy in America. "Hamilton was not only a monarchist," Jefferson concluded, "but for a monarchy bottomed on corruption. . . . [He was] bewitched and perverted by the British example."[4] "His system," Jefferson wrote in a letter to Washington, "flowed from principles averse to liberty, and was calculated to undermine and demolish the Republic."[5]

After John Adams's election in 1796, foreign affairs gave these domestic political debates a much more fevered cast. Politics began to take on an all-or-nothing, conspiracy-theory tone that was only inflamed by the international context, in which the possibility of war with France loomed. When Adams was elected, France was at war with Britain and other countries in Europe. American and French ships were attacking each other without an express declaration of war, a situation we now call the Quasi-War. It was against this background that Adams called Congress into a special session in May 1797 for the purposes of sending a mission of ambassadors to negotiate with France and strengthening national defenses. When the French refused to meet the American mission without bribes (the XYZ Affair, after the code names given to the private French citizens who claimed to be agents of Talleyrand) and issued a sweeping decree that all ships carrying British cargo could be stopped, it looked very much as though America would be in an open war with France at any moment.

The Federalists' worries about the Republicans' plan for extending the principles and practice of the French Revolution to the United States took on a more discernible shape in the wake of the XYZ Affair. Many Americans erupted in anger against the presumption of the French—"Millions for defence, but not one cent for tribute" was a popular slogan—and the Federalists in the Adams administration and in Congress found themselves riding a momentary wave of anti-French feeling that swept the country. Worries about immigrants were heightened in the atmosphere of impending war, especially Irish immigrants, who were more likely to sympathize with France and support the Republicans' "leveling" schemes. "Under the guise of patriotic purpose and internal security," writes the historian James Morton Smith, "the Federalists enacted a program designed to cripple, if not destroy, the Jeffersonian party. In the face of the emergence of an effective grass-roots democratic opposition to their domestic and foreign policies, they retreated to repression as a means of retaining political power."[6] Their program included calling Washington out of retirement to lead a stronger army, with Hamilton as his second-in-command. More infamously, it included the Alien, Sedition, and Naturalization Acts.

The bitter ideological divisions in which these acts arose were most marked in relation to what Americans thought about the French Revolution. One's view of the principles and practices of the revolutionary government in France was thought to indicate what one really believed to be the true nature of American citizenship. Was the French Revolution an expression of the best form of civic freedom or a cautionary example of democracy gone mad? Leading figures believed that this question went to the heart of their new nation's meaning.[7]

"THE CONSTITUTION WAS MADE FOR CITIZENS, NOT ALIENS"

The most ardent proponents of the Alien and Sedition Acts and the Naturalization Act of 1798 took longstanding concerns over national identity and belonging and pressed them to extreme conclusions. In the House of Representatives, Harrison Gray Otis, Robert Goodloe Harper, and John Allen were the key figures, particularly Otis and Harper. Otis, a moderate Massachusetts Federalist and supporter of John Adams, and Harper, a leading South Carolinian Federalist, were particularly close (Allen represented Connecticut). Although a number of their proposals were turned back, their vision of citizenship dominated the debates and drove the legislation in its most immoderate directions.

For Otis, Harper, and Allen, the country needed significant restrictive measures to protect itself from imminent attack by the French and French sympathizers. France, they claimed, had shown no compunction about toppling other governments in Europe, especially small republics, usually by attacking them from within and then invading them. In America, they believed, France was trying to gain a foothold through immigrants and democratic societies. Otis detailed these fears in a speech in the House of Representatives before the Alien and Sedition Acts were passed in June: "In my humble opinion, there is greater danger from this source [aliens] than from any other. I believe that it has been owing to this cause that all the Republics in Europe have been laid prostrate in the dust; . . . it is this system which has watered the tomb of William Tell with the blood of widows fighting over their slaughtered husbands, and with the tears of orphans who survive to swell the procession of the victors. . . . In the fate of the European Republics," Otis warned, "we might read our own."[8]

Proponents of the alien acts also dwelt extensively on what they considered the clear evidence that aliens currently coming to the United States lacked the proper habits and dispositions for self-governance. In a special session of Congress in May 1797, Otis echoed the worries about immigrant character that both Jefferson and Morris had raised in earlier debates and writings, but his position was more radical. He defended a proposal to tax heavily all certificates of naturalization, and hence to limit immigration. "The tax," he declared, "will tend to foreclose the mass of vicious and disorganizing characters who cannot live peaceably at home, and who, after unfurling the standard of rebellion in their own countries, may come hither to revolutionize ours. . . . I do not wish to invite hordes of wild Irishmen, nor the turbulent and disorderly of all parts of the world, to come here with a view to disturb our tranquillity, after having succeeded in the overthrow of their own Governments."[9]

Otis and his colleagues worried specifically about the political effects of the influx of great numbers of radical immigrants from Ireland and France. Men who had no or little property would have no interest in protecting private property, in their view one of the most important protections of the Constitution. Proponents of the alien acts also worried that a large number of aliens of any sort tended to threaten the purity of national character. "The grand cause of all our present difficulties," asserted William S. Shaw, Adams's nephew and secretary, "may be traced . . . to so many hordes of foreigners imigrating to America. . . . Let us no longer pray that America may become an asylum to all nations."[10]

To combat these threats, some of the Federalists made a number of far-reaching proposals. They advocated unlimited presidential authority to restrain and remove enemy aliens, subject only to subsequent congressional regulation, and left open to later definition the penalty American citizens would be subject to for harboring or concealing an enemy alien.[11] Otis wanted aliens to be deported as soon as war was declared between the United States and their home country. Allen went even further, saying that deportation should not be contingent upon war or invasion, nor should it be limited to alien enemies. "[T]here are citizens of several other countries who are as dangerous, who have dispositions equally hostile to this country with the French—he believed more so." Allen pointed especially to the significant rise in naturalizations in Philadelphia that increased support for the Republican Party. It was not "wise or prudent," he advised, "to wait for an invasion, or threatened invasion."[12] He further hinted at the need for some sort of legislation to deal with American citizens who harbored aliens.

In the alien friends debate, Federalists further argued for deporting aliens who were suspected of wrongdoing without a trial by jury or any specific finding of guilt. If an alien was deported and then returned to the United States, they proposed that the alien should be tried and, if convicted, banished for life or fined and sentenced to hard labor for a specific number of years. If the alien were apprehended after being banished, he was to be imprisoned without trial and confined to hard labor for life.[13] The original bill also proposed a national registration and surveillance system for all aliens. No alien was to be allowed into the country without obtaining a special permit that required the holder to remain in his locality. The failure to get this permit meant the offender could be tried and, if convicted, imprisoned during the life of the act or fined. Citizens could not "harbour, entertain or conceal any alien" without providing a notice to a federal judge in advance. The bill further sought to reverse the burden of proof in all these cases, requiring the alien to demonstrate he had conformed to the law and the Constitution in order to obtain a permit and that he had not violated the permit once obtained. The government need not prove anything.

Some of these proposals were incorporated into the final legislation, while others were turned back by Republican opponents. They indicate the extremes to which some Federalists were willing to take their concerns about protecting the character of the nation.

Other leading Federalists did not fully share these views and joined the Republicans in opposing some of these measures. They criticized a larger system of registration and surveillance that would have required aliens to receive permits to remain in specific localities and required citizens to report to a federal judge their intention to house an alien. They further objected to proposals that aliens who returned after having been deported would be sentenced to imprisonment and hard labor.[14] Although eager to restrict aliens' rights and extend the naturalization period, Samuel Sewall (Massachusetts), chairman of the House Committee on the Defense of the Country for the Protection of Commerce, contended that power over aliens should be as guarded and definite as possible, rather than open-ended and subject to abuse. Allen's fears, he declared, were delusional apprehensions that "arose from some defect in his own organization, or disease of his body (which he believed might be better cured by the physician, than by anything else) rather than from any real ground of alarm."[15]

Hamilton, who had returned to private life in 1795 but remained an influential Federalist, sought to temper the more radical measures, although his protests were relatively mild. "Let us not establish a tyranny," he cautioned Oliver Wolcott, Adams's secretary of the treasury. "Energy is a very different thing from violence."[16] President Adams later denied any responsibility for the measures, although at the time he publicly worried about the influence of aliens and approved the acts once they had been passed by Congress.[17]

Restrictions on aliens and extended naturalization requirements were, however, strongly supported by the more dominant Federalist strain. A powerful, well-defined notion of nationhood was a central component of their argument. This notion was even more constricted than the traditional ideas about instinctive attachment and early education that Morris and Sedgwick had articulated in earlier debates. For Otis and his compatriots, the conditions of the original act of consent, the need for national self-preservation, and the importance of native birth all meant rights applied only to citizens.

In the debate over the Alien Friends Act, Otis argued that aliens were not a part of the people who consented to the original Constitution. " '[W]e, the people of the United States,' " he observed, "were the only parties concerned in making that instrument. [I find] nothing in it which [binds] us to fraternize with the whole world." The Constitution's protections against governmental abrogations of rights were reserved for the citizenry; they did not extend to aliens. The Republicans' arguments were based on "the very erroneous hypothesis, that aliens are parties to our Constitution, that it was made for their benefit as well as our own, and that they may claim equal rights and privileges with our own citizens."[18] A supporter extended this claim: since aliens were not a party to the compact they "were not bound by it to the performance of any particular duty, nor did it confer upon them any rights."[19] And in a report to the House of Representatives arguing against repealing the Alien and Sedition Acts, a select committee asserted that "the Constitution was made for citizens, not for aliens, who of consequences have no rights under it."[20] The Republicans' complaint that the legislation provided the president with arbitrary authority in violation of basic rights was beside the point for the Federalists. In their view, constitutional limitations on governmental authority simply did not apply to aliens. If, for instance, the president deemed an alien to be a danger, that alien would have demonstrated that he lacked the proper qualities to become a citizen and hence could be deported. The issue was citizenship, not rights.[21]

Robert Harper sharpened the distinction between citizens and aliens further in responding to the accusation, made by Edward Livingston of New York, that the Federalists' constitutional theory would do nothing to prevent a similar bill from being adopted with regard to citizens. What would prevent this development, he asked? "What prevents me from cutting the throat of the gentleman from New York? The laws of God and of my country. In the same way should I be prevented from bringing in a bill of this kind against citizens." Harper acknowledged that citizens might be more dangerous than aliens, but he affirmed that the Constitution protected citizens against banishment.[22]

For the Federalists, Congress's authority to bestow on the president sweeping and largely unregulated control over aliens issued as well from a right to self-preservation and the Constitution's recognition of this critical principle. The preamble's injunction to provide for the common defense and the general welfare, Sewall said, furnished Congress the implied authority to restrain seditious persons and to banish dangerous aliens.[23] "If we find men in this country endeavoring to spread sedition and discord; who have assisted in laying other countries prostrate; whose hands are reeking with blood, and whose hearts rankle with hatred towards us," Otis asked, "have we not the power to shake off these firebrands?" If the Constitution did not allow Congress to restrain and banish aliens suspected of sedition, the Constitution "would not be worth a farthing."[24]

In their initial proposal to extend the naturalization process, the Federalists' inveighed against the current policy of admitting aliens to citizenship when there was "not sufficient evidence of their attachment to the laws and welfare of this country to entitle them to such privilege." To ensure that attachment, the House Committee on the Defense of the Country for the Protection of Commerce proposed that "a longer residence within the United States, before admission than the act provides is essential and ought to be required." Sewall, chairman of the committee, first recommended that the number of years of residency required before naturalization be raised from five to ten. France, he observed, required a much longer period.[25]

Others sought to place more extensive barriers to membership by consent and to limit the rights of naturalized citizens. Otis proposed that only native-born citizens should be allowed to hold public office. He moved to amend the Naturalization Act to read "that no alien born, who is not at present a citizen of the United States shall hereafter be capable of holding any office of honor, trust, or profit under the United States." Citizenship and suffrage were separable, Otis contended, and pointed to Great Britain as a good example to follow. And since Congress had the authority to establish a uniform rule of naturalization, it could make the period of residency equal to the life of the alien. Otis proposed a graded form of citizenship in which only native-born citizens would be eligible for high office. Harper called for an even more radical assertion of nativity. He insisted that "nothing but birth should entitle a man to citizenship in this country." This position was ruled out of order and dismissed without debate, but it indicated the extent to which some legislators were willing to go in pressing the exclusionary dimension of birthright citizenship.

When this proposal was rejected, Harper sought to extend Otis's motion to bar naturalized citizens from holding office by barring them from voting as well. Though he believed foreigners should be afforded civil rights, such as property ownership, he asserted that "it was an essential policy, which lay at the bottom of civil society, that none but persons born in the country should be permitted to take part in the Government." Even the most acceptable of strangers, he contended, "could not have the same views and attachment with native citizens." Besides, he added, immigrants came to the United States not because they wanted to hold office or vote but to live under a free government.[26]

Harper's proposal to deny the suffrage to non-native-born citizens failed because of constitutional concerns that the federal government could not restrain the states in their admission of citizens. Otis's proposal to bar naturalized citizens from holding office was shelved by other Federalists. They regarded it as also being too easily subject to constitutional objections. Instead, with Otis's support, they championed an extended residency period as the most effective way to prevent most aliens from naturalizing and becoming politically active. After little debate, and a very close vote, legislation passed that increased the residency period to fourteen years. This legislation also required that an alien make a declaration of intention to naturalize at least five years before becoming a citizen.[27]

By 1798 the Federalists had adopted a view of attachment and homogeneity similar in important ways to that of the Anti-Federalists during the debates over ratifying the Constitution. Otis, Harper, and Allen treated national identity as natural rather than created. They believed that attachment to others was fundamentally instinctive and had to be acquired early in life. Similarly, they thought that the republican habits of self-governance were most likely to flourish only when inculcated from birth. They married these views to a commercial, centralist conception of citizenship in which a large but homogeneous nation was best preserved by limiting immigration, access to naturalization, and the rights of aliens. In sum, proponents of the Alien and Sedition Acts increasingly tied the future of their new government to the particular habits, education, and history of those already in America and their children. America's civic principles would flourish only so long as the current American nation did.

These views were not anti-alien in the sense that they identified Americans as a naturally superior people, although they often incorporated such sentiments. Nor were they nativist in the sense that they grew out of a specific hostility toward aliens, although such hostility existed and conditioned these views. Rather, these were traditional, mainstream views that specific events forced their exponents to articulate in a more pointed way than during earlier debates.[28] In the context of the political battles of the 1790s, including the possibility of war with France, Federalist leaders gave specific meaning to the longstanding position that national cohesion becomes increasingly difficult to achieve in proportion to the diversity among the citizenry.

The Rights of Aliens, Citizens, and States

Critics of the Alien and Sedition Acts and the Naturalization Act of 1798, like their opponents, thought the government had the right to exclude newcomers from entry, and even to arbitrarily detain or deport alien enemies. Alien enemies, they acknowledged, were subject to the discretion of the Congress, a power that stems from the power to declare war. Critics of these acts also believed that the government should establish rules for becoming citizens and require newcomers to complete the naturalization process before they could become eligible to vote or hold public office. In their view, these requirements were all "favors," or privileges, properly determined and dispensed by Congress.

Yet Jefferson, Madison, and the rest of the Republicans could hardly fail to notice that most of the Federalists' worries were Republican hopes and vice versa, and that the proposals meant to defend the nation turned out to be directed mostly at the Republican position. In 1798, traditional fears of a standing army dominating an unarmed people at the behest of a strong executive seemed to be coming true in the form of a national army with Alexander Hamilton near the top. They were also outraged by the Alien and Sedition Acts, which put recent immigrants and critics of the Federalists at the caprice of the president and the Federalist-dominated judiciary, and at the Naturalization Act, which seemed designed to keep immigrants from voting—immigrants who tended to vote Republican.

The Republicans' objections to the various laws passed in 1798 were also deeply rooted in an understanding of the relation between the civic and the national dimensions of citizenship that differed from that of the Federalists in crucial ways. They stressed the rights of aliens, citizens, and states. Critics of the alien acts distinguished between favors subject to the discretion of the government and rights that cannot be abrogated—at least not without what we would today call "due process." They contended that once aliens had been lawfully admitted to the country and were living under its laws, civil rights could not be denied them without injustice. "[I]t cannot be a true inference," Madison insisted, "that because the administration of an alien is a favor, the favor may be revoked at pleasure. . . . [I]t cannot be pretended, that a person naturalized can be deprived of the benefit, any more than a native citizen can be disenfranchised."[29]

In their view, the civic principles that undergirded self-government required the government to treat aliens no differently than citizens with regard to civil rights. Aliens who were subject to the law ought to be protected by it. Representative Edward Livingston of New York declared that law, justice, and the practice of all civilized nations recognized the reciprocal relation between the temporary allegiance of aliens and the requirement of governmental protection for them. "If they are accused of violating this allegiance," he pointed out, "the same laws which interpose in the case of a citizen must determine the truth of the accusation, and if found guilty they are liable to the same punishment. This rule is consonant to the principles of common justice, for who would ever resort to another country, if he alone was marked out as the object of arbitrary power?" Livingston especially derided the idea that the Constitution applied only to citizens. The document made no distinction when it referred to all "persons accused," "all trials for crimes," all "judicial power," and all "criminal prosecutions." The Constitution, he asserted, made "[n]o distinction between citizen and alien, between high or low, friends or opposers to the Executive power, republican and royalist."[30]

Writing in 1800, Madison supported Livingston's analysis. "[I]t does not follow," he contended, "because aliens are not parties to the Constitution, as citizens are parties to it, that whilst they actually conform to it, they have no right to its protection." If this were true, he suggested, an alien could be put to death without a fair trial. This possibility was odious, and, moreover, it contradicted the principle that had been upheld throughout the United States that an alien not only had to receive a jury trial but had to have one in which up to half the jury were also aliens.[31]

During the congressional debates, Livingston had similarly criticized the extent to which the proponents of the Alien Friends Act had pushed the logic of national belonging. He contended that to justify their policies the Federalists had to call black white: "Good Heaven! To what absurdities does an overzealous attachment to particular measures lead us! In order to punish a particular act we are forced to say that treason is no crime and plotting against our Government is no offence! And, to support this fine hypothesis, we are obliged to plunge deeper in absurdity, and say that, as the acts spoken of in the bill, are no crimes, so the penalty contained in it is no punishment, it is only a prevention." To reach these ridiculous conclusions, Livingston charged, the Federalists had to undermine the commitment to the nation that all agreed should be inculcated in aliens and to violate the presumption of individual liberty to which the country was dedicated and which had attracted immigrants in the first place:

> An unfortunate stranger, disgusted with tyranny at home, thinks he shall find freedom here. . . . But, while he is patiently waiting the expiration of the period that is to crown the work, and entitle him to all the rights of a citizen, the tale of a domestic spy, or the calumny of a secret enemy, draws on him the suspicions of the President, and, unheard, he is ordered to quit the spot which he selected for his retreat, the country which he had chosen for his own, perhaps the family which was his only consolation in life, he is ordered to retire to a country whose Government, irritated by his renunciation of its authority, will receive only to punish him; and all this, we are told, is no punishment.[32]

On the question of naturalization, Republicans strongly defended a uniform conception of citizenship with regard to the status of aliens. In the debate over the Naturalization Act of 1798, Representative Abraham Venable of Virginia rejected Otis's proposal to deny eligibility for public office to naturalized citizens. Citizenship, he contended, was an all-or-nothing proposition: "Foreigners must . . . be refused the privilege of becoming citizens altogether, or admitted to all the rights of citizens." Representative Nathaniel Macon of North Carolina reinforced this position. No mere law, he asserted, could change the constitutional requirement that all citizens are equal and thus equally eligible for public office. To establish a second-class form of citizenship simply was not possible under the Constitution. (Second-class citizenship for free blacks, women, and Native Americans did not figure in these debates.)[33]

Macon's fellow North Carolinian, Representative Joseph McDowell, took a different tack. He agreed with the Federalists that it might be appropriate to require seven or even nine years of residency before an immigrant became eligible for citizenship. But he argued that anything beyond that was counterproductive. The Federalist plan to make citizenship so difficult to achieve would discourage "respectable foreigners" from emigrating to the United States. Moreover, when immigrants did come to the United States, it was "in our interest to attach them to us, and not always to look upon them as aliens and strangers."[34]

Opponents of the Alien Friends Act conceived of nationhood differently from those who urged greater restrictions on aliens. Their understanding of allegiance and identity was not threatened by recognizing aliens' rights within a broader framework based on core civic principles and practices. The greatest threat to the American people, in their mind, came from policies that subverted self-government, such as the act's creation of a class subject to the arbitrary authority of the president. To them, the act was an exercise of "preventive" justice, in which alien friends could be detained or deported without being accused of a specific crime. They also found the severity of its punishments too great to be applied without the safeguards against arbitrary power ensured by the judicial process. Echoing Livingston, Madison argued that deportation was so harsh that it could never be an appropriate response to mere suspicion.[35]

Opponents of the Alien Friends Act further contended that it constituted a threat not only to the liberty of alien friends but to all citizens' civic freedom. The act threatened that freedom indirectly by subverting the concept of limited government. The power conferred by the act was not enumerated in the Constitution, they pointed out, and the Tenth Amendment says that all powers not given to the federal government are reserved to the people or the states. The act thus opened the door to future usurpations of authority by the federal government by strengthening the claim that such authority is unlimited rather than enumerated.[36] In the Virginia House of Delegates debates, John Taylor added that the act also presented an immediate danger to the liberty of citizens by creating a class of persons dependent on the president. Such authority violated fundamental civic principles by making the president "a king of the aliens."[37]

The Republicans concurred with the Federalists that certain powers might be implied by the Constitution, but they insisted that the need for such powers must be demonstrated. Robert Williams of North Carolina declared that if the preamble conferred an open-ended grant of authority, as the Federalists suggested, then the rest of the Constitution would be superfluous. The preamble, he noted pointedly, "would swallow up the whole." And Albert Gallatin, the Geneva-born leader of the Jeffersonians in the House, inquired of Otis, "Did he like the Constitution only for the powers it gave, and not for the restraints it put on power?"[38]

The Federalists' constitutional theory, which seemed to turn limits on federal authority into grants of executive power, provoked revolutionary talk from its critics. Samuel Smith, an unaffiliated representative from Maryland, suggested that the Federalists' actions mirrored those of Great Britain that had provoked the American Revolution. The Declaration of Independence, he reminded his foes, included the complaint that the king of England had prevented emigration to the colonies and denied them the authority to naturalize new citizens. Livingston charged that the absence of distinctions between citizens and aliens in the Constitution meant that the same restraints and punishments contemplated for aliens would also be applied to citizens. He warned that neither the people nor the states would accept this infringement on their liberty. The effects of these measures "will be disaffection among the States, and opposition among the people to your Government—tumults, violations, and a recurrence to first revolutionary principles." Livingston concluded by calling explicit attention to the link between foreign affairs and domestic ideological divisions:

Do not let us be told, sir, that we excite a fervor against foreign aggression only to establish tyranny at home; that, like the arch traitor, we cry "*Hail Columbia!*" at the moment we are betraying her to destruction; that we sing out "*Happy land!*" when we are plunging it in ruin or disgrace; and that we are absurd enough to call ourselves *"free and enlightened,"* while we advocate principles that would have disgraced the age of Gothic barbarity, and establish a code, compared to which, the ordeal is wise, and the trial by battle is merciful and just.[39]

As the revolutionary talk of Smith and Livingston indicates, the Republicans' opposition to the Alien and Sedition Acts encompassed broader concerns than the rights of aliens. Indeed, their opposition to those measures was not based on an absolute prohibition on seditious libel laws or restrictions on aliens' rights. They did not object to state laws that were exactly the same as the ones passed by Congress. Proponents of the Alien and Sedition Acts had in fact called attention to this fact, noting that a number of states, including strongly Republican ones like Virginia, already had laws allowing for the deportation of aliens.[40] Otis had sought to use this contradiction against the Republicans. He quoted statutes from states that made libel a criminal offense and punished licentiousness and sedition even while those same states' constitutions expressly protected the right of free speech and freedom of the press.[41]

But where Otis saw a contradiction, most Republicans believed their views were entirely consistent. To be sure, the conflict over the federal Alien and Sedition Acts forced some Republicans to rethink the idea of prohibitions on seditious libel at any level of government. But their attacks on the federal package focused extensively on questions of federalism. Gallatin contended that "every nation had a right to permit or exclude alien friends from entering within the bounds of their society. [But] . . . in this country . . . the power to admit, or to exclude alien friends, does solely belong to each individual State." Republicans advanced similar arguments regarding the Sedition Act and limits on freedom of the press and freedom of speech. Macon, for instance, insisted that the sedition bill "directly violated the letter of the Constitution," but he found nothing objectionable in the law itself. After all, "persons might be prosecuted for a libel under the State Governments," he noted approvingly.[42]

This concern for states' rights became especially pronounced in the Kentucky and Virginia Resolutions. Drafted by Jefferson and Madison, respectively, they were protests by state legislatures against the perceived injustice and unconstitutionality of the Federalist-sponsored legislation. The Virginia legislature claimed there was "a design . . . to consolidate the States by degrees, into one sovereignty, the obvious tendency and inevitable consequence of which would be, to transform the present republican system of the United States, into an absolute, or at best a mixed monarchy." The Republicans' opposition to the Alien and Sedition Acts thus flowed from deeply held beliefs in states as the location in which liberty was best protected and from which citizens could most easily participate in public life.[43]

Their opposition was also profoundly rooted in the linkage between states' rights and slavery. They relied on a constitutional provision prohibiting Congress from ending the slave trade until 1808 to deny that Congress had the power to deport aliens. Article I, Section 9 of the Constitution barred Congress from prohibiting until that date "the Migration or Importation of such Persons as any of the States now existing shall think proper to admit." Gallatin argued that whereas the word "importation" applied to slaves, the word "migration" referred to free immigrants. Further, he said, the word "persons" was a general term and therefore did not exclude free immigrants. Both slaves and free immigrants had been expressly included in this provision, he contended, so as to cement a deal between the middle and southern states: the former had wanted to ensure that they would continue to receive new settlers, and the latter wanted to continue importing slaves. Gallatin did not support slavery or the slave trade, but most of his Republican allies were southerners who either opposed abolition or believed the fate of slavery ought to be determined by local communities. They worried that if Congress could deport aliens it likewise had the authority to remove slaves from the country despite the importation clause.[44]

This states' rights dimension to Republican thinking further indicates the extent to which more than simply partisanship was involved in the conflict over the Alien and Sedition Acts and the Naturalization Act of 1798. The political stakes were high because foundational beliefs about citizenship were at stake. Although at odds with the Federalist conception, the Republicans' understanding of the relation between the civic and the national dimensions of citizenship was not entirely distinct from that of their opponents. Republican arguments in favor of protecting the civil rights of aliens were a subset of a broader argument that the national government did not possess the authority to violate the rights of aliens or citizens. This argument fit within traditional concerns about self-government and community, concerns which, in the case of aliens, tended toward inclusionary policies and, in the case of blacks, undergirded their exclusion.[45]

The relevant distinction is thus not between an exclusionary nationalism championed by the Federalists and an inclusionary civic approach advanced by the Republicans. The proper distinction is between two models that both emerged from shared convictions about the value of individual freedom and national authority, and the different balances they struck between the two. Those shared convictions can be seen united in the figures of the Federalist John Marshall and the Republican James Madison.

MARSHALL, MADISON, AND MODERATE CIVIC NATIONALISM

John Marshall was the most notable moderate Federalist to question the wisdom of the Alien and Sedition Acts. James Madison, who made significant contributions to both the Federalists' and the Republicans' ideology, forthrightly opposed the acts. In these debates, both Marshall and Madison characterized American nationhood as defined by the "will of the people" rather than solely a matter of organic belonging or belief in abstract principles. This definition pitted principles against peoplehood in focusing attention on individual and states' rights versus majority rule. Yet Marshall and Madison also sought to balance these claims. Their efforts contributed to the emergence of a moderate civic nationalism while also revealing enduring tensions at the heart of that approach.[46]

Marshall had served as one of Adams's commissioners to France during the XYZ Affair and was at that time the leading Federalist in Virginia. In mid-August of 1798, he wrote to Timothy Pickering, Adams's secretary of state, that the Sedition Act was "viewed by a great many well meaning men as unwarranted by the Constitution." As a candidate for Congress in the fall of 1798, he responded to an anonymous letter published in the *Times and Virginia Advertiser* seeking his views on the Constitution, foreign affairs, and especially the alien and sedition bills.[47] Declaring himself "[i]n heart and sentiment, as well as by birth and interest . . . , an American; attached to the genuine principles of the constitution, as sanctioned by the will of the people," he assured his readers that he was "not an advocate of the alien sedition bills." Had he been a member of Congress during the previous session, Marshall contended, he would have unhesitatingly opposed these measures.

As a defender of national authority, Marshall did not say that the laws were unconstitutional or threatened to subvert the principles of self-governance. Rather, he deemed them "useless . . . ; [t]hey are calculated to create unnecessary discontents and jealousies at a time when our very existence, as a nation, may depend on our union."[48] Marshall believed that the laws would be quickly repealed and pledged that he would oppose any efforts to revive them. In fact, the laws were still in effect when he became a member of Congress and he joined with the Republicans in voting to repeal the sedition law; the vote was 50 to 48. Marshall's first biographer, Albert Beveridge, judges that "[h]ad he voted with his party, the Republican attack [on the sedition law] would have failed."[49]

During Marshall's campaign for office, the New England Federalists had been appalled by his views. Some, like Sedgwick, found them "mysterious and unpardonable" conduct that aided "French villainy," but dismissed them as carefully couched political statements designed to ensure Marshall's election in strongly Republican Virginia. Others believed that Marshall's statements reflected his true views. Writing about Marshall, Fisher Ames of Massachusetts declared that "[t]he moderates are the meanest of cowards, the falsest of hypocrites." And John Thompson from Virginia, writing under the pen name "Curtius," informed Marshall that he had "lost forever the affection of a nation and the applause of a world." As a moderate, Marshall was subject to these criticisms as well as those hurled at him by Republicans who still found his views far too dangerously "monarchist" and "aristocratic" and who assailed him as a "British agent," an "enemy of free speech," and a "destroyer of trial by jury."[50]

Despite his criticisms of the Alien and Sedition Acts, Marshall was a Federalist, and it was rumored he had authored or collaborated on authoring a defense of these measures against Jefferson and Madison's efforts to rally the states against them. That defense criticized the Virginia Resolution as part of a plan to break up the United States and contrasted "the happiness united America enjoys" with "the evils which disunited America must inevitably suffer." It articulated a conception of nationhood that distinguished between a union of citizens and a compact among states: "we, the people" authorized the Constitution, and thus individual states had no legitimate authority to object to laws passed by proper constitutional means. This focus reflects the moderate Federalists' preoccupation with grounding the legitimacy of the Constitution in the will of the people as a whole far more than in distinguishing between citizens and aliens. In their view, Americans had become a single people when they ratified the Constitution, bound together as a nation by this transformative act of consent as much as by the principles to which they consented.[51]

Marshall also represented a brand of national sovereignty that was willing to criticize its own excesses. His objections in 1798 to the Alien and Sedition Acts contributed to their eventual undoing. And in 1801 he voted in Congress to repeal the sedition law, despite the fact that this vote weakened his future as a Federalist leader. Marshall's criticism of the Alien and Sedition Acts had, nonetheless, been relatively muted. Preserving the Union clearly overrode his concerns about violations of individual liberty. His was a moderate civic nationalism willing to tolerate extreme measures in order to defend the sovereignty of federal authority. Marshall's views suggested the ways even a self-critical civic nationalism could still exact a price in individual liberty and the treatment of aliens.

Over the course of a long public career, Madison articulated a protean and moderate nationalism, one that at various stages placed greater emphasis on federal or state identity and authority and that continually aimed to balance individual rights and national sovereignty. His civic nationalism entailed a process of continual construction that does not rest on yesterday's formulations, but instead requires institutions and identities to be modified to meet new challenges. In reacting to the extreme proposals for unlimited presidential authority advanced by the Federalists, Madison stressed the central function played by the states in protecting rights and preserving liberty. But he also emphasized that the states played a role within a larger national framework of identity and governmental structure.

In his opposition to the Alien and Sedition Acts, Madison sought to secure all Americans' approval for Virginia's interpretation of the Constitution. "The test of the acts was not the immediate political will in *one* state," the political scientists Bradley Carter and Joseph Kobylka comment in explaining Madison's approach, "but rather the compatibility of the Acts, *in the public mind*, with the principles underlying the political community of all states."[52] In this sense, Madison's position was characterized by a distinctly communal and national dimension. He defended a "compound republic," a system neither "wholly national nor merely federal," in which individual states could not simply annul particular laws they disliked.[53]

The different emphases Madison placed on national or federal authority throughout his career reflected a careful effort to draw important distinctions as to the best way to prevent minority rule: in the 1780s and 1830s by emphasizing the national dimension, and in the 1790s by bolstering the states' roles as intermediaries. As the historian Drew McCoy points out about Madison's balancing act in the 1830s, he really had "two objectives and two audiences"—to draw Jeffersonians away from nullification and nationalists away from overweening federal demands.[54] Madison's views, like Marshall's, reflected an ongoing effort to manage the tension between civic principles of individual and states' rights and the national authority and identity necessary to counter minority tyranny. Madison represented a more decentralist vision than did Marshall, but he was, as Joseph Reisert writes, an advocate "of a balanced federalism, taking the side of national government when the fractiousness of the state governments threatened the union with anarchy and taking the side of the state governments when the national government overstepped its constitutional authority."[55] Thus, it was from the same set of concerns about community and creed that had driven the Federalists' nationalism and the Republicans' focus on self-governance that Madison's civic nationalism emerged as an alternative to both.

Yet Madison's views on the proper balance between state and federal authority and identity were not always clear. Did his arguments actually contemplate an ultimate right to revolution, to secession, if individual states did not believe the principles of a federal, republican government were being respected? Or did he believe that differences within the nation could only be resolved via an appeal to the whole people?[56] It seems implausible that if the people of the United States had decided that the Alien and Sedition Acts were acceptable, Madison would have humbly gone back to Virginia and accepted his error. After all, the whole point of his objection to the acts was that the federal government was violating basic civic principles and undermining the shared political truths that bind citizens into a nation. If Madison had stood by the logic of those principles he might have had to contemplate the dissolution of the American nation. As it happened, although Kentucky and Virginia's sister states rejected the resolutions, these statements did serve to rally opposition to the Federalist schemes and thus contribute to their quick demise. Because of these developments, Madison never had to give a final answer to a tension at the heart of his moderate civic nationalism: To what extent does the nation reflect a unitary people and to what extent does it embody civic principles—in this case the right to secession—that cannot be suppressed, even by that people? Madison did not resolve this tension, though his moderate approach and his focus on flexible political institutions suggests a way to manage it.

Civic nationalists like Madison and Marshall were pulled in different directions by their opponents, especially those who set the terms of debate by proposing significantly longer and more restrictive requirements. At times, the more exclusionary aspects of a shared concern for nationhood prevailed, and policy swung toward more restrictive requirements. These requirements were temporary, but they suggested the direction in which policy could be pressed by the competition among different kinds of nationalism.

Despite these swings and the tensions between civic principles and national identity, by the beginning of the nineteenth century a moderate civic nationalism emerged on the specific question of what laws should govern the rights of aliens and the requirements for naturalization. By the time Jefferson was elected president, the Quasi-War with France had evaporated and with it any popular support for Hamilton's army, which was still more a sketch than a fighting force. The Federalists' attempts to cut off immigrant support for the Republicans failed because they were not able to restrict citizenship to the native-born or to apply the extended residency requirement retroactively to immigrants who had come to America under the 1795 law. If the "wild Irish" were inclined to vote Republican before Otis's famous speech, they were so alienated by the Federalists' open disdain and mistrust that they supported the Republicans even more strongly afterward. For their part, the Republicans naturalized as many Irish and other immigrants as they could.[57]

The support of many of these new citizens contributed to Jefferson's victory in the election of 1800. No one was prosecuted under the Alien Friends Act, which expired in 1801, as did the Sedition Act. The Naturalization Act of 1798 was repealed by Congress in 1802. By then, even figures as widely disparate as the Republican Jefferson and the Federalist Hamilton had come to agree on a five-year residency requirement for naturalization. The temperate civic nationalism of Madison among the Republicans and Marshall among the Federalists had become the dominant position within both parties.[58]

That moderate nationalism also had real restrictions as to how inclusionary its advocates were willing to be when it came to issues of racial difference. We have already glimpsed those limits in the Republicans' capacity to champion both the rights of aliens and the necessity of slavery. To see them more clearly, to evaluate how widely shared they were, and to understand the reasons given for them requires returning to the 1790 naturalization act.

CHAPTER THREE

The Free White Clause of 1790

THE PRECISION with which arguments over immigration and alienage were carried out by the late 1790s stood in marked contrast to the Constitution itself, which did not define who a citizen was. The first legislation that determined who could become a citizen, however, was quite explicit in one respect. The Naturalization Act of 1790 used racial terminology to restrict citizenship to "free white persons." For over a century and a half this limitation had significant consequences. It contributed directly to the subordinate status of minority groups as well as to broader crises in American citizenship and nationhood. It was not abolished until 1952. Yet the authors of the act did not explain their decision. There was no recorded debate over the adoption of the free white clause. Who did the clause's framers intend to exclude and to include, and why?

Traditional accounts have glossed over these questions. They have instead emphasized the liberal, universalistic aspects of the Founding. The exclusion of non-whites from citizenship has been regarded as a regrettable fact that was naturally corrected by America's commitment to its broader civic principles of freedom and equality.[1] More recently, scholars of radically divergent ideological views have shown that the Founding generation's concerns for nationhood had significant bearing on the origins of the free white clause. Some have argued that its origins are fundamentally racist while others have claimed it was merely a prudential calculation that Europeans were more suited for U.S. citizenship.[2]

Arguments from silence are, of course, slippery things that depend heavily on the context into which the silence is set. The lack of debate might, for instance, have reflected a concession to the political reality of sectional differences over slavery rather than the expression of a fundamental theory of citizenship. In this view, some representatives may have had objections to the clause but agreed to its exclusionary language as the price for maintaining the Union. A dispute over the clause might have risked undoing the fragile compromise on the status of blacks and the studied ambiguity on state and national citizenship so recently concluded in ratifying the Constitution.

In fact, neither this rationale nor the traditional liberal nor the revisionist interpretations explain the exclusionary language in the first naturalization act. Instead, legislators in 1790 likely saw the free white clause in the context of arguments they had been having for years in several different contexts about what would happen *after* the abolition of slavery. Scholars have not found any debate over the free white clause because they have been looking in the wrong place—in the debates over naturalization rather than the controversy over emancipation.

What emerges from such a picture is not simply a matter of political compromise, a preference for a shared European heritage, or an unconflicted ideology of racism. Rather, these debates reveal how many leaders agonized over the tension between blacks' natural right to freedom and prudential concerns about an integrated nation. The free white clause terminology was consistent in the minds of those who opposed slavery with ensuring a cohesive community. The shared concern to establish a nationalist foundation for citizenship made it easier for all to agree on excluding blacks from citizenship. A careful examination of this concern highlights the limits of a moderate civic nationalism in balancing the universal thrust of democratic civic principles and the particular bond of nationalist sentiment. It focuses attention especially on the claims minorities can make based on historical treatment and the difficulties civic nationalism faces in acting on those claims.

WHY WHITE?

The use of the term "white" with regard to immigration and naturalization in 1790 at first seems puzzling. After all, few non-whites were emigrating to the United States at the time. "White" had nonetheless become a standard part of politics by the late eighteenth century. The term was used to exclude blacks and Indians and could be found throughout statutory law. It was widely used in restrictions on intermarriage, militia service, voting, and officeholding; on the right to serve as a lawyer, juror, or witness in court (with the exception of cases involving other blacks); and on the right to serve as an executor, make a will, or be a trustee of any land.[3] In this context, the free white clause is best understood as referring to domestic minorities, especially blacks, rather than to immigrants. In his *Commentaries on American Law* (1867), James Kent concurred with this view and gave some indication of the vexatious questions the clause would raise over citizenship in the United States:

> The act of congress confines the description of aliens capable of naturalization to "free white persons." I presume this excludes the inhabitants of Africa, and their descendants; and it may become a question, to what extent persons of mixed blood are excluded, and what shades and degrees of mixture of color disqualify an alien from application for the benefits of the act of naturalization. (a) Perhaps there might be difficulties also as to the copper-colored races of America, or the yellow or tawny races of the Asiatics, and it may well be doubted whether any of them are "white persons" within the purview of the law.[4]

The domestic focus of the free white clause is further suggested by elites' concerns with non-English immigration. As we have seen, many in the Founding generation were worried about an influx of radicals or monarchists from France. Gouverneur Morris articulated a commonly held belief when he observed that, owing to the lack of moderation in their character, *all* the French were unfit for self-government. Yet while the free white clause was distinctly exclusive in its treatment of non-whites, the Naturalization Act of 1790 itself was remarkably inclusive for its time, in bestowing citizenship on all European immigrants. Despite significant doubts about whether some Europeans were fit for self-government, only non-whites were actually excluded from citizenship. Neither the French in general, nor monarchists or radicals in particular, were barred from citizenship, although by 1795 applicants for naturalization had to renounce hereditary titles.

Racial restrictions on citizenship, unlike religious restrictions, carried over from the colonial laws of various states. State naturalization laws are the most plausible source for the actual language used in the Naturalization Act of 1790. The Virginia Act of 1779 enabled all white persons born in Virginia or residing there for the previous two years to be citizens. South Carolina granted citizenship to all "free white persons" who swore an oath and had lived in the state for one year. In Georgia, after the Revolutionary War, all "free white persons" who registered in the county of their residence had civil rights. As the Constitution had not resolved whether state or federal citizenship was primary, southern states would have especially wanted to ensure that black citizens of northern states could not claim national citizenship. By denying blacks the possibility of ever becoming citizens, the southern states protected themselves against having to afford them the privileges and immunities of full membership.[5] (The qualifying term "free" also suggests a southern concern to deny citizenship to indentured laborers—who were white—at least until they had completed their periods of servitude.)

Northerners and opponents of slavery also had powerful reasons to support the free white clause. To understand these reasons we must first consider the distinction most of the Founders drew between natural and political rights. Many opponents of slavery believed that slavery violated natural rights to life and liberty and ought to be ended. Eight of the thirteen original colonies passed laws abolishing slavery, and opponents of slavery pressed for the inclusion of clauses in the Constitution that would undermine the institution's vitality.[6] Both the constitutional provisions referring to slaves and the criminal law treated slaves as persons, observes the political theorist Herbert Storing, "as rational, and, to some degree, morally responsible human beings." The framers "understood quite clearly that Negroes, like men everywhere, were created equal and were endowed with unalienable rights. They did not say that all men were actually secured in the *exercise* of their rights or that they had the power to provide such security; but there was no doubt about the *rights*."[7]

The classic text of the framers on the injustice of slavery is Jefferson's discussion of his proposed bill to emancipate the slaves in Query 14 of the *Notes on the State of Virginia*. He argued that it is both an obligation and in the interest of whites to free the slaves. It is an obligation because slavery corrupts the principles of rights and justice. Consider the following passage, in which

Jefferson is discussing claims that blacks have an innate desire to steal from their masters:

> That disposition to theft with which they have been branded, must be ascribed to their situation, and not to any depravity of the moral sense. The man in whose favor no laws of property exist, probably feels himself less bound to respect those made in favor of others. When arguing for ourselves, we lay it down as a fundamental, that laws, to be just, must give a reciprocation of right; that, without this, they are mere arbitrary rules of conduct, founded in force, and not in conscience.[8]

As a piece of logic, one can hardly find a better refutation of the claim that the principles of the Declaration were inherently racist, that they could be and were applied to blacks as well as whites.

Later in the *Notes*, Jefferson argues that it is in the interest of whites to end slavery because the practice is bad for the master as well as for the slaves: it engenders habits of despotism (those used to ordering around their inferiors at home will eventually want to do so in politics as well) and laziness (in a warm climate no one will work if he can force someone else to do it for him). These bad character effects and the violation of fundamental principles of justice would eventually result in whites being justly punished:

> I tremble for my country when I reflect that God is just; that his justice cannot sleep forever; that considering numbers, nature and natural means only, a revolution of the wheel of fortune, an exchange of situation is among possible events; that it may become probable by supernatural interference! The Almighty has no attribute which can take side with us in such a contest.[9]

Despite these pronouncements, Jefferson, like many slaveholders, sustained slavery in harsh and uncompromising ways. Indeed, in some cases he appears to have gone further in supporting the practice of slavery than some of his contemporaries who were more reluctant to condemn it in principle. In 1776, for instance, Jefferson unsuccessfully sought to promulgate additional restrictions and penalties in Virginia that applied to free blacks and to miscegenation involving white women. In order to limit the growth of the free black population, he proposed that no free black could enter the state, nor could a slave freed in Virginia remain there for more than one year. Any white woman who gave birth to a mixed-blood child would also be required to leave Virginia within a year. Violators of these regulations would receive no legal protection.[10] Although he provided better conditions for his slaves than many others, nothing points up Jefferson's personal hypocrisy more than the harsh treatment he meted out to the more than forty slaves who sought to escape his plantation. "Jefferson," the historian William Cohen writes, was a sincere and dedicated foe of the slave trade who bought and sold men whenever he found it personally necessary. He believed that all men were entitled to life and liberty regardless of their abilities, yet he tracked down those slaves who had the courage to take their rights by running away. He believed that slavery was morally and politically wrong, but still he wrote a slave code for his state and opposed a national attempt in 1819 to limit the further expansion of the institution. He believed that one hour of slavery was worse than ages of British oppression, yet he was able to discuss the matter of slave breeding in much the same terms that one would use when speaking of the propagation of dogs and horses.[11]

While the contradiction between the Founders' principles and their practices is important to acknowledge, the widespread support for the free white clause is best understood from a different angle. That angle concentrates on the distinction between natural and political rights and the Founders' disbelief in the possibility of a multiracial nation. On these issues, it is the fate of free blacks, not slavery, that is most crucial. Despite Jefferson's trembling and his prophetic vision of divine punishment, he, like most of the Founding generation, did not believe that the immorality of slavery meant that blacks should be admitted to the civic body. Blacks' natural rights implied nothing about a right to citizenship.

As we have seen in the debates over immigration and citizenship, the Founders considered citizenship a political decision to be made by a self-governing people. Since political rights were understood to be dependent upon consent, prudential concerns played a central role in determining whether to give such consent. Few of the Founders believed that they were obligated to admit blacks into full political membership if they had reason to think that doing so would be a bad idea.[12] And on this count they most certainly did consider it a very bad idea. Most believed that emancipation followed by the assimilation of blacks into the body politic was impossible or impossibly risky. In making their case, they offered two primary reasons: blacks' unfitness for self-government and the threat of racial war.

"We Have the Wolf by the Ears": Obstacles to Integration

Some of the most ardent proponents of emancipation doubted whether blacks had the capacity for self-government. Some believed blacks to be innately inferior, while others attributed differences between blacks and whites to environmental factors. Jefferson thought there were "real distinctions" between whites and blacks. He viewed blacks as inferior in reason and "dull, tasteless, and anomalous" in imagination, though he wondered how many of those differences were due to environmental factors rather than innate features.[13] And while the Founders did not regard all emigrants from England as carriers of the proper civic skills and habits, their faith in European civilization did impart a geographic basis to the notion of "fitness for self-government." They regarded England as the source of political genius and European civilization as the source of their understanding of rights, reason, commerce, and religion. Anglo-Protestant culture, in particular, was understood as the source of immigrants best suited to take advantage of free institutions and live according to American civic principles.

Even opponents of slavery who did not believe blacks to be inherently inferior and incapable of self-government could not see how slaves could be assimilated into social and political life. Ferdinando Fairfax, a disciple of George Washington, wrote in 1790 that "there is something very repugnant to the general feelings even in the thought of [freed blacks] being allowed that free intercourse, and the privilege of intermarriage with the white inhabitants, which the other freemen of our country enjoy . . . and as a proof, where is the man of all those who have liberated their slaves, who would marry a son or a daughter to one of them? and if *he* would not, who would?" Jefferson reflected a similar view when he noted that "deep-rooted prejudices entertained by the whites" compounded by "ten thousand recollections, by the blacks, of the injuries they have sustained" and the certainty of "new provocations" will doom any hope for a peaceful nation. Even in the ostensibly more liberal North, free blacks suffered legal and social prohibitions that prevented them from attending most schools, serving on juries, worshiping in white churches, or working in white workshops. They were barred as well from public transport, libraries, and museums. "Nothing is more certainly written in the book of fate," Jefferson predicted, "than that these two people are to be free; nor is it less certain that the two races, equally free, cannot live in the same government."[14]

St. George Tucker, a leading Virginia judge and law professor, provides the fullest expression of the problem of assimilation and the obstacles that posed to emancipation. His *Dissertation on Slavery* captures the various strands in the pro-emancipation, anti-black citizenship position. Like Jefferson, Tucker starts his discussion from the premise that slavery is deeply inconsistent with the civic principles on which the United States was founded and which justified the Revolution:

> While we were offering up vows at the shrine of Liberty, and sacrificing hecatombs upon her altars; whilst we swore irreconcilable hostility to her enemies, and hurled defiance in their faces; whilst we adjured the God of Hosts to witness our resolution to live free, or die, and imprecated curses on their heads who refused to unite with us in establishing the empire of freedom; we were imposing upon our fellow men, who differed in complexion from us, a *slavery*, ten thousand times more cruel than the utmost extremity of those grievances and oppressions, of which we complained.

To the question "[W]hy not retain and *incorporate* the *blacks into the state*?" Tucker repeats and amplifies Jefferson's answer: "Shall we not relieve the necessities of the naked diseased beggar, unless we will invite him to a seat at our table; nor afford him shelter from the inclemencies of the night air, unless we admit him also to share our bed?"[15]

Tucker acknowledges that his views may "savour strongly of prejudice." But he regards the existence of those views, in himself and especially among his fellow whites, as a significant impediment to the incorporation of blacks into a single, united nation. "[W]hoever proposes any plan for the abolition of slavery will find that he must either encounter, or accommodate himself, to prejudice—I have preferred the latter; not that I pretend to be fully exempt from it, but that I may avoid as many obstacles as possible to the completion of so desirable a work, as the abolition of slavery."[16] Tucker is also explicit about his fear that freed slaves would start a racial conflagration. He worried about "the possibility of their becoming idle, dissipated, and finally a numerous banditti," and the likelihood of a civil war between whites and blacks.[17]

Like Jefferson, Tucker is clearly dubious about the justice of his views. A state of slavery, he writes, "is perfectly irreconcilable . . . to the principles of a democracy, which form the *basis* and *foundation* of our government."[18] But he believes with equal fervor that his natural right to self-preservation compels him to oppose any simple plan of emancipation. Both men recognized that, in an extreme situation, natural rights were not strong enough to bind them to what they thought was their duty.[19] Opponents of slavery who could not imagine a successful multiracial nation thus faced a quandary. For them the question of black citizenship posed a conflict not between right and wrong—freedom and slavery—but between the rights of blacks' claim to freedom and their own title to survival. "I can say, with conscious truth, that there is not a man on earth who would sacrifice more than I would to relieve us of this heavy reproach, in any *practicable* way," Jefferson wrote in 1820. "But as it is, we have the wolf by the ears, and we can neither hold him, nor safely let him go. Justice is in one scale, and self-preservation in the other."[20]

EMANCIPATION WITHOUT CITIZENSHIP

A minority of citizens disagreed with Jefferson and Tucker that justice and self-preservation were of equal weight. They argued that the only just course of action was to emancipate and then assimilate the slaves. In this view, not only was slavery wrong but the nation's civic principles dictated that the freed slaves should be allowed to consent to the government they found themselves under. In the late 1770s, for instance, the citizens of Sutton, Massachusetts, objected on these grounds to a proposed provision in the state constitution that would limit the right to vote to "[e]very male inhabitant of any town in this State, being free and twenty one years of age, excepting negroes, Indians, and mulattoes."[21] "[This] article appears to us to wear a very gross complextion of slavery," the citizens wrote, and is diametrically repugnant to the grand and Fundamental maxim of Humane Rights; viz. "*That Law to boind all must be assented to by all.*" This is manifestly ading to the already acumulated Load of guilt lying upon the Land in supporting the slave trade. . . . [I]f by any good Providence they or any of their Posterity, obtain their freedom and a handsome estate yet they must be excluded the privileges of Men![22]

A far more widely accepted position among the Founders who recognized slavery's injustice was that shared civic principles were insufficient to ensure that freed slaves and whites could live as fellow citizens. The problems posed by the prejudice of the whites and the expected desire for revenge of the blacks made it more plausible to them to look to some kind of emancipation scheme that did not include citizenship and assimilation into the American nation. "A general emancipation of slaves," Madison wrote, "ought to be 1. gradual. 2. equitable & satisfactory to the individuals immediately concerned. 3. consistent with the existing & durable prejudices of the nation."[23] Two options received the most consideration, both of which provide the context within which the free white clause was likely adopted in 1790. In the first instance, some proposed schemes for emancipation followed by colonization, whether within the United States or in Africa.[24] Writing in 1819, Madison summarized his long-standing views on the subject:

> The objections to a thorough incorporation of the two people are, with most of the Whites insuperable; and are admitted by all of them to be very powerful. If the blacks, strongly marked as they are by Physical & lasting peculiarities, be retained amid the Whites, under the degrading privation of equal rights political or social, they must be always dissatisfied with their condition as a change only from one to another species of oppression; always secretly confederated agst. the ruling & privileged class; and always uncontrulled by some of the most cogent motives to moral and respectable conduct. . . . The colonizing plan on foot, has as far as it extends, a due regard to these requisites; with the additional object of bestowing new blessings civil & religious on the quarter of the Globe most in need of them.[25]

Although colonization now appears an unlikely and unpitying plan, it was a commonly held view among abolitionists who sought to end slavery without bloodshed. Colonizers like Madison, and later leading figures like Henry Clay and Abraham Lincoln, "were forced to think deeply and deliberately, as statesmen rarely do, about the far future of their country," writes the journalist Benjamin Schwarz. "Knowing the enormous financial and moral cost of the course they proposed, they could nevertheless see no alternative."[26]

For opponents of slavery like Tucker, though, colonization suffered from too many prudential and principled objections. "If humanity plead[s] for their emancipation," he wrote, "it pleads more strongly against colonization." The cost of resettling blacks within the United States, and the dangers to which the colonists would be exposed, made such an undertaking unlikely. And the notion of shipping slaves back to Africa was even less plausible. To accomplish that scheme "without the most cruel oppression, would require the utmost exertion of all the maritime powers in Europe, united with those of America, and a territory of ten times the extent that all the powers of Europe possess in Africa."[27] To others, forced colonization was a prima facie injustice which, in trying to remedy the injustice of slavery, only made things worse. "A Freeman" wrote in the *Maryland Gazette* on December 30, 1790:

> We have no just right to export [or] banish any man, unless he previously violates some law, which inflicts transportation as a just punishment for his crime.—A different sentiment cannot correspond with the idea, that "*all men are born equally free, and in point of human rights to liberty, stand on equal ground.*" But where would you export them to? They are as much *Americans* now as we, and we as much *Europeans* as they are *Africans*—Nothing but a mind influenced by prejudice or partiality can countermand or contemn this idea or argument.[28]

Some opponents of colonization argued that blacks could stay in the country but should not be given full rights of citizens. As we have seen, Tucker explicitly linked Jefferson's discussion of the dilemmas caused by emancipation with the exclusion of freed blacks from citizenship. He distinguished between "domestic" and "civil" slavery. In civil slavery, different classes of men had different civil rights. Tucker said that civil slavery in America already existed in the case of free blacks and mulattos, "whose civil incapacities are almost as numerous as the civil rights of our free citizens," and include the right to vote, to serve in the militia or as a witness in court, or to be tried by a jury of one's peers. He contended that "[t]hose who secretly favour, whilst they affect to regret, domestic slavery, contend that in abolishing it, we must also abolish that scion from it, which I have denominated *civil* slavery. That there must be no distinction of rights." But Tucker rejected this analysis, offering his arguments that the prejudice of whites and the incapacity, whether natural or conventional, of blacks counsel against opening citizenship to free slaves and assimilating them into the polity.

Tucker therefore tried to find a middle road "between the tyrannical and iniquitous policy which holds so many human creatures in a state of grievous bondage, and that which would turn loose a numerous, starving, and enraged banditti, upon the innocent descendants of their former oppressors." To chart this middle course, Tucker proposed gradual emancipation, whereby every female born after the passage of the law would be free, as well as all of her children, but they would be denied all civil privileges. Freed blacks would, among other restrictions, be deprived of voting or holding public office, in the "hope that the seeds of ambition would be buried too deep, ever to germinate"; prevented from bearing arms, thus calming "our apprehensions of their resentments from past sufferings"; and banned from owning land, adding "one inducement more to emigration, and effectively remove the foundation of ambition, and party-struggles." Their personal rights and what property they were permitted would, however, be protected.

Tucker seemed to know deep down that the only real alternatives are separation or assimilation and that the "middle course" can only buy time and perhaps make it easier to accomplish one or the other. His basic strategy, then, was to make life in the United States so restricted for the freed slaves that they would leave of their own accord; alternatively, he hoped that under the cover of these civil disabilities the prejudices that made it impossible to assimilate blacks would disappear over time, though he did not seem to think that very likely. The immediate obstacle was slaveholders who "have been in the habit of considering their fellow creatures as no more than cattle," "who will shut their ears against this moral truth, that all men are by nature *free* and *equal*," and who will not sacrifice their property to their duty or their long-term self-interest in avoiding a violent slave revolt. But as the slave population grows the situation would worsen: "[E]very day renders the task more arduous to be performed." Tucker's discussion thus ends on a despairing note.[29]

Civic Nationalism and the Claims of History

Slavery opponents' hopes to emancipate the slaves and then either colonize them or not allow them to become citizens were the implicit justification for the free white clause. Opponents of slavery, who doubted whether an integrated nation could function, made prudential, if rather utopian, judgments that denying free blacks citizenship would lead to their voluntary exile or gradual incorporation. The clause was consistent in their minds with ensuring that citizens possessed the proper character and shared sense of nationhood and with protecting themselves against the dangers posed by freed slaves who might demand greater retribution than simple political equality would allow. The exclusion of non-whites from naturalization was, from this view, an entirely logical policy to adopt. The Founders' emphasis on the nationalist underpinnings to citizenship thus facilitated racially based limitations to it.

The Founders' judgments about nationhood and fitness for self-government did not, however, reflect an unambiguous ideology of racial supremacy, as some historians have recently claimed. These historians argue that the free white clause and the concerns over national survival that undergirded it were "inextricably linked" to racial categorizations. They conclude from the apparent lack of debate over the clause that there must have been an overarching ideology so pervasive and uncontroversial that no one saw any need to talk about it. In this context, the Naturalization Act of 1790 becomes an unequivocally white supremacist law.[30] In portraying many of the Founders as untroubled by slavery or the question of what would happen after slavery disappeared, this view disregards the widely shared belief that blacks had a natural right to freedom but that an integrated nation was not feasible. By lumping together the issues of slavery and citizenship, it overlooks the complexity of the Founding generation's contradictory thoughts in favor of a cleaner, starker story of racial ideology.[31]

Defenders of the Founding generation have also simplified the Founders' views in favor of absolving them of responsibility for the origins and consequences of excluding non-whites from citizenship. These defenders argue that the term "white" was merely a synonym for Europeans, whose political ideals and character traits made them best suited for citizenship in the new republic. The Founders' preference for Europeans reflected a common heritage, not an assertion of racial superiority. Yet those who doubted whether French immigrants possessed the characteristics necessary for American citizenship did not exclude them from naturalization. The free white clause sought to forestall the possibility of black citizenship rather than simply to favor immigrants considered most likely to become proper citizens.

In associating non-whites with a dangerous heterogeneity, and in treating European civilization as a marker of democratic fitness, the Founders significantly shaped the exclusionary contours of U.S. immigration and citizenship law. They set the nation on a course in which race would remain a dubious proxy for citizenship. The free white clause contributed to the denial of citizenship to free blacks in the 1850s, the outbreak of the Civil War, and the subsequent inscription of birthright citizenship into the Constitution via the Fourteenth Amendment. In the second half of the nineteenth century, the clause bolstered the Chinese exclusion movement, which culminated in the denial of citizenship to Chinese in 1882. And in the early twentieth century, it was central to legislation that severely restricted the entry of southern and eastern Europeans and to naturalization cases that disqualified applicants for citizenship based on their race.

By simplifying the Founders' views on immigration, race, and citizenship, both their critics and defenders miss the real meaning of the free white clause: its embodiment of inherent risks and tensions in balancing the universal thrust of democratic civic principles and the particular bond of nationalist sentiment. The more America is defined by the former the more difficult it is to identify an identity that provides a substratum of social solidarity. Yet too narrow a definition of nationhood threatens the civic principles to which the nation is committed. Hence the continual search for a nationalism powerful enough to bind citizens without crushing individual freedom and destroying democratic institutions.

Many of the Founders understood this dilemma and resisted offering too specific a vision of American citizenship. In defining an American civic nationalism they often mixed various and sometimes contradictory notions—civic principles, shared culture, common experience, providential mission, and inherited opinion. The Founding generation relied especially heavily on the obligations imposed by the past to establish a nationalist foundation to undergird civic principles. An ancient history linked to a recent conflict and to future civic aspirations offered a special appeal to leaders who had just broken with their mother country: such a combination appeared robust enough to resist a singular definition of nationhood that was rooted in racial or religious identity and flexible enough not to blindly stamp out individual freedom and social pluralism.

It is therefore of significant consequence for civic nationalism that the Founders were so unwilling or incapable of recognizing the particular claims of history when it came to the presence of blacks. "Whilst America hath been the land of promise to Europeans, and their descendants," Tucker wrote, "it hath been the vale of death to millions of the wretched sons of Africa." Blacks had a distinct claim they could press to be included as full citizens. Their historical standing provided the basis for a political right, one that supplemented their natural right to freedom. (By contrast, no direct injustice had been visited on immigrants and hence, following the distinction between natural and political rights, they could have plausibly been denied citizenship.) But, as we have seen, this claim was not one the Founders could bring themselves to recognize. It threatened national unity and self-preservation.

The Founders left unresolved the question of whether a civic nationalism defined in large part by claims to a common history could live up to the obligations that its history implied and take responsibility for all the elements of its past. Can a civic nationalism that is dependent on its past as a binding agent still account for the tensions within that history? Or is it always more likely to select only those elements that are easy to commemorate? The human propensity to favor one's self and one's immediate community may too easily weaken the impact of those aspects of a shared history that impose difficult obligations.[32] The Founders' treatment of the free white clause provides an especially telling example of the tension between the unifying dimension of any appeal to history and the limits to which such an appeal can be relied on when that history demands actions that are onerous and risky.

Law and policy governing immigration and citizenship at the Founding and in the early Republic thus emerged from the conflict within civic nationalism as well as the struggle between civic nationalism and more traditional forms of nationalism. The conflict within civic nationalism revealed significant limits to its inclusiveness and capacity to sustain a nationalist identity that supported rather than undermined civic principles. At the same time, throughout this period that capacity offered a compelling alternative to far more illiberal, exclusionary policies. This period indicated the ways in which nationalism was simultaneously the source of exclusion and a bulwark against it.

CHAPTER FOUR

Americanization and Pluralism in the Progressive Era

THE AMALGAM of exclusionary and inclusionary laws and policies governing immigration and citizenship that emerged from the Founding and the early Republic continued throughout much of the nineteenth century. No single standard for membership existed in that period; instead, modes of citizenship were multiple and often contradictory. By the end of the nineteenth century and the beginning of the twentieth, significant efforts were under way to codify the meaning of American citizenship. Radical changes in politics, the economy, and culture gave new impetus to the question of whether American nationalism would support or undermine civic ideals, whether it would protect against illiberal, exclusionary policies or serve as the basis for them. These fundamental changes to American life led to a broad argument about whether and how to construct a more felt sense of national identity. To presidents, policymakers, journalists, and intellectuals, society seemed more complex than at the Founding and in the early Republic. The scope and scale of change made the task of shaping citizens appear more difficult to them and raised fundamental questions about what could hold together an increasingly diverse citizenry and whether a mass democracy could govern itself.

Many elites doubted that political processes of incorporation were functioning adequately. They worried especially about whether new and old citizens could share a common citizenship. One result of these worries was the argument that significant limits needed to be placed on the influx of new immigrants. The period ended with the successful movement to reduce the overall level of immigration and to exclude southern and eastern Europeans and Asians. The Progressive Era's broad social changes also induced leaders to regularize naturalization requirements and to actively shape immigrants' allegiance to civic principles and their attachment to the American nation. In contrast to those who wanted to restrict immigration, these "Americanizers" believed that a common civic nationalism could be forged.

The Americanization movement emerged from the larger Progressive efforts to reorder society. Progressives' views on the civic and national dimensions of citizenship, on the conceptual and communal bases for belonging to America, varied considerably and these variations shaped the Americanization movement in crucial ways. Left-leaning Progressives such as the philosopher John Dewey and the journalist Randolph Bourne articulated a conception of America as the first "international nation" and expressed a desire to integrate immigrants' cultural heritages into a broader American cosmopolitanism. Jane Addams and the settlement house movement embodied in practice a similar view.[1] In contrast, right-leaning Progressives such as Theodore Roosevelt and Herbert Croly, editor of *The New Republic*, stressed a more explicitly nationalist vision of citizenship, one that welcomed immigrants but expected them to relinquish cultural and political habits thought to be at odds with a robust American identity.

Initially, both left and right Progressive views of nationality, ethnicity, and immigration offered moderate civic nationalist alternatives to more coercive and exclusionary forces of nationalism. Ultimately, however, the instability of the Progressive coalition would become most apparent on these questions.[2] Moreover, despite their significant differences, the Progressives' common concerns about cultural change and uniform civic principles would provide the seeds for the Americanization movement's turn toward compulsory methods of assimilation.

CITIZENSHIP AND NATIVISM, 1830–1911

In the nineteenth century, citizenship was defined and contested in many ways. The Constitution authorized Congress to provide for "an uniform rule of naturalization," but it did not indicate what the relationship should be between citizenship in an individual state and membership in the nation. Did an individual owe his primary allegiance to his state of residence or to the entire nation? Was state citizenship a consequence of national citizenship or the reverse?[3] Fundamental conflicts also arose over the membership status of non-whites. The doctrine of consensual citizenship that made immigration and naturalization easy for whites also permitted the government to deny citizenship to Indians and blacks.[4] In the 1830s, the Supreme Court defined Indians as members of "tributary states," a category that preserved Indians' autonomy from individual states but effectively denied them citizenship in the United States.[5] In *Dred Scott v. Sandford* (1857), the Court held that blacks could not be citizens because they had not been part of the original social contract that ratified the Constitution. Chief Justice Roger Taney invoked the exclusion of non-whites from naturalization in 1790 as evidence that the framers never intended free blacks to be citizens.[6]

In 1870, the Massachusetts radical Republican Charles Sumner proposed eliminating the bar on non-whites' eligibility for citizenship. "Sumner invoked the Declaration of Independence in a Fourth of July oration," notes the historian Reed Ueda, to contend "It is 'all men' and not a race or color that are placed under the protection of the Declaration. . . . The word 'white' wherever it appears as a limitation of rights, must disappear. Only in this way can you be consistent with the Declaration."[7] Western states, determined to prevent Chinese immigrants from becoming citizens, vociferously opposed Sumner. His proposal was defeated by a ratio of two to one. Congress did, however, soon provide for the naturalization of aliens of African descent or nativity.

In 1868 Congress had already moved to establish blacks' claim to citizenship by enshrining the nationalist notion of birthright citizenship in the Constitution as part of the Fourteenth Amendment: "All persons born or naturalized in the United States and subject to the jurisdiction thereof, are citizens of the United States and of the State wherein they reside." One day before it ratified the Fourteenth Amendment, Congress also passed the Expatriation Act of 1868, which codified the principle that acquiring and relinquishing American citizenship depended on the consent of the individual. The statute held that the right to expatriate (voluntarily relinquish citizenship) "is a natural and inherent right of all people, indispensable to the enjoyment of the rights of life, liberty and the pursuit of happiness."[8] Both the Fourteenth Amendment and the Expatriation Act aimed to establish a single status of citizenship. The Fourteenth Amendment enlarged the status of citizenship to include blacks and the Expatriation Act reduced the claims on allegiance another nation could make of American citizens. Both the nationalist emphasis on birthright and the civic stress on consent moved American citizenship in a more inclusionary direction. The joint effect of these measures, however, was to more firmly establish a conception of citizenship that combined an unsteady mix of nationalist ascription and civic consent.

The emphasis on consent as part of America's civic principles also played a key role in efforts to reduce the number of dual citizens. Since 1795, the oath of allegiance has required new citizens to "renounce and abjure" their previous allegiances. Despite this strong expectation favoring singular rather than dual citizenship, throughout much of the nineteenth century, individuals often maintained formal civic statuses in two countries as a matter of practice. So long as sending countries refused to recognize that their citizens or subjects had relinquished their nationality upon becoming U.S. citizens, there was little America could do to bring practice in line with principle. America's desire that immigrants break formal ties with their countries of origin also conflicted with its even stronger economic need for immigrants. Nonetheless, most sending countries eventually required expatriation when their citizens swore allegiance to the United States. The United States further agreed to treaties with several European states that included "the presumption that a naturalized American who returned to live in his homeland would lose his U.S. citizenship." Thus, the United States moved toward reducing this particular form of multiple citizenship status.[9]

In contrast, differential citizenship statuses increased in other parts of U.S. immigration and naturalization law during the nineteenth century. From 1800 to 1830, the United States witnessed low levels of immigration and a rough process of homogenization. By the 1840s, immigration to the United States had begun to increase significantly. Almost two million persons immigrated in that decade, a number that steadily increased and then peaked in the first decade of the twentieth century at nine million immigrants. Eligibility to enter the United States for much of the nineteenth century was regulated in a patchwork manner.[10] By 1875, however, federal rules governing and enforcing limits on entry were increasingly characterized by the different statutes that had emerged from the states, and more and more categories of immigrants were being excluded—for example, convicts and prostitutes in 1875, and epileptics, beggars, procurers, anarchists, and advocates of political violence in 1903.[11]

In 1882 Congress passed the Chinese Exclusion Act, the country's most restrictive measure since the Naturalization Act of 1790. The 1882 act denied Chinese laborers entry to the country for ten years, required legal Chinese workers who were already in the United States to carry certificates of identification, authorized the deportation of illegal Chinese workers, and prohibited any Chinese from becoming citizens via naturalization.[12] In signing the act, President Chester Arthur reflected widely held views that the "experiment of blending" Chinese and Americans had been "unwise, impolitic, and injurious to both nations."[13] The legal groundwork for denying eligibility for naturalization to Asians had been bolstered by the ruling in an 1878 case, *In re Ah Yup*. The question before Circuit Court Judge Sawyer in this case was whether a person of the "Mongolian race," as an immigrant from China was classified, could be considered white. The judge found it sufficient that neither scientists of racial classifications nor public opinion considered the Mongolian or "yellow race" to be Caucasian.[14] Even as applied to Asians, however, multiple and conflicting statuses existed. In key rulings in 1886 and 1898, the Supreme Court affirmed that Chinese present in the United States should be treated equally and that their children were citizens, thus reinforcing the organic ideal of birthright citizenship.[15]

In contrast, most white immigrants could gain entry and become citizens quite easily, though there was significant variation in standards for citizenship owing to corruption and local discretion. Prior to the Civil War, naturalization was largely available to whites who had lived in the United States for five years and sworn an oath of loyalty to the Constitution.[16] Political machines guided immigrants through the naturalization process in return for their votes. In New York, the Tammany Hall machine naturalized just over nine thousand immigrants each year between 1856 and 1867. In 1868, Tammany naturalized over forty-one thousand immigrants as part of its successful effort to wrest the governorship from the Republicans. Steven Erie describes a scene in which "[i]mmigrants fresh off the boat were given red tickets, allowing them to get their citizenship papers free." By the mid-1880s, Tammany was operating its "naturalization mill full blast" and had succeeded in naturalizing "nearly 80 percent of the city's Irish, German and other 'old' (Western European) immigrants."[17] Hence, if access to citizenship for white immigrants was formally a standardized affair, applicants' actual route to citizenship varied widely.

Local discretion with regard to naturalization contributed in other ways to the different rights available to noncitizens and to the categories of those eligible to become citizens. Twenty-two states and territories at one point extended voting rights to noncitizens. Most states offered this measure as a means of increasing their population and labor forces. In some cases, voting was seen as itself a form of citizenship education, one that stressed civic principles and attachment to the American nation. In 1863, for instance, the Vermont Supreme Court held that aliens could vote and serve on local school boards as "a preparatory fitting and training" and an appropriate effort to encourage newcomers to identify their "feelings and interests . . . with the government and the country."[18] Most states limited alien suffrage to immigrants who had declared their intention to naturalize. This approach cast alien suffrage as "a *pathway* to citizenship rather than a possible substitute for it: *non*citizen voting became *pre*-citizen voting."[19] Other states used their discretionary power to exclude groups that were entitled to citizenship. In Texas, for instance, Mexican immigrants were often deterred from naturalizing by local authorities who doubted their status as whites and their fitness for self-government (despite a Texas court's ruling that Mexicans had a right to naturalize).[20]

Courts early in the next century further sought to sort out who was eligible for naturalization. In doing so, they often offered inclusionary rulings that broadened who was white and therefore could become a citizen. At the same time, these rulings reinforced the association of citizenship with whiteness. In *In re Halladjian*, a 1909 Massachusetts case assessing whether four Armenians were eligible for citizenship, the court reaffirmed the idea that white simply meant not black or American Indian.[21] Similarly, in a 1910 case involving a Parsee (Syrian) applicant for citizenship, the Second Circuit Court of Appeals found it "absurd" that "Russians, Poles, Italians, Greeks, and others," simply because their ancestors had not immigrated to the United States in 1790, could be excluded. "If a Hebrew . . . had applied for naturalization in 1790," said the court, "we cannot believe he would have been excluded on the ground that he was not a white person."[22] This kind of reasoning meant that the courts could often issue inclusionary rulings, even as those rulings tended to reinforce the idea that, whatever its precise contours, white meant something distinct.

In the nineteenth century, law and policy governed immigrants and non-whites in complex ways. In treating whiteness as the core of American citizenship the courts strengthened a nationalist legal and cultural conception. Yet in emphasizing the importance of birthright citizenship and an often broad definition of who was white, the courts wielded the nationalist dimension of citizenship in ways that granted full legal status to many non-whites. For non-whites, especially blacks and Indians, the courts' civic emphasis on consent denied them citizenship, while many states' civic concern for educated and engaged citizens provided voting rights for white immigrants, even those who had not yet become naturalized. In the nineteenth century, there was no straight-line relation between civic principles and inclusion, or nationalist sentiment and exclusion. Instead, both the civic and the nationalist dimensions of citizenship each had inclusionary and exclusionary consequences.

The relative ease of naturalization for those deemed white reflected the confidence of most native-born Americans that such immigrants could become citizens regardless of national background, religion, or language. Nonetheless, individual doubters, supplemented by organized groups, periodically questioned whether any but the English or northern Europeans were capable of becoming Americans. Nativists in the nineteenth century offered civic and nationalist reasons for their objections to open immigration and citizenship laws. The consensual basis to citizenship meant for them that citizens could not simply be born; they had to be made. In their view, the fact that immigrants (especially the Irish) were "made" abroad under less democratic and less egalitarian conditions posed serious obstacles to their being "remade" once in America. Views like these drove the platform of the Know-Nothing Party, which sought to extend the residency requirement to twenty-one years. Americans, Massachusetts governor Henry J. Gardner declared, "must nationalize before we naturalize."[23] As Michael Walzer has observed, "despite their name, the Know-Nothings thought that citizenship was a subject about which a great deal had to be known."[24]

The Know-Nothing Party played a significant role in the presidential elections of 1852 and 1856, but it disappeared as quickly as it had arisen. Its brief success was due as much to the crisis in the American party system as to the appeal of its ideology.[25] Regional differences played an important role in the Know-Nothings' swift demise, as they could not hold together a national alliance in which northerners were preoccupied with Catholics, southerners apprehensive about blacks, and westerners worried about Chinese.[26] As a result, nativists' influence in much of the nineteenth century was short-lived and most Americans were "optimistic in the expectation that . . . [an immigrant's] experience in the new homeland would solidify his commitment to the principles of American democracy."[27]

Nativism revived as a more widespread movement at the end of the century, a time when Americans were confronted by large numbers of immigrants and by different ethnic groups arriving from southern and eastern Europe. Between 1880 and 1920, at least 25 million immigrants arrived in the United States, two and half times more than in the previous forty years. By 1900, less than one-half of the entire population was both white and born of two native parents. By 1930, immigrants and their children constituted 75 percent of New York City and Boston, 66 percent of Chicago, and more than 50 percent of San Francisco, Detroit, Minneapolis, and Philadelphia.[28] Many Americans perceived these newcomers as agents of the social and political unrest that was transforming Europe. They worried deeply about the significant economic changes reshaping American life, and they identified immigrants as the workers responsible for the increase in labor strife (from 1881 to 1905, the United States experienced at least 37,000 strikes). Naturalization figures further raised concerns that immigrants were not committed to becoming citizens. From 1900 to 1910, the number of naturalized males grew only 7 percent while the number of noncitizen males grew 73 percent. The percentage of nonnaturalized adult men among the foreign-born grew from 43 percent in 1900 to 55 percent in 1919.[29]

These worries were supplemented by concerns over the authoritarian political traditions with which immigrants were familiar and their consequent lack of experience in making independent political judgments. Immigrants from predominantly rural, agrarian backgrounds entered an increasingly urban and industrial society that required different skills, habits, and practices. This disjunction between an essentially nineteenth-century people and a twentieth-century economy could, some thought, serve as a barrier to the successful incorporation of immigrants into American life. And as these largely rural people crowded into American cities, significant social problems like crime and disease increased. Immigrants' Catholicism remained a serious concern. The explicitly anti-Catholic American Protective Association (APA) was founded in 1887 and gained more than two million members within a decade. It aimed to stem the influence of Catholicism in labor and politics. Among other policies, it required members to swear an oath not to employ or to vote for a Catholic.

This traditional form of American nativism was supplemented by a much greater emphasis on racial differences and capacities. As early as 1885, Josiah Strong had argued in *Our Country* that the new immigration would undermine the morals and virtues of the American people. Writing in 1902, Woodrow Wilson looked alarmingly at the "multitudes of men of the lowest class from the south of Italy and men of the meaner sort out of Hungary and Poland, men out of the ranks where there was neither skill nor energy nor any initiative or quick intelligence."[30] These views were represented by the Immigration Restriction League (IRL), an organization founded by New England lawyers, philanthropists, and educators.[31] The IRL warned that immigrants now entering the United States were "permanent failures" who threatened American character and citizenship. Just as the invading Goths and Vandals overwhelmed the Roman people by their sheer numbers, warned Prescott F. Hall, one of the league's leaders, America was threatened by a new invasion of barbarians who were "below the mental, moral, and physical average of both our country and their own."[32] The IRL's views converged with popular arguments in social science regarding the superiority and inferiority of different races. The doctrine of social Darwinism strengthened the beliefs of those who saw immigration as diluting American achievements of racial and cultural superiority. The pseudoscience of eugenics added to this idea the notion that intelligence and skills were rooted in genetic sources and were racially coded.

The restrictionist movement was given significant impetus by the publication in 1911 of the massive forty-two-volume *Reports of the Immigration Commission,*

headed by Senator William P. Dillingham of Vermont. The commission compared the new immigrants unfavorably with older arrivals, who were said to
possess a greater pioneering spirit, to have come for the purpose of remaining,
to have spread themselves throughout the country, and to have taken up a range
of positions in economy and society. Although many of these immigrants were
non-English-speaking, the commission contended that they had quickly integrated into society. The commission produced a dictionary of races or peoples
that transformed the Irish from the culturally deficient and politically dubious
Celts of the nineteenth century to members of the Anglo-Saxon race who had
been assimilated successfully.[33]

In contrast, the commission argued that the newer immigrants were largely
unskilled, poorly disciplined, and inefficient, and that they were only in America
to work long enough to raise some money to go home. Further, the commission
found, these immigrants tended to evade assimilatory forces by congregating in
the larger cities and by maintaining close links with their fellow nationals and
countries of origin. Following the lead of the IRL, the commission determined
that the new immigrants were intellectually inferior. It recommended that
Congress restrict the flow of new immigration; its proposals, including a literacy test and racial quotas, were embodied in law starting in 1917 and culminat-
ing in the Immigration Act of 1924.[34]

AMERICANIZATION, PROGRESSIVISM, AND JOHN DEWEY'S
INTERNATIONAL NATIONALISM

While restrictionists argued that the cultural deficiencies of the new immigrants and the English roots of American identity necessitated restricting the
entry of new ethnic groups, many leaders in government, industry, and philanthropy responded to the massive social changes of the Progressive Era by seeking
to assimilate immigrants.[35] The Americanization movement involved school
boards, the workplace, settlement houses, state and federal agencies, unions,
voluntary and patriotic organizations, and broad-based efforts at political reform. In its efforts to consciously form a new citizen, the Americanization
movement initially included a wide range of legal, political, medical, civic, and
cultural efforts to help immigrants adjust to their new surroundings and to
encourage Americans to accept them. Public and private agencies sought legislation to protect immigrants against exploitation by employers and landlords,
worked to formalize the rules governing naturalization and to increase the rate
by which newcomers became citizens, and offered courses by which immigrants could improve their proficiency in English and strengthen their understanding of American history and civic values. An introductory letter attached
to "An Outline Course in Citizenship," prepared by the Bureau of Naturalization
and sent to over 550 cities and towns throughout forty-three states, explained

that the purpose of Americanization was to transform "uninformed foreigners, not comprehending our language, customs, or governmental institutions, to intelligent, loyal, and productive members of society."[36]

Americanization is best understood as part of the broad Progressive movement to reorder society. Opinion-makers and political leaders in the Progressive Era were heirs to the Founders' belief that certain kinds of citizens were necessary to make free government work. But they differed both from those Founders who doubted that a cohesive national identity could be constructed out of a diverse population and those who believed that a shared national identity could be generated by the natural workings of social and political institutions. Unnerved by the massive changes in politics, economics, and culture that characterized the early twentieth century, they thought that forging citizens, whether native born or naturalized, required much greater conscious effort. The self-confident Progressive reformers offered the most comprehensive attempt to replace the lost faith in America's assimilative powers, to establish a harmonious national life based on modern notions of scientific order.

The Progressives were deeply concerned about the concentration of authority in large, corporate entities. They worried that unbridled economic power threatened democratic life directly and indirectly. Too much wealth in the hands of too few men was directly corrupting the political system. And the new, large-scale, wage labor system threatened to indirectly undermine the capacity of citizens to be self-sufficient and politically independent.[37] Progressives particularly fretted over the loss of control and individual autonomy in the new, desacralized industrial order.[38] They worried that what the prominent journalist Walter Lippmann called the "acids of modernity" were eroding the foundations of free societies. "The prime fact about modernity as it presents itself to us," Lippmann wrote, "is that it not merely denies the central ideas of our forefathers but dissolves the disposition to believe them."[39] What elites thought had been ruptured was not just belief in a particular set of civic principles; they feared that the very capacity to believe in any principles had been shaken. As a result, America's leadership class despaired that the possibility for independent, virtuous men to live by a set of common civic and cultural ideals had been lost.

Progressive elites worried as well about weakening party loyalties and a decline in voting, the rise of an increasingly secularized Protestantism, the mass migration not only of Europeans but of blacks from the South to the northern cities, and the ever more vigorous entry of women into politics.[40] The movement away from small, largely homogeneous communities toward an increasingly industrialized, bureaucratized, and nationally oriented society evoked, in particular, a sharper consciousness of ethnic difference. In the nineteenth century, ethnic groups could keep a greater distance from one another because power and loyalty were more localized. European immigrants and blacks tended to avoid each other, just as the different European groups tended to settle in distinct areas of the country (Germans in the middle West and Irish in the

Northeast) or in separate parts of a city (as in Detroit and Milwaukee).[41] The more nationally oriented American society became, the more different groups encountered each other. As local autonomy decreased and industrial disloca-tion increased, more native-born Americans felt exposed to a strange and hostile society. The fundamental changes reconfiguring American life thus unsettled elites' sense of a stable social order at the same time they revealed a society made of contending groups.

To prevent corruption and reinvigorate a dispirited citizenry, the Progres-sives succeeded in establishing significant structural changes in the political system. They standardized the electoral process, separated local from state and national elections, promoted at-large nonpartisan elections, and instituted the secret ballot. The Progressives also championed the civil service, city manager, and commission forms of governance; introduced popular elections of sena-tors, primaries, recalls, referendums, and initiatives; and removed barriers to voting based on gender and race. These changes aimed both to enhance the role of neutral experts and to open up the system to greater democratic participa-tion. For Progressive reform to succeed, however, it had go beyond structural or administrative changes; it demanded a thoroughgoing project of civic, cultural, and national reconstruction.

Politically, individuals would need to be educated, literate, and, above all, rational. Popular control could not be maintained, nor expertise properly channeled, if voters could not analyze issues and think clearly. Initiatives and referendums required far more of individual voters than broad-based party politics. Culturally, citizens' capacities for independence and virtue would have to be protected from assault by deleterious social forces. Prostitution was crim-inalized to prevent women from literally losing their virtue; Prohibition aimed at eradicating the cruder instincts that made it difficult for men in particular to regulate their passions; national standards were promulgated for foods, drugs, public sanitation, and the control of infectious diseases in an effort to cleanse society; and individual bodily cleanliness received increased attention.[42]

Nationally, citizens need to possess a common identity. A core element in the Progressives' reconstruction efforts was forging a cohesive American national-ism that could undergird all the other changes. Left-leaning Progressivism, which emphasized cultural pluralism and an open-ended project of cosmopoli-tanism as the heart of this identity, emerged most clearly in the universities and settlement houses, particularly in Chicago. As a professor at the University of Chicago, and later at Teachers College in New York, John Dewey worked closely with the settlement houses, especially with Jane Addams at Hull House, and their ideas and experiences were mutually informing and reinforcing. Dewey's views on nationality, especially with regard to ethnicity and immigration, were not always clear and they remain a matter of some dispute.[43] His ideas were nonetheless influential among social reformers, and it is possible to sketch a broad outline of them.

Dewey stressed a radical sense of social experimentation in response to fears of the loss of individual control and autonomy in the new industrial and scientific era, and the perceived demise of the family, church, and neighborhood that had knit society together. In the tradition of Emerson and Whitman, he celebrated the democratic individual. He focused on human agency, on the ways that individuals can make and remake themselves in new environments. Confronting the centralization of state power, the impersonality of the growing bureaucracy, and the ethos of consumerism fostered by capitalism, Dewey looked forward to the emergence of a new order rather than nostalgically backward to the simpler agrarian times pined for by figures like Henry Adams. That new order would be democratic in the fundamental sense that all citizens possessed equal rights to participate in public life as individuals. His vision was simultaneously participatory and inclusive, in contrast to traditional views that regarded active citizenship and diversity as conflicting. In those views, a polity could encourage greater participation because it was more exclusionary; or it could be more inclusionary because it demanded less participation. But it could not be, as Dewey demanded, both inclusionary and participatory.[44]

Dewey acknowledged differences between immigrant cultures and American society, but he attributed these differences to environmental factors rather than racial characteristics. As immigrants encountered the American environment, with its complex and differentiated modes of production, Dewey believed they would develop skills and capacities similar to those of natives.[45] He thus set himself firmly against a notion of American identity as Anglo-Saxon. Indeed, he objected to any single pattern of conformity that threatened to stifle experimentation. "No matter how loudly any one proclaims his Americanism, if he assumes that one racial strain, any one component culture, no matter how early settled it was in our territory, or how effective it has been in its own land, is to furnish a pattern to which all others are to conform, he is a traitor to American Nationalism."[46]

As this reference to American nationalism suggests, Dewey thought that unity, or what he called "like-mindedness," was crucial to the further evolution of society and the emancipation of individuals. He argued that humans needed smaller membership groups, such as towns, religious organizations, ethnic groups, and occupational associations, out of which to fashion their own sensibility and moral development. These smaller associations, especially in a democratic society with widespread social and political participation, depended on "shared aims, beliefs, aspirations, knowledge—a common understanding—like-mindedness" that could maintain stability and efficiently structure social needs.[47] But how to reconcile conflicts among democratic participation, social pluralism, and national unity? Dewey contended that human society had progressed from smaller social organizations such as tribes, sects, and regions and was moving toward a national form of life that "subordinates petty and selfish interests." The goal was to create an "international nationalism" that combined the contributions of myriad cultures without destroying them. "The way to deal with hyphenism," Dewey wrote, "is to welcome it, but to welcome it in the sense of extracting from each people its special good, so that it shall surrender into a common fund of wisdom and experience what it especially has to contribute. All of these surrenders and contributions taken together create the national spirit of America."[48]

Dewey recoiled at any description of this vision as a melting pot, even one that produced a new rather than solely Anglo-American identity. "The theory of the Melting Pot always gave me rather a pang. To maintain that all the constituent elements, geographical, racial and cultural in the United States should be put in the same pot and turned into a uniform and unchanging product is distasteful. . . . The concept of uniformity and unanimity in culture is rather repellent." While Europe had to provide political accommodation for its ethnic and national groups, Dewey believed that the United States could blunt the demand for political nationalism by accepting and respecting assertions of cultural nationalism.[49] In order to manage the tension between unity and diversity, an American civic nationalism would have to be sufficiently integrated to allow for the multiple membership statuses that actually made true individualism possible. A rich and experimental individualism depended on a variety of resources that could not exist under any single system of uniformity.

The purpose of American nationalism was thus the protection and promotion of voluntary groups that made the project of individual emancipation possible. It could not aim to deracinate immigrants—to do so would undermine the resources necessary for creating an individual's identity. "Dewey believed in Americanization and in multiculturalism simultaneously," notes the political theorist Alan Ryan. "That is, he believed it was possible to create an American identity that was distinctive and yet not at odds with the plural cultural resources on which it would draw."[50] In Dewey's vision, the nation should not itself become an object of worship. Instead, its purpose lay in "promoting multiple memberships and exchanges." Once the nation-state was firmly established, it became "just an instrumentality for promoting and protecting other and more voluntary forms of association." The nation-state as an organization is a vehicle for "multiplying effective points of contact" and must remain subordinated to the larger process of "associating in such ways that experiences, ideas, emotions [and] values are transmitted and made common." Like an orchestra conductor "who makes no music himself," Dewey wrote, the nation-state "harmonizes the activities of those who in producing it are doing the thing intrinsically worth while. The state remains highly important—but its importance consists more and more in its power to foster and coordinate the activities of voluntary groupings."[51]

Dewey further contended that recognizing the instrumental nature of the state was especially critical at a time when voluntary groupings were increasingly "trans-national" in nature. "Internationalism," he asserted, "is not an aspiration but a fact, not a sentimental ideal but a force." Scientific, business, labor, and religious organizations cross national boundaries because "the interests they represent are worldwide." The doctrine of national sovereignty as an end in itself thus represented, for Dewey, "the strongest barrier to the effective formation of an international mind which alone agrees with the moving forces of present-day labor, commerce, science, art and religion."[52]

RANDOLPH BOURNE, JANE ADDAMS, AND THE PRACTICE OF PLURALISM

Dewey's concerns about deracination and the possibility of generating a truly international nationalism were further developed by his one-time student, Randolph Bourne. (Indeed, by the end of the twentieth century, his work would be even more influential than Dewey's in shaping the arguments of both multiculturalists and civic nationalists.) As a journalist and an essayist, Bourne brought a distinctly cultural dimension to his analysis of ethnicity and American identity. He rejected what he saw as native-born Americans' tendency to substitute a "petrified" English culture for the development of a genuinely American one. "The Anglo-Saxon element is guilty of just what every dominant race is guilty of in every European country," Bourne wrote, "the imposition of its own culture on the minority peoples." Bourne's 1916 essay, "Trans-National America," opened with a frontal assault on the notion that immigrants were un-American because they felt deeply attached to their countries of origin. "We are all foreign-born," he announced, "or the descendants of foreign-born, and if distinctions are to be made between us they should rightly be on some other ground than indigenousness." Bourne pointed out that the early settlers did not come to the New World to adopt the culture of Native Americans. Indeed, he contended, "[i]n their folkways, in their social and political institutions, they were, like every colonial people, slavishly imitative of the mother-country."

This reverence for all things English had misled both native-born and naturalized citizens into missing what was genuinely unique about the new nation, its "distinctively American spirit." This spirit was fundamentally "pioneer"; it was about "bigness [and] action"; it was the "adventurous, forward-looking drive of a colonial empire." A conception of nationalism defined as the melting pot misunderstood that the American cultural tradition, paradoxically, lay in the future. This tradition had to be created, not formed in imitation. Bourne was excited by the prospects of creating something genuinely fresh, by the "incomparable opportunity of attacking the future with a new key." But his excitement at creating a new culture was tempered by what he regarded as American elites' insistence on "Anglo-Saxonizing" newcomers. He observed that the South remained the most purely English and compared it unfavorably to the "wisdom, intelligence, industry and social leadership" that had come out of the midwestern states, which had absorbed more immigrants. The homogeneity and uniformity so sought after by the most ardent nationalizers threatened to create "cultural half-breeds, neither assimilated Anglo-Saxons nor nationals of another culture."

Bourne distinguished between what he called centripetal and centrifugal forces in cultural life. He praised the distinctive qualities of individual cultures as centripetal, as providing the values that make it possible to locate oneself in the world, to make judgments, and, as such, to be better able to contribute to the American community. Americans should respect rather than denigrate "the Jew who sticks proudly to the faith of his fathers and boasts of that venerable culture" and the "Bohemian who supports the Bohemian schools in Chicago." Centrifugal forces, in contrast, operate at the fringes of particular cultures, such that immigrants who are detached from their cultures become mere "fragments of peoples. . . . This is the cultural wreckage of our time, and it is from the fringes of the Anglo-Saxon as well as the other stocks that it falls." Bourne thus joined his concern that a backward-looking Anglo-Saxonism stood in the way of the truly American pioneer spirit with his worry that immigrants were being pressed to lose the only identity that could keep them anchored in the absence of a future-oriented American identity.

The dominance of English tradition and the deculturation of newcomers, in fact, stood in the way of America's forging a radically new transnational identity. This identity would be simultaneously pluralist and cosmopolitan. America would make a place for groups to mingle but not to become uniform. Thus, what other Americans recoiled in horror at, the ostensible "failure of the melting pot," Bourne regarded as the beginning of the great American experiment in democracy. "In a world which has dreamed of internationalism, we find that we have all unawares been building up the first international nation. America is already the world-federation in miniature, the continent where for the first time in history has been achieved the miracle of hope, the peaceful living side by side, with character substantially preserved, of the most heterogeneous peoples under the sun."

While Bourne marveled at the possibility that European cultures would "merge" but not "fuse," he clearly thought that in the intersections among cultures citizens would engage in a dynamic "weaving back and forth" of traditions. Bourne coined a distinctive term for this process: citizens would be "acclimatized," rather than assimilated. In this process, even the "eager Anglo-Saxon" would be liberated to breathe "a larger air. In his new enthusiasm for continental literatures, for unplumbed Russian depths, for French clarity of thought, for Teuton philosophies of power, he feels himself a citizen of a larger world."[53] The hyphen that joins ethnicity and nationality (in, for example, "Italian-American") functioned for Bourne "as a plus sign," to use Michael Walzer's phrase.[54] Individuals' distinctive cultural heritages would serve as spurs to the development of an "intellectual sympathy," which aims to get to "the heart of the different cultural expressions, and [feel] as they feel." Bourne believed that under these circumstances it would be possible to understand other views and traditions while retaining one's own. Indeed, those differences would be made "creative" because they constituted the foundation of a "new cosmopolitan outlook."

This outlook would be America's true gift to the world even as it bound Americans together by their equal possession of it. "For Bourne," David Hollinger notes, "cosmopolitanism implied strength and resilience rather than a lack of deep character. Cosmopolitans engaged a world the complexity of which rendered provincial tastes and skills inadequate and uninspiring."[55] Bourne was an American nationalist who saw America serving a greater purpose, not one who saw preserving the nation as the primary aim. American civic nationalism would draw on subnational identities in the service of establishing a transnational identity. It would be the crucible through which acclimatized Jews, Germans, Italians, and Anglo-Saxons created "an intellectual internationalism [that makes] . . . understanding and not indignation its end." "Such a sympathy," Bourne assured, "will unite and not divide."

Although Bourne despised the ideology of patriotism, he did not favor "a policy of drift." Bourne wanted an "integrated and disciplined" American nation, one he thought could best be achieved by a set of policy ideas that coordinated rather than eradicated its diverse elements. His main concern was the integration of immigrants in America. He insisted that "we must have a policy and an ideal for an actual situation [of cultural pluralism]. Our question is, What shall we do with our America?" Bourne argued for policies that engaged new immigrants in social and political life coupled with a powerful antidiscriminatory ethic. Effective integration, he contended, required a spirit of joint cooperation. A free society was one in which all its members had an equal chance to determine its "ideals and purposes and industrial and social institutions." New and native-born citizens must feel a sense of enthusiasm and purpose; this depended on no ethnic group sensing "that its cultural base [was] being prejudged." Immigrants were more likely to embrace a country that included them as equal participants in an ongoing process of national self-definition rather than one that believed they had to lose their sense of self and ideals.

Bourne believed that multiple allegiances and identities strengthened American identity, as long as immigrants were properly engaged in a process of acclimatization. He therefore did not regard becoming an American citizen as the kind of transformative event that could or should sever an individual from his previous allegiances. Instead, Bourne favored dual citizenship. He further advocated "free and mobile passage of the immigrant between America and his native land" because it would enable America to spread its new ideology of cosmopolitanism. Rather than seeing immigrants who shuttled between the United States and their country of origin as parasites, Bourne saw them as "a symbol of the cosmopolitan interchange which is coming, in spite of all war and national exclusiveness." "Only the American," he wrote confidently, "and in this category I include the migratory alien who has lived with us and caught the pioneer spirit and a sense of new social vistas—has the chance to become that citizen of the world."[56]

While Bourne developed the cosmopolitan implications in Dewey's thought, Jane Addams practiced a pluralist, democratic conception of Americanization that highlighted immigrants' contributions to the national identity. Like Dewey and Bourne, she and her settlement house compatriots feared that the cultural change from southern and eastern Europe to urban, industrialized America was an alienating process for newcomers. The informal and formal pressures to adjust to new conditions threatened family life and bewildered individuals. Addams and her fellow reformers worried as well that America's treatment of immigrants violated its promise of political equality and social justice. In response, Addams opened Hull House in an immigrant neighborhood in Chicago in 1889, and other reformers opened four hundred other such houses across the country by 1910. These settlement houses attracted college-educated, middle-class women, and some men as well, who believed deeply that the universal ideals undergirding American democracy had to be given "tangible expression," as Addams wrote in 1892.[57]

Settlement workers understood that they were competing with the urban machines' informal and effective method of shaping immigrants. They recognized that ward bosses provided an array of social benefits—from patronage to medical care—that tied immigrants tightly to their provider. As Progressives, their objections to this relationship ran deep, focusing on the machines' vision of politics as personal, organic, and hierarchical. The ethnic machine offered an alternative process of naturalization and Americanization that seemed to contradict everything they hoped to achieve. The very notion of politics as an organic process that depended on personal loyalty and concrete benefits was at odds with their view of politics as above personal needs, issuing from universal laws and abstract principles applicable to all.[58]

The contrast between good government Progressives and corrupt ethnic politicians is easily overdone. Machine politicians supported some of the Progressives' reforms and, as Amy Bridges has pointed out, "the partisan abuse of public employment" was not simply a reflection of immigrants' cultural values but, in fact, had characterized the operations of city government as far back as the Federalists in the 1790s. Addams herself recognized that since "the so-called more enlightened members of the community accept public gifts from the man who buys up the Council, and the so-called less enlightened members accept individual gifts from the man who sells out the Council, we surely must take our punishment together."[59]

More so than other Progressives, settlement house leaders also understood that for immigrants to become emancipated politically they had to do so through the prism of their group identity and ethnic solidarity. "[W]hat headway can the notion of civic purity, of honesty of administration, make against this big manifestation of human friendliness, this stalking survival of village kindness?" Addams wrote, in describing the machine politician's vital connection to immigrants. "The notions of the civic reformer are negative and impotent before it. The reformers give themselves over largely to criticisms of the present state of affairs, to writing and talking of what the future must mean; but their goodness is not dramatic; it is not even concrete and human." Addams knew that for settlement workers to compete with ward bosses they would first have to "obtain a like sense of identification" and demonstrate "some solidarity in our ethical conceptions." She understood that ethnic partisanship was, as the historian John Buenker characterizes it, "a means by which millions of people of diverse backgrounds were integrated and socialized into the American political process. It allowed them to function as loyal citizens, without denying their sense of ethnic identification and 'peoplehood.' "[60]

Social reformers thus devised plans to compete with the urban machines in terms of the provision of social goods, protective legislation, the recognition of group identity, and citizenship training. They engaged in a wide range of legal, political, medical, civic, and cultural efforts to help immigrants adjust to their new surroundings and to press Americans to accept them. Reformers lobbied cities to provide sanitary conditions in which newcomers could live, including such basics as proper garbage collection. They urged immigrant mothers to provide "American breakfasts" that provided sufficient calcium and vitamin D to protect against rickets. They crusaded against landlords who exploited newcomers by providing substandard housing. When Chicago police raided immigrants' homes indiscriminately, social reformers understood that all the civics lessons in the world meant little when American law looked to newcomers like the rule of state functionaries in the world they had just escaped. When workers in the Chicago stockyards went on strike in 1904 protesting poor and unfair conditions, Addams and her compatriots lent their support. Their aim, as Graham Taylor, founder of the Commons settlement in Chicago, said in 1912, was to establish a coordinated program of public and private organizations "to receive, distribute and locate immigrants; to protect their persons and property from exploitation and abuse; to inform and train them for citizenship."[61]

Addams especially recognized that the larger task of incorporating newcomers entailed what the political scientist Peter Skerry describes as a shift from a tight-knit world of family and neighbors to a complex public world characterized by bureaucratic institutions, instrumental relations, and formal rules. "The early settlements practically staked their future upon an identification with the alien," Addams explained. "We stuck with this at some cost, for we believed that especially in times of crisis it was our mission to interpret American institutions to those who were bewildered concerning them." She did not, Skerry argues, draw a bright line between the private and the public; instead she sought to use private concerns to encourage an interest in the public good. Addams, he writes, "understood that enticing immigrants into the public square had to begin with their own quotidian concerns." She linked domestic issues of child care, nutrition, and housing to broader lessons about personal and social responsibility. "It is surprising," Addams remarked, "how a simple experience, if it be but genuine, affords an opening into citizenship altogether lacking to the more grandiose attempts. A Greek-American who slaughters sheep in a tenement-house yard on the basis of the Homeric tradition can be made to see the effect of the improvised shambles on his neighbors' health and the right of the city to prohibit him only as he perceives the development of city government upon its most modern basis."[62]

Mediating institutions like Hull House also helped immigrants develop what Harry Boyte and Jennifer O'Donoghue call "public identities" by teaching "the skills of give and take, instilling the importance of working with people different from oneself, fostering a commitment to democracy, and holding citizens accountable to common standards." By calling attention to the political dimensions of their circumstances, Addams believed that newcomers would expand the notion of what a shared public life meant. From sanitation needs to working conditions, they would bring a social and communal dimension to public life that was needed to constrain the American tendency toward unbridled individualism. Reformers like Addams thus sought to harness the social and civic resources provided by immigrants' ethnic identities and group interests while consciously seeking to widen those identities and interests.[63]

This approach was made possible in large part because social reformers rejected the distinction between old and new immigrants. Grace Abbott, director of the Immigrants' Protective League in Chicago, testified before Congress that the earlier waves of immigrants who were now being lionized as more fit to become Americans were no different than the current crop.[64] Abbott, Addams, and others who worked directly with immigrants believed strongly that environment rather than heredity was the factor that determined successful adjustment to American institutions and practices. Given the proper circumstances newcomers, like societies, could evolve and change. Reformers defended immigrants against the charges of inferiority leveled by restrictionists. Democracy, they contended, may have emerged from the Anglo-Saxon tradition but it was not limited to descendants of that tradition. "Here in the United States," Abbott wrote, "we have the opportunity of working out a democracy founded on internationalism."[65]

Like Dewey, Addams thought that just as the tribe and ethnic group represented steps on the ladder to the nation, the nation itself aimed toward its own transcendence into an international or universal brotherhood. The goal was to create spheres of openness and communication where groups and individuals could interact and break down barriers, including national ones. In this view, the United States was in the vanguard, the leader in showing how an ultimate stage of peaceful cooperation would replace conflict among groups.[66] Such methods as a club system that mixed ethnic groups would hasten the arrival of that stage by serving as what Dewey called a "social clearing-house." These clubs operated, the historian Rivka Shpak Lissak observes, as a

> laboratory for democracy and social and cultural assimilation. Ethnically mixed clubs were meeting places for otherwise segregated children and inculcated tolerance and respect for differences as a product of coexistence. They taught that the preconditions for democracy were the breaking down of national and cultural differences and the unification of American society on the basis of common interests, ideas, feelings, and norms of behavior, as opposed to segregation and preservation of ethnic identity.

Social clubs fit well as part of Addams's strategy of linking private to public concerns. "The value of social clubs," she wrote, "broadens out in one's mind to an instrument of companionship through which many may be led from a sense of isolation to one of civic responsibility."[67]

Like Dewey and Bourne, Addams and many social reformers believed that the best way to create this new, universal brotherhood was by treating immigrants as equals who would participate in shaping the American nation. In particular, social reformers sought to highlight the tremendous "gifts" the new immigrants would contribute. Immigrants' religiosity, their closeness to the agrarian life of independent labor and its attendant virtues, and their cultural expressions from sewing and embroidery to metalworking and woodworking were precisely what the reformers thought American society needed. Settlement workers "insisted that immigrants preserve the customs and traditions of the old country, assuring immigrants that it was not necessary to reject the past to become an American." To the social reformers, the new arrivals' innocence meant that they had important characteristics to offer Americans, characteristics they termed "things of the spirit."[68]

Addams's emphasis on immigrants' gifts and the contributions they could make to American identity served several purposes. For immigrants, it was meant to ease the assimilation process and to overcome their sense of alienation; they need not change their names to fit in. At the same time, their assimilation into American society would be greatly facilitated by showing American citizens that they had important things to contribute beyond their labor. For Americans, these gifts would help them retain a connection to their own roots, which were becoming fast attenuated in a mobile, industrial society. Further, they would help build a popular, vernacular culture that would simultaneously add color and richness to American society and link old and new citizens in a common culture.[69] This view corresponded to the reformers' evolutionary belief that contact and competition among cultures would produce the strongest, richest one. Their confidence in an environmentalist approach meant that they believed that immigrants' cultural habits and skills could make important public contributions. These habits and skills would help draw immigrants into a larger social and civic world and, in doing so, their group identity would foster rather than impede incorporation.

Left-leaning Progressives like Dewey, Bourne, and Addams saw in ethnic identity and democratic engagement a way to reduce the tension between the rational commitment to abstract ideals and the organic bond of nationalism. Rather than an obstacle to a genuine civic nationalism, ethnic identity provided the rootedness and emotional well-being from which immigrants could join Americans in creating a meaningful national culture that fostered the highest levels of individual emancipation and civic freedom. The national identity that resulted from the dynamic exchange between immigrants and American culture would itself be genuinely transnational and outward looking, capable of continual renewal and transformation even as it provided stability and cohesion. This dynamic would hasten rather than impede immigrants' integration into the American civic nation.

This celebration of a simultaneously open and coherent national identity was not universally shared, even on the left. Some social reformers held that American culture had become a thing in itself. In their view, America had absorbed the Hebraic and the Greek, the Egyptian and the Roman, and it had melded the Middle Ages, the Renaissance, and the Enlightenment into the foremost exemplar of a universal culture. That culture was not a finished product, and hence immigrants could contribute to it, but neither was it a vague projection into the future, a new identity that would be significantly different from what already existed. Social reformers who held this belief were less critical of American culture and tradition than were Dewey and Bourne. Dewey believed that America had "not yet so justified itself" in terms of art and science. Like Bourne, he criticized the upper-class American habit of aping European manners.[70] Addams, too, refused simply to venerate American culture, and she plainly objected to Americanization as homogenization. This tension between the incorporation of immigrants as an open-ended exchange among cultures and immigrants' imbibing and adjusting to an existing cultural identity was persistent throughout this period.[71]

The real cultural weight of ethnic identity posed other challenges to the left-leaning approach to civic nationalism. As part of a broader Progressive movement, the settlement workers' prized the formal processes of naturalization, the autonomous operations of neutral government institutions, and the centrality of individuals expressing rational judgments. Yet they also saw in the urban machines the importance of informal, local mediating institutions that addressed the realities of immigrants' daily experiences and embraced ethnic and communal solidarity. Reformers' attempts to compete with the urban machines in cultural and material terms thus produced a hybrid model of incorporation, one in which ethnic identity served as a bridge to a wider civic and national sensibility even as the civic ideals of individualism and neutrality before the law were stressed. The federal government's official organs of Americanization drew on the same civic ideals but combined them with a much stronger emphasis on the transfer of national allegiance. As we see in the next chapter, those organs, especially the Bureau of Naturalization and the Bureau of Education, were influenced to take a more aggressive approach by a different strand of Progressivism, the leading proponent of which was Teddy Roosevelt.

CHAPTER FIVE

Nationalism in the Progressive Era

WHILE Dewey, Bourne, and Addams reflected facets of a left-leaning tradition of American civic nationalism, Theodore Roosevelt and Herbert Croly articulated a more mainstream position. Their analysis and rhetoric shaped the context of public debate over immigration and citizenship throughout the first two decades of the twentieth century. Roosevelt and Croly shared with Dewey and Bourne the belief that American citizenship was defined by its core civic principle of individualism. In contrast, they saw the eradication of ethnic identity—and the establishment of a uniform national identity—as the prerequisite for advancing that principle. Roosevelt worried that a series of economic and political trends—materialism, localism, and globalism—was causing citizens to place the interests of the nation second and that this would make them incapable of self-government at a time when they needed to master significant domestic problems and manage America's growing authority in the world. In response to these trends, he called for a "New Nationalism" that reflected the unique nature of American life and pressed citizens to achieve great things. In an era dominated by industrialists and political bosses, Roosevelt promoted larger projects of national solidarity. In his mind, America's civic freedom depended on a distinct national culture inherited from Europe. To ensure the vigor of that culture, the entry of non-whites needed to be limited, and white immigrants had to be Americanized.

Roosevelt's nationalist ideology informed the work of the two primary federal vehicles for Americanization immediately before, during, and after World War I—the Bureau of Naturalization and the Bureau of Education. Richard Campbell, the commissioner of naturalization, and his deputy, Raymond Crist, saw their task as elevating "the most neglected of professions—the profession of self-government."[1] At the Bureau of Education, Roosevelt's disciple Frances Kellor wanted the national government to play a guiding role in incorporating newcomers. She saw the bureau as the way for the Americanization movement to achieve its "national goal of consciousness."[2]

Both bureaus strongly focused on ensuring a shared national sentiment between newcomers and native-born citizens. Rather than emphasizing the adoption of an American cultural identity inherited from Europe, these institutions focused on the naturalization requirement that new citizens demonstrate an attachment to the principles of the Constitution. Initially, they treated immigrants' embrace of American civic principles as the measure of their devotion to the American nation. The difficulty with this measure, they discovered, is that there was no definitive way to determine when an applicant had, in fact, embraced these principles. As a result, both bureaus turned to educational programs which stressed that, above all, immigrants must undergo a psychological transformation of devotion from their traditional ethnic identity to America's civic ideals. These programs sought to sidestep the tensions between individualism and nationalism by seeking to engender broad changes in attitude rather than the adoption of specific cultural attributes or ideologies.

ROOSEVELT'S NEW NATIONALISM

Roosevelt took aim at the notion that material success and laissez-faire government were the goals of individual life and a free society. At the same time, the absence of real equality of opportunity and "social and industrial justice" for average citizens was undermining their ability to believe in America's higher ideals. Roosevelt celebrated economic development and personal advancement, but he insisted that politics, patriotism, and duty were more important than material gain. "[O]ur country calls not for the life of ease but for the life of strenuous endeavor," he told the Hamilton Club in 1899. "[I]f we shrink from the hard contests where men must win at hazard of their lives and at the risk of all they hold dear, then the bolder and stronger peoples will pass us by."[3]

Roosevelt recognized that patriotism was a dangerous idea, one that could lead citizens to celebrate only what was their own. He acknowledged that the United States should be willing to learn from ideas developed in other nations, as long as such ideas were compatible with America's fundamental ideals and were adapted to the nation's particular circumstances. Those broader ideals, however, were not subject to adaptation or negotiation. His understanding of the civic dimension of American citizenship mixed a psychological emphasis on individualism, an economic focus on equality of opportunity, and a structural concern with the separation of church and state. Roosevelt regarded these ideas as distinctive hallmarks of a specifically American civic nationalism, one that could serve as a singular force for individual emancipation and social progress.

He thus defended American patriotism against those he derided as "parochialists" or "cosmopolitans." "Parochialism," Roosevelt argued, is the "patriotism of the village," the exaltation of the little community over the broader needs and purposes of the nation. The parochialist's impulse to love the particular was justifiable, he granted, but the object of his affection was too insular. Just as the patriotism of the village destroyed American strength, so, too, did a philosophy of cosmopolitanism that promoted the extinction of national feeling. Such a future might one day be possible, Roosevelt conceded, "where our patriotism will include the whole human race and all the world." But since that age "is still several eons distant," proponents of cosmopolitanism "are of no practical service to the present generation." In fact, they threaten the development of a robust American identity as the primary source for achieving good at home and abroad. "Nothing will more quickly or more surely disqualify a man from doing good work in the world than the acquirement of that flaccid habit of mind which its possessors style cosmopolitanism," he charged. "The patriotism of the village or the belfry is bad, but the lack of all patriotism is even worse. . . . Such a man is not a traitor; but he is a silly and undesirable citizen."[4]

The primary intellectual force behind Roosevelt's civic nationalism was Herbert Croly, a preeminent journalist and editor. In 1910, Croly helped draft Roosevelt's New Nationalism speech, which Roosevelt delivered at the dedication of the John Brown Cemetery at Osawotomie, Kansas. That speech drew on Croly's recently published book, *The Promise of American Life*, which set the broad moral agenda for centrist Progressivism. Croly sought to square a Jeffersonian commitment to democracy and individual emancipation with the scale and complexity of modern life. In his view, only a Hamiltonian vision of expanded national authority could control the economic forces that threatened to overwhelm democratic institutions and undermine citizens' opportunities for individual emancipation.

Such expanded authority required a commensurate sense of national identity to undergird it. Croly rejected the possibility that an American national identity could imitate the European nations' emphasis on shared blood, soil, or race. He also doubted the proposition that Americans could be held together on the basis of their civic ideals alone. Instead, Croly sketched a national identity that simultaneously reached backward into American history and looked forward to a new age of individual freedom. In America, individual rights depended on a sense of identity that was "chiefly a matter of actual historical association," he asserted. "A people that lack the power of basing their political association on an accumulated national tradition and purpose is not capable of either nationality or democracy."[5] Citizens exercising their rights then had to understand that they would only achieve true independence by finding their place, economically and morally, as contributors to a broader national life.

Economically, citizens had to find their particular niche in a modern industrial order. Morally, they had to identify with the needs and aspirations of their fellow citizens. As Alan Ryan observes, the emphasis in Croly's book was on the future, on the *promise* of American life. That promise was individual emancipation, but such emancipation depended entirely on a national state that could adequately meet social needs and a robust American nationalism that could support that state. Thus, for Croly, individual freedom and national purpose were intimately linked. "The task of individual and social regeneration," he wrote, "must remain incomplete and impoverished until the conviction and feeling of human brotherhood enters into the process of the human spirit."[6]

Roosevelt merged a distinctly racial vision of history and American culture with Croly's historical, economic, and moral nationalism. He drew from his study of history and natural science an understanding of social competition in which both heredity and environment played crucial roles. In his 1910 Oxford Lecture, Roosevelt rejected racial determinism in favor of a view in which nations and races could both advance and regress depending on the mix of racial traits and environmental influences.[7] Americans, in his view, combined the best racial traits of the English, German, Irish, and Norse, traits that then had been strengthened and improved by the hard frontier environment. From these racial strains Roosevelt understood that Americans had inherited the capacities to be "bold and hardy, cool and intelligent, quick with their hands and showing at their best in an emergency." Americans also possessed a special capacity for ruling themselves, for combining liberty with self-control, a trait they had inherited from their Teutonic ancestors.[8]

Non-white races, on the other hand, represented for Roosevelt inferior racial strains who would dilute Americans' special combination of self-assertion and self-control. Thus, the destiny of the white race, its "domineering masterful spirit," justified the seizure of Texas from Mexico. Mexicans were alien from whites in "blood, language, religion and habits of life," incapable of self-government, and thus naturally subject to dominion.[9] Similarly, the Chinese had lost their manly virtues and lacked the proper capacity for self-assertion. Roosevelt therefore supported the exclusion of Chinese immigrants in 1882 and reiterated his support for significant restrictions during his presidency. Slavery, in Roosevelt's estimation, was "a crime whose short-sighted folly was worse than its guilt," for it "brought hordes of African slaves, whose descendants now form immense populations in certain portions of the land." He supported emancipation but doubted that blacks would ever be capable of self-government or truly belong equally to the American nation.[10] In contrast, he expressed tremendous admiration for the achievement of Japanese civilization, even suggesting, at one point, that the Japanese had reached a higher degree of development in some respects than had Americans. Nonetheless, he supported the Gentlemen's Agreement of 1907 barring further immigration from Japan. He did so, in part, owing to his aversion to racial mixing with the Japanese and his doubts that America could assimilate those whose origins and customs were so fundamentally alien.[11]

Despite these views, Roosevelt rejected the more extreme nativist thinking and policies that were common currency in the late nineteenth and early twentieth centuries. His preoccupation with racial differences did not "translate into a full-blown hysteria about a 'yellow peril,'" as the historian Thomas Dyer points out. "[T]he association of barbarism with yellow skin made little sense" to Roosevelt. He lampooned plans to provide separate railroad cars for Japanese, calling them "silly" and "indefensible." Japanese who already were present in the United States had to be incorporated into the nation.[12] Roosevelt also condemned the Know-Nothings and Native American parties of the nineteenth century as un-American. Americans, he held, should neither persecute nor support anyone on the basis of their religion or ethnicity. He objected to voting against a man because of his religious creed, and he objected to voting for him on the same grounds. In either case, Roosevelt asserted, one imposes a religious test that violates the spirit of the Constitution.[13] In 1912, pressed by social workers and motivated in part by political needs, Roosevelt's Progressive Party pledged to protect the welfare of immigrants and to incorporate them as part of its nationalist ideology. This position earned Roosevelt the ire of the nativist Junior Order of United American Mechanics and secured for him a significant proportion of the immigrant vote. Three-quarters of the districts in New York City in which Roosevelt won a plurality were heavily populated by immigrants from eastern Europe.[14]

The historical and scientific theories of civilization development that had led Roosevelt to embrace imperialism abroad and restriction at home also caused him to reject or modify the dominant forms of nativist thinking. He believed that America was developing its own, distinct nationality. "We are making a new race, a new type, in this country," he wrote in 1906. This new ethnic type owed its development to the unique American environment, both "physical and spiritual," as well as to the mixture of blood found among the original settlers. He further contended that this new race "has never been fixed in blood" and could continue to absorb immigrants of appropriate racial stock, as each group "adds its blood" and, in the process of doing so, "changes [the nation] somewhat."[15]

Roosevelt thus promoted a distinctly ethnic process of nation building. He worried that economic and social modernization were hastening the general tendency of races to reach "a stationary state" where their fecundity and virility began to decline. These concerns resulted in his relentless championing of a traditional notion of motherhood in which women had a duty to their race to procreate. His support for restrictions on Asian immigration also reflected his project of nation building. Roosevelt advanced an ethnic and nationalist unity among working-class whites by limiting the entry of non-whites. He wanted to provide a buffer against both lower-class resentment and upper-class domination. By protecting whites from economic competition from imported labor, he argued, American democracy could avoid the class conflict that had destroyed aristocratic governments. He thus pursued restriction as part of an explicitly economic and ethnic nation-building strategy, which differed from that of the more explicitly white supremacist proponents of race-based exclusion.[16]

Roosevelt heartily approved of Israel Zangwill's 1908 play *The Melting Pot*, which Zangwill had dedicated to him. The idea and image of the melting pot seemed to suggest a fusing of nationalities into a new nationality that drew from all its ingredients. Roosevelt's own understanding was closer to the notion that non-Anglo-Saxon nationalities would be purified in the melting pot and shaped in the image of the majority culture. In his view, a single standard of behavior was necessary to reinforce a sense of commonality and a willingness to sacrifice. Immigrants therefore had to shed their foreign speech, habits, dress, and especially language. The most important demand American civic national-ism placed on its adherents was a sense of identification with America itself. Al-legiance "is a matter of the spirit and of the soul," Roosevelt told the Knights of Columbus. "The only man who is a good American is an American and nothing else. . . . There is no room in this country for hyphenated Americans."[17]

To achieve this uniform nationality required a formal process of American-ization. Initially, that meant a policy that was simultaneously generous in out-look and practical in outreach, and swift and harsh if standards were not met. Immigrants' rights had to be protected so that they felt neither bitterness nor resentment toward their new identity. In 1915, Roosevelt objected to a literacy test because, in his view, it barred many newcomers who might make excellent citizens. In its stead, he proposed admitting illiterate aliens and giving them an opportunity to learn English and to work. They would also be expected to par-ticipate in civic life. "The policy of 'Let alone' which we have hitherto pursued is thoroughly vicious from two standpoints," he declared.

> By this policy we have permitted the immigrants, and too often the native-born laborers as well, to suffer injustice. Moreover, by this policy we have failed to impress upon the immigrant and upon the native-born as well that they are expected to do justice as well as to receive justice. . . . We cannot secure . . . loyalty unless we make this a country where men shall feel that they have justice.[18]

Immigrants had to prove themselves willing to take up the duties of their new civic and national status. Roosevelt advocated deportation for those who, after a period of time, had not at least begun to acquire the language. As part of a broader transformation of identity and sentiment, he urged immigrants "to bear the most honorable of titles" by Americanizing their names. He made clear that U.S. citizenship was an all-or-nothing proposition, one in which devotion to the American flag not only came first but was singular—"no other flag should even come second." "Above all," Roosevelt demanded, "the immigrant must learn to talk and think and *be* United States."[19] This view shaped much of the initial federal effort to formalize the rules governing naturalization and to mold immigrants into citizens. The movement to Americanize immigrants re-flected Roosevelt's confidence in the absorptive capacities of civic nationalism in the United States.

Naturalization and Constitutional Attachment

Roosevelt's first and most direct link to formally incorporating new immigrants began with a commission he appointed in 1905 to standardize the administration of naturalization. The Commission on Naturalization's recommendations constituted the federal government's first serious effort to shift the process of becoming a citizen away from an informal and fragmented approach toward a single method. (The federal government would repeat this process throughout the century. Periodic bursts of attention to the naturalization process would dissipate as concerns about citizenship waned, the difficulties of reforming the system became apparent, and naturalization officers defended the discretion accorded them by the system.) Starting in 1903, the Bureau of Immigration had issued reports critical of the multiple ways in which state courts processed applicants for naturalization. The level of fraud in the states, the bureau concluded, was "appalling."[20] These reports coincided with growing concerns that the naturalization process was too easily abused by ethnic machines for political purposes. The combination of fraud and concerns about newcomers led Roosevelt to appoint an interagency commission.[21]

The commission's recommendations established the outlines for the system of naturalization that continues to this day. Congress, following the commission's proposals, centralized the administration of naturalization by establishing the Naturalization Division in the new Bureau of Immigration and Naturalization, which was located in the Department of Commerce and Labor. Local courts were stripped of the authority to grant citizenship, and local officials were disallowed from reviewing the credentials of applicants for citizenship. By 1907, the authority to grant citizenship had been almost entirely concentrated in the federal courts, and federal officials were tapped to investigate candidates' standing to become citizens.[22]

In addition to these procedural changes, Congress followed the recommendation of Roosevelt's commission when, in 1906, it mandated that applicants demonstrate speaking knowledge of English. The commissioners noted that an immigrant who did not speak English could become a citizen yet still "remain[ed] a foreigner." They objected to this practice:

> He can not understand the questions which the court may put to him when he applies for naturalization nor read the Constitution which he swears to support. When, afterwards, he votes, he can not read his ballot. The Commission is aware that some aliens who can not learn our language make good citizens. There are, however, exceptions, and the proposition is incontrovertible that no man is a desirable citizen of the United States who does not know the English language.[23]

Congress also excluded anarchists and polygamists from eligibility to naturalize. In 1907 Congress passed the Expatriation Act, which further sought to standardize the rules governing U.S. citizenship and to clearly establish that status as unitary rather than multiple. Although it was called the Expatriation Act, the law codified the formal conditions of conduct by which the government could denationalize citizens.[24]

In the drive to make the citizenship process uniform, the courts and the Bureau of Naturalization faced a difficult issue: how to determine whether an applicant for citizenship was attached to the principles of the Constitution.[25] Following the requirements established in the Naturalization Act of 1795, the Naturalization Act of 1906 required applicants to have conducted themselves as persons "of good moral character, attached to the principles of the Constitution of the United States, and well disposed to the good order and happiness of the United States." The bureau determined that whether an applicant had behaved as a person of good moral character could be best established by requiring the testimony of two witnesses. Whether someone was attached to the principles of the Constitution, however, proved far more vexing to determine. "This would appear to be by far the most indispensable requirement of a good citizen," an internal bureau memo concluded. "If it exists in any case it carries with it all the other personal qualifications prescribed by the law, but, as a matter of practical experience, the determination of the question of whether a petitioner is in fact attached to the principles of the Constitution of the United States is the point which in its establishment involves the most difficulty."[26]

While some courts held that attachment could be assessed on the same basis as character (by the applicants' conduct), other courts, as well as the bureau, began to consider this insufficient evidence. Attachment, they reasoned, reflects an interior rather than exterior state of affairs. As a state of mind, rather than a way of acting, it was difficult to assess. Conduct might reveal those who were not attached to the Constitution, but it could not demonstrate who was attached. Moreover, they pointed out, the law did not say that a court must or may be satisfied with the conduct standard. Instead, they began to emphasize a conceptual rather than behavioral standard for judging attachment to the Constitution. If they could not determine an applicant's interior state of mind, they could at least ascertain if an applicant knew what the principles of the Constitution were. By demonstrating that they understood those principles applicants could prove their attachment to the Constitution by proxy.[27]

Following passage of the 1906 law, the Bureau of Naturalization advised that, before and after taking out First Papers, the applicant should learn English, "the spirit of his new environment, the customs and laws of the community of which he forms a part, and his duty to the government."[28] During the ninety days the applicant awaited a judicial hearing, the bureau recommended that the alien "should be specially instructed in the duties of citizenship, not merely to be able to answer the questions authorized by the government, but rather that he may be able to relate himself intelligently and fully as an American citizen in accord with the oath of allegiance he is required to take." A form prepared in 1909 counseled applicants to use the ninety-day waiting period to

> read carefully the Constitution of the United States and also the Constitution of your own State. If you cannot, in a general way, grasp their meaning you

should have someone explain them to you. . . . You should learn about the origin of our country, the Declaration of Independence, the wars in which the United States have been engaged, and other important National matters. Unless you have a fair knowledge of the matters referred to above you cannot intelligently take the oath of allegiance or say that you believe in the principles of the Constitution of the United States or of your own State, or be considered sufficiently intelligent to assume the duties of American citizenship. As a rule no court will admit you to citizenship unless you have a fair knowledge of these matters.

This form also warned applicants, "You should bear in mind that what is said above is only by way of suggestion. Some Judges may not require so much while other Judges may insist upon more."[29] Indeed, regional examiners reported significant differences within their districts as well as among them in the administration of the naturalization process. Sometimes these differences related to "local conditions and the character of the local population," as the chief examiner in Colorado wrote. It was easier to maintain an "excellent standard" for industrial workers, he said, because they lived together and could easily get to the courthouse. In contrast, only the "most elementary standard" could be expected where applicants were poor, especially if they were homesteaders who lived far from town.[30]

The standards expected by judges and examiners varied considerably. One judge required an applicant to show that he had saved one hundred dollars before seeking to become a citizen.[31] Others were likely to make the examination difficult for applicants who revealed their support for socialism, communism, or anarchism. If an examiner had "reason to doubt the loyalty, desirability or ideological 'correctness' of an applicant," notes Michael Kammen, "the examination might become not merely rigorous, but bewildering and unfair."[32] In general, however, judges and examiners employed relatively lax standards. The chief examiner in Colorado characterized one judge's examination as a "farce," in that it "never results in disclosing any objections which may exist to the naturalization of any applicant."[33] In New York, the chief examiner described how applicants for citizenship gave "ridiculous answers to questions propounded to them on the Constitution of the United States and the institutions of this country . . . , answers [that] are usually ludicrous by reason of the fact that there was misunderstanding on the part of the alien as to just what was meant by the question propounded to him."[34]

Reports like this raised concerns about the value of citizenship. The *Christian Science Monitor* editorialized that "citizenship in the United States is held at too cheap a rate, else there would be more candid and brave discussion of all the fundamental issues involved in the franchise for both native and for alien." The paper predicted that "[s]tandards of admission to the franchise will steadily rise, as should standards of its retention. It should be oftener earned, and also often forfeited where there is betrayal of civic welfare. Now it seems to come too easily and automatically, to be exercised too indifferently, and consequently to be guarded with too little vigilance."[35]

The bureau, its regional examiners, and cooperating judges sought to raise these standards. In Alameda County, California, Judge I. W. Harris emphasized how important it was for a new citizen to understand the Constitution in order to "cast an intelligent ballot; one that really expresses what he thinks and not simply at the request of some self-seeking politician."[36] The commissioner of naturalization, Richard Campbell, who had served on Roosevelt's 1905 commission, stressed the importance of basic principles: "It seems to me the point to be impressed upon every intending citizen, as surely as it should have been on every actual citizen by birth in the course of his academic education, is that, as contra foreign governments, the initial power of the government is drawn from the mass of the people, and is not inherited by divine or any other right and is therefore not a personal possession either of any individual or any family."[37] Examiners began to develop lists of questions that aimed to draw out these fundamental points, such as:

> Can the Constitution be changed?
> Can Congress pass any law in regard to religion?
> What other guarantees are there in the Constitution?
> Can a citizen be deprived of life, liberty, or property?
> What is the form of our government? Who rules this country?
> What is a republic?
> What is a monarchy?
> How do kings and emperors get their offices?[38]

Judges and bureaucrats also linked applicants' understanding of these basic principles to the development of loyalty among new citizens. They held a fundamental faith that once immigrants understood American principles of governance they would naturally embrace their new nation. Commissioner Campbell wrote to the chief examiner in St. Paul to suggest that "a foreigner would quickly catch at the distinction [between his new and old nations' principles] and realize what a privilege it is to cast his vote, an expression of his will. . . . Self-respect and knowledge of one's own interest could not fail to impress a new citizen with affection for the country that grants such a privilege."[39] To emphasize this point, Campbell distinguished between the importance of understanding basic principles and detailed or extensive knowledge of American institutions and practices. He advised the assistant secretary of labor, Louis Post, to limit the knowledge required to the foundational principles of consent and the will of the people. "So far as the details by which those principles are made operative are concerned," he wrote, "while they are desirable to be known, they are not indispensable to the exercise of good citizenship."[40]

Nonetheless, it was becoming clear that most judges and examiners were relying on rote recitation. Frank Thompson, superintendent of schools in Boston, for instance, described "a parrot-like repetition by candidates of stereotyped answers to still more stereotyped questions."[41] The sheer volume of applicants for citizenship constituted a significant reason for the development of this process. There were simply too many applicants for the courts to examine their views in any depth. Indeed, the bureau concluded that the process involved "the consumption of so much time that the courts found it physically impossible to continue the use of this plan otherwise than in the most condensed form, and consequently became more profoundly convinced of its inadequacy and inconclusiveness." The emphasis on memorization further caused the bureau to acknowledge that there was something odd about treating factual information as proof of attachment to specific principles. "The storing of the memory with information," the bureau conceded, "is accepted, most illogically, as proof of attachment."[42]

The chief examiner in Seattle reported that although much progress had been made in applicants' recitation of factual knowledge, they still did not grasp the underlying principles. Applicants could often correctly answer what the Constitution was and what rights it guaranteed, he noted, even what it said about slavery. But when the examiner would ask the candidate, "What would happen if Congress would now make a new law saying that all persons born in the country from which the candidate came and are now living in the United States should become slaves on the first day of next month," the answers were disappointing. The examiner

> would embellish his question with a supposition that on the first of the month the Sheriff or U.S. Marshall comes to the applicant and wants him to put on a pair of handcuffs so that he might be carried off to the bull pen along with others of like nationality to be sold off at auction as slaves. And many candidates have been unable to answer the questions and others have said "Well I suppose I would have to be a slave, then." In this way they showed they had failed to grasp the great fundamental principle of our Constitution that the Constitution cannot be transgressed.[43]

Despite general acceptance of memorized answers, the standardization of the naturalization process resulted in two problems from the perspective of the Bureau of Naturalization: too many applicants were failing the examination because they were not able to meet even the most minimal requirements, *and* too many unfit applicants were still being passed.[44] These problems were further compounded by an informal system that developed to prepare applicants for their naturalization hearings. Private individuals and organizations prepared guides and lists of typical questions an applicant might expect to be asked in a naturalization hearing. For a fee, they provided these guides and offered advice on how to navigate through the naturalization process. Sometimes these informal advisers gave the court clerks 50 percent of any sales they produced.[45] The bureau objected that this process "opened the door to serious abuses in the way of making unjust exactions from a class of people who are unable to protect themselves."[46]

EDUCATION FOR CITIZENSHIP

The Bureau of Naturalization's solution to abuses of the system, to the tensions between conduct and belief, and to the tensions between factual knowledge and true attachment was to concentrate on more serious preparation of applicants. In a 1914 letter to Assistant Secretary of Labor Post, Judge Clarence Goodwin in Chicago had suggested that the government had a "golden opportunity to see that [the applicant] has a real and sympathetic knowledge of the process of government, an understanding of the reciprocal duties of nation and citizen and a feeling of loyal devotion of the Government of which he is to become a part." He believed that the government had a positive duty in this regard, and stressed that it was a duty "owed to the nation itself even if it is not owed to the applicant."[47] Goodwin's letter to Post received enthusiastic support from Deputy Commissioner Crist, who had long complained that the bureau was too passive. Its examiners could only object to the admission of what they considered unqualified applicants, a role he characterized as "heartless," especially since "it is known that there is no organization which he can be directed to go to obtain the necessary aid and instruction."[48] Crist observed that aliens' experience with arbitrary and autocratic government in their countries of origin made them "a fruitful source for the development of anarchy [and] disorder." The harsh and arbitrary nature of the naturalization process in the United States, he worried, would encourage rather than combat such tendencies.[49]

Campbell shared Crist's views. While acknowledging that 75 percent of current applicants might range from fairly admissible to unfit, he contended that "nearly all can be transformed through attendance at the public schools into desirable citizenship material." The courts needed help in "reaching the conclusion that [those who have been thus trained] have secured such a practical knowledge of the Constitution and laws of the US, and of all the American institutions as will afford them some reasonable ground for deciding that applicants for citizenship are definitely in some measure attached to those principles."[50] In 1914 the bureau sent a representative to meet with public school authorities in the larger cities, including Chicago, St. Louis, Milwaukee, St. Paul, Philadelphia, and New York. The bureau convened meetings in other cities the following year and met with government officials, jurists, and business organizations in its efforts to develop a national plan for the education of citizens. It conducted a survey of the entire country in March 1915, which revealed that many schools were interested in working with immigrants and that a variety of programs to educate newcomers already existed. New York City, for instance, had 1,000 classes attended by 40,000 immigrants.[51]

The problem, the survey concluded, was that this instruction did not exist in many places, that in others the programs flourished and faded periodically, and that instruction proceeded "in the usual academic way by which facts are committed to memory."[52] Coordination was necessary if these programs were to be turned into a nationwide project in civic education that had staying power and could offer the most sophisticated methods of instruction. Educators, judges, and representatives of private organizations, according to the bureau, all agreed that, as a federal agency, the bureau should take the lead in developing such a cooperative movement. The bureau envisioned an expanded citizenship program in the schools, which would at once benefit new citizens and the nation (by increasing naturalization and improving the quality of new citizens).[53] In 1916, Campbell reported on a conversation with a naturalization judge who doubted that even 50 percent of native-born citizens could answer correctly 50 percent of the questions suggested by the educational program developed by the bureau. Campbell took this discrepancy as all the more reason to establish a broad program of citizenship instruction to serve all students and provide a "more intimate sense of responsibility in the native-born citizen."[54]

The bureau's work with the schools did not aim merely at a practical adjustment in the mechanics of naturalization. For Campbell, it presented "the first linking together of the American public school with the Federal Government for the definite object of elevating the average understanding of . . . those principles enunciated in the American Declaration of Independence."[55] The civic nationalist energy devoted to incorporating immigrants was plainly revealed in this work. For the first time, immigrants were offered educational programs designed especially for them. By the 1920s, more than 750 cities and towns offered such programs, which ended up serving at least one million immigrants. Moreover, private organizations, labor unions, and employers also offered naturalization programs.[56] The bureau notified immigrants of the availability of classes by working with a variety of these organizations as well as foreign-language newspapers. It sent invitations to all applicants for citizenship. The bureau also extended its outreach beyond those already in the process of preparing to become citizens by sending letters to foreign-born adults with children in the public schools.

The most significant practical problem the schools faced was getting immigrants to complete courses, given that many of them worked at night or were exhausted by their day's labor. Some courses met once a week for ten weeks; others could last as long as seven months, meeting nearly every day.[57] The bureau worked energetically and creatively to ensure that students completed their courses of study. It encouraged the schools and private organizations to offer prizes to students for improving their English proficiency, for writing essays and conducting debates on the nature of American citizenship, and for doing well in "domestic arts" and manual training. To standardize the educational preparation, the bureau provided a variety of publications, including the *Student's Textbook, Teacher's Manual,* and *Syllabus of the Naturalization Law.* The *Student's Textbook* was distributed free of charge to schools and was given to immigrants when they filed their First Papers declaring their intention to naturalize.[58] Perhaps most important, the bureau offered certificates of graduation. In addition to offering public recognition to the programs and to the achievements of immigrants, these certificates provided a tangible inducement for immigrants to complete a course: naturalization judges in many cases agreed to treat them as proof that the applicant was attached to the principles of the Constitution.[59]

The link between education and citizenship was often reinforced when communities presented the certificates of course completion at the same time that applicants received their certificates of naturalization. This linkage helped the bureau invest the naturalization proceedings with greater dignity. As part of the broader Americanization movement, the oath of allegiance and the renunciation of previous allegiances took on greater symbolic significance. The bureau treated these events as important opportunities for it to develop a shared sense of American identity. It consciously aimed to join new and native-born citizens in public ceremonies that included patriotic speeches and singing the national anthem. In this scheme, "the new citizen is made to feel that he is welcomed to a place in his adopted country and the old citizen has a new sense of the dignity and importance of American citizenship."[60]

The actual naturalization courses sought to inculcate a basic conceptual understanding of democratic principles. Some courses also emphasized the importance of political and social participation. The participatory dimension reflected the bureau's and educators' belief that citizenship meant engaging actively and independently in a common public sphere. Some courses thus sought to include "practical means by which the actual performance of citizenship responsibilities and duties might be undertaken by the prospective candidate for citizenship, and that this be carried on in such manner as to cause the public schools to be used as community centers."[61] This instruction could be as simple as showing students how to vote by marking ballots or as involved as organizing the students into mock courts or miniature governments. One class practiced its citizenship skills by petitioning the local government to provide better public works service for parts of the city with significant concentrations of immigrants.[62] Frank Thompson praised this approach: "Here an organization of immigrants is learning citizenship through responsible, reciprocal relations with a department of government. The actual collective decisions of the education committee are exercises in group self-direction." Thompson linked open discussion of political and economic issues in the classroom to the development of the capacity for robust public deliberation.

In Los Angeles, judges and educators also developed a program of civic instruction that emphasized immigrants' role in contributing to the development of democracy in America. Fifty percent of the petitioners for naturalization in Los Angeles attended these courses, which were often touted by the bureau as models for other cities.[63] At the New Citizens Civic Club in Los Angeles, the instructor, Charles Kelso, emphasized current political topics. He wanted immigrants to regard American democracy as a great but unfulfilled experiment:

> You are not satisfied with what has been done, are you? I am not and don't want you to be; I want you to feel we have just laid the foundation for democracy in America. We have just repeated the second paragraph of the Declaration of Independence, and yet it was a long time after the Declaration was adopted before that was realized fully. Who had the right to vote after the Declaration of Independence? Did women? Did black men? No, only white men with property. The Declaration was not realized all at once but gradually.[64]

Courses like those offered by Kelso were, however, exceptions. Most courses relied on rote memorization of facts and uniform interpretations of political values. In part, the low educational level of students and their poor English skills significantly restricted the complexity of discussion. Educators reduced complex questions to catechisms that typically stressed allegiance over understanding:

Q: Do you believe in our form of government?
A: Yes.
Q: Will you support the Constitution?
A: Yes.
Q: What do you mean or understand by supporting the Constitution?
A: By living according to its laws, and seeing that all others do the same, and if necessary fight for its defence.
Q: What color is the American flag?
A: Red, white and blue.[65]

The elementary nature of most courses was reinforced by tedious methods of teaching. Teachers often employed the "direct method" of instruction, which meant constant drilling and recitation. This method did not appeal to many students; the largest drop-off in course attendance usually came as students encountered it near the beginning of the program.[66]

Despite Campbell and Crist's declared interest in emphasizing fundamental principles of governance, the bureau produced a set of federal texts that combined dry facts about the national government with details about community life. The *Textbook* "does not give enough instruction along the line of 'What is a Democracy, how did it originate and why it is the best form of Government,'" complained Judge Bingham from Salem, Oregon. "[It] ought to contain, in simple language, a little more of the history of the formation of governments and the theory of political science." While the textbook included only nine pages on American history, it devoted twenty pages to "some things the house-wife should know in order to keep herself and her family happy."[67] Educators and the adult education textbooks they used did focus extensively on the importance of participating with other citizens at the local level. This focus reflected their view that immigrants needed to abandon their traditional culture as a precondition for acceptance of American political principles. "Foreigners tend to be clannish," observed William Sharlip and Albert Owens, authors of *Adult Immigrant Education: Its Scope, Content and Methods*, "to consider the welfare of those belonging to their own particular group and to ignore the outside and the community at large." Hence, courses in civic instruction devoted extensive attention to showing immigrants the importance of moving away from their ethnic community and culture in order to prove themselves to be fully American.[68]

Progressive educators also stressed that to become proper citizens in the new, democratic age, immigrants had to develop a new set of personal virtues. To inculcate these virtues and to shape a common culture, immigrants were exhorted to adopt everything from the American way to clean one's house and brush one's teeth to the Protestant value of self-reliance. Thus, immigrants who progressed beyond basic instruction in English spent a considerable amount of time studying home economics and personal hygiene. "The linking of patriotism and the toothbrush," writes John McClymer, "effectively conveyed the Americanizer's basic message: 100 percent Americanism was just that, a total way of life. Becoming an American, immigrants were taught, involved making yourself over entirely."[69] It required a psychological break with one's previous identity, as well as a conceptual one.

"We Mutually Pledge to Each Our Lives, Our Fortunes, and Our Sacred Honor": Frances Kellor and the National Americanization Committee

Roosevelt's nationalist ideology was even more apparent in the Bureau of Education's work with immigrants. Frances Kellor and the National Americanization Committee she directed were the conduit for this influence. Kellor studied sociology at the University of Chicago and lived in Jane Addams's Hull House, where she witnessed the rigors of immigrant life in America. Since 1906, she had served as a key adviser to Roosevelt on immigration; later she took over research and publicity work for the Progressive Party where she sought to combine social reform, coherent planning, and national discipline. Kellor was "an apostle of industrial efficiency," the historian John Higham aptly notes. "[S]he abhorred the chaos and waste of *laissez faire*."[70]

In 1904, Kellor published a hard-hitting investigation of the poor treatment immigrants and women received from employment agencies, and she continued to analyze urban ills as a researcher for the Inter-Municipal Research Committee.[71] In 1908, Governor Charles Evans Hughes appointed her secretary of the New York Commission on Immigration, under whose auspices she engaged in an intensive examination of immigrant living conditions, education, and employment. Her study helped create the New York State Bureau of Industries and Immigration. Under Kellor's direction, the bureau conducted further investigations into the treatment of immigrants and took an active role in protecting newcomers by advising them, mediating on their behalf, and pressing for legislation to protect their interests in housing, banking, and travel.

In 1909, Kellor convinced a group of influential New Yorkers to establish a branch of the North American Civic League (NACL), a vehicle for New England businessmen who believed that unskilled immigrants needed help to become productive workers and good citizens.[72] The New York branch, which emphasized social welfare and protective legislation, formed the Committee for Immigrants in America and the National Americanization Committee (NAC), with Kellor as vice chair and the primary driving force. The NAC became the leading force in coordinating the rapidly spreading Americanization movement. In 1915 alone, it organized July Fourth "Americanization Day" receptions in 150 cities. As one member later boasted, "We put 'Americanization' in the dictionary and on the map."[73]

By the time the Dillingham Commission issued its report in 1911, the extent of Americanization efforts that Kellor would seek to coordinate was apparent. The commission devoted little attention to the question of Americanization, though it briefly discussed what it saw as the causes behind newcomers' lack of assimilation. Judged by immigrants' rates of naturalization, acquisition of English, and loss of traditional customs, the commission found that most new immigrants were "backward in this regard." It attributed problems with assimilation primarily to the fact that most immigrants were single men who had little contact with native-born Americans "and consequently have little or no incentive to learn the English language, become acquainted with American institutions, or adopt American standards."[74] The commission further contended that many did not seek to naturalize because they regarded their stay in the United States as temporary. It noted approvingly the efforts of private groups to assimilate immigrants, but it did not believe that the federal government should play a formal role in this process.[75]

In contrast, Kellor aimed to coordinate the existing work on Americanization among private and public organizations while lobbying for a federal agency to direct and expand the movement.[76] But no government agency wanted to take on the task. Only the Bureau of Education expressed interest, and its resources were hardly sufficient. Kellor solved this problem by using the Committee for Immigrants in America to fund the Division for Immigrant

Education in the bureau, a use of private funds that was entirely legal at the time.[77] Kellor directed most of the programming of the new division and worked tightly with Franklin K. Lane (secretary of the interior) and Philander P. Claxton (commissioner of education under Lane).[78] Lane acknowledged that the Bureau of Naturalization did "much in the way of giving definite instruction in matters of citizenship to those who have applied for citizenship papers," but he reserved for his own Bureau of Education the "larger task of educating all aliens in the use of the English language, in the history and resources of the country, in our industrial requirements, in our manners and customs and in our civic, social and political ideals."[79]

Like Roosevelt, Kellor offered a wide-ranging analysis of the crisis she believed threatened American civic nationalism. This crisis was deeply rooted in the conditions of American life, not simply imported from abroad. The fundamental problem was that the conditions for liberty had been lost. Liberty had been a chastened and disciplined conception—chastened by a threat to rights and disciplined by a duty to defend those rights. Quoting from the Declaration of Independence's preamble, she argued that America's progress and prosperity had made the meaning and importance of liberty and opportunity clear to all. "But," Kellor emphasized, "to these words this pledge was added: 'And for the support of this Declaration with a firm reliance on the protection of Divine Providence, we mutually pledge to each our Lives, our Fortunes, and our sacred Honor.' " In Kellor's analysis, Americans had lost this sense of obligation, without which liberty and opportunity could not be sustained. She linked this loss to a deterioration in personal virtue and national cohesion. Under the influence of prosperity, the traditional "American religion of individualism," which had stressed independence, had now simply become irresponsibility. Now, with conflict abroad and dissension at home, virtue and community had to be rediscovered.

The first problem the nation faced, Kellor asserted, was how to "nationalize our native-born American into doing his duty in the military training camp, in his industry, at the polls, with the welfare of the nation in his mind, and national service as his purpose." She placed little faith in legal or administrative requirements. Significant changes required bold leaders and an extensive program of education. Americans needed to learn, via military methods of drilling, "obedience, promptness, precision, regularity of habits, abstinence, economy, avoidance of waste, and respect for authority." Actual military training would also provide the best means for forging national cohesion across class and race lines. Where the factory had failed, she wrote, the "dog tent may succeed. It may become the best school of practical civics that there is—a place where all Americans can meet together for the common good of America."

For Kellor, the problem of individual dissoluteness and national dissolution was compounded because native-born citizens cared little about the condition of newcomers. "[T]he native American," she wrote, actually becomes "anti-American" by perpetuating "class consciousness and race hatred," favoring immigrant "colonies" with "different standards of living, different law enforcement and isolation from American influences," and leaving "his immigrant neighbor . . . unprotected and living in filth and disorder." Kellor further decried politicians who use "newly naturalized immigrants to swing the American vote in this direction or that, but who [do] nothing to make the immigrant a good citizen, or even to see that he understands American political ideals," calling them "menaces to a united America." She was particularly critical of "First Americans" who wanted to restrict immigration and limit the rights of aliens.

Kellor acknowledged that the Founders might not have imagined the shift in immigration patterns toward southern and eastern Europe. But she dismissed that point as irrelevant and questioned First Americans' understanding of what it meant to be American. Their view, she wrote derisively, was too timid. "I question if the vision [of new and different immigrants] would have disturbed [the framers], or whether it could ever have put greater caution and reserve into the instrument they were drawing up." She imagined instead a more robust and future-oriented conception of nationalism. "The magnanimity of spirit there expressed is based upon something greater than philosophy. It is based on a quality that had nothing to do with changes of times or conditions, a quality of stern fearlessness, a national conviction that the destiny of this nation was to be above all else the safeguard and champion of liberty."

Kellor argued that the extent to which Americans had deviated from the Founders' vision "is best measured by the way we have come to regard and to treat the most helpless and trusting of our people—the immigrants who come to our shores." She described as vast the difference between the American ideals immigrants were made to study for the citizenship examination and the reality of their actual experiences. These experiences included being ignored by government agencies, exploited by criminals and employers, and used by politicians for personal gain. How, she asked, could immigrants possibly "square [the Constitution's] teachings with . . . sentences they receive for minor offenses in justice-of-the peace courts which have no interpreters; with the prohibition that they cannot work at certain trades; with the double standard of living under which they see their American neighbors protected and themselves neglected and exploited?"

Kellor did not "despise" the conclusion of ethnologists regarding the notion of a specifically Anglo-Saxon racial type. But she doubted its practical usefulness—"so few conclusions and so many theories"—and suggested that the theorists were motivated more by apprehension than experience. What she *knew*, because she had seen it, was that recent immigrants could become Americans "in spirit and loyalty." She ridiculed proposals for a literacy test for admission to the United States as a negative, arbitrary policy "based on race and class theories and antagonisms that bear no real or lasting relation to the fundamental needs of the country." Instead, she emphasized the need to reach out to immigrants in a positive way.[80]

As commissioner of education and director of the Department of Interior's Americanization work, Philander Claxton shared Kellor's views on the need to embrace newcomers. Claxton, a former superintendent of schools in North Carolina, emphasized that "Americanization is a process of education, of winning the mind and heart through instruction and enlightenment." Government and private groups have an obligation to provide immigrants with an opportunity to understand democratic principles in the American mold. They must "offer the opportunity, make the appeal and inspire the desire." But true Americanization can only issue from the immigrants' own acceptance and engagement with their new country. A program of assimilation that became "narrow or fixed and exclusive" would itself be un-American, violating the very principles upon which it was based. A coercive program of Americanization would have lost "its faith in humanity" and improperly rejected "vital and enriching elements from any source whatsoever." Americanization, he asserted, combines all that is best in other countries and then "transfuse[s] and transform[s]" them into a "common possession." This common possession is "incomplete and in the formative stage" and continually requires renewal. To become Americanized, therefore, meant sharing and being inspired by the country's ideals, understanding its institutions and how they preserve freedom and protect rights, and putting the common good and welfare of the nation before "purely selfish means."[81]

Fred Butler, who worked directly under Claxton as director of the Americanization Division of the Bureau of Education, shared his faith in conversion rather than coercion and in what he called "citizenship training." In his mind, democracy was a living organism and "it would be a mistake for any government to so crystallize and harden points of view as to obstruct the development and change of American ideas in the future." America represented a specific set of ideas, but they were general principles rather than narrowly defined practices. Americans have always believed in the right of private property, he noted, but they also have the right to demand its abolition. Americanization thus meant teaching basic American political principles while acknowledging that citizens could disagree over their application. Butler contrasted this approach with the prevailing view of Americanization as a process "of getting hold of certain foreign-born people and making them sufficiently American so that they will not be a danger to us." He deemed this approach "the essence of Prussianism" and worried that Americans were swinging from an inappropriate indifference toward immigrants to a patronizing approach that did not understand or reflect the American spirit.[82]

Butler proposed to temper such a swing by adopting an approach that combined aspects of Roosevelt's New Nationalism and Bourne's cultural pluralism. Good schools are a central means for preparing immigrants and Americans to be intelligent, rational citizens. But good citizens are best shaped not simply by civics classes, he observed, but by their entire environment, by their "contact with life." "America is a democracy and a foreigner who puts his foot on our shore has imbibed enough Americanization within a few months to resent any patronage [i.e., patronizing] on the part of Americans." He therefore prescribed that Americanizers undergo a "thorough schooling of themselves in humility." The purposes of Americanization would be further served by good schools and the development of what he called "community life." "We are all drawn together by emotional experiences more than intellectual experiences," Butler wrote in praising the shared sensibility generated by the war. The challenge for Americanizers was to create a similarly binding set of experiences in their local communities: "We must make these people come together with us where their hearts and ours beat to the same tune that we may all feel ourselves parts of the same people and not parts of separate groups."[83]

For mainstream civic nationalists like Kellor, Roosevelt, and Croly, the principle of individualism was at the core of American citizenship. At the same time, advancing this principle required a widely shared sense of national culture and destiny. Roosevelt especially believed that individual emancipation had to be set within a racialized nationalism that eradicated ethnic identity. This view contrasted sharply with those of Bourne, Dewey, and Addams, who thought that democratic individualism could best be advanced by an American nationalism that drew on ethnic identities to establish a broader cosmopolitan ethos. Among prominent architects of civic nationalism in the Progressive Era, the meaning of that nation—and of what one had to give up in order to belong to it—was deeply contested.

In practice, the institutions of American civic nationalism—the Bureau of Naturalization, the Bureau of Education, and the settlement houses—formed a broadly common front. They saw their goal of assimilating immigrants as an alternative to more coercive and exclusionary measures. Both bureaus and Hull House pioneered outreach programs that aimed to prepare newcomers for their new role as American citizens. They established institutions and programs to meld knowledge, experience, and commitment in ways that connected immigrants to American public life. These institutions and programs mediated between the raw experiences of new immigrants and the operations of government bureaucracies, employers, and American cultural traditions. They treated citizenship as a complex combination of community engagement, civic principles, and national bonding. Fred Butler at the Bureau of Education was emblematic of this approach. He described society in biological terms, emphasizing that new needs and possibilities continually arise and require citizens capable of meeting them. As new citizens, immigrants required instruction in basic civic principles and practical experience in the operations of social and political institutions. They also needed opportunities to bond with native-born citizens in pursuit of a shared goal, to find in "common emotions . . . a binding force."

Butler sought to combine the civic and the national dimensions of citizenship, but such efforts often encountered practical difficulties and were fraught with tensions. While the Bureaus of Naturalization and Education hoped to raise the standards expected of an applicant for naturalization, judges and naturalization examiners most often settled for some basic familiarity with facts about American government as proof of attachment. The bureaus, the courts, and especially the schools also often taught millions of immigrants that American political principles had definite meanings that were not open to discussion or alteration. These approaches revealed the problems involved in conveying meaningfully the debates over, and conflicts among, the abstract principles in the civic dimension of citizenship. They also indicated the conceptual difficulty of treating America as an open-ended proposition while viewing it as the embodiment of specific civic principles and cultural traits and attitudes. While some of the leading Americanizers in the federal government treated immigrants' ethnic heritage with respect, others tended to view immigrants' cultural attachments as temporary. These twin concerns—teaching uniform political principles and requiring cultural change—opened the door to a more coercive and exclusionary program of Americanization. The next chapter explores this transformation and the dynamics that led to it.

CHAPTER SIX

World War I and the Turn to Coercion

BETWEEN THE elections of 1912 and 1916 elite and popular opinion about immigrants and Americanization shifted significantly. In 1912, Roosevelt's Progressive Party vowed to safeguard the well-being of immigrants and to integrate them into the American nation. On the Democratic side, Woodrow Wilson sought to overcome his past statements denigrating new immigrants by heaping praise on his newfound constituents. William Howard Taft and the Republicans promised to veto the literacy test and spent lavishly on advertising in foreign-language newspapers. All three parties set up special arms of their campaigns that were dedicated to addressing the concerns of immigrants. By the election of 1916, however, the emphasis had shifted to vitriolic denunciation of "hyphenated Americans." Roosevelt denounced the "politico-racial hyphen" as a "breeder of moral treason" and insisted on "America for Americans." The Democrats, too, warned against ethnic conspiracies to weaken "the indivisibility and coherent strength of the nation."[1]

During World War I, broad concerns about whether new immigrants would or could assimilate became specific concerns about threats to industrial production and national security, as well as the possibility of conflict among nationalities within the United States. When the war ended, Americans' concerns shifted from German nationalism to Russian Bolshevism. Most proponents of socialism, communism, or anarchism operated peacefully, but attacks on public officials in Philadelphia and other cities stoked fears that subversion of American principles and structures remained a real threat. Attorney General A. Mitchell Palmer reflected a common sentiment when he estimated that "[f]ully 90 percent of Communist and anarchist agitation is traceable to aliens."[2]

The hypernationalism associated with America's entry into World War I and with its looming battle with communism radically altered the Americanization movement. Americanization came to be seen primarily as an antidote to labor unrest and political radicalism, a means by which to assure the true loyalty of immigrants and to deport or at least deny citizenship to those who failed to demonstrate sufficiently their fidelity to America. Yet a focus on the war and subsequent ideological struggles can be misleading. It makes it easy to ascribe the Americanization movement's shift to a more coercive approach to extreme circumstances. In fact, moderate Americanizers' civic nationalist ideology also contributed to this shift. Their ideas were shouldered aside by more assertive positions that offered specific answers to the question of what it meant to be and to become an American. In some cases, moderate Americanizers' civic nationalist desire to balance ethnic connectedness, national belonging, and civic freedom made it hard to articulate a lucid, commanding response. They found it difficult to muster a sufficiently robust alternative to the position that immigrants ought to be compelled, not simply persuaded, to become fully Americanized. In other cases, the logic inherent in their own ideas of national solidarity opened the way to more coercive and exclusionary policies.

Tightening the Boundaries of Citizenship

Eligibility for and the significance of citizenship changed radically from the early 1910s to the early 1920s. Courts established racial and ideological boundaries that more formally and fully excluded non-whites and radicals. Courts also increased differences between citizens and aliens, and states revoked voting rights for noncitizens. In many of these cases, especially those involving race, Prohibition, socialism, and alien suffrage, the seeds of a shift toward more restrictive and exclusionary laws were present well before the war. The conflict in Europe, and at home, provided fertile soil for those seeds to grow. The war also focused new attention on other cases, especially those involving military service and competing national allegiances.

In the decade before the war, the courts had sometimes broadened who they considered to be white and therefore eligible for citizenship. By the 1920s, courts increasingly reinforced the correspondence between citizenship and whiteness *and* limited the range of those eligible to naturalize. Despite the differences in outcome—admitting Armenians and Syrians before the war and denying Japanese and immigrants from the Indian subcontinent after the war—the concern for whiteness linked judicial reasoning in both periods. In *In re Halladjian*, the 1909 Massachusetts case involving Armenians, the government had unsuccessfully advanced the theory that white was not a biological category but a cultural one tied to "the ideals, standards, and aspirations of the people of Europe."[3] In this view, civilization, rather than race, ought to be the deciding factor in naturalization cases. By the 1920s, these arguments about fitness for self-government met with greater success. In *Terrace v. Thompson* (1921), for instance, a district judge explained that the denial of citizenship to Asians "is not due to color, as color, but only to color as evidence of a type of civilization which it characterizes."[4]

The Supreme Court increasingly relied on a combination of racial science, popular views, and the historical meaning of whiteness to deny citizenship to non-whites. In the 1922 case *Ozawa v. United States*, the Court determined that Japanese were not eligible for naturalization. Prior to 1922, some courts had admitted Japanese as free whites and others had excluded them. Takao Ozawa contended that "white" meant only neither black nor American Indian.

Moreover, he asserted, Japanese were capable of self-government and could be assimilated. While the Court acknowledged that it was often difficult to determine who was a member of the Caucasian race, it decided that membership in that race was the defining characteristic of those eligible for citizenship. Relying on the logic of *Ah Yup*, the 1878 case denying eligibility to naturalize to Chinese, the Court turned to public opinion to determine that the Japanese were clearly not Caucasians. It further argued that white meant those who were considered so in 1790 and supported the government's contention that the framers of that law were "white men from Europe. . . . They were eager for more of their kind to come, and it was to men of their own kind that they held out the opportunity for citizenship in the new nation."[5]

In the following year, the Court heard *United States v. Bhagat Singh Thind*, a case involving an Indian (whom the Court categorized as "Hindu"). Here, the Court denounced the very idea of scientific racialism, noting that scientists had stretched the term "Caucasian" to include "not only the Hindu, but some of the Polynesians . . . [and] the Hamites of Africa." Yet while Indians might lay claim to being Caucasian, they were nonetheless ineligible to naturalize, for while "it may be true that the blond Scandinavian and the brown Hindu have a common ancestor in the dim reaches of antiquity . . . the average man knows perfectly well that there are unmistakable and profound differences between them today."[6] Thus, the notion of a popular understanding of whiteness had become the dominant mode of determining who was eligible for naturalization. As Matthew Frye Jacobson points out, in *Ozawa* the Court itself observed that race is a " 'practical line of separation,' not a natural one."[7]

In addition to racial characteristics, ideological ones became crucial determinants of fitness for citizenship in the late 1910s and 1920s. In a significant number of cases, courts expressed the Progressives' belief in the link between personal virtue and democratic citizenship by denying citizenship or revoking certificates of naturalization for violations of Prohibition laws.[8] More broadly, these cases related to the conflict between an abstemious Protestant establishment and the influx of Catholic immigrants. Courts worried that violators of Prohibition were especially likely to breed "disorder and unhappiness," and thus indicated that applicants were not "well disposed to the good order and happiness of nation and peoples."[9] A significant number of cases interpreting what it meant to be attached to the principles of the Constitution also turned on identifying incompatible political ideologies. In 1912 the Court for the Western District of Washington cancelled a certificate of naturalization because the applicant was a socialist. In 1918 an Oregon court cancelled a certificate of naturalization that had been issued to a member of the International Workers of the World, which advocated overthrowing the U.S. government. The judges reasoned that such views made applicants' declarations of attachment to the Constitution false.[10] The courts regarded anarchists as incapable of being attached to the principles of the Constitution.[11]

World War I also brought new attention to the obligation of citizens to serve in the military. By the time the conflict in Europe had ended, the refusal to bear arms had become grounds upon which to deny citizenship. State courts reasoned that applicants could not take the oath of allegiance to support the Constitution with reservations.[12] This logic of attachment culminated in the case of a fifty-year-old woman who objected to bearing arms out of pacifist principles. "[S]he is an uncompromising pacifist, with no sense of nationalism but only a cosmic sense of belonging to the human family," Justice Butler wrote for the Supreme Court, and is therefore "not well bound or held by the ties of affection to any nation or government." He echoed the doubts about cosmopolitanism expressed by Gouverneur Morris at the Constitutional Convention and by Teddy Roosevelt before the war. "Such persons," Butler contended, "are liable to be incapable of the attachment for and devotion to the principles of our Constitution that are required of aliens seeking naturalization."[13]

If applicants with "cosmic" attachments to humankind could not be trusted as citizens, neither could those with attachments to competing national identities. The Expatriation Act of 1907 had sought to enforce the rules prohibiting dual citizenship by identifying a series of actions by which native-born and naturalized citizens could be stripped of their membership status in the United States. In 1922 the Circuit Court of Appeals went further in determining that advocacy on behalf of one's country of origin, at least a country at war with the United States, was incommensurate with U.S. citizenship. The court affirmed the District Court for the Territory of Hawaii's cancellation of a 1904 certificate of naturalization on the grounds that the applicant, an immigrant from Germany, had publicly supported his native country during the war, including its sinking of the *Lusitania*. The District Court held that, owing to these views, the applicant had sworn a false oath of allegiance: "[I]t was in the crucial times of 1917 that the respondent failed in the fundamental obligation to his oath of true faith and allegiance in 1904. . . . [His] frequent expressions were so plainly against the United States and in favor of Germany, [that he] must have taken the oath of full faith and allegiance with a reserved determination to [keep down his true loyalty] until a momentous time might come."[14]

Before the war, the courts, as well as individual states, had begun to harden the line between citizens and aliens. The Supreme Court sustained state regulations prohibiting aliens from working on public construction contracts in 1914 and permitting only citizens the privilege of harvesting wildlife in 1915.[15] It continued this trend after the war, permitting, for instance, a state to prohibit an alien from owning land.[16] The Court allowed such restrictions because it did not consider the treatment of aliens a question of constitutional rights but rather of the allocation of resources, which states were best suited to determine. These were not, however, merely technical decisions, as they coincided with both greater mistrust of aliens and an increased desire to emphasize the distinctiveness of citizenship.[17] Americans were especially concerned about foreign values and foreign influence with regard to voting. Between 1901 and 1914, Alabama, Colorado, Wisconsin, and Oregon amended their constitutions to prohibit alien suffrage. The number of aliens in the United States, especially the strategic location of many of them with regard to war-related production, brought a swift end to alien suffrage in the seven remaining states that allowed the practice.[18] "For the first time in over a hundred years," the political scientist Leon Aylsworth remarked in 1931, "a national election was held in 1928 in which no alien in any state had the right to cast a vote for candidate for any office—national, state, or local."[19]

As courts and states heightened the legal distinctions between citizens and aliens, many Americanizers adopted more coercive means to induce immigrants to naturalize. Industrialists gave job promotions only to citizens or those in the process of becoming citizens. A bill to deport aliens who would not apply for citizenship within three months was introduced in Congress in 1916, and during the war the idea was frequently discussed. The Congressional Revenue Act of 1918 taxed "non-resident" aliens at double the rate of citizens and resident aliens.[20] As citizenship became more dear, carrying with it greater benefits and rights, and as Americanizers turned toward more coercive mechanisms, immigrants rushed to declare their intent to naturalize. Their haste increased worries among private Americanization groups that unqualified immigrants would be granted citizenship. As with the courts and state governments, the hypernationalism of the war period amplified traditional doubts among Americans about the loyalty of immigrants.

Since the turn of the century, organizations like the Daughters of the American Revolution (DAR) had designed programs of patriotic education to inculcate in immigrants a strong sense of loyalty to America. By 1907 the Sons of the American Revolution (SAR) was spending half its income on making aliens into citizens, primarily by producing a patriotic pamphlet in fifteen languages. The DAR and SAR worried especially about the radical ideas they believed immigrants were importing. They articulated what Higham deemed a "nervously nationalistic strain" that feared contamination by other cultures and preached "a loyalty that consisted essentially of willing submissiveness."[21] By the war years, these groups were joined by organizations such as the National Security League, which attempted to investigate applicants' qualifications for citizenship. "The present system of granting application for naturalization," the vice chairman of the American Legion's National Legislative Committee complained to the secretary of labor, "[leaves] untested the alien's capacity for citizenship."[22] The Veterans of Foreign Wars of the United States urged that aliens "prepare to become citizens or prepare to leave the country and all aliens who for cause have been refused citizenship be deported at once."[23] Patriotic societies further called for the deportation of alien radicals. The war aggravated old worries about the radical influence exerted by immigrants and, as a result, the means of dealing with those concerns became increasingly harsh.

Patriotic societies were especially vigorous in their efforts to restrict the use of languages other than English. In their view, language was the central link between foreign cultures and foreign allegiances. The American Legion thus successfully pressured state governments to pass laws requiring the public schools (and in some cases private schools) to use only English. Idaho and Utah went further and required immigrants who did not speak English to enroll in Americanization classes. Nebraska legislated that English be used for all meetings, making exceptions only for religious or lodge gatherings.[24] F. F. Beall of the Packard Motor Company reflected a growing view that eliminating foreign-language newspapers was crucial to any serious program of Americanization. He accused these papers of trying to "disrupt our Civic affairs. . . . If these people are so desirous of retaining their own language, they ought to go back to the Country where they were born."[25] Despite their pro-American positions, the German-language newspapers in particular were designated for suppression, and public and private organizations even pressured the schools to cease teaching German.[26]

Private groups and individual states also focused extensively on the question of loyalty in the public schools. The American Legion and other patriotic organizations linked allegiance to American democracy to an understanding of, and reverence for, American history and identity. In their view, immigrants needed to associate their new nation's democratic principles with its English heritage and shed any hint of political attachment or loyalty to their native land. Woodrow Wilson's ambassador to Britain in 1917, Walter Hines Page, captured this view when he declared, "We Americans have to throw away our provincial ignorance, hang our Irish agitators and shoot our hyphenates, and bring up our children with reverence for English history and in awe of English literature."[27] The American Legion further recommended that teaching disloyalty in the schools be an offense. Both the Legion and the National Security League pressured public schools to hire only American citizens as teachers. New York and a number of other states passed legislation requiring citizenship as a qualification for teaching in the public schools. Nebraska went even further in requiring private as well as public schools to adopt a citizens-only employment policy. Oregon outdid Nebraska when it outlawed private schooling entirely for elementary students in 1922.

POSTWAR AMERICANIZATION AND THE SPECTER OF SEPARATISM

Before the war, Philander Claxton at the Bureau of Education and Frances Kellor at the National Americanization Committee (NAC) aimed to create a moderate civic nationalism of service and duty. But they began to shift toward a more aggressive approach as early as the fall of 1915, when the NAC officially changed its slogan from "Many People, But One Nation" to "America First."

During and immediately after the war, the committee increasingly emphasized the development of social and industrial programs that incorporated military preparedness, coercive educational and regulatory schemes, and, finally, active efforts to recruit ethnic leaders to its cause as a way of fostering loyalty and adjustment to the American way of life.

Kellor contended that the massive military preparedness campaign required more than armaments. To succeed, it required organized economic and social action. America's capacity to coordinate all these features depended, in turn, on a sense of dedication to the nation over individual or group interests. She became increasingly concerned about the threats immigrants posed to a unified sense of nationalism:

> Security and prosperity have blinded us to the fact that we do not all speak the same language nor follow the same flag. . . . America has neglected, even forgotten, its task of making Americans of the people that come to its shores. Men may be workmen and voters and taxpayers and bosses, but the final question for this nation to answer is—are they loyal American citizens?

Kellor charged that ethnic separation was breeding un-American habits and encouraging immigrants to think of the United States as a place to gain an economic stake and then return home. This tendency for "birds of passage" to exploit America was encouraged by "a conglomeration of colonies and ghettos and immigrant sections in our large cities, and the country dotted with settlements quite as un-American as anything to be found abroad."

In addition, newcomers were open to three kinds of pernicious influences: cosmopolitans who aimed to "substitute the 'brotherhood of man' for loyalties and obligations and relationships of life"; socialists, who urged immigrants to "ignore national lines and unite only as 'Workers of the World' "; and machine politicians, who "desecrate American citizenship." These influences were especially dangerous because they easily found impressionable minds among immigrants who had no experience with America's political ideals. To combat these ills, as well as to forestall Americans' mistreatment of immigrants, Kellor wanted to forge what she called a true American nationalism.[28]

Kellor rejected the suggestion that she limit her work to "foreign-born Americans," because such a title "made no appeal to the children of foreign-born or the Americans and when men become citizens they hated to be called foreign-born Americans." The term "Americanization," she predicted, "has a future and will be increasingly liked."[29] In her view, Americanization required native-born citizens and immigrants each to meet particular obligations. Americans had to understand that racial prejudice ran contrary to American ideals and that they should therefore tolerate and welcome new arrivals. In the economic sphere, industry needed efficient workers who understood English and modern methods, and who believed in the principles of American democracy. Efficient workers made for safer working conditions, and Americanized workers would resist the efforts of unions and radicals. She stressed the relationship among cultural assimilation, economic development, and national security. But American citizens had to do more than merely provide equal opportunities for newcomers; they had to recognize the "human, social, and civic" dimensions to immigrants' lives, as well as the economic dimension.[30]

Immigrants' obligations were more specific than those of American citizens. They were responsible for learning English, becoming "literate, efficient citizens," loyally supporting "the best ideals and traditions of America," and adopting "American standards of living." To ensure that immigrants met these responsibilities, Kellor, the NAC, and the Bureau of Education embarked on a broad educational and regulatory campaign. On the educational front, the NAC published materials on teaching English and civics for immigrants as well as for public school teachers. It prodded universities and colleges to play an active role in training teachers in Americanization and provided reading lists and produced a monthly newsletter. The NAC also emphasized the need for legislation that protected immigrants against unfair and dangerous working conditions and housing.

Kellor and the NAC's main attention, however, was increasingly directed toward regulating the lives of immigrants. "[A]gainst an ounce of accommodation," Higham notes of the NAC, "it balanced a pound of coercion." In 1917 the NAC issued a document titled "War Policy for Aliens," in which it asserted that "a man born on another soil . . . had to *prove* himself for America." "[P]acifists, agitators, and other Anti-American groups," the committee contended, were finding fertile ground in immigrant communities to "ferment unrest, dissatisfaction and disloyalty." The country's "go-where-you-will-do-as-you-please" approach to incorporating immigrants had, in its view, resulted in "ignorance of where they are, what they are doing and of their attitude toward America." To respond to these problems, the NAC pressed hard for registering aliens as a means of tracking their activities, tightening citizenship requirements—including deporting aliens after three years if they had failed to apply for citizenship and learn English—interning aliens who were considered anti-American and potentially disloyal, and exposing them to Americanization courses. The NAC and other Americanization groups sought to "bring all the races together," which, as Desmond King observes, came to mean "breaking up the ethnic communities into which many immigrants settled."[31]

In addition to forwarding the NAC's "War Policy for Aliens," Kellor urged that agencies reach out to non-English-speaking immigrants. Simply teaching English and civics, she contended, was too passive an approach.[32] Most immigrants were being shaped more by the "thousands of foreign-language organizations in the United States fighting among themselves for independent and united native countries or to preserve their racial solidarity here."[33] In 1918, Kellor set up the War Works Extension program to counter the influence of foreign presses and foreign-language associations. Her idea was to shift from training American teachers, schools, and other organizations to working directly with immigrants. To this end, the Bureau of Education moved into the New York City offices of the NAC and began establishing relationships with ethnic organizations and publications. The War Works Extension aimed to create loyal ethnic associations, recruit "racial leaders," provide patriotic copy to presses, and establish a nationwide information network that would place correspondents inside the foreign-language papers.[34]

Kellor continued to distance herself from some of the more extreme measures being proposed by other Americanizers. "[A]lien baiting" and other "repressive measures," she argued, would not protect immigrants from socialist and Communist propaganda. The appropriate response to immigration and radicalism was a proper program of assimilation, one that introduced immigrants to the true meaning of American ideals and gave them an opportunity to succeed economically. Despite these protests, Kellor's own views and policies had become more coercive. Yet even as her work emphasized more sharp-edged means, she was pushed aside by forces that were committed to an ideologically pure Americanism and had no interest in programs that directly aided newcomers. By the time her efforts to coordinate a nationwide Americanization movement had ended—in 1919, when Congress banned private subsidies of governmental agencies—Kellor had already lost the battle to maintain a moderate approach to incorporating immigrants.

The ideological crackdown and the transformation of naturalization education from outreach to control can also be seen in the Bureau of Naturalization's turn toward more intrusive means, especially the system of annual registration of aliens. In 1918, the bureau gained the authority to use naturalization fees to support its textbook publications and distribution program. The following year, under Deputy Commissioner of Naturalization Raymond Crist, the agency established the Division of Citizenship Training. Crist, by this time, was eager for employers to intimate that employees' jobs depended on their becoming citizens.[35] While Crist continued his work with the courts and public schools, by 1922 it was James J. Davis, the secretary of labor, who most actively sought to open up a new front in the Americanization of immigrants. Davis was a naturalized citizen, having immigrated from Wales when he was eight years old, and had been concerned about immigration and naturalization throughout his tenure in the Harding and Coolidge administrations. He worked closely with Albert Johnson, chair of the House Immigration Committee, and Samuel Shortridge in the Senate to establish a registration system for aliens and to mandate their attendance at Americanization courses.

Such an approach, Davis declared, would make it "possible for the alien to become not only a good citizen . . . but one fully understanding America and what it stands for, at the same time making it hard, and justly so, for undesirables to get their papers." It would have the added advantage of "automatically bring[ing] into notice the alien who declares himself or is known to be an anarchist, whose intentions are hostile or resistive or who is for any reason undesirable."[36] A publication signed "100% American," which described "Jewish and Roman Catholic efforts to seize America by gradual usurpation," quoted Davis prominently on its front cover: "Immigration, in the final working out of the problem, is an American issue. It is the right—yes it is the duty of the United States to protect every American citizen of to-day and of tomorrow from contact with the mental, moral and physical delinquents of all the world."[37] In addition to his own strong views on the subject, Davis was responding to growing public sentiment. "We need to know who the aliens are and where they live," one correspondent wrote. "[Some have objected] to this method because foreigners come here to gain freedom and escape the registration required in their native land. That is all the more reason we should compel these to win the spurs they desire to wear. We have been making citizenship entirely too cheap."[38]

Davis's proposals also received sharp criticisms. The Union of American Hebrew Congregations (UAHC) charged that mandatory registration and Americanization were patterned on the Alien and Sedition Acts and the Chinese exclusionary law. In a resolution adopted in 1923, the UAHC termed the former measure unpopular and the latter harsh and repressive. It objected that an annual registration of aliens "would give unlimited opportunity for blackmail, extortion and oppression that are apt to cause injuries to the seven million aliens in this country," and that would "lead to an enormous number of deportations to foreign lands on purely technical grounds, without time limit, of persons having their family ties and all their interests here." The UAHC especially worried about giving a single agency simultaneous control over civic education and deportation.[39]

Employers also made pointed criticisms of the bill. William Rogers, president of Brown Iron Company in Buffalo, New York, objected that he did not see any connection between improved educational preparation for aliens and the need for a nationwide system of registration. Such a system, he predicated, "will be very annoying," and the machinery to enforce it "would be vast and complex. It would be impossible to keep track of all the actions of the subordinate officials charged with enforcing these provisions. They would apparently go into the homes of the immigrants with the authority of the United States Government back of them, and the opportunities for graft, oppression and espionage would be unlimited."[40]

Davis attributed opposition to his proposals to either "the red or anarchistic element" or misinformation. Far from denying that his proposals were patterned on the Chinese exclusion law and on the even earlier Alien and Sedition Acts, Davis cast his proposals as part of this tradition of American citizenship. Following Roosevelt, he distinguished between Europeans who were capable of being assimilated—including the "Hebrew people," whom he congratulated for having "to some extent been successful in teaching their people" about American ideals—and non-white races. The "Chinese and other Eastern races," he asserted, "will never become assimilated into a united American Republic. They are not of us. Their economic and moral standards are those of a thousand years ago."[41] Davis defended the Alien and Sedition Acts as entirely appropriate, given the circumstances of the time. He contended that those who worried that the power to deport would be abused revealed the extent to which they had yet to become fully Americanized themselves—there was something deficient in the UAHC's lack of faith in the American courts to dispense justice fairly. "We might well fear for the future of the Republic when the efforts of national leaders to teach fundamental principles . . . are openly opposed by a dominant foreign race."[42]

Perhaps most revealing was Davis's response to the UAHC and other correspondents who charged that his plan amounted to coercing immigrants into becoming citizens. "Citizenship must not be forced upon the foreign born, however desirable it might be to have a people all owing allegiance to the same flag," he wrote to Simon Wolf, chairman of the UAHC's Board of Delegates on Civil Rights. "Citizenship can come only from the heart." He then added, "But without a knowledge of America, the heart will never change in its attitudes toward the things which have been impressed upon it in the early years. If we compel the alien to know America, I have no fear that there will come that change of heart necessary to produce an American citizen." "America," he was certain, "never suffers by contrast."[43]

Davis compared his plan to the compulsory education of children. Why, he asked, should adult foreigners be any different? "We are all agreed that citizenship is a matter of the growth of a desire to be created in the breasts of the foreigners and that it cannot be forced," he wrote to Robert C. Deming, in the Department of Americanization in Connecticut. "But why object to the enrollment for training to help create that desire? You register to vote, and I have to go to Pittsburgh from Washington and pay to register for the privilege of exercising the franchise. What more harm would it do for the good alien to have to register?"[44] Davis's words offered little comfort to his critics, who, in the context of the Palmer raids and heightened mistrust of aliens, found it difficult to see how a system of registration could not help but lead to deportations and discrimination against immigrants and minorities.

In the end, the dominant vision of citizenship in the Progressive Era came to depend on both limiting the entry of newcomers and coercing those already present. Immigrants whom Roosevelt and Kellor had considered assimilable were increasingly regarded as racially deficient by a wide range of legislators, opinion leaders, and the public. Such views contributed heavily to the establishment in 1924 of a yearly quota of 150,000 immigrants from European countries, based on the proportion of foreign-born residents in the United States in 1890, a practice that discriminated against southern and eastern Europeans. This statute also excluded the Japanese altogether. Roosevelt died in 1919, but by then even his confidence in the absorptive capacities of American nationalism had been shaken. His "booming, belligerent optimism," in Thomas Dyer's words, gave way to a sense of "impending racial disaster."[45]

THE PERIL AND THE PROMISE OF CIVIC NATIONALISM

The war clearly accelerated the shift from programs designed to foster loyalty through an understanding of American ideals to those intent on inculcating a reverence for all things American. In the face of this nationalist fervor, neither left-leaning nor centrist Americanizers could forestall the emergence of coercive Americanization programs and exclusionary immigration policies. Jane Addams criticized methods she considered "cruel, undemocratic, and in any case counterproductive"; others, such as Graham Taylor, who, by 1918 had become president of the National Federation of Settlements, protested the compulsory nature of state laws regarding language and naturalization.[46] Addams and Taylor sought to turn the energy generated by the war toward their own purposes, arguing that their methods were more likely to result in Americanization. The war opened new opportunities not only for teaching English and citizenship, Addams wrote, but also for establishing a "new center and perspective" through "mutual effort with the alien population." But most left-leaning Progressives did not offer a vision distinct enough to alter the direction in which Americanization was moving. Even Addams, who, more than anyone else, had articulated an alternative ideology, recognized that her pleas often had a "remote sound." "[T]o advocate the restraint of overzealous officialism as a method of Americanizing the alien would indeed be considered strange doctrine," she acknowledged in 1919. "[F]or there is no doubt that at the present moment one finds in the United States the same manifestation of the worldwide tendency toward national dogmatism, the exaltation of blind patriotism above intelligent citizenship."[47] As the war ended, some new groups arose that sought to maintain a moderate approach to Americanization; they, too, could not withstand the rush to conformity.[48] For most left-leaning Progressives, their own beliefs that there were American habits, practices, and ideals that immigrants needed to adopt meant that their views often seemed merely a pallid version of the more aggressive and distinct nationalism that shaped law, policy, and public debate, rather than a distinct alternative.

Left-leaning intellectuals as well as practitioners gave way to the passions unleashed by the war. They shrank from the coercive and intolerant nature of the Americanization movement, worrying, according to the historian Gary Gerstle, that their ideas and programs "too easily contributed to group antagonisms" and "were a spur to virulent nativism and racism. Feeling themselves impotent in the face of a reactionary nationalism, and perhaps guilty as well for helping to create this cultural Frankenstein, liberals gave up the fight to create a new culture and new nationalism for the masses."[49] Dewey, in particular, simply stopped addressing questions of diversity and nationalism. His only objection to the restrictive and racial immigration laws of the early 1920s was that they might offend the Japanese and contribute to the prospects for military conflict.

Dewey's goal of constructing a common national spirit by extracting from each ethnic group its special contributions suggested a rational process at odds with the passionate nature of nationalism. Even as he invoked ideals of shared aims and common understandings, what he called "like-mindedness," Dewey could not grapple with the emotional wellsprings of American nationalism. He retreated from the cultural conflict over the meaning of America, Gerstle suggests, because, like many of his fellow liberals, he regarded that sphere as fundamentally irrational. Ethnic and national identities and the passions they spawned were too difficult to control, whereas the economy, where liberals now focused their attention, was the sphere of reason and planning. If, in the grip of emotion and prejudice, Americans had turned to coercive means of incorporation and racially restrictive immigration laws, there was little that could be done to change those outcomes. "The simple fact of the case," Dewey told an audience of political scientists in China in 1921, "is that at present the world is not sufficiently civilized to permit close contact of people of widely different cultures without deplorable consequences."[50]

Bourne died before Dewey made these comments, but earlier he had bitterly criticized Dewey for allowing the war to overcome their shared vision of an international nationalism. "War is the health of the state," Bourne famously declared, arguing that war benefitted the state (and its bureaucracy). Unlike Dewey, he was more comfortable with the cultural and emotional dimension of ethnic and national identity. Bourne eagerly castigated the fear and illiberalism he believed undergirded the dominant culture's reaction to the growing ethnic diversity of the United States. But he was a literary and cultural critic who lacked organizational support, and he never developed his ideas into a coherent, compelling account of transnational America that could effectively compete with more easily grasped ideologies of nationalism.[51] These ideologies clearly delineated the singular nature of American identity and the necessity that newcomers shed their ethnic identities and previous national allegiances. In contrast, Bourne avoided questions about the conflicts that might develop between the left and the right side of the hyphen, about whether the group consciousness he applauded would overwhelm the cosmopolitanism he sought to engender, or whether the cosmopolitanism would corrode the group consciousness. His attention to the importance of inherited identities often seemed at odds with his emphasis on the dynamic "weaving back and forth" between new and native-born citizens.

Bourne wrote of "a future America, on which all can unite, which pulls us irresistibly toward it," and he set out a process for arriving at this destination. But he never gave it substance. He never fully addressed the potential conflict between a citizenship rooted in an unchanging set of civic principles and a national culture devoted to a continual process of becoming. Nor did he confront the question of whether a dynamic national culture would require some greater sense of stability and form. Bourne made it easier for his views to be swept aside because he left unanswered the question of how a national identity based on the "pioneer spirit" could become the integrating force he thought necessary as well. Bourne's critique of Americanization and evocation of a new cosmopolitanism gained some ground in the 1930s and 1940s, especially among socialists and modernists. But the confusion between the persistence of difference and the emergence of a genuinely new culture still characterizes debates over multiculturalism today.[52]

The vagueness and confusion among left-leaning Progressives made it difficult to identify a clear, coherent, and compelling moderate alternative position. At the same time, it allowed the coercive and exclusionary aspects within civic nationalism to become more prominent. Those aspects were most apparent in the intellectual architects and practitioners of a centrist civic nationalism, who also left key questions unanswered. As much as Roosevelt tied civic principles and democratic politics to national solidarity, his vision of nationalism could also be remarkably vague. Allegiance to the American nation was crucial, but crucial to what end? Nationalism was necessary, but what was a nation for? At times, Roosevelt invoked moral greatness, civilizational and racial superiority, and individual freedom, among other purposes to which the American nation was devoted to achieving. But his nationalism, his celebration of America and American deeds above all else, was ultimately unclear as to what, if any, limits should or could be placed on that nation and on its exploits. Roosevelt's ideas about racial evolution, and devolution, in combination with his conception of allegiance as singular and unbending thus provided fertile ground for more coercive policies directed only at immigrants.[53]

The failure of Kellor's efforts to maintain a moderate Americanization position illustrates some of the problems posed by the unbounded nature of Roosevelt's civic nationalism. Roosevelt and Kellor had sought to defend a uniquely American nationalism, one that rejected the notion of hyphenation for native white Americans as well as for ethnics. As part of this ideology, native-born Americans were obligated to accept and help new immigrants, to demonstrate tolerance even as they demanded assimilation. Educators insisted that Americanization was a mutual process of exchange, one in which immigrants' cultures, values, and experiences should be mixed with those of Americans to create something new and stronger. But Americanizers' belief in the basic superiority of American culture and ideals left the door open for the more moderate two-way program of exchange to become a one-way process of assimilation.

The idea of Americanization as a two-way process also masked the fact that it was easier to articulate and enforce the obligations of immigrants than those of citizens. Although liberal and centrist civic nationalists alike emphasized the need for Americans to fulfill their responsibilities—at a minimum to be tolerant, accepting, and helpful to immigrants—few programs found ways to ensure that these demands were met. By default, attention focused almost entirely on immigrants. Even here, public officials proved unwilling to support Americanization programs if doing so required them to provide funding. The files of the Bureau of Naturalization, the Bureau of Education, and the National Americanization Committee are filled with plaintive pleas to the federal government to support their work financially, support they never received. There simply was no broad-based willingness among Americans to fulfill the demands that assimilating immigrants placed on citizens. And as the exhortations for Americans to become more tolerant waned, efforts to deracinate newcomers gained strength.

The emphasis on encouraging a voluntary commitment to citizenship developed into a mandatory one that relied on a powerful logic: Why simply provide an option to naturalize when immigrants can be compelled to do so? Under the pressures of a war-driven nationalism, efforts to encourage naturalization and the acquisition of English came to seem insufficiently robust. For many Americanizers, the idea of allegiance became a zero-sum calculation. Following Roosevelt, they viewed any hint of attachment to an immigrant's culture or native land as evidence of disloyalty and a lack of commitment to America. In this way, the moderate civic nationalism that characterized the early stages of the Americanization movement opened the door to the harsher ideology that emerged in the later stages.[54]

To say that there were links between the different stages of the movement is not to argue, as some have, that Americanization was a coercive and exclusionary project from its inception.[55] The direction that Americanization eventually took was far from foreordained—the nativist tendencies in America were not themselves sufficient to have created a compulsory program of assimilation. It required the fear and insecurity of the war to legitimate otherwise objectionable policies. Moreover, however harsh the exhortations and schemes became, in most cases they were not carried out with actual force. The government did not intern large numbers, as it would during the next war. Proposals to deport aliens who failed to naturalize or learn English within specified time periods were never enacted. The Council on National Defense rejected the NAC's "War Policy for Aliens," declaring that the "alien problem" was largely an educational problem. Despite a flurry of federal legislative efforts to enforce compulsory Americanization, all such attempts failed, while state laws, such as California's ordering every adult male alien to register and pay a poll tax, were declared unconstitutional.[56]

Americanization died in part because many of its proponents were simply not willing to pursue compulsory assimilatory measures to their logical extremes. Their fundamental commitments had been based on conversion, not coercion, and they lacked a substantial appetite for implementing the more forcible measures. Public support for stringent Americanization measures also

faded once the flow of immigrants had been restricted. A newfound commitment to individual rights, especially on the part of the courts, further stemmed
the turn toward coercion, as did resistance on the part of immigrants and their
leaders. The Supreme Court upheld linguistic and religious rights, striking
down laws that limited the use of German language and limiting the influence
of parochial schools. Citizenship, Justice J. C. Reynolds argued in the German-
language case, is a civic relationship, not an ethnic one.[57] A Polish newspaper
reflected a similar sentiment when it argued that the Americanization movement had "in it not the smallest particles of the true American spirit, the bright-
est virtue of which is the broadest tolerance."[58] Thus, in conjunction with the
resurgence of a civic preoccupation with rights and tolerance, the moderate
civic nationalism that the most active Americanizers embodied imposed its
own limits on coercion.[59]

In the Progressive Era, the combination of massive immigration, significant
social change, and international conflict pressed the question of whether a
workable balance between the civic and national dimensions of citizenship depended on some degree of coercion and exclusion. What kind of political or
cultural coherence could be forged among the different domestic and newly arriving groups, given the expansion in languages, cultures, religious beliefs, and
political traditions? These were real questions and reflected real problems.[60]
The Americanizers' responses to these questions and problems intertwined
their beliefs in social efficiency and social justice, moral and institutional stability, and both civic ideals and national cohesion.

In the end, the great wave of immigrants to the United States that arrived before 1924 eventually became citizens and full-fledged members of the American civic nation. As just one measure of this incorporation, by the 1940s and
1950s their rates of naturalization had increased significantly.[61] Whether and
how the Americanization movement contributed to this process of incorporation is difficult to assess. Samuel Huntington suggests that without the Americanization movement "the dramatic 1924 reduction in immigration . . . would
in all likelihood have come much earlier. . . . The success of the movement was
manifest when immigrants and their children rallied to the colors and marched
off to fight their country's wars."[62] Yet many immigrants' negative reaction to
Americanization may well have delayed their sense of belonging in their new
land. Their willingness—and that of their children—to fight in America's wars
can also be attributed to their desire to prove their Americanness, not a confir-
mation of it.

Still, in conjunction with other real and symbolic pressures on diversity—
restrictions on cultural and religious pluralism, limitations on the entry and
naturalization of Asians, restrictions on immigration from southern and eastern Europe, and a powerful ideology of ethnic nation-building championed by
Roosevelt and others—centrist Americanization seemed to reduce the concerns of native-born citizens. Immigration was less troubling so long as it was

tied to robust programs of assimilation. The greater clarity Americans felt about the meaning of their nationhood, the more welcoming they could be toward those deemed capable of becoming part of it. Immigrants who had previously been considered dubious candidates for citizenship and nationhood—Irish, Italian, Polish, Jewish, and others—became American.

As for left-leaning approaches, even the movement's most acerbic critic, Randolph Bourne, considered Americanization's achievements remarkable: "What has been offered the newcomers has been the chance to learn English, to become a citizen, to salute the flag. And those elements of our ruling classes who are responsible for the public schools, the settlements, all the organizations for amelioration in the cities, have every reason to be proud of the care and labor which they have devoted to absorbing the immigrants."[63] Americanizers lobbied for legislation to protect immigrants from unscrupulous landlords and tyrannical employers. They offered large-scale practical assistance to immigrants for the first time in American history. Americanizers also for the first time established an outreach program to encourage and prepare immigrants to become citizens, in the process improving the naturalization system and developing the first formal programs in adult education.

Americanizers rejected both an individualist, laissez-faire approach to incorporating newcomers as well as the ethnic machine's group-based strategy. Some pressed for a complete transfer of allegiance and identity, while others wanted immigrants to manage the tensions between their ethnic and American identities as they became citizens and participated in public life. Both kinds of Americanizers tried to find ways to overcome native-born citizens' prejudice toward newcomers. As we see in the next chapter, the Americanization movement and the civic nationalist energy that infused it differed significantly from the general neglect of immigrants and of strategies to balance the civic and the national dimensions of citizenship that followed upon its demise.

CHAPTER SEVEN

Immigration and Citizenship at Century's End

THE SENSE of a truly national citizenship that the Progressives sought to forge became increasingly solidified in the period between the New Deal and the Great Society. This identity undergirded an expanding democratic, tolerant, and multicultural ethos. The United States extended rights and offered opportunities for political participation to those previously excluded from the full protection of the state and from engagement in public affairs—African Americans and immigrants in particular. The nation rejected racial quotas in the admission of immigrants and coercive programs of assimilation. By the 1960s, U.S. immigration laws no longer favored whites over Asians and Latinos, and minority voices successfully decried the notion that newcomers ought to shed their ethnic identities. The prospects for an inclusive and robust moderate civic nationalism seemed to be improving.

Yet by the 1980s and 1990s, premillennial rumblings could be heard as to whether that identity was sufficient to meet the challenges of the next century. Americans again confronted questions about the link between peoplehood and principles, this time in an era when individual alienation, group fragmentation, and global dislocation posed new challenges to the meaning of nationhood, the exercise of self-government, and the protection of rights. "What," asked the sociologist Nathan Glazer, "can national loyalty mean in a world of changing nation-states, ever more closely bound together?"[1]

Controversies arose over the full range of policies regarding immigration and citizenship. In the 1980s, much of the debate revolved around questions of admission criteria, continuing a longstanding dispute over whether immigrants are an asset or an economic liability.[2] As the decade wore on, attention turned to questions of how many and what kind of immigrants should be allowed entry. Controversies also erupted over what sort of naturalization process was appropriate in an increasingly multicultural and transnational age. Similar disputes arose over ending the entitlement to birthright citizenship and denying citizenship to the U.S.-born children of undocumented aliens.

Even the terms used were hotly contested. For some, "assimilation," like "Americanization," was a dirty word; for others, assimilation was essential to immigrants' and the nation's well-being.[3] Bilingual education and affirmative action policies were strongly promoted and then equally fervently resisted, especially as they applied to new immigrants. The importance of citizenship status in determining access to rights and benefits also caused significant controversy, as the courts and Congress shifted back and forth. By the end of the century it had also become clear that the United States would likely have more dual citizens than ever before. Debates over these issues reflected fundamental disagreements over the meaning of America's civic principles, the sources of its national identity, and the value of U.S. citizenship.

Beginning in the 1960s, two different conceptions of the civic dimension of citizenship became increasingly dominant. One view stressed that a truly democratic polity depends on universal rights rather than nationalism. This view was espoused by leading law professors, political theorists, and sociologists, as well as philanthropic organizations and ethnic advocacy groups. It often overlapped with a second view advanced by other minority and immigrant advocacy groups and scholars that emphasized political participation and ethnic representation as the key to protecting immigrants' rights and furthering their position in American life. Both positions drew on strands in the civic dimension of citizenship— individual rights and political representation—even while they doubted that Americans shared a unique set of political principles and questioned whether abstract principles had united or could unite Americans.

As these two views became entrenched, especially among ethnic advocates and academics, a significantly different set of views became prominent in popular political discourse. Voters and legislators argued about restricting immigration, strengthening citizenship, and limiting the rights of aliens. These policies reflected, in particular, two conceptions of nationalism. The first celebrated the notion that Americans share a homogeneous and distinctly European cultural heritage. Its proponents included conservative journalists and advocacy organizations, as well as the presidential aspirant Patrick Buchanan. The second conception emerged most clearly in neoconservative journals and think tanks. It stressed that American nationhood was rooted in a voluntary commitment to a set of universal civic principles.

The rights, representation, cultural, and universal positions were neither monolithic nor mutually exclusive. Nevertheless, each position represented a distinct view of the civic and the national dimensions of citizenship and the relation between the two. Each position developed one (or more) key ideas that were present in earlier debates at the Founding and in the Progressive Era. What distinguishes these views and the broader debate among them from debates in those periods is the separation of civic nationalist positions into civic *or* national positions alone and the increasingly extreme definitions given to each.

From New Deal Nationalism to Nationality as a Human Right

From the 1930s to the 1960s the national and the civic dimensions of citizenship were strengthened individually and mutually reinforced one another. A series of critical public events solidified a growing sense of national unity, common political ideals, and the acceptance of minorities. The Great Depression painfully demonstrated the economic and social interconnections among Americans. The New Deal built on these interconnections to establish that a basic degree of economic and social rights were necessary for a meaningful citizenship. "Necessitous men," Franklin Roosevelt famously proclaimed, "are not free men."[4] The historian Gary Gerstle suggests that "because the disciplinary campaign of the 1920s, and especially its immigration restriction component, had been successful in silencing those who might have challenged the cultural and political boundaries of the American nation, FDR and his fellow New Dealers felt little need to emulate TR's commitment to identifying and ostracizing the nation's alleged enemies. FDR liked to stress the openness of American society, not its rigidities." Gerstle describes how, as the New Deal gave way to World War II, a new public image emerged of a diverse nation that recognized ethnic minorities as fully American, though racial minorities, especially African Americans, were still excluded from participation in the shared experience of unity that the war produced.[5]

The civil rights movement of the 1960s spoke to that exclusion. It emphasized that the American story of a national community dedicated to upholding core civic principles depended on black Americans' succeeding in their struggle for freedom. When Martin Luther King cast the aims of the civil rights movement as nothing less than the "transformation of a whole people," he was speaking as much of the American people as of black Americans.[6] The Great Society promised to provide the education, training, and social safety net that would enable black as well as other poor Americans to become full members of the national community. The purpose of the Great Society, said Lyndon Johnson, was to involve Americans in "a common enterprise, a cause greater than themselves. . . . Without this, we will simply become a nation of strangers."[7] Immigrants, too, played a central role in reinforcing the notion of a unified American nation dedicated to the principles of individual liberty and equality. A "real historical melting pot that was neither Anglo conformist nor homogeneous had formed," the historian Reed Ueda notes. "It produced a shared national culture and a heterogenous and constantly changing set of ethnic cultures. . . . New cultural elements, once recognizably foreign, over time became quintessentially American."[8] By the mid-1960s, at the height of the civil rights movement's moral authority and the Great Society's political influence, America seemed to be finding its way toward a citizenship that valued the contributions of minorities, and diversity more broadly, within a broader sense of national unity and civic pride.

At same time, a variety of new forces arose that challenged this unity and the legitimacy of the country's ideals. Watergate, Vietnam, the racial crisis, counterculture New Left radicalism, and feminism all both reflected and shaped doubts about the justness of American institutions, especially on the part of influential elites. Their rejection of the melting pot as a cover for Anglo conformity was especially notable. Advocates for minorities described American history as a story of ethnic oppression and characterized the nation as a community held together by few common bonds or principles. They further contended that members of minority groups must possess special group representation rights (such as racially drawn voting districts) as well as special group cultural rights (such as bilingual and bicultural education). Some proponents of these policies regarded them primarily as a method for redressing historical injustices, while others defended them as fundamental requirements of justice that would be permanently necessary. A bicultural and bilingual curriculum in this latter view was intended to affirm students' culture by conveying that no transformation of identity was necessary to become American. Critics of multiculturalism worried that these more radical claims betrayed the civic promise of equal treatment before the law and a shared nationality in favor of group rights and a plurality of ethnic nationalisms. The often vitriolic disputes between multiculturalists and their critics led to an increasingly fragile sense of the meaning of the civic and the national dimensions of American citizenship and the linkage between the two.[9]

That fragility was heightened by a growing sense of individual alienation. As the federal government took on more responsibilities and became more complex, citizens' confidence about their shared political life, ironically, diminished. Government seemed increasingly remote from individual citizens who doubted its capacity to operate efficiently and equitably. "Americans view politics with boredom and detachment," the journalist E. J. Dionne wrote in 1991. "For many years we have been running down the public sector and public life. Voters doubt that elections give them any real control of what the government does, and half of them don't bother to cast ballots."[10] American legal and political cultures' emphasis on rights further obscured the importance of obligations and responsibilities, and the market economy put strains on stable local communities, intact families, and an ethos of deferred gratification. These trends weakened any sense of a common national identity as well as the local communities that help citizens understand civic principles and exercise their civic duties.[11]

The linkage between peoplehood and principles was also under pressure from external forces. While the extent and newness of globalization has often been overstated, by the mid-1980s it had become clear that the United States and other nations were operating in a radically changed world. As capital markets became increasingly global they exercised greater authority over governments' economic and social policies. This influence in some cases reduced a government's accountability to its own population and diminished feelings of efficacy among its citizenry. The growth of multinational corporations also raised questions about individual nation-states as the primary site of political order.[12]

The growth of international rights codes and conventions further challenged the civic and the national dimensions of citizenship. These codes and conventions require states to provide positive rights deemed universal to all persons within their territory, ranging from protection against torture and freedom of speech to social and economic well-being and cultural survival. The form of governance preferred is often multicultural and consociational.[13] The influence of international rights codes and conventions was most evident in the limitations placed on the ability of Western European countries to control immigration and to treat aliens differently from citizens. The European Court of Human Rights (ECHR), for instance, pressured states not to restrict entry on the basis of national or ethnic criteria and emphasized the membership rights of aliens based on their presence in a polity. "The ECHR does not recognize a right to nationality per se," notes the sociologist David Jacobson, "but in restricting the border control of states on the basis of universal (not national) criteria, and in recognizing the rights of aliens on the basis of attachments they may have to a territory (through marriage, for example) . . . the convention recognizes, in effect, a right to nationality as a human right."[14]

While the rights accorded to aliens in the United States did not go as far as in some European countries, during the 1970s and 1980s U.S. courts accorded greater procedural and substantive rights to legal as well as illegal immigrants. Citizenship, the courts increasingly made clear, should be considered irrelevant for the provision of various social benefits.[15] Although little attention was paid to it at the time, in 1967 the U.S. Supreme Court made it virtually impossible for persons to lose their citizenship. The Nationality Act of 1907 had codified the acts by which persons could lose their citizenship. The Court worried that the connection between acts such as naturalizing, serving in the armed forces, or voting in the election of a foreign state and a person's intention to renounce their U.S. citizenship was so opaque, and the punishment so severe, that Congress could not strip a person of citizenship absent the consent of that person.[16] Justice Earl Warren called citizenship "man's basic right for it is nothing less than the right to have rights."[17]

These court decisions in the United States and the rights codes in Europe strongly shaped much of the political discourse among Western elites over immigration and citizenship starting in the 1970s. That discourse reflected an ideology that emphasized the equality of all persons. The nation, in this view, was a collection of individuals, not a people, and one's personhood is what mattered, not one's peoplehood. From this cosmopolitan perspective, love of country was a threat to the achievement of justice, and national identity should be a morally irrelevant characteristic.[18]

Between the New Deal and the Great Society, other key components of U.S. immigration and citizenship policy also shifted away from civic or nationalist categorizations. Initially, in the 1940s and 1950s, Congress reinforced specific civic categorizations by denying citizenship to members of the Communist Party or organizations that advocated anarchism, polygamy, or political assassination. (Congress also strengthened the federal government's deportation powers and widened its surveillance of alien residents. In addition, Congress raised the standards for naturalization by requiring that applicants read and write English, not just speak and understand it, and that they demonstrate a basic knowledge of U.S. civics and history.)[19] By the 1990s, however, these ideological criteria had diminished to the point of irrelevancy. Starting in the 1940s, Congress also repealed the Chinese Exclusion Act and eliminated all racial or marital qualifications for citizenship, allowing for the first time all persons to apply as individuals.[20] In 1965 Congress ended all ethnically discriminatory immigration quotas and instead stressed family reunification and labor qualifications. Proponents of family reunification as a cornerstone of American policy thought it would draw immigrants primarily from the traditional emigration countries of Europe. Instead, Asians and Latin Americans far outdistanced Europeans. The act also fundamentally changed the politics of immigration. Where once civic and nationalist constructs governed admission, now interest groups shaped policy by lobbying for increased immigration and special dispensations to increase the numbers of groups admitted from particular regions.[21]

In the United States, immigration rates rose dramatically following the 1965 amendments and surged in the 1970s and 1980s. Not since the 1920s had so many immigrants from such a variety of cultures come to the United States. The 1990 census recorded 19.7 million foreign-born residents, the largest number in American history, although the proportion of foreign-born (6.2 percent in 1980) remained far below the level reached in the late nineteenth and early twentieth centuries (13 percent). There were more than double the number of nationalities present in the 1980s than in the 1920s, and illegal immigration increased from apprehensions totaling less than one hundred thousand in the early 1960s to over one million by the early 1980s.[22] The Immigration Act of 1965 also fed changes in the nature of migration that raised particularly thorny questions about the meaning of American nationhood. Improved communication, better transportation, free trade laws, the proliferation of dual citizenship, and a discourse celebrating universal personhood and cultural difference meant that by the 1980s and 1990s the link between migrant and home country seemed to be persisting and possibly even strengthening over time. Mexicans living in the United States, for example, used modern communications technology to shape public works projects that they funded in Mexico. And for some illegal immigrants, a continuous "circuit of migration and return" seemed the most apt characterization of the way they worked and lived.[23]

Migrant groups pressing for dual citizenship and other rights in their home countries, and home governments seeking to exert influence on economically and politically important diaspora communities, also created new forms of transnational economic and political fusion. Political leaders from a variety of Latin American countries began raising funds and campaigning in American cities. Jean Bertrand Aristide went so far as to designate Haitians living abroad the "Tenth Department" of Haiti—"thereby granting them," observed the sociologist Robert Smith, "symbolically, at least, equal status with Haitians in the nine geographical departments (provinces) of the country." In 1990 the Mexican government established the Foreign Affairs Ministry's Directorate General for Mexican Communities Abroad. The first director of this program described its purpose as creating "the Mexican global nation."[24]

While diasporas are often made up of new or recent immigrants, they increasingly drew support from those seeking to revitalize long-lost connections. Transnational networks of Armenians or Irish, many of whom were descendants of immigrants from more than a century ago, became increasingly active players in the politics of their countries of origin. These kinds of diasporic politics were not new in American history—in the 1840s the Irish in the United States campaigned strongly against alliances with England, to cite just one example—but they seemed to be increasing in intensity and multiplying in number.[25] At a time when the coherence of U.S. politics and culture was itself at issue, these heightened forms of transnational identities prompted renewed questions about immigration and American nationhood: How would immigrants be incorporated and how would they—and native-born citizens—conceive of their shared identity? Latino immigrants in particular exhibited relatively low rates of naturalization, voter registration, political participation, educational achievement, and language retention.

There were many political, economic, and cultural reasons for these low rates. Some reasons new arrivals chose not to naturalize, for instance, were the same as those in earlier eras—continued attachment to their native lands, the hope to remigrate, personal and pecuniary disadvantages, administrative difficulties associated with the INS, and the experience of discrimination.[26] Yet there were new reasons, too. Return trips home were much easier for Latin Americans than for Europeans. Whereas no single language predominated among earlier waves of immigrants, by the 1980s Spanish was the native tongue of more than 50 percent of the new immigrants. Immigrants were less evenly dispersed, and their communities enjoyed constant replenishment from their native countries. While these factors combined to make adjustment to life in the United States less traumatic, it was unclear whether they would also weaken the incentive to adopt America's civic principles and identify as a member of the American nation.

The United States had itself undergone significant structural changes that made it more difficult for newcomers to become incorporated. The institutions of civil society that had helped integrate immigrants into American life, such as churches, unions, and political machines, played a quite different and generally more attenuated role. The Catholic Church in particular no longer mediated as effectively between immigrant cultures and American life as it once did. Although Latinos made up a sizable portion of its membership, especially in the West and Southwest, the church's influence was greatly reduced, and its interest in playing a similar role diminished. Other arenas in which immigrants could both gain protection and acquire the skills and values of a democratic society, such as labor unions, had also suffered serious setbacks.[27] In addition, immigrants were heavily concentrated in the large "reformed" western and south-western cities, where political parties possessed insufficient patronage to spend on incorporating newcomers and did not need their support to the same extent as in the past. The more bureaucratic mode of politics that predominated in these cities caused white political officials to perceive immigrants largely as a drain on local resources.[28] And while ethnic politicians needed newcomers to be counted for representation purposes they did not necessarily need them to naturalize or participate in politics. Under the amended Voting Rights Act, the censuses' enumeration of permanent residents and illegal aliens provides the basis for single-member districts, which are designed to ensure the election of minority representatives. Officials elected into single-member districts with sizable populations of noncitizens had little incentive to mobilize them into politics when, as was often the case, they differed from their constituents on important issues such as immigration, abortion, and bilingual education.[29]

By the end of the 1980s, the very structure of modern U.S. and international politics posed new challenges to the incorporation of immigrants into a traditional notion of citizenship that embraced both its civic and nationalist dimensions. Broad shifts in America's legal and political culture, as well as other changes, such as the abandonment of the public schools in many areas by the upper middle class and the dissolution of common military service, had contributed to changes and perhaps a contraction of the public sphere. The growth in transnational relations and the decline of domestic institutions had introduced greater uncertainty into what was meant by being American and into whether and how immigrants might become Americans.

"NAME ONE BENEFIT OF BEING A CITIZEN OF THE UNITED STATES": AMNESTY AND THE NEW NATURALIZATION PROCESS

At the same time that fundamental questions were being raised about the institutional capacities for incorporating immigrants into a unified American citizenship, few public or private organizations were paying attention to the role of naturalization in this process. From the 1930s through the 1960s, the INS had carried out its basic naturalization work in collaboration with schools, bar associations, and social service organizations. A combination of community and governmental institutions quietly continued much of the preparation for citizenship and testing that had been initiated during the Progressive Era. Communities celebrated "Citizenship Day" and "I Am an American Day" annually but without the fervor associated with the Americanization movement.[30]

Throughout this period, the INS sought to improve its approach to naturalization. In 1936 the INS established the Citizenship Program, which found an arbitrary set of procedures and a lack of uniformity in the kinds of questions asked by examiners, despite the earlier efforts of Roosevelt and the bureaucracy. In response, it directed examiners to be "fair, courteous, patient and sympathetic," and to ask questions that were "frank, clear and expressed in simple language." The Citizenship Program also sought to shift from technical questions that depended on memorization to questions that emphasized basic principles. "This does not meant that they [the applicants] must be familiar with every principle enunciated in the Constitution," the program instructed its examiners. An applicant for citizenship was to demonstrate a simple understanding of basic principles and functions of government "which would affect him in his daily life as a citizen." The program also explicitly cautioned against seeking to teach or test for a single understanding of democratic principles, given "the diversity of opinion in [the Supreme Court] on the meaning of some of the principles of the Constitution."[31] In reviewing this process of "follow-through and fine tuning," the historian Michael Kammen concludes that "constitutionalism in the education of immigrants made halting yet substantial strides between 1914 and 1939."[32]

The agency also increased its efforts to improve immigrants' understanding of American values and history by providing more substantive civic education. In 1946 Attorney General Tom C. Clark pointed out that it made little sense to wait until five years had passed to offer an immigrant the opportunity to learn American values and history. It would make more sense, he contended, to provide this opportunity as soon as a visa was granted. To that end, he initiated "a comprehensive program to emphasize the work and meaning of American citizenship."[33]

This steady and unspectacular attention to the naturalization process began to change in the late 1960s. Budget problems forced cutbacks in the schools, and the women who had volunteered their time in community organizations were now entering the workforce in significant numbers. At the same time, less demand was placed on the system as fewer immigrants were entering the United States. The INS stopped updating its naturalization materials. This indifference toward the citizenship process occurred despite the fact that in 1950 Congress raised the standards for naturalization. By the time naturalization rates began to rise again, around the mid-1970s, the INS was beset by management problems and focused primarily on enforcement and border control. As a result, the INS became far more concerned with keeping immigrants out than with welcoming those already here.[34]

Ethnic groups also paid little attention to naturalization. The political scientist Louis DeSipio describes how traditional associations like the League of United Latin American Citizens were skeptical about increased immigration and did not focus on naturalization. At the other end of the spectrum, more radical Chicano groups' commitment to separatism left little room for a conventional process like naturalization. For their part, civil rights groups adopted a strategy that emphasized rights regardless of citizenship or legal status. Rather than encouraging naturalization, these strategies reduced the incentives for immigrants to become citizens.[35]

Not until the 1980s did the naturalization process begin to receive significant attention. Ironically, this attention emerged from deeply contentious debates over an amnesty program for illegal aliens, debates that culminated in the Immigration and Reform Control Act of 1986 (IRCA). In contrast to earlier guest worker policies—the *bracero* programs—IRCA enabled migrant laborers to apply for permanent residence and citizenship. It doubled the number of successful applicants for permanent residence and ensured that, for the first time, migrant agricultural workers would be free to join unions and to leave agricultural work.[36] In the mid-1980s, however, leaders in the House of Representatives could not construct a majority out of two opposing groups: those set on increasing patrol of the borders and levying sanctions against employers of illegal aliens and those who favored a legalization program for illegal aliens. Jim Wright (D-Texas), the majority leader, proposed adding a civics and English-language requirement that would play a key role in securing the bill's passage.[37] He argued that his proposal would "reinforce the sense [that becoming a citizen was] worthwhile" and aid the applicant's capacity to participate in American society, especially in the economy. "I do not think we have to pour all these great strains into one great melting pot and come out with a single stream of sameness," Wright explained. "But I do not believe either [that] we want to create the temptations to a balkanization of American society into little subcultures."[38]

Proponents of legalization opposed Wright's amendment. They regarded the addition of an English and civics requirement as onerous and discriminatory. Edward Roybal (D-California) chastised him for requiring immigrants to prove their commitment to the polity. Native-born citizens, he pointed out, bear no equivalent obligation. Ted Weiss (D-New York) attacked Wright's proposal as a thinly veiled attempt to discriminate against the principal beneficiaries of amnesty: Hispanics and Caribbean blacks. In Wright's view, by contrast, the ultimate goal of the amnesty program was to strengthen citizenship, not confer rights: "[W]e dignify the applicant when we give that applicant the assumption of an ability to learn and the opportunity to learn to participate fully, not as a substandard member, but as a full-fledged member of our society." Wright distinguished between undocumented workers who "desire to be here only a short time, to make a little bit of money, a grubstake, and then to return to their native lands" and those who want to be incorporated into the American community. Simply pursuing a course of study would meet his requirement, he stressed, and would "test the sincerity and the seriousness of purpose of the immigrant who would cast his or her lot with us and with our Nation for the rest of his or her life." In turn, the United States had a responsibility to "provide opportunities for people to master knowledge of this country, knowledge of our laws, knowledge of our language, opportunities that have existed in the past for other waves of immigrants who have enriched our society." The educational amendment passed by a vote of 248 to 169.[39]

The programs in English and civics that developed under IRCA sparked a controversy similar to the debates that raged in the Progressive Era, but with noticeably different outcomes. As in the 1910s and 1920s, Congress left it to the INS to determine who would carry out the program, the substance of the education, and how aliens would be tested. More than 1,200 organizations responded to an initial congressional allocation of four billion dollars, including public schools, private for-profit agencies, state offices, legal services corporations, ethnic, religious, and community organizations, labor unions, farm labor groups, and associations of agricultural employers.[40] Many educators regarded the civics program "as an unprecedented adult education program for immigrants, particularly for Hispanic immigrants, who . . . had not been historically heavy users of pre-existing adult education services." Some wanted to develop even more extensive programs than Wright had proposed.[41] In contrast, Congress, the Bush administration, the INS, and ethnic and immigrant advocacy groups all treated the program in civic education with skepticism. In 1989, members of Congress proposed diverting amnesty funds to health research and the resettlement of Soviet Jews. In the same year, the Bush administration sought to finance its drug enforcement programs with these monies.[42] For its part, the INS failed to produce useful materials promptly. Educators repeatedly pressed the INS to provide adequate guidelines and materials for the program in civics and English.[43]

Ethnic and immigrant advocacy groups also regarded a program in civic education with skepticism. They argued that undocumented immigrants' social and material contributions to the United States entitled them to inclusion in the political community. The amnesty program should therefore extend to illegal aliens the rights that come with legitimating one's membership status in the community, not establish an extended naturalization process.[44] Linda Wong, cochair of the forty-three-member Coalition for Humane Immigrant Rights of Los Angeles, cautioned, "We should do everything possible . . . to minimize any attrition that might occur as a result of excessive demands." She proposed that the INS allow applicants to take their exams in their native language and be tested by community organizations. Similarly, a handbook prepared for the National Council of La Raza warned that "the education programs provided for newly legalized aliens must bear in mind that the foremost goal is to help the newly legalized alien adjust her/his status to permanent residence."[45] Ethnic and immigrant advocacy groups sought to lessen the program's requirements. The INS initially required a minimum of sixty hours of a one-hundred-hour program, and these groups proposed ten hours instead. Educators argued that this would be insufficient and the INS settled on forty hours of a sixty-hour program.[46]

In addition to intense lobbying by ethnic and immigrant advocacy groups, the education program was shaped by a number of practical considerations (which mirrored those in the Progressive Era): a majority of aliens needed basic language instruction; educators found it impossible to design an elaborate program for the three million aliens to be legalized in a short period; and the programs induced demand and created a problem of supply.[47] Immigrant advocates had predicted that these courses would fail to attract participants. Yet the programs were oversubscribed and applicants often attended class well beyond the required forty hours. After three times as many students as expected showed up for classes, the Los Angeles School District established a twenty-four-hour school for citizenship.[48]

In contrast to its counterpart in the Progressive Era, the 1986 amnesty program placed few civic or nationalist demands on applicants. The INS issued a clear policy that an educational certificate did not indicate that "the applicant learned specific information or has reached a certain level of comprehension. It merely certifies attendance at a recognized program."[49] These programs did not reflect an active effort to devalue or diminish the status of citizenship, but neither did they strengthen citizenship and the naturalization process in the manner envisioned by Jim Wright. In the end the overarching goal of these programs became to make legalization easier, a result of the across-the-board lack of interest in the citizenship process.

IRCA's civic education programs did unintentionally move the citizenship process in one new direction: toward a more standardized approach to the naturalization examination. As we have seen, naturalization standards have varied widely at different times in different locales. In some cases, officials upheld a stringent set of requirements; in other cases, applicants who simply showed up became citizens. Officials and commentators have complained that the lack of standardization permits abuse, creates confusion, and makes the process an arbitrary one. In response, the INS has periodically sought to make the process more uniform and more focused on understanding than on memorization. These efforts resulted in some changes, but as the periodic bursts of concern over naturalization waned so, too, did the energy and authority to sustain these changes. The INS itself has also resisted making the test too standardized, as the current system gives examiners opportunities to exercise professional discretion. Some interviewers willingly passed applicants who had prepared for the examination but failed it nonetheless. Standardization, some officials have objected, would unfairly require less educated immigrants to answer the same questions as doctoral students.

Under IRCA, advocates successfully argued that given the educational background of the applicant pool and the large numbers, providing sample questions and some greater degree of standardization was necessary. Over a weekend, two INS officers developed one hundred questions and answers to be provided to applicants preparing for the exam. Some of the approved answers suggested that citizenship has only material value, such as one that lists only government jobs, travel with a U.S. passport, and petitioning for close relatives to come to the

United States as acceptable responses to the statement, "Name one benefit of being a citizen of the United States." Several questions dealt with the benefits, rights, and freedoms of citizenship, but none spoke of its obligations. This is in contrast to the oath of allegiance, which dwells almost exclusively on requirements.

By the mid-1990s, a typical examination required that an applicant answer seven out of ten or twelve questions correctly from the list developed under IRCA or related questions. In effect, the examination tested memory more than knowledge. Few applicants for citizenship were denied citizenship because they failed the exam. Most applicants got 80 to 90 percent of the questions right and many scored a perfect 100 percent. Indeed, while immigrants still regarded the naturalization examination with trepidation, immigrants who actually went through the process reported that the exam was easy. Almost 80 percent found the examiner helpful.[50]

Alien Rights and Minority Representation

In the debate over legalization, ethnic and immigrant advocacy organizations defended the rights of migrants, regardless of citizenship or legal status. They pressed for amnesty on the grounds that the ties illegal immigrants had established in the United States, and the contributions they had made to the economy and to society, meant that they had earned the right to legal status. The conflict over legalization reveals the growing influence in the 1980s and 1990s of a new conception of the meaning of citizenship, one that both reflected and shaped the thinking of advocacy organizations. This conception was fully articulated by legal scholars, political theorists, and sociologists. It stressed the universal rather than national foundation of America's civic principles. Advocates for this position insisted that we should promote liberal democratic citizenship, not American citizenship. In their view, the United States placed too great an emphasis on a distinctively American conception of citizenship. In doing so, it fostered exclusivity and worked against promoting a salutary universal vision of freedom. In contrast, they emphasized how democratic nation-states can expand human values by according full rights to migrants.

Proponents of the rights position applauded the court decisions of the 1970s and 1980s that deemed citizenship irrelevant for the provision of various social benefits. In their view, fashioning citizens on the basis of citizenship in the nation-state would compel conformity to a "discourse [that] is neither neutral nor all-inclusive." It would result in the reemergence of exclusionary definitions of citizenship: the Alien and Sedition Acts and the Chinese exclusion laws, the legal scholar Alexander Aleinikoff has pointed out, reflected majority preferences for maintaining "communities of character." For Aleinikoff, who in the mid-1990s held high policy positions at the INS, claims about national community merely reflected "the norms and culture of dominant groups."[51] Others argued that naturalization itself, in reinvigorating the mythical act of consent and legitimating the American nation-state, "obscures the nonconsensual and ascriptive bases and present-day practices of American democracy."[52]

From a rights perspective, a liberal democracy cannot demand that newcomers believe in its civic principles. A liberal democracy may expect immigrants to adopt certain social behaviors and attitudes, and it may hope that they come to believe in the core values of the society, but it cannot *require* that newcomers demonstrate such beliefs. This is so, the political theorist Joseph Carens argued, because civil society is morally prior to political society. The web of social, familial, and economic ties that an immigrant forms by living in a country properly constitutes the basis for formal membership. Like some of the Republicans during the debates at the Founding and in the early Republic, rights advocates emphasized the reciprocity between aliens' obligations to obey the law and governments' responsibility to protect them; they saw the principle of no taxation without representation as applicable to aliens upon entry.[53]

Carens and other contemporary proponents of a rights perspective further contended that civic and history tests for citizenship establish an unduly high threshold of knowledge and serve only as a barrier to full legal standing. Moreover, civic knowledge does not necessarily make someone a virtuous citizen—and native-born U.S. citizens do not have to take a test. In any case, tests of this sort often improperly favor some groups at the expense of others.[54] Even more fundamentally, Americans have never agreed on the meaning of their core principles. "Which traditions are the ones that the alien must appreciate and understand?" asked the law professor Gerald Rosberg. "The tradition of those who were once slaves or once masters; those who won the Mexican-American War or those who lost it; those who came from Ireland or those who despised the Irish and would have sent them back?" This disagreement makes it implausible to suggest that there is any one set of principles immigrants must adopt.[55]

Rights advocates were especially critical of efforts to make national citizenship a mechanism for inclusion in an increasingly transnational age. Some argued that the nation-state was obsolete in a time when people, images, ideas, capital, labor, and even government flowed across borders. The constitutional scholar Sanford Levinson described national citizenship as becoming like citizenship in individual American states. National citizenship "might supply us with teams to root for . . . and a place from which to vote," he wrote. "It is, though, ever more unlikely to be of any real import in structuring our identities." In this context, some proponents of the rights position dismissed entirely the importance of strong feelings of attachment among citizens.[56] In their view, the phrase "national community" is an oxymoron.[57]

Others emphasized how emotional bonds of attachment develop only through social interaction in small, intimate settings. Participation in local community affairs, observed law professor Jamin Raskin, helps all persons to develop a sense of "empathy, virtue, and feelings of community." Raskin counseled that the tradition of giving political rights to aliens should be resurrected and expanded. "The move toward local noncitizen voting," he contended, "can be seen as part of the trend of communities accepting responsibility for participating in the enforcement of global human rights norms. . . . Eventually, we may define a human right to democratic participation."[58] Similarly, the Ford Foundation's Changing Relations Project identified the exclusion of immigrants from economic, social, and political opportunities as one of the major barriers to more harmonious relations between newcomers and citizens. Its authors, including Robert Bach, a sociologist who in the mid-1990s became the director of policy planning for the INS, contended that, among other policies, local political participation by noncitizens could best address economic, community safety, and environmental issues and overcome "ethnic alienation and nativism."[59]

The political theorist Bonnie Honig further suggested that immigrants and their advocates should favor a democratic cosmopolitanism in which legal and illegal immigrants exercise "the rights of democratic citizens while they are here" and band together to "take and redistribute power." Migrants of all kinds should participate in social and worker movements as ways to help them demand their rights, including the right to vote, and they should forge ties with transnational groups like Amnesty International and Greenpeace as a way to denationalize democracy. Participation in these movements and groups, Honig concluded, "is an education in democratic citizenship far worthier of the name than the citizenship classes offered by the state in preparation for naturalization."[60]

For proponents of a rights perspective, multiple loyalties are a fact of modern life. As ties among people and institutions become more numerous and cross national boundaries, they argued, we should accept that American citizens might be members of many different groupings. From this perspective, noted Peter Schuck, a leading analyst of U.S. and comparative citizenship law, dual citizenship gives individuals more choices as to where they can "live, work, and invest," while providing them with "additional sources of rights, obligations, and communal ties."[61] Old worries about dual loyalties and conflicting jurisdictions are less relevant in a world where international ties have proliferated and where the likelihood of war among liberal states seems remote. If there is no direct conflict between two countries, why object to an individual's asserting one set of interests in American elections and another set elsewhere?[62]

A second conception of the civic dimension of citizenship also undergirded the legalization debate, as well as other disputes. In common with the rights perspective, this conception downplayed the importance of immigrants' attaining a conceptual understanding of American political principles and was deeply wary of claims about national identity. It further shared a central concern for protecting immigrants and minorities. Scholars and advocates for ethnic groups and immigrants who advanced this conception differed from the rights perspective in according greater legitimacy to U.S. legal citizenship and in emphasizing more the importance of immigrant and ethnic groups being represented in national politics. Ethnic politics and increased minority representation, in this view, are the best way to ensure that America lives up to its civic ideals.

The minority representation view typically affirmed that a core of abstract principles holds together the different groups within the United States. Yet what it means to be an American can mean different things to different people, and each experience contributes to the national story. Indeed, diversity is an important basis for an "American" identity. Ethnic communities are critical to providing a sense of identity, fulfillment, and self-confidence for many. Core democratic values thus require all Americans to support the flourishing of ethnic communities. Americans must respect newcomers' differences, not merely begrudgingly accept immigrants if they change their ways.[63] The minority representation approach is similar to that of the cultural pluralists and social reformers of the Progressive Era in its aim to be inclusive and to treat national citizenship and cultural diversity as compatible, even harmonious. Following Dewey, Bourne, and Addams, its proponents believed that immigrants have an important role to play in building a democratic culture. In practice, they differed from Progressives like Addams in seeing ethnic politics and legally mandated group preferences as appropriate vehicles for ensuring this end.

Minority group advocates objected to what they saw as the prevailing view of American history as a heroic struggle to put its principles into practice—a struggle in which discrimination against minorities was a mere footnote rather than the main story. Americans are so deeply affected by racism and exclusionary practices, the law professor Juan Perea asserted, that allowing popular sentiment to determine immigration and immigrant policy is a recipe for self-replication and stasis. Americans would opt for the familiar, for themselves. Instead, immigrant incorporation must be viewed as the dual responsibility of the immigrant and the native born. Native-born citizens, however, need to change even more than immigrants do.[64]

While citizenship is important to attain, legal permanent residents should, advocates of this approach argued, enjoy similar rights and benefits to Americans. The only rights that can be justifiably denied to legal aliens are those that concern certain political activities (such as voting). Excluding legal residents from the welfare safety net compromises their socioeconomic integration and creates a group of permanently marginalized residents.[65] Such an approach also encouraged immigrants to become citizens solely because the alternative was serious economic hardship. Further, the naturalization process itself mistakenly stressed attitudinal rather than behavioral attachment. Participation in electoral and organizational politics is crucial to good citizenship but, as the political scientists Louis Desipio and Harry Pachon (the latter of whom served as president of the National Association of Latino Elected Officials [NALEO]), pointed out, the current naturalization process does not create such citizens. Indeed, the fundamental threat to citizenship is an overly bureaucratic naturalization process that has discouraged many applicants from attempting or completing the process.[66]

What, then, should be done? Proponents of greater minority group representation applauded rights advocates' arguments for noncitizen voting rights. But they worried that the demographic characteristics of most Latino noncitizens suggested that they would not exercise the franchise. Noncitizens, most of whom are Latino, have had the right to vote in New York school board elections since 1968, but few have done so.[67] DeSipio and Rodolfo de la Garza proposed instead an additional way for immigrants to naturalize. They suggested "that a limited five-year noncitizen voting privilege be granted to new immigrants. If during this five-year period, the immigrant regularly exercises the vote, he or she will have been deemed to have demonstrated the behavior of a good citizen and will have the naturalization examination requirements waived."[68] Latino organizations followed a second strategy that DeSipio called a civil rights approach. They emphasized that the large number of Latino noncitizens limited their ethnic political power. In response, these groups experimented with different strategies for increasing naturalization rates and went on to "make demands for some form of redress, specifically federal support for and encouragement of naturalization." The first group to follow this strategy, NALEO, launched a combined research, advocacy, and outreach program in the mid-1980s. NALEO developed citizenship services centers that were adopted by other local and national ethnic and immigrant advocacy groups.[69]

Proponents of greater minority representation saw dual citizenship as another way to increase political engagement. Immigrants who view American citizenship as inclusive would naturalize sooner and integrate faster, argued Gary Rubin, public policy director of the New York Association for New Americans.[70] In their view, dual citizenship posed no challenges to the civic or national dimensions of U.S. citizenship: "Dual Mexican-Americans who advocate policies that benefit Mexico are little different from Catholics who advocate policies endorsed by the Church or members of Amnesty International who write their congressman at their organization's behest," law professor Peter Spiro suggested. "There are no questions of disloyalty here, only of interests and identities and of different modes of social contribution."[71] Indeed, immigrants' attachment to their country of origin had not prevented them from acting loyally toward their adopted country, indeed, from fighting and dying for it.[72] One can be a member of two families, a birth family and a marriage family, and feel equally, if differently, committed to both. Becoming a citizen, therefore, is not an end in itself but a part of the process of ensuring that immigrants come to be represented in American politics.

The Return of the Nation

As the rights and the representative perspectives became entrenched among ethnic advocates and academics in the 1980s and 1990s, a significantly different response became prominent in popular political discourse. This response reflected a range of views and concerns, and its proponents did not clearly articulate a unique model of membership. Several resolutions were introduced in Congress to revise the Fourteenth Amendment, ending the entitlement to birthright citizenship and denying citizenship to the U.S.-born children of undocumented aliens. In California, Proposition 187 denied medical services in public hospitals and education in public schools to illegal aliens. At the federal level, in 1996 Congress denied social benefits such as food stamps and supplemental security income to many legal permanent residents; this welfare legislation signaled a revival of the distinction between citizens and aliens.

In response to the Oklahoma City bombing, in 1996 Congress passed the Anti-Terrorism and Effective Death Penalty Act, which required the rapid detention and removal of criminal and illegal aliens and secret deportation tribunals for those who could be tied to foreign terrorist organizations. It also limited conventional hardship waivers and appeal rights for certain categories of aliens and made many of these changes retroactive.[73] Controversies also broke out over accusations that the INS, under pressure from the Democratic Party, was lowering its standards for naturalization, enabling more new citizens to participate in the 1996 elections and cheapening the meaning of citizenship. And in California again, voters in 1998 approved Proposition 227, which required English to be the primary language of educational instruction. Throughout this period advocates of restricting immigration became more vocal, and a national commission proposed reducing the level of legal immigration by one-third.

Some of the major groups pressing for limits on immigration in the 1980s and 1990s emerged from traditionally liberal constituencies. Concerns about population growth and ecological stability drove some environmentalists to become leading advocates of restricting immigration.[74] Other groups that sprang up to press for limits argued that the U.S. asylum and refugee policies, coupled with increases in illegal immigration, had overwhelmed the courts and the bureaucracy to such a degree that the INS could not control the borders and the police could not deal with the rise in immigrant-related crime, and that illegal aliens were placing an especially heavy burden on the social welfare system, especially in health care.[75]

Traditional nativist views that emphasized Americans' racial superiority and immigrant cultures' deficiencies surfaced, but it was difficult to determine whether those with environmental and regulatory concerns shared those beliefs. Public opinion surveys found that most Americans' beliefs about immigrants were inconsistent, ambivalent, and weakly held.[76] When citizens were asked in the late 1980s about their definition of American identity, they emphasized belief in God and speaking English.[77] Compared to Americans' attitudes toward immigrants in the early and mid-twentieth century, these concerns over religion and language were considerably less exclusionary. Whatever the role of racial beliefs, it was also clear that these proposals were driven by a complex mix of concerns about a loss of sovereignty and the erosion of law, the insulation of immigration policy from public control, and the assimilation of newcomers. "[W]hile Americans are frequently depicted as anti-immigrant," Peter Schuck noted, "Americans will tolerate relatively high levels of immigration, and even increases in certain categories, as long as they are satisfied that newcomers pay their own way, don't get special breaks and obey the law."[78]

In the 1980s and early 1990s, many Americans responded to a prolonged period in which law and policy emphasized individual and group rights by turning to their majoritarian institutions and instruments of rule—Congress and the initiative process—to "revalue" a citizenship they feared had been cheapened. These efforts were part of a broader movement to revalue citizenship among native-born citizens, a movement that aimed to balance rights with obligations and sparked proposals ranging from character education and national service for the middle class to work requirements for the poor and corporate responsibility for the wealthy. This larger effort to restore social cohesion was carried out at all levels of government and society, including, for example, federal efforts to control or at least label violent television programming and local initiatives to gain control over quality of life issues by imposing penalties for panhandling, vagrancy, and public drinking, and by emphasizing community policing programs.[79]

In the debates over immigration and citizenship, two conceptions of citizenship came to be articulated especially clearly. The first celebrated the notion that what it means to be an American is defined by sharing a distinctly European cultural heritage. To a variety of commentators, the large influx of immigrants from a diverse set of cultures threatened to undermine the cultural homogeneity that makes democratic politics possible. For cultural nationalists, the object of affection is the nation, not universal political principles or the Constitution. The Constitution is merely an instrument of a people already formed by their cultural affinity. The preamble's aspiration to "secure the blessings of liberty to ourselves and our posterity," observed Peter Brimelow, a *Forbes* magazine journalist and author of the influential book *Alien Nation*, meant only "the specific posterity of those men who signed that document. They represented a full-fledged nation." Cultural nationalists acknowledged that the colonists broke with England by emphasizing individual allegiance to a set of political principles. But they thought this revolution was only possible, and that the Founders understood it as such, because the colonists possessed an Anglo-Saxon cultural and racial heritage that made them especially prepared for the demands of free government.[80]

Cultural nationalists argued that Americans must subscribe to a set of common political principles. Their affection, however, is reserved for their countrymen, not for those principles. Indeed, they contended that such cultural homogeneity is a precondition for the emotional attachment that makes free government possible. Abstract political principles are only realizable in a thick cultural or racial context.

Citizenship is "natural" rather than synthetic or created and America embodies—and has since its inception—an already existing people. America is a stable concept, both culturally and ideologically, unfolding its providential role in history rather than evolving toward an uncertain future.

Some immigrants, cultural nationalists asserted, are simply not suited to assimilate and to adopt American principles, habits, and culture. "If we had to take a million immigrants in, say Zulus, next year, or Englishmen, and put them in Virginia," asked the 1992 presidential candidate Patrick Buchanan, "what group would be easier to assimilate and would cause less problems for the people of Virginia?"[81] Cultural nationalists, like the Federalists Gouverneur Morris and Theodore Sedgwick in the 1780s and 1790s, further contended that the diversity a multiethnic society brings invites conflicts that cannot be managed by shared political principles. They differed from their Federalist predecessors in that the latter group doubted that immigrants *in general* lacked the instinctive patriotism that government needs, whereas the former focused more on the cultural deficits possessed by non-white and non-European immigrants. "Racial justice," Lawrence Auster of the American Immigration Control Foundation explained, "means that the majority in a country treats minorities fairly and equally; it does not mean that the majority is required to turn itself into a minority."[82] Yet this is precisely what Auster believed was happening:

> It is only since the 1960s, with the great increase in the numbers of people from non-European backgrounds, that the battle cry of cultural relativism has become ideologically dominant. In demanding that non-European national cultures, as cultures, be given the same importance as the European-American national culture, the multiculturalists are declaring that the non-European groups are unable or unwilling to assimilate as European immigrants have in the past, and that for the sake of these nonassimilating groups American society must be radically transformed.[83]

The problems that concern cultural nationalists related more to admissions policy than to citizenship. To the extent that they paid attention to naturalization policy, they advocated lengthening the residency requirement from five to ten or more years, rigorously enforcing the English-language requirement, abolishing exemptions, and generally discouraging foreign residents access to the political community. In their view the qualities of American citizenship are difficult for immigrants to learn, especially those from Latin America. For immigrants America does admit, however unwisely, vigorous programs of Americanization are necessary. Americans have "the right to insist that immigrants, whatever their race, become Americans."[84]

The cultural position dismissed the notion of human rights as itself an oxymoron, at least insofar as those rights are anything but abstract notions of negative freedom. Its proponents shared with Gouverneur Morris a basic distrust of those Morris derided as "citizens of the world." Cultural nationalists specifically favored reducing the scope of rights and protections immigrants enjoy. Their goal was to make migration to the United States less desirable by firmly distinguishing the rights of citizens from those due aliens. For cultural nationalists, it was especially important to reject all forms of dual citizenship. In their view, individuals cannot maintain dual nationalities without damaging one society or the other. After all, individuals can only maintain a single identification with an ethnic group if a well-ordered world is to remain stable. Dual citizenship is especially worrisome with regard to a contiguous nation like Mexico, said Dan Stein, executive director of the Federation for American Immigration Reform, given the view championed by some Mexican American advocates that the Southwest should be returned to Mexico.[85]

The cultural nationalist position was sharply censured by neoconservative scholars, opinion writers, and policymakers who believed that immigrants can and should be turned into Americans through a process of assimilation. In contrast to the cultural nationalists, these analysts stressed that American identity is primarily defined by consent to a set of shared civic principles. In contrast to advocates of increased minority representation, they regarded these principles as fixed goals to which Americans aspire, not principles subject to interpretation or negotiation. America's steadfast progress toward realizing these principles for all its citizens has made it a "universal nation," a nation based on universal principles and uniquely open to citizens from all nations.

Universal nationalists attended as well to the nationalist dimension of citizenship. They held that the English language, the Protestant work ethic, and a deep love of country are necessary supports for a nation based on shared political principles. These characteristics, as well as civic principles, can be learned and need not be formed solely by birth or early education. Universal nationalists followed Madison in his conviction that immigrants can and will become good citizens if they enter a nation committed to a strong form of civic education. And like Madison's compatriot, James Wilson, they linked immigration and liberty, believing that new immigrants who are not led astray by ethnic advocates will strengthen a culture committed to individual rather than group rights and achievement. The Irish, Italians, and Jews were all regarded as racially distinct at the time of their arrival, observes Michael Barone, a senior writer at *U.S. News and World Report*. The transformation of these groups into Americans, one fraught with tensions and far from painless, should be celebrated as a harbinger of a future America that will likewise incorporate blacks, Latinos, and Asians.[86]

Universal nationalists distinguished between what Peter Salins, a senior fellow at the Manhattan Institute, calls "assimilation" and "acculturation." The former involves identifying with the nation's ideals, the latter with a particular culture. Assimilation represents a civic commitment that requires the acceptance of the liberal, universalist ideas embedded in the U.S. Constitution, basic civic and social competencies, and a recognition of oneself as an American. In this view, the maintenance of cultural ethnicity by immigrants does not preclude their ability to maintain civic commitments. Salins notes that Timothy McVeigh was acculturated but not assimilated; while he shared similar cultural characteristics with other Americans, his hatred of America's ethnic diversity and the universalist principles that generated and legitimated that diversity meant that he was not assimilated. In contrast, Salins approvingly points to Hasidic Jews, Mormons, and insular groups of Chinese Americans as examples of groups that are assimilated but not acculturated.[87]

For universal nationalists, Americans' acceptance of immigrants who assimilate has been a key to how the United States has successfully forged a multiethnic, democratic polity. Native-born citizens have accepted newcomers by "letting them come, letting them quickly become citizens, according them a full complement of American civil rights, and treating them in myriad ways, both large and small, as equals. They have employed them, let them buy homes in their neighborhoods, let them join their social organizations, even let them marry their sons and daughters."[88] That acceptance, however, is based on immigrants' becoming patriotic Americans—taking pride in their new national identity and seeing themselves and their children as belonging to the American people. It does not entail providing public protection for immigrants' ethnic identities. While universal nationalists acknowledged that some aspects of the first Americanization movement went too far, they affirmed the movement as an honorable effort to create harmony.[89]

The naturalization process, in their view, should infuse new citizens with a sense of duty, responsibility, and loyalty; it should do more than merely grant a set of political entitlements. Newcomers should study America's values and history and make a considered act of commitment to their new identity. "Preparation for the tests and the ceremony of citizenship has long been a powerful instrument of unity," commented John J. Miller, vice president of the Center for Equal Opportunity, "an engine of assimilation that turns newcomers into citizens who understand our political traditions and are proud to be Americans." The syndicated columnist Georgie Anne Geyer described previous waves of immigrants as deeply committed to becoming citizens and Americans as having always thought the citizenship process mattered tremendously. Naturalization procedures rigorously tested applicants for their understanding of and commitment to an uncontested notion of American identity. In the early 1990s, however, Geyer, Miller, and other universal nationalists worried that Americanization had been unfairly discredited as a nativist concept and that the central role naturalization plays in this process had been devalued. Few immigrants, they charged, cared enough to become citizens. By the middle of the decade, these worries changed to concerns that immigrants were rushing to naturalize for purely material reasons—to retain benefits that the federal government was threatening to take away. In both cases, the naturalization process had lost its integrity and the value of citizenship had been denigrated.[90]

Geyer and other universal nationalists worried as well that the greater prevalence of dual citizenship would inhibit assimilation and divide immigrants' loyalty and attention. As a person's affection and commitment are divided among different interests that affection and commitment will also weaken. Indeed, Geyer asserted that dual nationality may dilute loyalty so significantly that rather than doubling their loyalties dual nationals will have none.[91] Others argued that America represents a distinct set of moral and political values that are not compatible with those of other nations, even other liberal democracies. Dual citizenship threatened the core of American self-government, the concept of "we the people," a people consisting of individual citizens with equal rights and obligations. "Dual citizenship violates the concept of equal citizenship," charged the American Enterprise Institute's John Fonte. "It means that some individuals are more equal than others. It means that some individuals are supercitizens; like medieval Electors in the Holy Roman Empire they have voting power in more than one polity and are loyal to more than one constitutional order."[92]

These four conceptions of citizenship—immigrant rights, minority representation, cultural nationalism, and universal nationalism—are still prominent today. They draw on different strands in the American tradition of citizenship. The rights position stresses the fundamentally human (rather than civic or national) basis to freedom and equality. It especially dismisses feelings of belonging at the national level. The minority representation perspective is also wary of claims about national attachment; it prizes ethnic coalition building and multicultural policies that advance the standing of immigrants. The cultural position values abstract civic ideals, especially notions of negative freedom, but regards them as realizable only in a thick cultural or racial context. In contrast, universal nationalists believe that citizenship is a matter of political artifice and who constitutes "we the people" is more a matter of consent than culture. What distinguishes these views and the broader debate among them from debates at the Founding and in the Progressive Era is the separation of civic nationalist positions into civic *or* national positions alone and the increasingly extreme definitions given to each. By the mid-1990s, the separation of these strands would be challenged by a disparate group of moderate civic nationalists, a challenge to which we now turn.

CHAPTER EIGHT

A New Civic Nationalism

BEGINNING in the mid-1990s, a remarkably wide variety of moderate civic nationalist policymakers, politicians, opinion makers, and scholars began to articulate a new position. These nationalists have treated the United States as
more than a set of abstract political principles. They see that a robust national
identity is required to bind Americans. At the same time, this school contends
that America is based on neither racial nor religious superiority. This revived
civic nationalism combines ideas that today are often considered antithetical—
inclusiveness and nationalism—and covers a significant swath of the political
spectrum from left to right. Its perspective is shared by influential intellectuals
from the social democratic left, the communitarian center, and, to varying degrees, the neoconservative right, and its sensibility is represented in Congress
and in state government.[1]

This new ordering of the intellectual and, potentially, the political universe
in the United States is reminiscent of the Progressive Era. Then, as today, Americans were pressed to address the nature of their Union by a combination of
economic dislocation, cultural upheaval, demographic change, and challenges
to established moral and scientific paradigms. A broadly defined civic nationalism emerged from that era and from the crucibles of the Depression, World
War II, the civil rights movement, and the Great Society. During the last thirty
years, that nationalism has been challenged internally by group discontent and
individual alienation and externally by the globalization of markets and the
movement of people. Over the course of the twenty-first century, that identity
will be further tested by simultaneous trends toward political devolution and
supranational evolution, massive demographic shifts and mounting cultural
tensions, the advent of new technologies, and the forces of global markets.

Modern civic nationalists often note the parallels between the Progressive
Era and today. They draw extensively on writers and political leaders from that
period in articulating their solutions for our time. Yet, for all their agreement,
modern civic nationalists draw on distinctly different ideas of national identity
developed at the beginning of this century: Randolph Bourne's vision of a
transnational America and the new nationalism of Teddy Roosevelt. Bourne
and Roosevelt shared a concern for the cultural and conceptual dimensions of
citizenship, even as they offered radically divergent conceptions of allegiance,
nationality, and ethnicity. At critical junctures, each of their views was ambiguous and unclear as to its limits. Roosevelt could not compete with the more

exclusionary and coercive forces of nationalism that he had helped unleash, even as his own vision and associated social movement became more restrictive. Bourne was tossed aside more easily than Roosevelt, in part because he was not allied with any significant political movement and, in part, because of the inscrutability of his vision of American life. Neither view prevailed and both men died depressed and dispirited within two weeks of each other.

The Progressive coalition that for a while included both men's ideas was ultimately riven apart. Can civic nationalism today offer a coherent and compelling vision that avoids that fate? The effort to revive a moderate and civic nationalism involves risks and trade-offs, but I believe it can sustain a robust and diverse America in an era when new forms of political community are emerging and contending with one another. The version of civic nationalism that offers the most promise today, I argue, is one that draws on James Madison, as well as Roosevelt and Bourne. Madison's supple and versatile nationalism is particularly well suited to confronting the problems posed by both too strong and too weak a sense of national identity. This versatility can best advance a shared sense of national citizenship that is responsive to the major challenges of the twenty-first century.

BOURNEIAN AND ROOSEVELTIAN CIVIC NATIONALISM

There are two primary strands of civic nationalism today: Bourneian and Rooseveltian. These strands are neither monolithic nor mutually exclusive—some civic nationalists draw on both Bourne and Roosevelt—but they are sufficiently different that it is useful to distinguish between them.[2] The Bourneian strand argues that a multicultural nationalism is consistent with both the new realities of global life and the highest aspirations of the American people. It regards a unitary American identity as neither possible nor desirable. More than ever before, immigrants enter an ethnically diverse America where they are able to maintain cultural, political, and economic connections with their home countries. This acceptance of a more multicultural society undermines what the prominent immigration analyst Alexander Aleinikoff derides as the Rooseveltian aim "to mold new immigrants into an American stock, reasserting Western values and excluding people who do not abide by them."[3] In contrast, Aleinikoff celebrates rather than laments the proliferation of multiple loyalties. In his view, attachment to one identity does not necessarily mean less attachment to another. Nor is it clear that one's national allegiance crowds out all other commitments. "People talk about symbolic problems of dual nationality," he notes. "It's very hard to identify concrete problems with it. . . . People are a bundle of allegiances, to families, nations, even the schools they attended."[4]

Nonetheless, as a practical matter, the nation-state remains the primary vehicle for protecting rights and practicing democracy, and Bourneians like Aleinikoff embrace it in contrast to their earlier, rights-oriented criticisms. The nation-state, in their view, remains the best means to encourage "us to look beyond the immediate demands of those alive today to the interest of future generations." Bourneian civic nationalists like David Hollinger, a well-known historian who helped revise the National History Standards, see the American nation as a vehicle for advancing the values of a "rooted cosmopolitanism," including "recognition, acceptance, and eager exploration of diversity" as well as "a push for solidarities less all-inclusive than the species-wide 'we.' "[5] A sense of shared American purpose is necessary for redistributing resources within the United States, helping minorities achieve greater equality, and expanding the circle of humans whom Americans care about and feel responsible for.

Bourneian civic nationalists distinguish their notion of allegiance from an emphasis on unchanging civic principles. In their view, a commitment to shared principles produces only an agreement to disagree, rather than a more robust sense of identification. What is needed, instead, is a sense of "mutuality," a Bourneian commitment to go beyond mere nondiscrimination and to actively engage others on their own terms.[6] This emphasis on mutuality and identification with the whole over the parts diverges from a multiculturalism that emphasizes the permanency of group differences. It sets itself against any view that would interfere with the "open-ended interaction [that changes] both immigrant and native cultures." This brand of nationalism embraces Bourne's notion of a dynamic relationship between new and old, a process that rejects the idea of America as a fixed entity. For Aleinikoff, America is a "contract under constant renegotiation." Hollinger, too, emphasizes dynamic interaction among groups, but he devotes equal attention to the historical roots of the American nation. Americans, he emphasizes, share a past that consists of quarrels over the meaning of American identity as well as a common project of expanding human freedom.[7]

Proponents of a Rooseveltian nationalism deride the Bourneian emphasis on an America constituted by mutually respecting groups; they place their faith in the melting pot and are sharply critical of group-based polices like affirmative action. Some, like Michael Lind, who in the 1980s managed the neoconservative policy journal *The Public Interest* and in the 1990s became a senior fellow at the New America Foundation, stress that the American nation, like all other nations, is formed by language and habits, by "common folkways and a common vernacular culture." This is not a patriotism based on ideology; "it has more to do with family, neighborhood, customs, and historical memories than with constitutions or political philosophies." Lind aims to use this patriotism to establish a new "trans-American melting pot" by means of "universal miscegenation and upward-leveling, race-blending, and class-blurring."[8]

Lind worries especially about the undemocratic consequences of concentrated economic authority and the separatism bred by an inflated devotion to material success. He calls this the "Brazilianization" of American life, in which the danger to the American nation stems less from balkanization along racial lines than from a division along class lines, in which non-whites and poor whites are consigned to the bottom of the social hierarchy. Such a system is characterized by the withdrawal of elites, including some minorities, into private neighborhoods, schools, police protection, and health care—"a nation-within-a-nation."[9]

Other proponents of a Rooseveltian civic nationalism, like the duo of William Kristol, former chief of staff to Vice President Dan Quayle and, in the 1990s, the founding editor of the leading neoconservative magazine *The Weekly Standard*, and David Brooks, a senior editor at *The Weekly Standard* who in 2003 became an op-ed columnist for the *New York Times*, aim to rescue conservatives from an antigovernment, libertarian philosophy. They want to rejuvenate national citizenship, to remind Americans that "citizenship entails more than just voting, and the business of America is more than just business."[10] Kristol and Brooks's arguments are rooted in patriotism rather than religion, appealing to public virtues like "courage, honor, integrity, and duty," and shifting the roots of nationalism "from religious faith to the Declaration of Independence, from the cross to America." This shift means to them a Roosevelt-like stance against selfish private interests—"tobacco companies, pork-barrel spenders, special interests, overreaching federal regulators"—rather than a crusade to regulate morality in private life.[11]

While the ideology of "leave us alone" made sense in moving the American people away from a large, active federal government, Kristol and Brooks say, "wishing to be left alone isn't a governing doctrine." "How," they ask, "can Americans love their nation if they hate its government?" That ideology is merely a politics of resentment at a time when conservatives should be inspiring citizens to enlarge their aspirations. Without larger purposes, Brooks fears, "democracy has a tendency to slide into nihilistic mediocrity." This mediocrity is embodied by a new upper class of temperate, tolerant strivers for self-actualization, a class he insists needs to see that politics is about more than personal discovery or self-interest. Politics, in his view, is a noble calling; its fundamental aim is to get Americans to "think of ourselves as citizens, not merely consumers; we should serve the public good, not merely private interest. We should be represented in Washington as Americans, not merely as members of interest groups or taxpayers."[12]

When civic nationalism came onto the scene in the mid-1990s, it offered to transcend traditional political divisions. In our hypereconomy of ideas, the fissures within it have rapidly become apparent. Across the wide range of nationalists who are committed to an inclusive and robust civic America, many of those fissures cannot be bridged. A multicultural nationalism, to take one example, is a goal for some and an oxymoron for others. Still, these nationalists differ from ardent multiculturalists and fervent globalists in their shared view that America is a remarkable nation. To some, America is an exceptional nation, unique in human history; to others it occupies a special, if not unique, position among nation-states. Like both Roosevelt and Bourne before them, they believe America must create its own traditions and play a distinctive role in the world.[13] But if a modern American nationalism is to avoid the fate of its Progressive Era predecessor, its proponents will need to confront difficult questions about how the civic and national dimensions of American citizenship can reinforce rather than undermine each other. In this, Bourneian and Rooseveltian civic nationalists face distinct challenges.

Bourneian civic nationalists advance a conception of American identity and ideals that seems radically open to change. They stress that Americans have different ideas about what being an American means and emphasize a process of dynamic interaction that privileges flux over fixity. This preference for process raises the same questions as Bourne's emphasis on the "pioneer spirit": How does a predilection for change relate to established conceptions of national identity and civic principles? Does an identity based on commitment and process have sufficiently integrative force? Bourneian proponents of a civic nationalism do not sufficiently address what, if any, limits they would place on a transformative conception of national solidarity, one in which citizens may believe in new principles and ideals and the nation may be reconfigured. These broad conceptual questions require answers, and not simply as a matter of political theory. If, as it sometimes seems, the Bourneians' embrace of nationalism is primarily directed toward transcending the nation itself in favor of broader forms of governance and identification, citizens who disagree with those aims will not subscribe to their vision. Moreover, it seems unlikely that citizens will continue to regard their nation with deep affection and attachment if its purposes are defined too instrumentally. To the extent that those purposes reflect a worldview that privileges individual liberty, critical judgment, and chosen obligations, they may be especially at odds with the reverence and affection for the nation that Bourneian nationalists depend on.[14]

If Bourneian nationalists' affection for global institutions risks increasing civic alienation, Rooseveltian nationalists can be insufficiently attentive to meeting the demands of a rapidly globalizing world.[15] The Rooseveltian nationalists' uniform and unbending conception of allegiance does not adequately account for the reality of individuals' lives and international relations in a world characterized by significant increases in sociocultural, economic, and political exchange. Even if the United States projects its military and economic power more strenuously in the twenty-first century, new forms of regional and global political institutions are likely to develop, forms that introduce new questions about the meaning of citizenship and loyalty. The changing structure of the global economy has not made the nation-state obsolete, but it has raised important issues of scale and the design of political institutions that can attend to the complex interrelation of national, subnational, and supranational interests and identities.[16] Rooseveltian civic nationalists downplay these difficult issues.

Both Bourneian and Rooseveltian civic nationalists clearly reject any notion of ethnic federalism. Yet Bourneians sometimes treat groups rather than individuals as the key components of American nationalism. The characterization of America as a "contract under constant renegotiation" by contending racial groups suggests more than simply acknowledging the role group consciousness and group effort has played throughout American history; it suggests a continuing and publicly acknowledged and rewarded role for group rights. This possibility raises the question of whether "a commitment to the continued flourishing of the country" can bind citizens when their views of the country's meaning and values are sufficiently divergent and the process for managing those differences is negotiation among groups.

Rooseveltians explicitly counterpose their project to "talk about building a bridge to a multicultural, diverse and politically correct 21st century."[17] For them, a vigorous, unified, national identity requires opposition to bilingual education, affirmative action, and other group-based policies. Yet merely to condemn all policies that attend to group recognition and benefits hardly seems sufficient. As Peter Skerry points out, such a stance ignores the extent to which Rooseveltian nationalists' own favorite policies, such as charter schools or faith-based social services, depend on the existence of robust ethnic ties. This stance also slights the critical role group recognition and benefits played in the assimilation of earlier waves of immigrants.[18]

Most civic nationalists recognize that building national community in the United States has often proceeded in tandem with the exclusion of minorities and restrictions on individual rights. Yet civic nationalism has also served as a prophylactic against both more coercive forms of nationalism and utopian ideas of free-floating rights, as well as a tool for marshaling the social resources required to achieve large-scale goals. At the Founding, it was the moderate nationalism championed by James Madison and John Marshall that proved most resistant to narrower forms of nationalism. In the Progressive Era, it was the moderate civic nationalism of Jane Addams and Frances Kellor that fueled the development of the first large-scale programs of practical assistance to immigrants in American history. And it was Roosevelt's and Croly's new nationalism that offered the most realistic alternative to unalloyed nativism and succeeded in expanding who was included in the American nation.

Some contemporary Rooseveltian nationalists distinguish between a nativist dark side to Roosevelt's nationalism and a constructive and inclusive side, though it remains to be seen whether the latter can be achieved without the former.[19] Bourneian civic nationalists especially acknowledge that there are risks in stressing the centrality of national solidarity: "[C]oercion is obviously a large part of the story of American belonging," Hollinger states flatly. But simply because the moderate nationalism of the Progressive Era gave way to more coercive, exclusionary policies does not mean such a dynamic has to repeat itself today. The limits on diversity imposed by the Immigration Act of 1924 and by the Americanization movement may well have strengthened Americans' sense of a shared nationality in ways that helped Franklin Roosevelt gain support for his New Deal. But how decisive these events proved remains unclear. Would Eisenhower not have ordered the National Guard to enforce the integration of schools in Little Rock, Hollinger asks, if blacks, Asians, and Germans had not been excluded or subordinated earlier?[20]

Whether the dangers of coercion and exclusion are worth risking today depends on both the promise of civic nationalism and on what the realistic alternatives are to it. In the previous chapter I described four models of citizenship as dominating debates over immigration and citizenship at the end of the twentieth century. Are these models—the rights, representation, cultural, or universal models—preferable to a civic nationalist one?

Alternatives to Civic Nationalism

Rights advocates correctly suggest that new conceptions of political community linking the local to the international may evolve in the twenty-first century. But combining commitment to others with respect for pluralism is an even more difficult project when moved from the national to the transnational level. The capacity to enforce rights depends on a sense of community that creates a recognition of such rights and a willingness to sacrifice for their achievement.[21] Rights advocates tend to dismiss particularist elements that contribute to national loyalty as inappropriate attempts to establish cultural preconditions for citizenship. They thus miss the extent to which democratic reforms have emerged from civic nationalist movements, not simply from context-transcending rights claims. They further confuse a cultural monism that is no longer demanded of immigrants in the United States with the sense of trust that must be continually generated. By separating rights from nationalism, rights' advocates underestimate the extent to which a sense of nationhood makes both liberty and justice possible.

Rights advocates approve of the disagreggation of collective identity, political membership, and social rights taking place in many European countries. The Europeans, on the whole, provide a wide range of social benefits and local voting rights to noncitizens. The United States provides fewer social benefits to noncitizens and has resisted sporadic efforts to offer local voting rights to immigrants before they naturalize. For many rights advocates, the American model is seriously deficient. Yet that model presumes that newcomers will eventually be recognized as Americans. By contrast, the European approach has offered a way to avoid the higher costs of fully incorporating immigrants as equal citizens and members of a shared national identity. The generous provision of social rights, and in some cases local voting rights, can be seen as a way of responding to the needs of immigrants while maintaining an ethnic definition of citizenship and nationhood.[22] The American model faces serious challenges today, but the turmoil over immigration that is roiling Europe indicates the perils involved in disaggreggating collective identity, political membership, and social rights.[23]

Advocates of increased minority group representation championed naturalization when it was neglected by the INS, the political parties, and most private, voluntary organizations. Their approach is a reminder that naturalization and group representation have always played important roles in both the advancement and incorporation of ethnic groups and the general health of a democratic society. They also correctly call attention to the fact that, for many immigrants, the difficulty of becoming a citizen is less related to substance and symbolism and more to the capacity to endure long lines, insensitive staff, and confusing forms. The trouble with this vision is that it tends to reduce citizenship to one aspect of its civic dimension—electoral and organizational politics—at a time when that politics has been weakened and partly replaced by an approach that accents what Harry Boyte and Jennifer O'Donoghue call "service delivery—be it of language classes, job training, or welfare provisions." "In this approach," they write, "immigrants are perceived as deficient, needy, and powerless. The role of organizations is to provide services for them. Immigrants enter public life largely as consumers and claimants, demanding their 'right' to a fair share. . . . [T]hey are encouraged to compete in an arena of grievances and deficiencies."[24]

The structure of the political system further exacerbates this emphasis on grievances in the way it rewards the "virtual" representation of minorities rather than actual representation. This system diminishes the opportunities for newcomers to understand American civic principles and to engage in democratic politics. It teaches a subgroup ethnic nationalism that discourages identification with the nation as a whole and enables politicians to sustain extreme positions that are at odds with those of their immigrant constituents. Nor does the representation approach address the deeper issues when it comes to naturalization. The issue is not how to make naturalization easier, which is how the representation advocates tend to frame matters, but whether we can make it more coherent and meaningful and ensure that applicants are well prepared to become citizens.

Both the rights and the representation frameworks make it difficult to understand the importance of a robust national identity. Advocates of these views tend to dismiss all proposals to alter the social or civic status of immigrants as motivated simply by racial and economic fears and as reflective of the fundamentally illiberal nature of appeals to nationhood in the United States.[25] Criminal justice professor Susan Bibler Coutin, for instance, writes that Proposition 187 and challenges to affirmative action in higher education and to bilingual education in public schools are "systematically interrelated" with the "racism, sexism, and xenophobia" apparent in the Rodney King verdict and the rioting that followed, and "the searing debates about race and domestic violence during the O. J. Simpson trial." For American studies professor George Sanchez, the

1980s and 1990s witnessed the resurgence of "a nativism that is as virulent as any that has gone before." Every invocation of the American nation, the historian Matthew Frye Jacobson writes, is itself evidence of a coercive, exclusionary nativism as bad as or worse than in previous eras.[26]

These charges of nativism and racism make it difficult to discuss a range of issues relating to immigration and citizenship. Real concerns about the rate of Latinos' acquisition of English, or worries that policies like bilingual education have actually delayed that acquisition, are dismissed by rights and representation advocates as fantasies promulgated by English speakers who "fear being alienated amidst other languages." Similarly, arguments made by both liberals and conservatives that the racial preferences developed to aid blacks should not apply in the same way to Latinos and Asians, especially those who are recent immigrants, as well as worries that multicultural education places too much stress on separatist identities, are dismissed as akin to "papist conspiracy theories." And serious, complex debates over whether immigrants are an asset or an economic liability are reduced to a conflict between careful analysts who appreciate the contributions made by immigrants and those who traffic in stereotypes.[27]

These blunderbuss assessments do not address the needs of immigrants or the concerns of citizens. Instead, they encourage the policies that rights and representation advocates most fear. Take, for example, immigrant advocates' strategy of clogging the asylum system until a blanket amnesty can be attained and their efforts to teach immigrants that law is arbitrary and naturalization is a purely political strategy to gain power. Coutin celebrates these strategies as intermediate efforts toward a "moral order in which citizenship and justice would be linked."[28] In this order, social citizenship would be primary and legal citizenship irrelevant. Yet these legal strategies and the normative worldview that undergirds them risk weakening the political support necessary to protect the most vulnerable. Such maneuvers bolster critics' contention that temporary programs of protection are merely ruses to gain time until permanent settlement can be won, and that the naturalization process has been hijacked by advocates who disdain its very purpose of making citizens who are committed to their new identity as Americans.

Some of the recent changes in U.S. policy toward immigrants are misguided, such as barring new immigrants from receiving certain welfare benefits; other changes pose real threats to the procedural rights of the foreign born. Proposition 187 was discriminatory and divisive, although it called attention to the unequal burdensome impacts of immigrants on state and especially local governments. (It was also struck down in federal court on the grounds that only the nation can make decisions about membership, not the states.)[29] Still other policies seem contradictory, such as increased border enforcement coupled with provisions for new amnesties for illegal aliens, or hypocritical, such as placing limits on health care for illegal aliens in light of the economy's heavy dependence on such workers. As the sociologist Alan Wolfe comments, "From an economic standpoint as well as a moral standpoint, there can be few more unattractive sights than apathetic Californians born on one side of the border turning their backs on hard-working Mexicans born on the other side."[30]

To note the hypocrisies, contradictions, and injustices in U.S. immigration and integration policies does not require the further claim that all policy changes are motivated by nativism and intended to further marginalize immigrants. Another California initiative, Proposition 227, ended the disastrous programs of bilingual education and cut through a political system incapable of responding to both popular will and the needs of immigrants, although it remains unclear whether a provision for money to be appropriated for adult English classes will be heeded. "Distinctions," the Bournean civic nationalist David Hollinger writes, "are in order":

> Not all criticisms of multiculturalism are at odds with the ideal of a culturally diverse nation. Nor are all proposals for imposing restrictions on immigration racist. Stronger efforts to restrict illegal immigration may be justified. Within legal immigration, the priority of family reunification may not be as defensible as other bases for selecting immigrants. There is nothing inherently wrong, moreover, in the idea that a society should periodically reassess the number of immigrants it can absorb. Some pressures on foreigners to conform to American norms may not be pernicious.[31]

The rights and representation frameworks are not open to such distinctions. They especially have trouble distinguishing among a range of nationalist concerns. Rights and representation advocates miss how the initial success of some of the more extreme positions reflected, in part, a peculiar logic of citizenship: too little attention to national community left a vacuum in which illiberal nationalisms temporarily crowded out moderate ones.

Contemporary proponents of a European-based cultural nationalism offer the most vigorous defense of illiberal nationalism. They advance a conception of political identity that arises as the result of what Alexander Hamilton called "accident and force," rather than "reflection and choice." This emphasis on homogeneity had a certain logic in the context of a small republic, though even at the Founding the difficulties with its approach were apparent. But if the cultural nationalists' vision was ever a realistic possibility, it has long ceased to be so. The United States has become an irrevocably heterogenous polity and its citizens are characterized by a wide variety of overlapping and contending allegiances. Those allegiances engender all sorts of conflicts, but, as the legal scholar and former general counsel for the INS David Martin observes, "such conflict simply comes with living in a rich and complex civil society. It can usually be managed, bridged, accommodated."[32] Indeed, in the United States an important purpose of our political system and social structure is to bring contending allegiances and values into the public square where they can clash, and where individuals and groups can be accommodated.

The national community plays a key role in integrating those allegiances, but it is not sacrosanct. An environmentalist who is a U.S. citizen need not prefer that nation's interest over his or her views of what is best for the global environment. Similarly, the United States has a long history of conflicts between religious communities and the nation.[33] In a democratic society, the reality and the desirability of multiple identities engender tragic dilemmas for many citizens as they struggle with the conflicts that sometimes arise among the values propagated by familial, religious, ethnic, and national communities. On a lot of questions there may be two right answers, and citizens often have to make unpalatable and difficult choices between values that are perhaps ultimately irreconcilable.

The cultural nationalist position is eager to suppress these conflicts and the identities from which they arise. Rather than responding to a widespread sense of disaffection and distrust among citizens, then, the cultural nationalist contributes to that alienation. In a nation as diverse as the United States, the cultural position cannot generate attachment to the nation because its picture of the world does not correspond to the complexity of most citizens' lives. Further, in pressing citizens to prioritize their national identity in every circumstance, cultural nationalism threatens to overwhelm the intermediate institutions of civil society, the very sources of meaning that prevent citizens from becoming alienated in a large, heterogenous, and bureaucratic society. Its aim to explicitly reintroduce racial categorizations into immigration and immigrant policy also promises to breed considerable resentment and social fragmentation.[34]

Cultural nationalists further contribute to disaffection and distrust among citizens by drawing attention away from broader problems of membership. They suggest that the primary source of turmoil in American life is the greater cultural diversity fostered by immigration over the last thirty years. But the sources of disaffection in American life are multiple. Indeed, conflicts over identity owe less to immigration than to disagreements among Americans over issues like affirmative action and bilingual education. Immigration has even contributed to a reaction against these policies by exposing the ways in which they have been expanded far beyond their original intentions and the ways in which they have held back rather than incorporated newcomers. By drawing attention away from the domestic sources of America's problems, the cultural position falsely suggests easy answers to complex problems.[35]

Universal nationalism aims to solve the problems posed by a cultural conception of identity. It imagines that conflicts among citizens' identities can be resolved if they give their primary allegiance to a set of shared political principles that are embodied in the U.S. Constitution. It emphasizes the Constitution as a symbol of overarching unity and as the center of an American civil religion. Yet America's sacred texts, like those of most religions, have been a significant source of conflict as well as cohesion. Those constitutional values are subject to competing interpretations and are often in tension with each other, so much so as to raise the question of what, in fact, is shared. Americans may agree on the importance of individual rights such as the right to free expression, but they disagree deeply over whether this means it is constitutional to burn the American flag. Nor has the American emphasis on individualism forestalled pitched battles over group-oriented policies such as affirmative action. Despite these disagreements, shared public values do play a critical role in limiting conflicts among citizens and thus forging some degree of unity. But the sharing means less that Americans agree on the content of these values than that they recognize them as public values and carry out their debates within the context set by them.[36]

Universal nationalists also tend to paint an idealized picture of American history. They do not acknowledge the extent to which the meaning of citizenship has long been contested among competing ideals, not simply a conflict between civic ideals and political practice. They accord little weight to the racial restrictions on who could become a citizen for three-quarters of American history. Yet, as I argued in chapter 4, these restrictions reflect the challenges that competing claims of justice, history, and human nature have presented to maintaining a balance between the civic and the nationalist dimensions of citizenship. In fact, much of what Americans now think of as the nation's fundamental commitments—the expansion of democracy in the Jacksonian Era, the demise of slavery following the Civil War, the growth of a national welfare state beginning in the Progressive Era—were not foreordained; they emerged from competing interpretations about the meaning of shared political principles as well as from competition among divergent models of nationhood.[37] The danger in the universal nationalist approach is that it will sap that history of its vitality and hence diminish its capacity to engage and inspire both new and old citizens. This is especially the case when it comes to the relationship between group identity and the incorporation of immigrants. Universal nationalists' view that the melting pot has enabled anyone to become an American ignores the ways in which immigrants have been able to do so partly by distancing themselves from blacks.[38] It underplays as well the extent to which group consciousness and ethnic politics have been critical mediums through which immigrants have elbowed their way into American public life and will continue to do so.

Too much attention to civic principles also begs the question, why care about the American people? If I do not get what I want, why should I not leave, either literally by emigration or secession, or figuratively by withdrawal into a privatized world or fragmentation into subgroups? National identity includes a reverential element, what Abraham Lincoln called a "prejudice" in favor of the nation that was earned by dint of its venerability and a "conviction born of the sense of the awful price exacted by the truths of its votaries."[39] In the 1980s and 1990s, universal nationalists often underplayed this emotional, historical, and rooted dimension of citizenship in favor of a commitment to abstract, general principles.

Some did clearly indicate the need for new citizens to identify as Americans— "placing that identification ahead of any associated with their birthplace or ethnic homeland," as Peter Salins puts it.[40] But this demand was more faint in others who emphasized adherence to the American creed. Despite this faintness, some of the more fervent universal nationalists unfavorably compared contemporary immigrants to earlier waves of newcomers who, they claimed (incorrectly), had transferred their identity and allegiance immediately upon naturalization. Nor did they confront the fact that it is America's civic principles, particularly the emphasis on individual rights over communal duties, that make it especially difficult to form citizens who are committed to their country when that commitment conflicts with their personal desires or their company's bottom line. "Why should such a man who institutes government in order to secure private rights have any concern for anyone else?" Walter Berns of the American Enterprise Institute asked in 2001. "Why should he be public-spirited?"[41] This question has particularly great force in an age when the individualistic values of the free market have extended so far that they threaten the sense of obligation upon which a sturdy citizenship is dependent.

Recently, universal nationalists have devoted more attention to these questions and to the emotional and cultural wellsprings of citizenship. The Hudson Institute's John Fonte helped establish a new federal Office of Citizenship and rallied the American Legion to oppose changes in the oath of allegiance by advancing the concept of "patriotic assimilation" in which loyalty to the American nation-state is paramount. Patriotic assimilation means that a newcomer "adopts American civic values and the American heritage as his or her own" and begins "to think of American history as 'our' history, not 'their' history."[42] Fonte, like Salins, rightly emphasizes the importance of immigrants' coming to use the word "we," signifying their identification as members of the American nation. Yet loyalty is notoriously difficult to capture—and even harder to define—in a free society in which citizens manage their own multiple identities and the sometimes conflicting allegiances they produce. "My country right or wrong cannot serve as a moral injunction if, as during the Civil War, the question is which country is mine?" observes Alan Wolfe. "Religious pluralism encourages multiple loyalties. Hyphenated Americans have at least two; global capitalists often have none." Wolfe further points out that "not only was the United States created through a singular act of disloyalty, it has been continually replenished by immigrants willing to break the bonds of family, faith, and community."[43] Americans' old and new identities—cultural, religious, political—and the associations that nourish them serve as a source of meaning, a personal mooring, in a market-oriented and freedom-worshiping society, as well as a bulwark against the intrusiveness of the nation and the government. Finding ways to encourage loyalty and to stimulate attachment to the American civic nation in these circumstances is therefore as complex as it is critical. Such efforts must be undertaken in a supple and realistic manner, one that recognizes how the habits of loyalty and attachment are formed by actual experiences over time as well as by inspirational events.

A different tack is taken by the influential political thinker Samuel Huntington, who, in his 2004 book *Who Are We?* identifies an Anglo-Protestant culture as the core of American identity. This position is a significant shift from his 1981 book *American Politics*, which highlights the civic principles of the American creed. In both books, Huntington acknowledges the role of culture and creed, and recalibrating the balance between the two is entirely in line with the civic nationalist approach advanced in these pages. Indeed, his recent book is an important reminder that the American creed has cultural origins and that culture cannot simply be jettisoned like a used-up booster rocket. But his changed views are also an indicator of how bifurcated analyses of citizenship and nationalism have become. Huntington's conversion from a position that is almost entirely creedal to one that is so overwhelmingly cultural suggests how hard it is to wrestle with the difficult, messy, and ultimately necessary tensions between the two. There is something brittle and timid about any position that forces such a stark choice, a timidity that does not contrast well with a more confident, pragmatic approach that melds the two.[44]

The Evasion of Politics and the Madisonian Moment

Despite the radical differences among contemporary models of citizenship, all four models share a curious similarity: they evade the political challenge of combining civic principles with national allegiance in a way that is mutually reinforcing and that accounts for actual political practice. We can see this evasion especially clearly in the two positions most opposed to one another: immigrant rights and cultural nationalism. Both reflect the ascendence of a static conception of citizenship. Cultural conservatives see no need to turn immigrants into citizens, or to make native-born Americans into citizens, because the project of self-government is complete once a culturally defined people governs itself. Similarly, proponents of the rights perspective do not ask immigrants to undergo any transformation of consciousness. In their view, immigrants already possess what is necessary to be a full member of the polity: their personhood and their capacity to discover common interests through local political interaction. For both groups, the fact of citizenship in a particular nation-state and constitutional order is essentially redundant, since in their view social identity trumps political identity. The rights group insists that mere presence is sufficient to merit membership and that a culture of rights is sufficient to undergird democracy; the cultural nationalists believe that citizenship and democratic politics can only be sustained by a relatively homogeneous culture. In both cases, disagreement is limited to minor issues and little is left for political life to decide.

The universal and the representation models of membership seek to create citizens and hence give more space for changes on the part of immigrants and citizens. But both emphasize a narrow conception of political identity that does not go far enough in simultaneously forging national attachment and teaching civic principles. If only Americans would end discrimination, say the proponents of a representation model of citizenship, or end affirmative action, say the universal nationalists, then the new immigrants, like the old, will join the mainstream and contribute to America.

Yet the story is not as simple as either side would have us believe. Immigrants have always come to the United States for a mixture of economic, ideological, and personal reasons. Most have become full participants in American life, committed to the broader community and supportive of its constitutional values. Although many Americans feared earlier waves of immigrants, a significant expansion of democracy has often taken place after the arrival of newcomers, as it did following the surge of immigration early in the last century. But Americans' doubts about their own national identity and the weakening of many institutional capacities for incorporating newcomers have introduced greater uncertainty into whether new arrivals and current citizens will regard one another as equals who bear mutual obligations and share a common civic and national identity. The decline in local government, common public schooling, and military service, coupled with the rise of a rights-oriented culture and the celebration of individual consumption unconnected to social ends threaten the notion of a public sphere into which immigrants can become incorporated. Moreover, the 1960s and 1970s left a legacy of doubt about the fact or value of a common national identity, doubts seen most clearly in the versions of multiculturalism that characterize America as held together by few commonalities.

In these circumstances, the tensions are especially pronounced between civic principles and national allegiance as components of an American citizenship that can inform political practice and social interaction. But they are tensions that appropriately reflect the delicate balance among creating a shared sensibility, sustaining self-governance, and protecting rights. Achieving that balance is not simply a matter of combining the rights, representation, cultural, and universal perspectives. Some of these views are clearly opposed to one another. We need, instead, a conception of citizenship that can recognize some of the contributions of the four positions while advancing a holistic model of citizenship. We need a conception of citizenship that can engage citizens in negotiating multiple identities and institutional relations, while emphasizing a sense of attachment to a broader whole that integrates those commitments. How to achieve that delicate balance is an enormously difficult task for which there is no easy answer. The model of citizenship that offers the most promise is, I think, a civic nationalist one.

The most salient difference between civic nationalism today and the competing rights, representation, cultural, and universal approaches is the attention the former pays to the dynamic interdependence of allegiance and ideas. From a civic nationalist perspective, there is no one set of relationships among those dimensions of citizenship that always and everywhere applies. The civic nationalist policies forged at the Founding and in the Progressive Era emerged from competing aspirations of national identity, civic ideals, and the exigencies of political life. These policies reflected distinct challenges and called forth distinct responses that cannot be understood as part of any simple story charting the rise of a single concept of citizenship and the fall of another. They do not lend themselves to a uniform theory of citizenship. Instead, they point to the continuous political work that must be done to knit those dimensions of citizenship into a workable whole.

Both Bourneian and Rooseveltian civic nationalists continue this tradition. They aim to navigate the strains that arise between civic aspirations and the claims of both broader and narrower forms of solidarity, not eliminate them. The debate between and within these strands of civic nationalism has helped focus our attention on the content of a renewed nationalism and the groups toward whom it is directed, as well as the process by which that renewal might be carried out, and the safeguards that can be built in for dissent and disagreement.[45] Yet for all that a modern civic nationalism can learn from these forebears, it is an even earlier proponent of moderate nationalism, James Madison, whose views merit emphasizing.[46] Madison did not resolve the tensions—between universality and particularity, between civic ideals and national identity—that lay at the heart of the political order he established. He offered no general theory for all time—and that is precisely what recommends his approach to us today. In lieu of a general theory, Madison's legacy suggests an approach, a temperament, that contrasts favorably with that of Bourne and Roosevelt.

Madison articulated a supple and versatile nationalism. Unlike Roosevelt's romanticism, his sober approach was conscious of its limits and the dangers presented by too strong a sense of national identity. Madison knew that the line between a moderate and an extreme nationalism is difficult to maintain under the pressure of politics. He also saw that to sustain itself a community needed to define its boundaries and that this necessity would limit who is eligible to possess rights and how extensively those rights were protected against the incursions of the nation. A modern Madisonian civic nationalism would thus remain alert to the logic that the need for social solidarity allows more exclusionary, illiberal ideologies to prosper. It would understand that more extreme positions can offer powerful, compelling claims because they do not have to moderate their views by accounting for the protection of individual and minority rights. A Madisonian civic nationalism would attend to the dangers presented by America's illiberal traditions and seek to limit the opportunities for their resurgence.

Such an approach would further be built on the Madisonian conviction that disagreement and deliberation in the context of a commitment to the American nation are critical if every generation of citizens is to grasp the meaning of U.S. civic principles. His approach acknowledged that the search for political understanding can never be a simple process and that it will usually involve a good deal of struggle. From this perspective, shared meaning is possible even in the face of pluralism and uncertainty. Indeed, for Madison the fact of difference was one reason *to* form the United States as a political community that binds people without making them into idol worshipers. This is so, in part, because disagreement urges citizens toward reflection and choice and therefore keeps alive the project of free government.[47]

A Madisonian civic nationalism would also attend to the design and the actual function of political institutions, as well as to the difficult decisions that the realities of politics force leaders to make. In contrast to Bourne's inattention to political strategy and structures, a civic nationalism that followed Madison's example would focus intensely on what kinds of new and different forms of governance and membership are best suited to a world of porous borders and global linkages.[48] It would focus on the role of actual social practices in forging new models of civic engagement. Depending on the situation, Madison sometimes argued that a strong federal government undergirded by a robust national identity was critical to maintaining a republican system of politics; at other times he believed that the states' roles as intermediaries between the national government and citizens had to be bolstered. A Madisonian civic nationalism would thus pay close attention to the voluntary associations of civil society as important places to develop the habits of belonging and political engagement that can resist overweening claims to nationhood and bolster frail ones.

These local associations must, however, be linked to broader communities to ensure that those habits do not become simply parochial and defensive. A Madisonian civic nationalism would understand that, at least in the United States at present, those social practices and the deliberative nature of a robust citizenship will not flourish if they are too easily or frivolously disconnected from a shared sense of national citizenship.[49] Conceptions of citizenship that pay too little attention to national community deprive us of the social resources we desperately need to share a common space and engage in common projects. In doing so, they further risk creating a vacuum in which illiberal ideologies can crowd out moderate ones. From a Madisonian perspective, democratic practices may engender commitments to those different from oneself, but they also presuppose that one has commitments. How can rights and practices themselves bind citizens in the absence of citizens' commitment to a people and a place? At the supranational level, the movement toward a European-wide citizenship and set of institutions raises a similar set of questions. From a Madisonian perspective, the challenge in Europe is to ensure that political integration—whatever form it takes—keeps pace with market integration and that civic principles are undergirded by a sufficient degree of trust to make them meaningful sources of deliberation and self-governance.[50]

In the United States the kind of commitment necessary to make diversity function has often stemmed from particularist sources. Those sources have included race, religion, language, culture, and history, as well as a civic creed and constitutional faith. Today, Americans face the difficult task of sustaining a civic nation in the absence of a dominant culture, ethnic identity, or consensus on the meaning of constitutional values. These absences make the challenge of forging unity out of diversity even more difficult than at the Founding or in the Progressive Era. Yet Americans possess something that was missing from those periods—a real history, "a record of specific tragedies, successes, failures, contradictions, and provincial conceits."[51] Where Madison had, in part, to invent a history of unity, civic nationalists today can draw on a rich national narrative, a central theme of which is the extension of citizenship to those previously excluded from it. Equality is not the only theme in that storyline, and a civic nation need not extend citizenship to the whole world. But for naturalized and native-born citizens the American narrative offers a powerful sense of belonging to those who adopt it, one that contains within it an opening to broader cosmopolitan commitments. A history that is, all told, inspirational, makes it easier to manage the tension between national solidarity and universal principles. A civic nation that contains significant diversity requires, of course, more than a storyline—equal rights, vibrant public institutions, shared social interactions, and public values all matter significantly. Americans' faith in their own and their nation's future is especially critical in this regard. That faith has contributed significantly to the nation's capacity to absorb immigrants, and it is a faith that continues to attract like-minded newcomers.

Tolerance, Neglect, and Governance by Proposition

The kind of protean, moderate nationalism advocated by Madison is especially critical today, as the central challenge may well come from too weak rather than too strong a nationalist commitment. The fate of populist efforts to restrict immigration and the rights and benefits of noncitizens, as well as the response of citizens and politicians to the September 11, 2001, terrorist attacks are telling in this regard. To be sure, the most significant changes barring new immigrants from receiving certain welfare benefits did alter the social contract offered to newcomers.[52] Nonetheless, more extreme efforts to shift U.S. immigration policy, such as Patrick Buchanan's nativist-tinged campaign, failed to catch fire. Throughout this period, restrictionists made no headway in reducing the number of legal immigrants, and illegal immigration increased. When George W. Bush took office in 2000 he explicitly repudiated restrictions on immigration, and he urged the creation of a new guest worker program. In sum, while Americans around the turn of the millennium expressed a variety of concerns about immigration, the actively exclusionary consequences of those concerns were, from a historical perspective, quite limited.

Even following the attacks of September 11, the initial treatment of Arab and Muslim Americans was strikingly mild compared to the past. The FBI and INS did detain, interview, and register Muslim and Arab immigrants, leading to criticisms that such policies were discriminatory and violated civil liberties. But these actions seemed more the result of a woeful lack of information coupled with a period of extraordinary danger and the fact that only Muslims can be members of Al Qaeda. "Mistreated immigrants were the victims not of governmental discrimination but of government unpreparedness," Robert Leiken writes. "Blind like Cyclops and lame like Odysseus, we had no choice but to grope in the dark, hoping to disrupt enemy plots and cells."[53] While the balance could shift toward greater repression, and blunderbuss strategies have already alienated Arab and Muslim citizens, fears that these minorities would be treated like Japanese Americans during World War II seem unfounded. The terrorist attacks will reshape the debate over immigration, particularly with regard to security issues such as border control and visas for foreign students. It remains unclear, however, whether any fundamental changes will occur in U.S. policy regarding the numbers and origins of immigrants seeking entry to the country, their rights and benefits once admitted, and the requirements governing access to citizenship.

Americans' attitudes toward these issues mirror their general, milder outlook. On a range of issues, America today is clearly a more tolerant nation that at the Founding and in the Progressive Era. Americans, Alan Wolfe suggests, have come to value tolerance as their primary virtue. They prefer what he calls a "small-scale morality" in which tolerance and respect for diversity loom large and judgmentalism is resisted. The Americans Wolfe interviewed exhibit a morality "modest in its ambitions and quiet in its proclamations." Wolfe's analysis may overstate how deep and wide this tolerance runs, but he has surely identified a significant driving force in contemporary American politics. Americans' nonjudgmentalism has contributed to the ascendancy of what David Brooks calls "reconciling banners" such as compassionate conservatism, smart growth, prosperity with a purpose, and sustainable development.[54]

These are appealing ideas, and each has much to recommend it. But the small-scale morality that undergirds our politics also poses problems. In these circumstances, it is difficult to imagine how current American habits, especially as those are increasingly shaped by participation in a modern consumer culture, provide a sufficiently robust basis for a renewed nationalist commitment to any particularly strenuous project. As William Galston observes: "Today, fewer and fewer have any experience (civilian or military) of service undertaken out of civic, moral, and legal duty rather than a personal quest for meaning (or college subsidies). This new morality—do what you choose, when you choose, without fear of legal coercion or social disapproval—is an experiment without precedent in human history."[55]

That toleration indicates not that traditions of American illiberalism are too strong but rather that even a moderate effort to forge a cohesive civic nationalism may prove too demanding. In modern rights-oriented America, it seems less likely that policymakers or citizens are willing to limit immigration significantly or pressure newcomers to assimilate on the terms of earlier eras. This unwillingness to make such demands on immigrants represents an important gain for the civic principles of tolerance and respect for diversity. At the same time, it poses a challenge for nationalism. Under these conditions, can a civic nationalist revival be vigorous enough? If not, then it seems harder to imagine how a milder version of nationalism can accomplish the same assimilation and nation building as Roosevelt's coercive one.

This difficulty is compounded by changes in American institutional life since the Progressive Era. Civic nationalists cannot rely on the same civic sinews as Roosevelt did—churches, unions, and political machines—to mediate cultural differences, incorporate immigrants, and link elites and citizens. The challenge today is to knit together a nation of nonjudgmental, middle-class citizens who are increasingly disconnected from one another and estranged from their poorer, racially diverse fellow citizens. The problem to be overcome is thus not active exclusion but passive neglect. This neglect is especially prominent in the case of incorporating immigrants, where an unhealthy divide separates groups that work directly with immigrants and groups concerned about the declining value of citizenship. Many organizations that aid newcomers focus on protecting immigrants' rights and easing their adjustment to American life; they are wary of engaging in a broader program of integration. On the other hand, organizations that decry the dissolution of a common American identity, the erosion of citizenship as a meaningful category, and weakened civic attachment have very little to do with newcomers.

The disjunction between these two groups and the general neglect of programs to incorporate newcomers effectively into the American civic nation were made clear by the failure of the 1997 bipartisan Commission on Immigration Reform. The commission offered elements of a civic and a universal nationalist approach to issues of immigration and citizenship. Its inability to promote this approach successfully holds useful lessons for any future effort to do so.

As chair of the bipartisan commission, former congresswoman Barbara Jordan called for reviving programs that Americanize new immigrants.[56] She claimed that "Americanization earned a bad reputation when it was stolen by racists and xenophobes in the 1920s." "But," she added provocatively, "it is our word and we are taking it back." In its report to Congress, the immigration commission reminded Americans that the country had paid little attention to programs that integrate immigrants into American society and civic culture. It pointedly asked, "What do we expect of the immigrants we admit, and how will we receive them?" Like its Progressive Era forebears, the commission characterized Americanization as a two-way process: immigrants must obey U.S. laws, pay taxes, and respect other cultures and ethnic groups; and citizens must provide an environment in which newcomers can become fully participating members of American society.[57]

The commission asked the federal government to help immigrants and their new communities learn about their mutual rights and responsibilities, to provide the information they needed for successful integration, and to encourage the development of local resources for mediation. It urged a renewed commitment to the education of immigrant children and a new goal—the rapid acquisition of English for all through immigrant language instruction programs.[58] While the commission's proposals to reduce legal immigration and to revive the concept and institutions of Americanization generated significant controversy, neither of them was adopted. The combination of forces that defeated the proposal to reduce immigration are relatively clear: both business and ethnic advocates have concentrated interests in maintaining or increasing immigration while opposition tends to be diffuse. But why was Jordan's nationalist call to "take back" Americanization not heeded by policymakers or the general public? In part, Jordan's call never generated sufficient interest because her own voice was stilled; she died before the commission issued its final report.

Another reason was the vagueness of the commission's definition of Americanization and the deep disagreements over its meaning. Many observers applauded the commission for characterizing Americanization as a two-way street. But what, they asked, does this metaphor actually mean? How wide are the lanes? Do traffic patterns reflect rush hour, with most people traveling in one direction? In the Progressive Era, Americanizers like Frances Kellor had also called for a mutual process of exchange between immigrants and Americans. As we have seen, the vagueness of this process left the door open for a moderate two-way program of exchange to become a one-way process of assimilation. The commission's work did not create a similar dynamic; instead, its views were lost in a welter of confusion and conflict over competing views of American identity, assimilation, and multiculturalism, and the past and future of Americanization.

Amid these deep divisions among elites, the commission lacked an identifiable constituency to advance its call to revive Americanization. For universal and cultural nationalists the commission's recommendations were too weak. They wanted the commission to have clearly spelled out its opposition to affirmative action and bilingual education. In contrast, proponents of immigrant rights and representation found the commission's proposals far too strong. They regarded the word "Americanization" as irredeemable, smacking of the xenophobia of an earlier age. The commission had few direct links to average Americans, native born or naturalized, nor to immigrants, and its recommendations did not precipitate any greater involvement by any of these groups.[59]

When Jordan died, the most powerful civic nationalist voice in favor of integrating immigrants was silenced. Instead, the policy approaches that gained the most attention at the turn of the century issued from the initiative process, such as the efforts in California to deny benefits to illegal aliens and to end bilingual education. Whatever the merits and problems with either proposition, both were fueled by sentiments that are essentially laissez-faire—that if we just get out of the way—and especially get misguided ethnic advocates out of the way—then things will be fine with immigration. As a result, while some observers worried that a revival of the Americanization movement would lead to coercion and exclusion, in fact the entire issue of integration was ignored.

Perhaps this is the most, and the best, that can be expected today. Americans have generally tended to view naturalization and assimilation as an obligation newcomers must undertake. Even in the Progressive Era, Americanizers found it difficult to get citizens to assume responsibility for helping immigrants in any sustained fashion. Moreover, we cannot say with any precision how much earlier Americanization efforts contributed to the incorporation of immigrants. And we do know that there are real dangers in pursuing a more active approach to integration. We are also in a poor place from which to judge how serious issues of assimilation and acceptance are today, as these processes are by their nature slow ones that accrete over generations. Finally, there are always real limits to what any particular public policy can accomplish, especially when it deals with issues as slippery as citizenship, identity, and nationhood. "Belonging," the legal scholar Kenneth Karst writes, "is a soupy gerund."[60]

In this regard, we should be cautious about asking too much of our citizenship policy. Silver-bullet solutions like splitting the Immigration and Naturalization Service into separate services and enforcement divisions or revamping the naturalization examination can be misleading. Whatever their merits, if pressed too strenuously they suggest that these changes can end our troubles, when the causes of those troubles tend to be much further upstream. We should also be mindful of the human costs that abstractions can impose on those in the most desperate situations. "In thinking about immigration and naturalization," the philosopher and naturalized U.S. citizen Kwame Anthony Appiah writes,

> we should always bear in mind that it is a process engaged in by particular human beings with their particular circumstances, purposes, and needs. Theories of naturalization that require too much of these particular persons will only invite them to feign feelings and beliefs that they do not have. What Locke, that great liberal, said apropos of religious conviction goes as well for patriotic sentiment and belief: you cannot coerce the "voluntary and secret choice of the mind."[61]

Yet it is also true that if we settle for a tolerance that breeds neglect we are left with a number of critical problems. In the first place, as I argued earlier, the important issues are less about cultural assimilation than they are about political institutions and communal obligation. Immigrants and their children will learn English, many will become citizens, and, as Peter Skerry puts it, in Los Angeles most will go to Dodgers games at Chavez Ravine. But, Skerry asks, will they come to view themselves as individuals and fellow citizens or as persecuted racial minorities?[62] And how will native-born citizens regard them? Absent social and political institutions that bridge communities and link private concerns to the public good, will they come to know them at all? The capacity to generate social trust and a commitment to common standards will be tested by the increasingly privatized nature of American society. Can an increasingly privatized society generate social trust and a commitment to common standards? Citizenship policy governing issues like naturalization, dual citizenship, and social welfare benefits play a role in shaping these dynamics. But they are subsets of a much larger question about whether American institutions—political parties, courts, bureaucracies, schools, voluntary associations—have the capacity to respond to the various needs of multiple constituencies while knitting together new and old citizens. Our policy of benign neglect has little to say about this challenge.

This silence is especially worrisome in the event that, as in the Progressive Era, a war-driven hypernationalism produces coercive policies aimed at immigrants. Absent such a development, the alternative to neglecting immigrants is not so much coercing them as it is coping with wild swings between emotionally fraught, divisive positions and radical proposals: either we end all immigration or we open our borders to virtually anyone; either immigrants are a burden on taxpayers and any responsibility for integration rests solely with newcomers or all newcomers should be given substantial public assistance and helped to maintain their cultures, languages, and identities; either all illegal immigrants should be deported immediately or the United States should make no distinction between legal and illegal immigrants. These divisions are then expressed in initiatives and propositions where scorched-earth battles are waged over up or down votes cast on a single issue. This "governance by proposition" approach to dealing with immigration has meant that public and private efforts are now less likely to focus on what sorts of policies and alliances need to be forged in order to build the institutional infrastructure for incorporating newcomers and strengthening a common citizenship. The culture war among elites that raged over the concept of Americanization and the lack of any broad constituency to advance the commission's strategy for incorporating immigrants strongly indicate the difficulties that any civic nationalist efforts are likely to encounter.

In citizenship policy, typical reform proposals tend either to demand more of immigrants (lowering social benefits and raising naturalization standards) or to provide more for them (lowering naturalization standards and increasing social benefits). The former approach loads too much onto the citizenship process, expecting it to solve in blunderbuss fashion problems of understanding and commitment that require a range of properly calibrated responses; the latter approach does not ask enough of the citizenship process, creating a system that neither helps immigrants make their way nor gains public support for their inclusion.

The result of settling for a policy of neglect that is undergirded by a benign tolerance is a standoff between these two positions. Our policy toward immigrants and the making of citizens has become another reconciling banner: "Don't invest, don't expect." On the one hand, this approach says, America will not provide sufficient social benefits or educational programs for immigrants so that they quickly and efficiently gain the skills and knowledge they need to become committed citizens and economic assets. On the other hand, America does not expect that newcomers will learn much about the history and values of their new country or actively engage in its public life—except in times of stress, especially wartime, where immigrants' commitment is expected to be total—nor does it expect native-born citizens to help immigrants become a part of the nation.

Unlike those other reconciling banners that dominate our politics today, such as compassionate conservatism or smart growth, this one is entirely negative. Rather than marry caring to restraint or intelligence to expansion, it couples nothing to nothing. In this it resembles President Clinton's "don't ask, don't tell" policy governing the role of gays in the military. Like that policy, the preferred response to conflict is to ignore it. This is not always a mistaken approach—sometimes it both advances a principle and maintains social peace by not constitutionalizing a policy and thus making it difficult to change—but in the case of immigration and citizenship it has left us less capable of responding to real needs among newcomers and real stresses in the social fabric. The next and final chapter considers whether there is an alternative to this situation.

Epilogue

THERE ARE many obstacles to developing a more coherent and cohesive approach to immigration, the incorporation of newcomers, and U.S. citizenship. Nevertheless, significant changes at home and abroad offer an opportunity to move ahead in new ways. The global war on terrorism has made security a major factor in debates over immigration. This war and the broader clash between democratic pluralism and religious fundamentalism have also focused renewed attention on the value of U.S. citizenship and the meaning of American nationhood. While this attention could lead to restrictive policies toward immigrants, it also opens the possibility of recasting the incorporation of immigrants as a sign of the strength of the American civic nation rather than as a threat, a drain on resources, or an obligation better left to immigrants themselves.

A renewed effort to turn newcomers into citizens could become a symbolic and real advantage in the conflict with forces that reject America's civic principles and national standing. Immigrants who feel welcomed, who are met with clear, meaningful standards in the process of becoming citizens, and who find institutions that help them understand and participate in American public life are more likely to bear "true faith and allegiance" to the Constitution and to be committed to the "good order and happiness" of the United States, as the oath of allegiance requires. This is especially the case if we compare U.S. and European policies. As I argued in the previous chapter, European difficulties with incorporating immigrants are exacerbated by a peculiar combination of generous welfare benefits and restrictive notions of citizenship and national identity. In contrast, the U.S. civic national approach allows citizens to maintain their ethnic and religious identity *and* their national identity, albeit not without tensions and difficult choices, which makes it easier for immigrants to see themselves as loyal and patriotic Americans. Immigrants who recognize this opportunity and see themselves as part of the American civic nation are more likely to protect the United States by tempering extremism in their communities and identifying actual security threats. A more serious effort to attend to both the practical and the profound dimensions of integrating newcomers can thus be a far more effective security strategy than heavy-handed approaches that risk treating entire groups of ethnic or religious minorities as suspect.

The possibility of recasting policy toward immigrants in a civic nationalist mode also depends heavily on U.S. foreign relations, particularly with Latin America. However much national security and concerns about terrorism and Islam will effect policymaking, much of the debate over immigration and incorporation policies will continue to turn on these relations, especially with Mexico.

In this context, the election of Vincente Fox simultaneously raised the possibility of real democratic reforms in Mexico and called attention to the need for realistic, long-term planning between the United States and Mexico on a range of issues. Fox focused the luster of his democratic victory on the idea of turning the North American Free Trade Agreement into a broader movement toward the integration of North America. Whether he can convert that luster into real changes in regional and immigration policy remains an open question, but his election has given impetus to a new dynamic between Mexican and American policymakers. From a civic nationalist perspective, the central question is whether the policies spawned by this dynamic will pit regulating labor flows against strengthening U.S. citizenship. Most Mexicans who enter the United States, Fox has said, are "not going to become American citizens, nor do they want U.S. citizenship. What they are interested in is having their rights respected."[1]

Significant changes within the United States, changes bringing to the fore new players and new coalitions, also offer opportunities to regulate immigration and to establish policies that actively incorporate newcomers into the nation. Both Democrats and Republicans are actively courting minority voters, and Latino political leaders are increasingly major players who address a broader set of concerns than those advanced by ethnic advocacy groups.[2] In California, the journalist Gregory Rodriguez pointed out in 1999 that the lieutenant governor, assembly speaker, assembly minority leader, and Senate majority leader "are all Latino politicians who have sought to broaden their bases and deftly balance both ethnic and mainstream concerns. . . . This represents the maturation of the Latino political establishment from grievance-oriented identity politics to a more confident, broad-based style that seeks to forge alliances with other groups and interests."[3]

New institutions and ethnic leaders are also emerging among immigrants themselves. There are more than 1,500 hometown associations (HTAs) in the United States which link immigrants to their community and culture. These associations offer their members valuable material benefits while serving as arenas for formal and informal engagement with the larger society. As a by-product of their organizing, HTAs have involved immigrants in learning how voluntary associations operate in the United States. These associations can be vehicles of assimilation, the political scientist Robert Leiken explains, insofar as "members learn to attend and conduct meetings, form non-profit organizations, understand something of our legal system, and meet other Mexican immigrants (often immigrants' first step toward the larger society)."[4] HTAs are not neat Tocquevillean democratic institutions and, unlike the political machines that helped incorporate immigrants during the Progressive Era, they have no patronage to provide. But they are broadly representative and often the only institutions that directly reflect the interests of immigrants in some locales. The leadership emerging from these associations is simultaneously having a democratizing influence on Mexican politics while it offers a more traditional view of assimilation in the United States. The HTA leadership emphasizes virtues like responsibility, individualism, and family values, Leiken observes, and thus may well take a very different view of bilingual education and affirmative action than the leadership of current civil rights groups.[5]

These changes in immigration and ethnic politics, in relations with Mexico, and especially in the greater attention now paid to American nationhood in the wake of September 11 present an opportunity to conduct the public debate over immigration, assimilation, and citizenship in a different way. This epilogue briefly charts the implications of this opportunity for immigration and immigrant policy, especially for naturalization and dual citizenship.

IMMIGRATION AND IMMIGRANT POLICY

In this book I have been concerned with the policies governing citizenship and the incorporation of immigrants rather than immigration policy itself. Nonetheless, the capacity to develop appropriate integration policies depends on our ability to manage our borders. If citizens do not believe that policymakers can regulate the inflow of immigrants, they will be less likely to support public spending for programs that teach English or provide medical care. Border control and the removal of visa overstayers, employer sanctions, enforcement of health, safety, and minimum wage laws, and perhaps even a national identity card for all legal residents will have to be part of any approach that aims to create an effective, publically defensible system.

The emergence of serious programs to incorporate immigrants also depends on the public's capacity to assess benefits and costs associated with current immigration policies.[6] For instance, since most skilled foreign workers who obtain temporary visas (Congress increased the number from 115,000 to 195,000 in 2000) become permanent residents and citizens, these visas obscure the fact that they are essentially conditional green cards.[7] A different kind of dilemma can be seen in calls for the United States to establish a guest worker program. These calls respond to the reality that even with robust enforcement policies, America will continue to see some level of illegal migration and migrants who stay in the country for long periods of time. They accurately reflect the need to find some means for managing the flow of migrants who are drawn by employers willing to pay them and a country that has become dependent on their cheap labor. But guest worker programs have historically spurred rather than reduced illegal immigration. Once workers put down ties in a community they usually find a way to stay illegally and are then joined by family members. This means that the public, not employers, is left to deal with the social and economic fallout associated with increases in illegal immigration. Guest worker programs are especially problematic if they do not include a path for those workers to become citizens. There are strong civic nationalist grounds for preventing the development of a large group of residents who are barred from access to citizenship. If citizenship is not a realistic goal for guest workers then the United States risks establishing a permanent class who are likely to be exploited by and alienated from the political system.[8] A policy that addresses these concerns would merit serious consideration.

Another approach is to make decisions up front about the kind of immigrants the nation wants. Then the government can provide permanent status for those admitted and facilitate their access to citizenship, rather than continue the fiction of temporary statuses that keep getting extended so that migrants become de facto permanent residents. While at odds with political forces on the left and the right today, this approach has the advantage of making our policies more transparent and allows citizens to more accurately assess the way immigration is shaping the national economy and political demographics; it can also dampen the fires of extreme proposals that are lit in part by the insulation of immigration from public debate and democratic control. This approach further strengthens a civic nationalism by moving toward the earliest possible opportunities for immigrants to become incorporated into the national community.

As this discussion suggests, U.S. policies regulating levels of immigration and control of the borders have an important impact on questions of integration and immigrant policy. Even the pluralist Randolph Bourne conceded that "it would be folly to absorb the nations faster than we could weave them." Sound and transparent criteria of the admission of immigrants coupled with the capacity to enforce these laws will make it easier to absorb the diversity immigration brings. Whatever immigration policies the country adopts, though, it will still need a policy for integrating those who are here. As Bourne put it, "What concerns us is the fact that the strands are here. We must have a policy and an ideal for an actual situation."

While many Americans have expressed concern over immigration and the naturalization process, few have helped newcomers become a part of the civic nation. The mainstream organizations of the Progressive Era that were concerned about Americanization have long since ceded their territory to ethnic advocates who object to the concept. Yet nation building is an ongoing process, and there is important political work to be done. We must challenge a bland politics of reconciliation by urging Americans to live up to the demands of preserving our national union and to reject the double negative model of "don't invest, don't expect." Instead, America must develop the policies and strengthen the communities that can build support for an approach that invests more in and expects more of all involved.

A modern approach to incorporating immigrants should integrate social, civic, and nation-building policies. It could, for instance, provide a safety net of programs for newcomers that ensures that their basic needs for food, shelter, and health care are met. Such a policy could actively protect immigrants' rights, ensure access to the labor market, and expand opportunities for them to learn

English and become citizens. At the same time, the government could obligate immigrants to demonstrate that they are making progress toward English acquisition, employment, and citizenship within a certain period.[9] Like welfare reform under President Clinton, the goal here would be to balance the obligations of society and of the individual, to protect rights while demanding responsibility. Some—though fewer—rights and benefits for permanent residents who choose not to naturalize after the five-year waiting period should still be protected—basing eligibility for assistance on citizenship can have the effect of emphasizing only the instrumental reasons for naturalizing. But the goal should be to treat immigrants as citizens-in-training and permanent residence as a transition period toward citizenship.[10]

What Naturalization Can Do

While the political, social, and emotional processes involved in becoming an American take place in a variety of venues over an extended period of time, naturalization can be a critical component in this process. Civic knowledge does not in itself make one a good citizen; nor can we reduce democratic ideals to a multiple choice exam, especially if it is to account for the varying educational levels of applicants. Yet civic knowledge helps citizens understand political events and alters and enlarges their views on specific public issues; it makes them less likely to express alienation from public life, more tolerant, and promotes political engagement.[11] A naturalization process that takes seriously the ideals and history that have formed the American civic nation can also inspire in new citizens a considered act of commitment to their new identity. The naturalization process cannot test attachment to the Constitution, but it can foster allegiance.

This sincere embrace of a new civic and emotional standing is best accomplished if preparation for the naturalization exam acknowledges both the successes and failures of the American civic nation and thus the responsibility that all citizens bear for fulfilling its promise. Naturalization programs need to stress that the applicant who swears "true faith and allegiance" to the Constitution does not become the subject of a government but, rather, a citizen of a text rooted in both nationalist fervor and civic freedom. Constitutional citizenship of this sort demands a commitment to continually constructing the political community rather than a passive acceptance of a static identity based on principles or culture. In place of yesterday's formulations, this kind of citizenship requires a willingness to wrestle with the tensions between the civic and the national and to rethink policies and revise institutions in light of current challenges. It requires a capacity for what the political scientist Charles Merriam called, in his 1931 comparative study of civic instruction, "invention, adaptability, and adjustment in a changing world."[12]

This commitment to constructing a common future depends equally on immigrants' developing a heartfelt embrace of the American civic nation. Too often, naturalization preparation today emphasizes what are called "life-coping skills," such as how to use public transportation and vocational English, and devotes little attention to civic and patriotic teachings. Even efforts to rectify this situation, such as a $70 million annual appropriation for English-language and civic instruction launched under President Clinton and continued by President Bush, have ended up being used primarily for instruction in English as a second language. A better approach would be to infuse meaningful ideas and experiences into English instruction and to combine English and civics instruction in ways that engage students.[13] A formal process of incorporation for immigrants should also encourage newcomers to see themselves as part of a new people. Just as the pledge of allegiance helps young Americans develop bonds with the nation, naturalization ceremonies should convey "the feeling of joining an important community," as Gary Rubin urged when he was public policy director for the New York Association for New Americans in the mid-1990s. "We need to think not only of knowledge *about* America," he stressed, "but how to publicly express allegiance *to* the country as well." The solemnity and celebratory nature of these occasions should be reinforced. As part of this process, we should consider the symbolic means by which the American people can affirm *their* commitment to new citizens, such as by a pledge that can be given in response to new citizens' oath of allegiance.[14]

A more substantive and symbolic naturalization process can serve as a ritual that binds new and old citizens and invites broadened community participation. It proclaims to citizens immigrants' commitment to their new identity, thereby strengthening the importance of citizenship as a category of mutual obligation. The Americanization movement in the 1910s and 1920s offers an example of how the commitments newcomers make increase support for their inclusion. An equilibrium between commitment and support also characterized the debate over the Immigration and Reform Control Act of 1986. The amnesty for illegal immigrants in that legislation received support in part because it stressed that a commitment to citizenship would be expected of qualified applicants and because it was balanced by employer sanctions. By emphasizing the process of civic education and the obligations aliens would undertake, proponents of the bill overcame the reluctance of some representatives to support the newcomers.

A naturalization process that treats citizenship as a valued and substantive status can also give applicants a reason to prize their new standing. Some barriers are, as Alan Wolfe points out, "necessary for achievement and growth, as rites of passage that make an identity worth having."[15] Moreover, a more serious naturalization process need not mean fewer successful applicants. The Americanization courses pressed on immigrants in the 1910s and 1920s presented obstacles for newcomers who worked at night or were worn out from their day job. Yet, although a course could last seven months and meet nearly every day, attendance rates remained high.[16] Similarly, when in 1952 applicants for citizenship were required to read and write as well as speak and understand English, the number of failed applicants after 1952 was two-thirds lower than during the previous decade.[17] And in the 1980s, immigrants flocked to IRCA's civic education programs, often attending class well beyond the required forty hours, compelling some localities to establish twenty-four-hour schools for citizenship. Such efforts could be repeated today by offering intensive, integrated English and civics courses that enable poorly educated or handicapped immigrants to adequately prepare for citizenship—or even, if the courses were sufficiently rigorous, to bypass what some applicants regard as an intimidating, high-stakes test for naturalization. For immigrants, the whole process of applying for citizenship should help them enter into American life. It should provide immigrants with educational opportunities and symbolic occasions that foster their development as full members of the civic nation.

That naturalization has not provided these opportunities or occasions for some time is attested to by most everyone involved—frustrated bureaucrats, poorly funded providers of civics and English classes, doubtful citizens, and, most especially, confused and worried immigrants—and by the absence of employers, patriotic associations, and other groups who played such a prominent role in the Progressive Era. Yet recent changes in the governmental bodies charged with turning immigrants into citizens make an effective and meaningful approach to naturalization more plausible. In March 2003 the responsibilities of the INS were transferred to the newly created Department of Homeland Security and split into three bureaus: Citizenship and Immigration Services, Immigration and Customs Enforcement, and Customs and Border Protection. Declaring that "citizenship is a journey, not an event," the first director of the Bureau of Citizenship and Immigration Services (BCIS), Eduardo Aguirre Jr., proposed a plan to integrate legal immigrants that includes revamping the naturalization examination, emphasizing the citizenship process to newcomers upon their arrival, and matching them with community volunteers. "Citizenship," he has said, "begins within the individual but is nurtured by the country." The Homeland Security Act also created a new Office of Citizenship within the BCIS to promote the training and instruction of citizenship responsibilities for immigrants.[18]

Whether the BCIS and the Office of Citizenship can overcome the neglect of naturalization and integration strategies remains to be seen. As we saw in the Progressive Era, restructuring the government organizations charged with incorporating immigrants does not guarantee the creation of successful new programs. And the Office of Citizenship is a small operation whose leadership acknowledges the difficulties in fostering allegiance and civic understanding among immigrants in a nation that is often indifferent to such education. Yet this awareness of pitfalls coupled with a more aggressive approach to promoting citizenship has drawn support from across the political spectrum. The liberal

National Immigration Forum, the neoconservative Manhattan Institute, and the conservative Heritage Foundation have all praised the BCIS's efforts to revitalize the government's citizenship agenda, and they have pressed it to do even more to engage immigrants in American civic life. They have urged that a renewed focus on naturalization can trigger a new understanding and appreciation of what it means to be American.[19]

BEYOND NATURALIZATION

Bolstering naturalization is a critical step in building a broader program of incorporation. But the history of similar attempts makes clear that such a program must go well beyond naturalization. We need fresh thinking about other ways to strengthen citizenship and engage immigrants. Writing in 1996, Louis DeSipio rightly argued that the context of naturalization is important to understanding what kind of citizens we can expect from the process. Naturalization had not spurred Mexican Americans to enter electoral or organizational politics, since Mexican Americans had tended to naturalize for individual reasons. For Cuban Americans, on the other hand, naturalization had often been part of a community-wide initiative and had been linked to larger goals of political empowerment. (The mistaken impression that naturalization necessarily leads to participation had been promoted, DeSipio contends, by studies that have paid too much attention to two exceptional periods in American history, the New Deal and the era of machine politics.) Although I have serious reservations about a proposal DeSipio and Rodolfo de la Garza advanced in the late 1990s to overcome this problem—a five-year voting privilege for noncitizens which, if they exercised it regularly, would allow them to become citizens without having to take the naturalization exam—their idea suggests we can think more creatively about different ways to foster political engagement, psychological attachment, and an understanding of American civic principles.[20]

Consider, for instance, the counterintuitive proposition that an amnesty for illegal immigrants could become a vehicle for building new coalitions in support of citizenship. Amnesties are typically regarded as evidence of the decline of the nation-state: its inability to control its borders results in rolling legalizations of de facto members of society. Yet what if civic groups joined forces with new immigrant associations to couple legalization with incorporation? Hometown associations are already becoming political players, joining with the AFL-CIO to back a new amnesty. Their combination of pro-amnesty and potential pro-assimilation politics suggests that they might be open to other kinds of alliances, including traditional civic groups that have decried the dissolution of citizenship but have yet to reach out to newcomers. In this approach, amnesty might be balanced with required English and citizenship classes, which could aid immigrants, involve the local community, and make clear some of the financial costs of integration.

An even more promising way to open up new possibilities is to move the debate beyond amnesty or naturalization as the dominant alternatives. These alternatives present a false choice between helping immigrants and strengthening citizenship. They ignore strategies that link immigrants' needs and interests to American principles and peoplehood. These strategies were best exemplified by Progressive Era social reformers like Jane Addams at Hull House in Chicago and Francis Kellor at the New York State Bureau of Industries and Immigration and in the early stages of her work at the National Americanization Committee. Addams and Kellor valued naturalization highly and believed it was a key part in a larger process of incorporation. They believed deeply in the importance of the public good and in the need for immigrants to embrace America and its ideals. The notion that social and civic rights are due persons based on their presence in a country would have made little sense to them, as would the idea that immigrants or Americans would be best served by a political strategy that demanded power for migrants while denigrating the nation and its values as unjust and exploitative. (This is the strategy favored today by too many self-styled advocates for immigrants.) But they also regarded instruction in lofty principles and the attainment of formal citizenship as insufficient elements in the incorporation of newcomers. Both Addams and Kellor understood that genuine attention to the needs of immigrant communities was critical to fostering in immigrants an understanding of American ideals and allegiance to the American nation.

These reformers especially believed that newcomers needed structures and strategies for negotiating the often bewildering challenges of making a new life in a new place. Kellor railed against government agencies for ignoring immigrants and chastised employers and ethnic machines for exploiting them. She interceded on behalf of immigrants, seeking to protect their interests on matters from housing and banking to travel. Addams likewise pressed for protective legislation against unscrupulous landlords and employers and provided practical assistance, such as getting garbage picked up and children properly fed. Both Kellor and Addams helped launch massive new ventures in adult education. Equally important, they believed immigrants had to develop the habits and skills that would enable them to cope with the demands of living in an open society. As a result, Addams and Kellor sought to make real the connections between the experiences of immigrant families and communities and the functions of American public institutions. They viewed the integration of immigrants, Jean Bethke Elshtain writes, as "a form of housekeeping writ large; one must tend to food, garbage, child-care, misbehavior, the breakdown of social relationships, a budget."[21] All of these issues required attention in order to draw newcomers and their children from their private worlds of tight-knit families and institutions into their larger public role as informed, committed participants in American social and civic life. In sum, Addams and Kellor offered a holistic approach to the process of turning strangers into fully rounded citizens.

This approach is needed again today, especially in bridging the gap between immigrant and native-born communities. For at least the last decade or so, Americans have been worrying over the erosion of community ties, civic institutions, and social trust. What has been too easily overlooked in these debates is that there are sources of social capital even in beleaguered immigrant communities which, against significant odds, are putting together robust local institutions. It is important not to exaggerate the social capital in immigrant organizations that deal with a relatively unskilled, uneducated population. But some of these institutions are socially "thick" in that they encompass numerous different activities of their members. They are thus relevant not only in terms of their engagement in public affairs but, as the sociologist Amitai Etzioni observes, because of "the richness of informal social norms and controls, the trust people put into one another, the extent to which they are tolerant and civil to one another." In the ongoing process of nation building, immigrants are in many ways contributing by developing their own social and civic organizations. Policymakers need to find ways to support these organizations and to link them to government institutions and civic associations.[22]

There are also local efforts under way to tap into the social capital among immigrant groups and to expand their interests and sympathies. In St. Paul, the Jane Addams School for Democracy is experimenting with ways young Americans and immigrants can undertake community programs while learning about citizenship, including helping the latter prepare for the naturalization examination. The school "is a creative, fluid public space where people's talents and contributions are valued and developed," writes Harry Boyte, "[w]here the question, 'what is citizenship?' is a constant topic of discussion and debate; where people who are marginalized develop the political savvy to be otherwise; and where power dynamics change from expert-dominated interactions (which treat immigrants as clients or customers) to public interactions where people learn and work together, and in the process create power." Another example comes from Chicago, where a community organization called the Resurrection Project offers a faith-based approach to simultaneously increasing home ownership, inculcating habits of personal responsibility, and molding community leaders in Latino neighborhoods. "The biggest challenge is forming people and [their] critical consciousness," explains a pastor who works with the Resurrection Project. "When we serve somebody, we want that person to be involved. And we have to have the structure for that involvement, we have to have a formation so they understand [what we're about] and get committed. . . . If they just come for a basket of food and they get the basket and they go away . . . what difference have we made?" A decentralized policy approach that encouraged programs like the Jane Addams School for Democracy and the Resurrection Project could strengthen the democratic sinews Roosevelt and Madison relied on and civic nationalists today so desperately need.[23]

DUAL CITIZENSHIP AND GLOBAL LINKAGES

A policy approach that links local and national identity and institutions should also attend to the social practices that connect these levels of governance to the global arena. On this issue, the advent of dual and plural citizenship statuses presents a different kind of challenge to civic nationalism. It offers an excellent opportunity to consider the relation of allegiance to democratic governance by focusing on a very real change in how societies organize themselves. One can be a Catholic, an African American, a member of the North Carolina Bar Association, and a supporter of the National Rifle Association. But plural citizenship may constitute a crucial shift away from the civic nationalism that enables the integration of all those identities. Rather than simply facilitating the integration of immigrants into an existing political system rooted in individual nation-states, it is possible that plural citizenship is a key step on the way to regional forms of governance or supranational confederations, or other systems of political organization, each of which would have different implications for nations—peoples with a sense of common identity—and for civic principles.[24]

To evaluate plural citizenship requires us to think more clearly about which, if any, of these directions we wish to move in and what the best ways are to reach our destinations. The next century will likely witness new and different forms of community and governance, but there are prudent and perilous methods for extending democratic values and political rule. Plural citizenship may be one of the most prudent methods for accomplishing those goals. It supports individuals' commitments to multiple polities and peoples, thus enlarging communal identity in the wake of economic and political globalization. It facilitates the spread of transnational communities of descent, diasporic communities whose members have often sought to strengthen democratic arrangements in their home countries. But pursued indiscriminately, plural citizenship risks exacerbating the process of alienation and fragmentation already at work within the United States. If, as seems likely, multiple citizenship proves popular among high-end professionals, its increasing availability may exacerbate the secession of elites from individual societies. As the historian Christopher Lasch has written, these elites' mobility is "not a perspective likely to encourage a passionate devotion to democracy."[25]

It is not far-fetched to envision the emergence of a class of professionals spread across the globe whose commitment to any particular country may depend more on the tax or employment advantages available to them than their commitment to a people or a place. Place of residence will no doubt always exert considerable influence on an individual's interests and commitments, but if only a quarter of the predictions being made now about the dawning of a postnational world come true, this picture will be a real possibility indeed. As Mark Fritz, a reporter for the *Los Angeles Times*, observes, "signs of portable patriotism, a sort of citizenship of convenience, are everywhere. In Denver, an American sells passports from Belize to Russian nouveaux riches looking to broaden their travel privileges. In Toronto, an immigration lawyer custom fits his clients with whatever citizenships will help them navigate global markets. One Canadian tried to get his son an Italian passport as a graduation present."[26] As the common spaces professionals inhabit increasingly deviate from those of the less well-off, including now the holders of only a single citizenship, it may prove harder to foster the sense of community and identity that undergirds democratic decision making.[27] Thus, at the same time that plural citizenship promises to diminish conflicts among nations, it risks contributing to the emergence of a new form of strife between global citizens and citizens attached to the principles and claims of their single nation.

Under these conditions, prudence calls for a cautious approach toward plural citizenship. Despite its benefits and the obstacles to enforcing a rigorous ban on the practice, a wholehearted endorsement of it could contribute to undermining the link between the nation and the state when alternative identities and institutional relations are unclear and may well prove destructive. In the meantime, civic nationalism desperately needs citizens who respond to disagreement and disaffection through "voice" rather than "exit," who stay and fight rather than pick up and leave, either literally or figuratively.[28] The writer Mario Varga Llosa offers a revealing example of the damage to democratic citizenship that formal membership in multiple nation-states can inflict. When he was defeated in seeking the presidency of his native Peru, Llosa promptly acquired a second citizenship in Spain. "Ever since I was young, it has been my ideal to become a citizen of the world," he commented by way of explanation.[29] In other words, when I do not get my way at home, I leave for the world. Politics, with its patient efforts to build a stronger coalition and forge more appealing policies in order to contest the next election, is decidedly out of fashion in this formulation.

If the United States can reinvigorate its sense of civic nationalism and cultivate in citizens a sense of commitment and sacrifice, then these concerns about multiple citizenship statuses may well fade. But that revitalization remains an open question. Civic nationalism looks to citizenship policy as one means of generating (or at least not undermining) a commitment to a particular people, place, and set of principles. This goal does not provide a simple policy prescription for how the United States should treat plural citizenship. It does suggest that on some bright-line issues the United States should err on the side of caution. Serving in the army of a country at war with the United States easily crosses the line. Holding a high public office in another country also presents too high a potential for significant conflicts of interests and values. Voting in a foreign election raises difficult questions about the role multiple citizenships play in diminishing devotion to one community, as well as questions about affording greater political influence to some citizens, especially the elites most likely to exercise such an option. It thus might be best to limit voting to dual nationals' country of residence, rather than allowing people to vote in whatever countries they happen to hold citizenship. David Martin has advanced the same position and defends it succinctly: "In a democratizing world, this rule focuses political activity in a way that corresponds closely with the locus of primary obligations [based on residence]. It also helps promote mature deliberation and seriousness about the vote, because the voter will have to live with the consequences in the most direct way. Focusing political activity in the place where you live encourages a deeper engagement in the political process—perhaps even civic virtue—and also helps develop affective citizenship and a sense of solidarity."[30]

Frances Stead Sellers, a British-born journalist and naturalized American citizen, captures what this moderate position looks like as a lived experience. In contrast to those who praise her for being a global citizen and those who vilify her as a bigamist, she replies, "[O]ne underestimates the importance of belonging while the other oversimplifies the realities of modern life." Instead, she describes "a gradual evolution in one's sense of belonging that the dual citizen experiences much like any other immigrant." This is a process of attachment Sellers thinks needs encouragement, part of which involves giving up certain rights and voting in only one country. It is also a process that takes time as dual citizens make sense of their hybrid identities. That time, she says, "is what assimilation is all about. The privilege of retaining my old citizenship has made it a more haphazard process, but that is no excuse for being an American of convenience, a paper citizen."[31]

As for the oath of allegiance, I would not urge Congress to revise it. Archaic words and the repetition of phrases add an elegance, cadence, and solemnity to the language. Nothing in the current oath of allegiance suggests that new citizens should not retain their affection for their country of origin, and it properly encourages newcomers to think of themselves as part of a new people. If applicants have difficulty following the oath, then reading and understanding it should be a key part of preparing newcomers for citizenship. Should Congress elect to revise the oath, there are good opportunities to clarify what allegiance requires and what it does not require, and a number of useful proposals have been made. The Commission on Immigration Reform's proposal, for example, is clear and carefully calibrated, though it transmutes "true faith and allegiance" to the Constitution into "political fidelity" to the United States of America. If we are to make changes in our traditional oath, we should be clear that the required declaration of fidelity aspires to something more than merely the political; it aspires to reverence as well as reason.

We should also be clear about the object of that blend of reverence and reason. This is a more difficult task than it might seem. If by "fidelity to the United

States of America" the commission means our exact form of government or economic system then it has wrongly substituted these for a more basic commitment to the Constitution as a vehicle for self-governance. If, instead, the commission means the American nation, then it has highlighted only the organic and emotional dimension of citizenship. The Constitution—understood as both our most sacred document and containing the political principles ratified by the people—seems uniquely suited to receive the true faith and allegiance of new citizens. Yet this may prove too bloodless for some, and the best approach would be a variation on the pledge of allegiance—a robust declaration of faith in the principles of the U.S. Constitution and the people for whom it stands.[32]

The term "naturalized citizen" implies the importance of manufacturing political commitment; to "make natural" suggests the artifice in shaping an American citizen. To guide this work we need a conception of citizenship that acknowledges the complexities within the American tradition while still projecting a vigorous—indeed, inspirational—sense of identity. This conception must combine a rational commitment to abstract ideals of civic freedom and an inherited and organic sense of belonging—a delicate task in any age and one made more difficult today by competing subnational and transnational forces. These forces challenge the core notion that a unitary U.S. citizenship is the best means for integrating our allegiances to the multiple communities to which we belong. Yet an American citizenship that continuously wrestles with the tensions between reason and reverence, between principles and peoplehood, is precisely what our age demands. America needs citizens who feel an emotional attachment to the nation, who are committed to the principles of the Constitution, and who are willing to engage in the constant political work it will take to balance that attachment and commitment. It needs civic nationalists.

Notes

INTRODUCTION

1. Naturalization Act of June 29, 1906, 34 Stat. 596. New citizens have been required to affirm their support for the Constitution since passage of the nation's first naturalization act in 1790, but it was not until 1929 that a prescribed text was officially adopted and promulgated.

2. Article VI of the U.S. Constitution requires officeholders to swear or affirm their support for the Constitution. This requirement is immediately followed by the statement that "no religious Test shall ever be required," thus making explicit the substitution of a sacred constitutional faith for a sectarian religious one.

3. The oath also includes a renunciation clause that requires new citizens to "renounce and abjure all allegiance and fidelity to any foreign prince, potentate, state, or sovereignty, of whom or which I have heretofore been a subject or citizen." Recently, there has been much debate among policymakers, activists, and academics over the possibility of revising the naturalization oath, especially the renunciation clause. In 2003, the Bureau of Citizenship and Immigration Services proposed making the language "less arcane so it would be more meaningful" ("Rewritten Citizenship Oath Will Get Another Revision," *New York Times*, September 14, 2003, 19); and in 2001 Representative George Gekas (R-Pennsylvania), head of the House immigration subcommittee, suggested making the oath "more modern and less legal" (John J. Miller and Ramesh Ponnuru, "Dividing Loyalties," *National Review Online*, March 30, 2001). These proposals are firmly opposed by those who believe that any changes in the oath risk weakening its substance and symbolism. For a range of opinions, see Tamar Jacoby, "Making Citizenship Oath Relevant, User Friendly," *Miami Herald*, September 26, 2003; John J. Miller, "Swearing Oaths: Damaging the Oath of Allegiance," *National Review Online*, September 5, 2003, http://www.nationalreview.com/miller/miller090503.asp; U.S. Commission on Immigration Reform, *Becoming an American: Immigration and Immigrant Policy* (Washington, DC: U.S. Commission on Immigration Reform, 1997), 51; Noah Pickus, *Becoming American, America Becoming* (Durham, NC: Terry Sanford Institute of Public Policy, 1997), 22–26, 31–32; Testimony of Lawrence Fuchs, U.S. Senate Committee on the Judiciary Subcommittee on Immigration, October 22, 1996; T. Alexander Aleinikoff, *Between Principles and Politics: The Direction of U.S. Citizenship Policy* (Washington, DC: Carnegie Endowment for International Peace, 1998); Peter Spiro, "Dual Nationality and the Meaning of Citizenship," *Emory Law Journal* 46, no. 4 (fall 1997): 1411–85; Peter Schuck, "Plural Citizenships," in *Immigration and Citizenship in the 21st Century*, ed. Noah Pickus (Lanham, MD: Rowman and Littlefield, 1998), 141–91. In Britain, too, there is controversy over the meaning of loyalty and allegiance. A report examining the causes of race riots in the summer of 2001 suggested that immigrants should be required to swear an oath of allegiance to Britain ("Race Riot Reports Urge Immigrant 'Loyalty,' " *The Guardian*, December 11, 2001). The previous year a report issued by the Commission on the Future of Multi-Ethnic Britain, chaired by the political theorist

Bhiku Parekh, concluded that "British has largely unspoken racial connotations" and proposed that the nation alter its self-understanding to see itself instead as "a community of communities" (Alexander MacLeod, "What's in a Name? Maybe a Lot, If You're 'British,'" *Christian Science Monitor*, October 13, 2000).

4. Alejandro Portes, "Global Villagers: The Rise of Transnational Communities," *American Prospect*, March–April 1996, 77.

5. Robert S. Leiken, *Bearers of Global Jihad? Immigration and National Security after 9/11* (Washington, DC: The Nixon Center, 2004), 6. Leiken points out that with the important exception of the Oklahoma City bombing, immigrants have been involved in the major terrorist attacks of the last ten years.

6. Representative Lamar Smith (R-Texas), for instance, charged that Vice President Al Gore had pressured the Immigration and Naturalization Service to lower its standards for naturalization, enabling more new citizens to participate in the 1996 elections and cheapening the meaning of citizenship in the process. "This is the first time . . . to my knowledge that politics has ever been mixed with this sort of sacrosanct procedure that we call naturalization or becoming a citizen," he asserted. Smith, as quoted on *Morning Edition*, National Public Radio, March 25, 1997. See also John J. Miller, "The Naturalizers," *Policy Review*, July–August 1996; Georgie Anne Geyer, *Americans No More: The Death of Citizenship* (New York: Atlantic Monthly Press, 1996).

7. Wilson cautioned, though, that "it is one thing to love the place where you were born and it is another thing to dedicate yourself to the place to which you go. You cannot dedicate yourself to America unless you become in every respect and with every purpose of your will thorough Americans." Hyphenated Americans, he made clear, were not true Americans. Woodrow Wilson, "Address at Convention Hall," in *Immigration and Americanization: Selected Readings*, ed. Philip Davis (Boston: Ginn and Company, 1920), 611–14. These views did not mean that Wilson favored all kinds of immigration. See chapter 5 in this book.

8. *Terrace v. Thompson*, 274 F. 841, 849 (1921).

9. Michael Walzer, "What Does it Mean to Be an 'American'?" *Social Research* 57, no. 3 (fall 1990): 602. On American political thought and politics, see Gunnar Myrdal, *An American Dilemma: The Negro Problem and American Democracy* (New York: Harper, 1944); Louis Hartz, *The Liberal Tradition in America* (New York: Harcourt Brace, 1955); Seymour Martin Lipset, *The First New Nation* (New York: Basic Books, 1963); and Samuel P. Huntington, *American Politics: The Promise of Disharmony* (Cambridge, MA: Harvard University Press, 1981). On American nationalism, see Hans Kohn, *American Nationalism: An Interpretive Essay* (New York: Collier Books, 1961), and Yehoshua Arieli, *Individualism and Nationalism in American Ideology* (Cambridge, MA: Harvard University Press, 1964). On immigration and citizenship, see Nathan Glazer, *Affirmative Discrimination: Ethnic Inequality and Public Policy* (New York: Basic Books, 1975); Philip Gleason, "American Identity and Americanization," in *The Harvard Encyclopedia of American Ethnic Groups*, ed. Stephan Thernstrom (Cambridge, MA: Harvard University Press, 1980), 31–53; and Lawrence Fuchs, *The American Kaleidoscope: Race, Ethnicity, and the Civic Culture* (Hanover, NH: University Press of New England, 1990). Some of these writers have modified their views in recent years. See Nathan Glazer, "Reflections on Citizenship and Diversity," in *Diversity and Citizenship: Rediscovering American Nationhood*, ed. Gary Jeffrey Jacobsohn and Susan Dunn (Lanham, MD: Rowman and Littlefield, 1996), 92; Glazer, "Is There an American People?" in *"What, Then, Is the American, This New Man?"* 9; and Samuel Huntington, *Who Are We? The Challenges to America's National Identity* (New York: Simon and Schuster, 2004).

10. Matthew Frye Jacobson, *Whiteness of a Different Color: European Immigrants and the Alchemy of Race* (Cambridge, MA: Belknap Press of Harvard University Press, 1998), 7. See also Ronald Takaki, *Iron Cages* (New York: Knopf, 1979); Ian Haney-Lopez, *White by Law: The Legal Construction of Race* (New York: New York University Press, 1996); Juan F. Perea, " 'Am I an American or Not?' Reflections on Citizenship, Americanization, and Race," in *Immigration and Citizenship in the 21st Century*, ed. Pickus, 49–76.

11. David Hollinger, "Nationalism, Cosmopolitanism, and the United States," in *Immigration and Citizenship in the 21st Century*, ed. Pickus, 86.

12. George Fredrickson, *The Black Image in the White Mind* (New York: Harper and Row, 1971); Daniel Walker Howe, *The Political Culture of American Whigs* (Chicago: University of Chicago Press, 1979); Reginald Horsman, *Race and Manifest Destiny* (Cambridge, MA: Harvard University Press, 1981).

13. J.G.A. Pocock, *The Machiavellian Moment* (Princeton: Princeton University Press, 1975); Herbert Storing, *What the Anti-Federalists Were For* (Chicago: University of Chicago Press, 1981).

14. Ralph Lerner, *The Thinking Revolutionary: Principle and Practice in the New Republic* (Ithaca: Cornell University Press, 1979); Thomas L. Pangle, *The Ennobling of Democracy: The Postmodern Age* (Baltimore: Johns Hopkins University Press, 1992).

15. Jeremy Rabkin, "Elective Citizenship?" *The Public Interest*, no. 131 (spring 1998): 117–21.

16. This range of views of nationhood, and their various consequences for citizenship, has been obscured by the debate between communitarian and liberal political theorists, as well as that between traditional and revisionist historians. Communitarians have criticized liberals for not attending to the social dimensions of public life and thus contributing to Americans' sense that their shared identity is fraying. Liberals have responded that the emphasis on the communal dimensions of public life is inherently exclusionary and has consistently promoted liberty only for some. These disputes have drawn out important distinctions on the relation of the individual to the community, the rights and responsibilities of citizenship, and the appropriate line between private and public concerns. But liberals have been too quick to see dangers in every invocation of social solidarity. Communitarians, on the other hand, have too easily assumed that it is possible to separate the more attractive aspects of community from their darker side. For representative statements, see Don Herzog, "Some Questions for Republicans," *Political Theory* 14, no. 3 (August 1986): 473–93; Michael J. Sandel, *Democracy's Discontent: America in Search of a Public Philosophy* (Cambridge, MA: Harvard University Press, 1996).

17. Rogers M. Smith, "The 'American Creed' and American Identity: The Limits of Liberal Citizenship in the United States," *Western Political Quarterly* 41 (1988): 228. Smith's massive *Civic Ideals* is a searching historical analysis of U.S. citizenship and the relationship between the inclusionary and exclusionary expressions of nationhood in American history. He traces the multiple conceptions of national identity that Americans have invoked to support liberal ideals. But while Smith acknowledges the need for political leaders to invoke conceptions of nationhood, he treats historical appeals to community largely as pernicious. Smith extensively covers the movement to restrict immigration in the late nineteenth and early twentieth centuries, for instance, but he relegates to two paragraphs the remarkable surge of immigrants from eastern Europe in this same period. As the political scientist Jennifer Hochschild points out, "[I]n 1893, three-quarters of Chicago was of foreign parentage. This is not a portrait of a nation that really wanted to

keep all but WASPS out." I build on Smith's mapping of the "multiple traditions" of American citizenship while seeking to plumb when the emphasis on nationhood has been a necessary and valuable support for civic principles and when it has undermined them. In contrast to Smith, I concentrate on when nationalism in the United States has helped incorporate immigrants as well as when it has thwarted that process. Rogers M. Smith, *Civic Ideals: Conflicting Visions of Citizenship in U.S. History* (New Haven: Yale University Press, 1997); Jennifer L. Hochschild, review of *Civic Ideals*, by Rogers M. Smith, *Political Science Quarterly* 113, no. 2 (summer 1998): 322.

18. Why the debate at the end of the twentieth century has been conducted so differently from that at the beginning of the century and at the Founding is a complex question. I suspect it is partly a reflection of a broader trend unrelated to immigration and citizenship. The specialization of tasks and professionalization of roles that characterizes modern society has led ideas, policies, and political strategies to be less tightly connected than in those earlier periods. At the Founding, profound thinkers were often politically influential—Madison, Hamilton, and Jay, in their defense of the proposed constitution, offered a sophisticated political philosophy as well as a strategic intervention in public debate. In the Progressive Era, the separation between thinking and doing increased but remained relatively narrow. Powerful figures like Roosevelt were also influential theorists, and journalists and philosophers like Herbert Croly and John Dewey were deeply involved in public debate and the design of institutions and policies. By the 1980s and 1990s American intellectual life had become separated into the realms of academia, the media, and think tanks. The analysts of this period had also become further separated from public officials and practitioners, although some individuals shuttled back and forth between policy analysis and policymaking. As a result, today's theorists are not forced to account simultaneously for the different demands imposed by intellectual rigor, policy implementation, and political strategy. They are more free to stake out extreme ideas because their positions rarely depend on the virtue of moderation.

19. The historian Gary Gerstle counts in this group of civic nationalists influential intellectuals such as Arthur Schlesinger Jr., Diane Ravitch, Jim Sleeper, Alan Wolfe, E. J. Dionne, Stanley Crouch, and Shelby Steele. He notes that their views overlap in some ways with those on the left, in the center, and on the right in both academia and politics (Gerstle, *American Crucible: Race and Nation in the Twentieth Century* [Princeton: Princeton University Press, 2001], 366). Civic nationalism also shares much with the revival of "liberal nationalism" among political theorists, many of whom who do not work in the American context. See, for example, the work of the British political theorist David Miller (*On Nationality* [New York: Clarendon Press, 1995], 185) and that of the Israeli theorist Yael Tamir (*Liberal Nationalism* [Princeton: Princeton University Press, 1993], 6).

20. For doubts about the possibility of reviving a liberal or a civic nationalism, see Sanford Levinson, "Is Liberal Nationalism an Oxymoron? An Essay for Judith Shklar," *Ethics* 105 (April 1995): 626–45; Judith Lichtenberg, "How Liberal Can Nationalism Be?" in *Theorizing Nationalism*, ed. Ronald Beiner (Albany: State University of New York Press, 1999), 167–88. Gary Gerstle's historical analysis is especially useful on this question. His recent book *American Crucible* describes some of the same contending and intertwined conceptions of American nationalism that I discuss, though he concentrates on the twentieth century and I on three periods in the eighteenth, nineteenth, and twentieth centuries. Gerstle offers a broad-gauged analysis of the cultural and political dimensions of race and nation in the United States, in contrast to my focus on citizenship questions

pertaining to naturalization and on particular policy alternatives. We share a suspicion that the American nation commands less definitional authority than in the past and that this loss makes it more difficult for the United States to demand much from its citizenry. We differ in our understanding of the degree of coercion and exclusion required by civic nationalists in the past as well as in policies toward immigrants over the last decade, and in the sources of those policies. Gerstle also accords race greater centrality as an analytical category than I do.

21. See, for example, Wayne A. Cornelius, "America in the Era of Limits: Nativist Reactions to the 'New' Immigration," *Research Report Series,* 3 (Center for U.S.-Mexican Studies, University of California, San Diego, D-010). Thomas J. Espenshade and Charles A. Calhoun summarize this proclivity among political scientists who analyze public opinion in "Public Opinion toward Illegal Immigration and Undocumented Migrants in Southern California," Office of Population Research, Princeton University, Working Paper #92-2, March 1992.

22. Amy Bridges, *A City in the Republic: Antebellum New York and the Origins of Machine Politics* (Ithaca: Cornell University Press, 1984), 12; Nathan Glazer, "The Emergence of an American Ethnic Pattern," in *From Different Shores: Perspectives on Race and Ethnicity in America,* ed. Ronald Takaki (New York: Oxford University Press), 19; Rogers Smith, *The Policy Challenges of American Illiberalism* (Washington, DC: Carnegie Endowment for International Peace, 1998), 4–9.

23. Smith, *The Policy Challenges of American Illiberalism,* 7.

24. Nathan Glazer, "The New Immigration and the American City," in *Immigrants in Two Democracies: European and North America,* ed. Donald Horowitz and Gerard Noiriel (New York: New York University Press, 1993), 278.

25. Peter Skerry, "The Racialization of Immigration Policy," in *Taking Stock: American Government in the Twentieth Century,* ed. Morton Keller and R. Shep Melnick (New York: Cambridge University Press, 1999).

26. James Ceaser, "Reconstructing Political Science," in *A New Constitutionalism: Designing Political Institutions for a Good Society,* ed. Stephen Elkin and Karol Soltan (Chicago: University of Chicago Press, 1993), 41–69; Karol Soltan, "What Is the New Constitutionalism?" in *A New Constitutionalism,* ed. Elkin and Soltan, 3–19.

27. Robert Goodin, *Political Theory and Public Policy* (Chicago: University of Chicago Press, 1982), chap. 1.

28. Joseph Carens, "Aliens and Citizens: The Case for Open Borders," *Review of Politics* 49 (1987): 251–73. See also Bruce Ackerman, *Social Justice in the Liberal State* (New Haven: Yale University Press, 1980); Judith Lichtenberg, "National Boundaries and Moral Boundaries: A Cosmopolitan View," in *Boundaries: National Autonomy and Its Limits,* ed. Peter Brown and Henry Shue (Totowa, NJ: Rowman and Littlefield, 1981). Carens also contends that the universalist liberalism he champions is a core part of American tradition and culture, and, as a result, his claims on behalf of more open borders are not simply a matter of deduction from abstract premises. But, as Peter Meilaender comments, "the correctness of his conclusion depends entirely upon whether he has accurately described [Americans'] beliefs, and about that they must argue and decide for themselves" (Meilaender, *Toward a Theory of Immigration* [New York: Palgrave, 2001], 53). Carens has modified and clarified his views over the last fifteen years—though he has consistently pressed for more open borders—and his arguments have come to include what he calls "realistic" and "idealistic" approaches to ethics. Indeed, Meilaender points to another article that Carens published

in the late 1980s in which he articulated well the approach I take in this book: "We may learn more about the ethics of immigration by trying to explore the moral views embedded in the political practices and policies of different states," Carens wrote. "In this view, any important question of political morality is bound to have complex, local dimensions tied to the history and culture of particular communities. We need not accept local understandings uncritically, but we should begin with these understandings if we wish to inhabit the same moral world as those about whom we write" (Carens, "Nationalism and the Exclusion of Immigrants: Lessons from Australian Immigration Policy," in *Open Borders? Closed Societies? The Ethical and Political Issues*, ed. Mark Gibney (Westport, CT: Greenwood, 1988), 42.

29. Peter Berkowitz, "The Debating Society," *The New Republic*, November 25, 1996; Soltan, "What Is the New Constitutionalism?"

30. Ceaser, "Reconstructing Political Science."

31. John Rawls, *A Theory of Justice* (New York: Oxford University Press, 1971).

32. Marc Landy, "Policy Analysis as a Vocation," *World Politics* 33 (April 1981).

33. Will Kymlicka and Wayne Norman, "The Return of the Citizen: A Survey of Recent Work on Citizenship Theory," *Ethics* 104 (January 1994): 352. For political theory, see also Beiner, *Theorizing Citizenship*; Gershon Shafir, ed., *The Citizenship Debates* (Minneapolis: University of Minnesota Press, 1998); and William Galston, *Liberal Purposes: Goods, Virtues, and Duties in the Liberal States* (Cambridge: Cambridge University Press, 1991). For public policy, see Helen Ingram and Steven Rathgeb Smith, eds., *Public Policy for Democracy* (Washington, DC: Brookings Institution, 1993); Henry J. Aaron, Thomas E. Mann, and Timothy Taylor, *Values and Public Policy* (Washington, DC: Brookings Institution, 1994). For official government efforts to promote citizenship, see Britain's Commission on Citizenship, *Encouraging Citizenship* (1990), Senate of Australia, *Active Citizenship Revisited* (1991), and Senate of Canada, *Canadian Citizenship: Sharing the Responsibility* (1993), cited in Kymlicka and Norman, "The Return of the Citizen." See also the U.S. Commission on Immigration Reform, *Becoming an American*.

34. Kymlicka and Norman, "The Return of the Citizen," 352–53.

CHAPTER ONE
IMMIGRATION, CITIZENSHIP, AND THE NATION'S FOUNDING

1. Alexander Hamilton, James Madison, and John Jay, *The Federalist Papers* 10, ed. Clinton Rossiter (New York: Mentor Books, 1961), 80. The tension between consent and rights was exacerbated by the framers' dubious view of human nature. They thought that men were worse in groups, extending their natural propensity for greed in proportion to their greater power achieved through such mobilization. See *Federalist* 6, 54; *Federalist* 13, 97–99.

2. Madison, *Federalist* 10, 80. Madison's embrace of diversity went along with his distrust of direct democracy. In this view, national government should be at some distance from the people and insulated from their momentary passions because the people did not always want to do the right thing. Public passions and popularly based factions threatened liberty as much as or more than strong governments. To succeed, a free government depended on "a chosen body of citizens, whose wisdom may best discern the true interest of the country, and whose patriotism and love of justice, will be least likely to sacrifice it to temporary or partial considerations" (82).

3. Modern commentators have also often taken this "new science of politics" to mean that Madison did not think the political system depended on the virtue of its citizenry. "The aim of political organization was not to educate men," the liberal political theorist Sheldon Wolin commented in summarizing this view of Madison, "but to deploy them; not to alter their moral character but to arrange institutions in such a manner that human drives would cancel each other" (Wolin, *Politics and Vision: Continuity and Innovation in Western Political Thought* [Boston: Little, Brown, 1960], 389). Wolin's position is shared by other liberal and radical political theorists, as well as by historians from Charles Beard to Gordon Wood and John Patrick Diggins. Conservative thinkers like George Will provide a similar diagnosis, treating Madison's vision of American identity as the progenitor of an interest group liberalism that obscures the importance of virtue. See Mason Drukman, *Community and Purpose in America: An Analysis of American Political Thought* (New York: McGraw-Hill, 1971); David Schuman, *Preface to Politics* (Lexington, MA: D. C. Heath, 1977); Martin Diamond, "Democracy and the Federalist: A Reconsideration of the Framers' Intent," *American Political Science Review* 53 (1959): 52–68; Gordon Wood, *The Creation of the American Republic, 1776–1787* (Chapel Hill: University of North Carolina Press, 1969); George Will, *Statecraft as Soulcraft: What Government Does* (New York: Simon and Schuster, 1983), chap. 2.

4. Madison, Virginia Convention, June 20, 1788, in *The Complete Madison: His Basic Writings*, ed. Saul K. Padaver (New York: Harper, 1953), 48.

5. The legal system, for instance, should teach citizens to be "plainspoken, self-possessed, manly in a quiet rather than gallus-tugging fashion; jealous of his rights, but aware of his duties and the self-esteem of others." Through their charges to the jury and later through their reasoned opinions, the early justices sought to "introduce the language of the law into the vulgar tongue . . . [and] transfer to the minds of citizens the modes of thought lying behind legal language and the notions of right fundamental to the regime" (Lerner, *The Thinking Revolutionary*, 102, 136). The law was also seen as a tool to enforce the moral virtues thought necessary for individuals to govern themselves. Laws encouraging respect for religion, such as Sunday-closing regulations; prohibitions on public immorality, such as laws against prostitution; and regulations supporting moderate habits, such as taxes on alcohol, were widely supported. See Thomas G. West, *Vindicating the Founders: Race, Sex, Class, and Justice in the Origins of America* (New York: Rowman and Littlefield, 1997), 172.

6. "First Annual Address to Congress," January 8, 1790, in *Basic Writings of George Washington*, ed. Saxe Commins (New York: Random House, 1948), 569.

7. "First Inaugural Address," March 4, 1801, in *The Life and Selected Writings of Thomas Jefferson*, edited and with an introduction by Adrienne Koch and William Peden (New York: Modern Library, 1944), 322.

8. Presidents Washington, Jefferson, Madison, and John Quincy Adams all sent messages to Congress calling for a national university that would, as Washington explained, assimilate "the principles, opinions, and manners of our Country men." Thomas Pangle, "Commentary," in *Forging Unity Out of Diversity: The Approaches of Eight Nations*, ed. Robert A. Goldwin, Art Kaufman, and William A. Schambra (Washington, DC: American Enterprise Institute, 1989), 88; see also Pangle, *The Ennobling of Democracy: The Postmodern Age* (Baltimore: Johns Hopkins University Press, 1992), chap. 9, and William F. Harris II, *The Interpretable Constitution* (Baltimore: Johns Hopkins University Press, 1993), 59n. 19. Benjamin Rush imagined an entire educational system, not just the universities, that

would "render the mass of people more homogeneous, and thereby fit them more easily for uniform and peaceable government" (quoted in Pangle, "Commentary," 87–88).

9. This instrumental view contrasts with classical republicanism's emphasis on political life as *the* human good and its extreme veneration of civic virtue and self-sacrifice. Herbert Storing criticizes Gordon Wood's treatment of the Anti-Federalists as being part of this tradition of civic republicanism stretching back to Aristotle. See Storing, *What the Anti-Federalists Were For* 83, and chap. 3, n. 7. See also Linda K. Kerber, "The Revolutionary Generation: Ideology, Politics, and Culture in the Early Republic," in *The New American History*, ed. Eric Foner (Philadelphia: Temple University Press, 1990), 42; James W. Ceaser, *Liberal Democracy and Political Science* (Baltimore: Johns Hopkins University Press, 1990), chap. 1.

10. Max Farrand, ed., *Records of the Federal Convention of 1787* (New Haven: Yale University Press, 1937), 1:422.

11. Agrippa, letter IX, December 28, 1787, in *The Anti-Federalist: Writings by the Opponents of the Constitution*, ed. Herbert Storing, selected by Murray Dry (Chicago: University of Chicago Press, 1985), 245.

12. Agrippa, Letter IV, December 3, 1787, in Storing, *The Anti-Federalist*, 234–36.

13. The Impartial Examiner, February 27, 1788, in Storing, *The Anti-Federalist*, 283.

14. Brutus, "To the Citizens of the State of New-York," October 18, 1787, in Storing, *The Anti-Federalist*, 114. Brutus's identity is still a matter of speculation, although scholars have pointed toward Robert Yates, a New York judge.

15. Letter I, October 1787, in Storing, *The Anti-Federalist*, 14.

16. "[A] constitution," says Agrippa, "does not in itself imply any more than a declaration of the relation which the different parts of government bear to each other, but does not in any degree imply security to the rights of individuals." Agrippa, Letter XIV, January 20, 1788, in Cecelia M. Kenyon, ed., *The AntiFederalists* (Boston: Northeastern University Press, 1955), 149. Agrippa explained the basis for this approach by offering a theory of the genesis of politics in which governments are not made but exist naturally. See Noah Pickus, " 'Hearken Not to the Unnatural Voice': Publius and the Artifice of Attachment,' " in *Diversity and Citizenship*, ed. Jacobsohn and Dunn, 9–70.

17. Storing, *What the Anti-Federalists Were For*, 22–23.

18. Charles Kesler, "The Promise of American Citizenship," in *Immigration and Citizenship in the 21st Century*, ed. Pickus, 19.

19. Jay, *Federalist* 2, 38.

20. *Historical Statistics of the United States: Colonial Time to 1970* (Washington, DC: Bureau of the Census, 1975), 1152, 1168.

21. Thomas J. Archdeacon, *Becoming American: An Ethnic History* (New York: Free Press, 1983), 12.

22. See Fuchs, *American Kaleidoscope*, chap. 1.

23. Archdeacon, *Becoming American*, 12.

24. Benjamin Franklin, "Observations Concerning the Increase of Mankind, Peopling of Countries, etc." (1751), in Franklin, *Writings*, ed. J. A. Leo Lemay (New York: Library of America, 1987), 374.

25. Willi Paul Adams, "The Founding Fathers and the Immigrants," in *La Revolution Americaine et L'Europe* (Paris: City/State Editions du Centre National de la Recherche Scientifique, 1979), 138.

26. Henry Cabot Lodge, ed., *The Works of Alexander Hamilton*, Collector's Federal Edition (New York: G. P. Putnam's Sons, 1904), 8:217.

27. Hamilton, *Federalist* 27, 176.

28. Hamilton, *Report Relative to a Provision for the Support of Public Credit* (1790), in *The Reports of Alexander Hamilton*, ed. Jacob E. Cooke (New York: Harper and Row, 1964), 1–45.

29. Madison, *Federalist* 14, 103–4.

30. Madison, *Federalist* 39, 240.

31. Madison's belief in the importance of public deliberation did not mean that he thought everything was subject to revision—natural and prepolitical rights are clearly central to his and the other framers' thought. But he did believe that what those rights meant in particular circumstances was very much a political matter. Although Madison came to defend the Bill of Rights as having an important educative function, for instance, he also worried deeply that it would mislead citizens into thinking that reflection and choice were not part of an ongoing process. A bill of rights would limit public life to questions of what that list did or did not permit. This focus on enumerated rights would diminish rather than enhance citizens' capacity to reason together about the proper balance between the protection of rights and the need for effective governance. As a result, citizens' grasp of the reasoning behind the principles would wane. See Pickus, " 'Hearken Not,' " 73–80, for a fuller discussion of Madison's argument regarding a bill of rights. See also Storing, "The Constitution and the Bill of Rights," in *Toward a More Perfect Union: Writings of Herbert J. Storing*, ed. Joseph M. Bessette (Washington, DC: AEI Press, 1995), 108–28. and Hadley Arkes, *Beyond the Constitution* (Princeton: Princeton University Press, 1990), chap. 4.

32. Walter Berns mistakenly attributes this position to Madison, and in doing so he misses the extent to which the Constitution itself played a role in creating a people. See his *Taking the Constitution Seriously* (New York: Simon and Schuster, 1987), 23.

33. James Kettner, *The Development of American Citizenship, 1608–1870* (Chapel Hill: University of North Carolina Press for the Institute of Early American History and Culture, 1978), 248–86. See also Peter H. Schuck and Rogers M. Smith, *Citizenship without Consent: Illegal Aliens in the American Polity* (New Haven: Yale University Press, 1985), 52–53.

34. Kettner, *The Development of American Citizenship*, 8–9.

35. See Adams, "The Founding Fathers and the Immigrants," 137.

36. "Common Sense," in *The Complete Writings of Thomas Paine*, collected and edited by Philip S. Foner (New York: Citadel Press, 1945), 1:26.

37. Fuchs, *American Kaleidoscope*, 14; on state policies, see 7–19.

38. "General Orders," April 18, 1783, in *George Washington: A Collection*, ed. W. B. Allen (Indianapolis: Library Classics, 1988), 237; "Letter to the Volunteer Association of Ireland," December 2, 1783, in *Writings of George Washington*, ed. John C. Fitzpatrick (Washington, DC: GPO, 1931–44), 27:254.

39. This view did not mean that Americans had no duty toward noncitizens. Life, liberty, or property could not be taken indiscriminately. Madison addressed this point in discussing what obligations a new government would have toward citizens of states that did not ratify the Constitution. The "claims of justice," he wrote "both on one side and on the other, will be in force, and must be fulfilled; the rights of humanity must in all cases be duly and mutually respected" (*Federalist* 43, 280). On matters of immigration,

this meant that the United States might be obliged to protect and admit refugees in dire straits. It further required governments to respect citizens' right to exercise their liberty by leaving: "All men have a natural inherent right to emigrate from one state to another that will receive them," Pennsylvania's Declaration of Rights affirmed in 1776. Samuel Eliot Morison, ed., *Sources and Documents Illustrating the American Revolution* (New York: Oxford University Press, 1923), 164.

These obligations did not, however, extend to an unregulated right to enter or to become a citizen of the United States. The right to emigration did not imply a right to immigration, since a state had to consent to receive the immigrant. Gouverneur Morris, a Pennsylvania delegate to the Constitutional Convention, articulated a widely shared sentiment when he declared that "[e]very society from a great nation down to a club, had the right of declaring the conditions on which new members should be admitted" (Farrand, *Records*, 2:238). The framers' and legislators' debates on this topic reflect a continual balancing process, one that accounts for the needs of individual states and the new nation as well as the polity's commitment to civic liberty and dependence on personal virtue.

40. "Letter to the Volunteer Association of Ireland," 27:253–54.

41. Benjamin Franklin, "Information to Those Who Would Remove to America" (1784), in Franklin, *Writings*, ed. Lemay, 982.

42. Jefferson, *The Life and Selected Writings of Thomas Jefferson*, ed. Koch and Peden, 217. These sentiments did not make Jefferson an opponent of immigration, though he did doubt the usefulness of actively recruiting newcomers, especially unskilled workers. He recognized that many immigrants would be escaping monarchical rule and therefore prove eager to embrace republican principles.

43. "Examination" #8, January 12, 1802, in *The Papers of Alexander Hamilton*, ed. Harold C. Syrett et al. (New York: Columbia University Press, 1977), 25:496. Emphasis in the original. See also "Examination" #7, 491–95.

44. *Annals of the Congress of the United States*, 3rd Cong. (Washington, DC: Gales and Seaton, 1849), 1007 (henceforth cited as *Annals*).

45. Ibid.

46. *Notes of Debates in the Federal Convention of 1787*, reported by James Madison, with an introduction by Adrienne Koch (Athens: Ohio University Press, 1966; reprinted New York: W. W. Norton, 1987), 406, 408, 418.

47. Ibid., 421.

48. *Annals* 1, 1156.

49. *Annals* 3, 1007.

50. Ibid., 1006. See also the remarks of Pennsylvania Representative Thomas Hartley, in *Annals* 1, 1147–48.

51. *Annals* 3, 1006.

52. Ibid., 1008.

53. Ibid.

54. *Notes of Debates*, 438, 419, 438.

55. Ibid., 420–21.

56. Ibid., 419.

57. *The Correspondence and Public Papers of John Jay*, 1782–93, ed. Henry P. Johnston (New York: G. P. Putnam's Sons, 1891), 3:250. Jay's argument further suggests the way in which he had exaggerated the shared ancestry and common bonds possessed by Americans in *Federalist* 2, for he does not rely on this claim here.

58. *Notes of Debates*, 420.

59. *Annals* 1, 1162.

60. Farrand, *Records*, 2:269. Of the fifty-five members of the Constitutional Convention, eight were foreign born, including Alexander Hamilton. Wilson came from Scotland in 1765; Hamilton migrated from the island of Nevis; William Paterson, Thomas Fitzhugh, James McHenry, and Pierce Butler were born in Ireland; and Robert Morris and William Richardson came from England. Adams, "The Founding Fathers and the Immigrants," 144n. 35.

61. *Notes of Debates*, 420.

62. *Journal of William Maclay, United States senator from Pennsylvania, 1789–1791*, ed. Edgar S. Maclay (New York: D. A. Appleton, 1890), 210.

63. *Notes of Debates*, 420.

64. *Annals* 1, 1149.

65. Ibid., 1148–49, 1153. Page moderated his views later in the debate. He maintained that residency requirements for voting were of "less importance" but was willing to countenance them so long as no constraints were placed on landholding other than an oath of allegiance and declaration of intention to remain.

66. *Annals* 3, 1004.

67. Ibid.

68. Wilson contended that raising the citizenship requirement for senators from four to fourteen years would give the entire political system an "illiberal complexion." Madison also objected to the 1795 requirement that an applicant for citizenship prove he had behaved as a man attached to the principles of the Constitution. Such a requirement, he argued, went unduly beyond the obligation to support the Constitution. "It was hard to make a man swear that he preferred the Constitution of the United States, or to give any general opinion, because he may, in his own private judgment, think Monarchy or Aristocracy better, and yet be honestly determined to support this Government as he finds it." *Notes on Debates*, 420; *Annals* 3, 1022–23.

69. *Annals* 1, 1150.

CHAPTER TWO
ALIENAGE AND NATIONALISM IN THE EARLY REPUBLIC

1. See Lance Banning, *The Jeffersonian Persuasion: Evolution of a Party Ideology* (Ithaca: Cornell University Press, 1978), 113–14, 125.

2. Alien Act of June 25, 1798 (1 Stat. 570).

3. Hamilton to Edward Carrington, May 26, 1792, in *The Papers of Alexander Hamilton*, ed. Syrett et al., 11:439.

4. Thomas Jefferson, "The Anas," in *The Life and Selected Writings of Thomas Jefferson*, ed. Koch and Peden, 126–27.

5. Jefferson to Washington, September 9, 1792, *The Life and Selected Writings of Thomas Jefferson*, ed. Koch and Peden, 518. See also Jefferson's May 23, 1792, letter to Washington, 512–13.

6. James Morton Smith, *Freedom's Fetters: The Alien and Sedition Laws and American Civil Liberties* (Ithaca: Cornell University Press, 1956), 21. The connection between domestic battles over ideology and relations to the volatile foreign situation emerges clearly

in Washington's Farewell Address in 1796, where he links the dangers of "entangling alliances" to the spirit of faction and party. Foreign influence, he warned, finds its way into the government itself "through the channels of party passion," and "the policy and will of one country, are subjected to the policy and will of another." *Writings of George Washington*, ed. Fitzpatrick, 35:227. See also Stanley Elkins and Eric McKitrick, *The Age of Federalism* (New York: Oxford University Press, 1993), 494–95.

7. Americans were both attracted to and repelled by France in the 1790s. An example is the 1793 visit of "Citizen Genet," who sought to raise money for the French revolutionary government. He was at first met with wild support, but by 1798 Federalists remembered Genet's expedition as a disaster. Genet helped spark a flurry of "democratic-republican" societies that were loosely connected with the political machinations of Jefferson, Madison, and their friends. The Whiskey Rebellion in Pennsylvania in 1794 was widely believed to have had something to do with these societies and was seen by some among those leading the rebellion as a parallel to the French Revolution. See Conor Cruise O'Brien, *The Long Affair: Thomas Jefferson and the French Revolution, 1785–1800* (Chicago: University of Chicago Press, 1996), chap. 5.

8. *Annals* 5, 1961, 1962.

9. Ibid., 429.

10. William S. Shaw to Abigail Adams, Cambridge, May 20, 1798, in Smith, *Freedom's Fetters*, 24.

11. *Annals* 5, 1631, 1785.

12. Ibid., 1578.

13. Smith, *Freedom's Fetters*, 51. For the bill, see the *Aurora*, May 8, 1798.

14. Elkins and McKitrick, *The Age of Federalism*, 590.

15. *Annals* 5, 1579–80.

16. Hamilton to Oliver Wolcott, J., June 29, 1798, in *Papers of Alexander Hamilton*, ed. Syrett et al., 31:522.

17. Adams's defenders have tended to accept his explanations and to downplay the danger to liberty posed by the Alien and Sedition Acts (see Page Smith, *John Adams* [Garden City, NY: Doubleday, 1962], 2:975–78). James Morton Smith, in his classic work on the acts, was much more severe (*Freedom's Fetters*, 92). Joseph Ellis offered a carefully modulated account, as did Elkins and McKitrick, who noted that while it "[m]ight be suspected that he relished the thought of his opponents being punished for abusive utterances, ... [there is] no evidence that the campaign against sedition was one of his primary concerns" (Ellis, *Founding Brothers: The Revolutionary Generation* [New York: Alfred A. Knopf, 2001], 190–91; Elkins and McKitrick, *The Age of Federalism*, 590.)

18. *Annals* 5, 2018. See also the remarks of William Gordon, a representative from New Hampshire, *Annals* 5, 1984–85.

19. Debate on Virginia Resolutions, reprinted in *The Virginia Report of 1799–1800, Touching on the Alien and Sedition Laws; Together with the Virginia Resolutions of December 21, 1798, the Debate and Proceedings Thereon in the House of Delegates of Virginia, and Several Other Documents Illustrative of the Report and Resolutions* 34–35 (1850): 34.

20. *Annals* 9, 2987 (1799), quoted in Gerald L. Neuman, *Strangers to the Constitution* (Princeton: Princeton University Press, 1996), 223n. 17.

21. Otis, *Annals* 5, 2019–20. See also 1960, 1988; Sewall, 1958, Gordon, 1984–85.

22. *Annals* 5, 2023–26.

23. Sewall, *Annals* 5, 1957–58.

24. Otis, *Annals* 5, 1960. See also the comments of Connecticut representative Samuel Dana, 1970; Gordon, 1983; Harper, 1990, 2026.

25. *Annals* 5, 1566.

26. Ibid., 1567–68.

27. Ibid., 1569–73. Federalists also sought to make the Naturalization Act retroactive. Albert Gallatin and the Republicans undermined this effort and the final bill allowed aliens prior to the 1795 act to have one year of grace to naturalize and those who had declared intention to naturalize under the 1795 law to complete the process within four years.

28. These views make it hard to see the Federalists as cosmopolitans who felt compelled to make nativist appeals to shore up their position, as Rogers Smith has recently argued (*Civic Ideals*, 162–63). The more fanatical Federalists, such as Otis, Harper, and Allen, offered a narrow view of citizenship as a logical extension of republican themes that had been sounded publicly for some time. There was also nothing strange in figures like Washington or Hamilton emphasizing the common bonds of nationhood. Neither man had been accused of harboring wildly cosmopolitan views that he was now abandoning. Both men had long stressed the importance of forging a cohesive national identity and creating the conditions in which republican virtue could best be nurtured.

29. *The Kentucky-Virginia Resolutions and Mr. Madison's Report of 1800* (Richmond: Virginia Commission on Constitutional Government, 1960), 35.

30. *Annals* 5, 2012.

31. *The Kentucky-Virginia Resolutions*, 35.

32. *Annals* 5, 2011.

33. *Annals* 5, 1570–1572.

34. *Annals* 5, 1775.

35. *The Kentucky-Virginia Resolutions*, 34.

36. Ibid., 27.

37. John Taylor, "An Inquiry into the Principles and Policy of the Government of the United States," (1814), 25, quoted in Neuman, *Strangers to the Constitution*, 57.

38. Williams, *Annals* 5, 1962; Gallatin, *Annals* 5, 1977.

39. Smith, *Annals* 5, 2022–23; Livingston, *Annals* 5, 2013–15 (emphasis in the original).

40. In Virginia, the law authorized the governor to detain and deport aliens whom the president thought dangerous. Although the Virginia constitution held trial by jury to be a sacred right, the state alien law, enacted in 1792, did not require a trial in cases of deportation. Walter Berns, *The First Amendment and the Future of American Democracy* (New York: Basic Books, 1976), 95.

41. *Annals* 5, 2148–49.

42. Gallatin, *Annals* 5, 1955; Macon, *Annals* 5, 2105–6. A few days later, Macon returned to this point, urging the Federalists to see that "there was nowhere any complaint of a want of proper laws under the State governments" (ibid., 2152). Even Livingston, who spoke passionately against the despotic powers the Alien and Sedition Acts would confer on the president, concurred that laws against sedition were necessary for a properly functioning democracy (ibid., 2153). Jefferson, too, shared such views. In his Second Inaugural Address he demurred, "No inference is here intended that the laws provided by the State against false and defamatory publications, should not be enforced" (Second Inaugural Address, March 4, 1805, *The Life and Selected Writings of Thomas Jefferson*, ed. Koch and

Peden, 343). See also Jefferson to Abigail Adams, September 11, 1804, in *The Writings of Thomas Jefferson*, ed. Andrew A. Lipscomb and Albert E. Bergh (Washington, DC: Thomas Jefferson Memorial Association, 1903–37), 11:51. On federalism and the Alien and Sedition Acts, see Berns, *The First Amendment*, 107–11. See also Leonard Levy, *Legacy of Suppression: Freedom of Speech and Press in Early American History* (Cambridge, MA: Belknap Press of Harvard University Press, 1960), and Levy, *Jefferson and Civil Liberties: The Darker Side* (Cambridge, MA: Belknap Press of Harvard University Press, 1963).

43. *The Kentucky-Virginia Resolutions*, 11. The Kentucky and Virginia Resolutions moved toward—even if they did not explicitly use—the language of nullification and secession. The Kentucky legislation read that "whensoever the General Government assumes undelegated powers, its acts are unauthoritative, void, and of no force." Jefferson's original draft of the Kentucky legislation was even more explicit and provocative. Calling the Alien and Sedition Acts "altogether void and of no force," he argued that in all such cases "every state has a natural right . . . to nullify of their own authority all assumptions of power by others within their limits." Madison appears to have moderated Jefferson's more radical language on these points. But it is no accident that "the principles of '98" was a rallying cry for John Calhoun and the rest of the South during the nullification crisis in the 1830s and still later in the years leading up to the Civil War. Virginia, anticipating that the Alien and Sedition Acts would be enforced, had mobilized its militia. And when the other states repudiated the radical states rights claims in the Kentucky and Virginia Resolutions, Jefferson wrote to Madison that they must make clear that these two states would rather "sever ourselves from the union we so much value, rather than give up the rights of self government which we have reserved, & in which alone we see liberty, safety & happiness." Jefferson to Madison, August 23, 1799, Rives Papers, Library of Congress, reprinted in Adrienne Koch and Harry Ammon, "The Virginia and Kentucky Resolutions: An Episode in Jefferson's and Madison's Defense of Civil Liberties," *William and Mary Quarterly*, 3rd ser., 5, no. 2 (April 1948): 174.

44. As Walter Berns has pointed out, the Alien Friends Act passed in the House by the slim margin of 46 to 40, and 30 of the votes against it came from slave states. In the Senate, the bill passed by a larger margin of 16 to 7, and all the "nay" votes came from southern slave states. Berns, *The First Amendment*, 92.

45. For an argument that the Republicans' emphasis on the reciprocity between aliens' obligations to obey the law and government's responsibility to protect them constituted a rights-oriented alternative to the Federalists' views, see Neuman, *Strangers to the Constitution*, chap. 4.

46. Madison clearly differed from Marshall in important ways. He was especially critical of Marshall's opinions as chief justice, which enlarged the power of the federal government—in particular Congress—against local and state authority. He criticized Marshall's expansive reading of the "necessary and proper" clause for unduly extending Congress's authority. But Madison sided with Marshall against Jefferson in defending the courts as the appropriate "Constitutional resort for determining the line between federal and State jurisdictions." See Drew R. McCoy, *The Last of the Fathers: James Madison and the Republican Legacy* (Cambridge: Cambridge University Press, 1989), 68–73, 99–101, 114–15.

47. Marshall likely encouraged the anonymous letter writer to pose these questions and may even have written the letter himself. See Albert J. Beveridge, *The Life of John Marshall* (Boston: Houghton Mifflin, 1916), 2:387n. 1.

48. "Marshall's Answers to Freeholder's Questions," October 11, 1798, *Times and Virginia Advertiser*, in Beveridge, *The Life of John Marshall*, 577.

49. Beveridge, *The Life of John Marshall*, 451.

50. Ibid. 390–97; Jean Edward Smith, *John Marshall: Definer of a Nation* (New York: Henry Holt, 1996), 240–44.

51. *The Address of the Minority in the Virginia Legislature to the People of That State: Containing a Vindication of the Alien and Sedition Laws*, (Virginia) Journal of the House of Delegates, December 1798. The address was reprinted in the *Virginia Gazette*, January 29, 1799, and in a supplement, February 5, 1799. The abridged version is in John P. Roche, ed., *John Marshall: Major Opinion and Other Writings* (Indianapolis: Bobbs-Merrill, 1967), 34–38. Beveridge identifies Marshall as the author of this defense, but more recent biographies cast doubt on this assertion. See Smith, *John Marshall*, 601n. 79; David Robarge, *A Chief Justice's Progress* (Westport, CT: Greenwood, 2000), 206. Although Marshall's contribution to this response is unclear, its basic understanding of nationhood fits well with his own views. The most likely author of *The Address of the Minority*, Henry Lee, had published a series of essays titled "Plain Truth" in the *Virginia Gazette*, in which he articulated a Federalist conception of the Union shared by Marshall (*Plain Truth: Addressed to the People of Virginia. Written in February 1799—By a Citizen of Westmoreland County, [Virg.]* [Richmond, VA, 1799]).

52. Bradley Kent Carter and Joseph F. Kobylka, "The Dialogic Community: Education, Leadership, and Participation in James Madison's Thought," *Review of Politics* 52 (winter 1990): 54 (emphasis in the original).

53. Madison to Edward Everett, August 1830, in *Letters and Other Writings of James Madison*, ed. William C. Rives and Philip R. Fendall (Philadelphia: J. B. Lippincott, 1865), 4:95–97; McCoy, *The Last of the Fathers*, 134–35. Three decades later, Madison compared his approach to South Carolina's assertion that it had authority to nullify federal laws, and withdraw from the polity, without attempting to persuade the rest of the Union. "[T]he doctrine of the present day in South Carolina," Madison wrote in 1829, "asserts that in a case of not greater magnitude than the degree of inequality in the operation of a tariff in favor of manufactures, she may of herself decide, by virtue of her sovereignty, that the Constitution has been violated; and that if not yielded to by the Federal government, tho' supported by all the other states, she may rightfully resist it and withdraw herself from the Union" (Madison to Joseph C. Cabell, August 16, 1829, in *The Writings of James Madison*, ed. Galliard Hunt (New York: G. P. Putnam's Sons, 1908), 9:343–44.

54. McCoy, *The Last of the Fathers*, 147–48. My interpretation of Madison's career and political thought, which acknowledges that he opened the door to some of the nullifiers' claims but was by and large consistent in distinguishing between his arguments in 1798–1800 and Calhoun's in the 1830s, is similar to the ones offered by McCoy and Banning. This view contrasts with Adrienne Koch and Harry Ammon, who treat the Kentucky and Virginia episode as primarily a defense of civil liberties and see southern invocations of the principles of '98 as misuses. It differs as well from Kevin Gutzman and from William Watkins, who see Madison as a forerunner of South Carolina's doctrines of nullification and interposition in the 1830s and later of the right to secession. Lance Banning, *The Sacred Fire of Liberty: James Madison and the Founding of the Federal Republic* (Ithaca: Cornell University Press, 1995); Koch and Ammon, "The Virginia and Kentucky Resolutions," 145–76; Kevin R. Gutzman, "A Troublesome Legacy: James

Madison and 'The Principles of '98,'" *Journal of the Early Republic* 15 (winter 1995): 569–89; William J. Watkins Jr., "The Kentucky and Virginia Resolutions: Guideposts of Limited Government," *Independent Review* 3 (winter 1999): 385–411.

55. Joseph Reisert, review of *The Political Philosophy of James Madison*, by Garret Ward Sheldon, *Law and Politics Book Review* 11, no. 6 (June 2001): 305–7.

56. Historians have often suggested that Madison's views were more temperate than Jefferson's on this question, and there is clearly some truth to that observation. Joseph Ellis concludes that "Madison's prudent and silent intervention rescued Jefferson from the secessionist implications of his revolutionary principles and artfully concealed the huge discrepancy between their respective views of the Constitution" (*Founding Brothers*, 201). But, as Lance Banning points out, the distinction between Jefferson and Madison can be overemphasized. Madison may well have prevented Jefferson from inserting into the Virginia Resolution a provocative reference to the federal laws as "not law, but utterly null, void and of no effect," but he did refer to these laws as "unconstitutional," a point on which there is little difference. Madison himself acknowledged that the language in the Kentucky and Virginia Resolutions and in his *Report of 1800* was vague on the precise line between protest and nullification. Banning, *The Sacred Fire of Liberty*, 387–95, 533n. 65.

57. In Philadelphia alone, 870 Irish immigrants naturalized in 1798 and 1799, compared to 85 in 1796 and 1797. Edward C. Carter, "A 'Wild Irishman' under Every Federalist's Bed: Naturalization in Philadelphia, 1789–1806," *Pennsylvania Magazine of History and Biography* 94 (1970): 331–83.

58. Part of this convergence of opinion can be attributed to the strategic political reasons Jefferson and Hamilton had for emphasizing common ground. Jefferson needed to consolidate his victory and govern effectively. Hamilton wanted to distance himself from the extremist rhetoric of his allies, which had contributed to their electoral loss. Both leaders would also continue to disagree fundamentally as to the proper economic basis for a flourishing republican citizenry. Yet it is also clear that Jefferson and Hamilton were drawing on deeply shared views about character and community.

CHAPTER THREE
THE FREE WHITE CLAUSE OF 1970

1. Franklin G. Franklin's 1906 survey of naturalization law follows the debate in Congress and is silent on the free white clause (*Legislative History* [Chicago: University of Chicago Press, 1906], 33–48). Luella Gettys's 1934 survey of citizenship law recounts the confusing and contradictory judicial efforts to interpret the meaning of the free white clause (*The Law of Citizenship in the United States* [Chicago: University of Chicago Press, 1934]). More recently, some prominent analyses of American citizenship and nationality do not mention the Naturalization Act of 1790 at all, while others acknowledge it in passing (Arieli, *Individualism and Nationalism in American Ideology*; Kohn, *American Nationalism*; Lipset, *The First New Nation*; Huntington, *American Politics*). These scholars are keenly aware of the denial of citizenship to blacks, Indians, and Asians, but they tend to treat that exclusion as an exception to American principles of inclusion. See also Reed Ueda, "Naturalization and Citizenship," in *Harvard Encyclopedia of American Ethnic Groups*, ed. Thernstrom, 734; Fuchs, *American Kaleidoscope*, 112; and Kettner, *The Development of American Citizenship*, 236.

2. West, *Vindicating the Founders*, chap. 7; Jacobson, *Whiteness of a Different Color*, chap. 1.

3. St. George Tucker, *A Dissertation on Slavery, with a Proposal for the Gradual Abolition of It in the State of Virginia* (Philadelphia: Mathew Carey, 1796; reprinted 1861), 17–20.

4. James Kent, *Commentaries on American Law*, 9th ed. (Boston: Little, Brown, 1867), 2:37.

5. Kettner, *The Development of American Citizenship*, 216, 311–33.

6. In a remarkable if not entirely convincing textual analysis, the former slave Frederick Douglass argued in 1860 that the so-called slaveholding provisions in the Constitution—Article I, Section 9, securing the slave trade until 1808; Article IV, Section 9, providing for the recovery of fugitive slaves; Article I, section 2, counting blacks as three-fifths of a person; and Article I, Section 8, requiring suppression of slave insurrections—all in fact indicated that the Constitution tended toward the abolition of slavery. "The Constitution of the United States: Is It Pro-slavery or Anti-Slavery?" speech delivered in Glasgow, Scotland, March 26, 1860, in *Life and Writings of Frederick Douglass*, ed. Philip S. Foner (New York: International Publishers, 1950), 2:467–80. For an exploration of Douglass's faith in the constitutional order, see Sanford Levinson, *Constitutional Faith* (Princeton: Princeton University Press, 1988), chap. 2.

7. Herbert Storing, "Slavery and the Moral Foundations of the American Republic," in *Toward a More Perfect Union*, 134 (emphasis in the original).

8. *The Life and Selected Writings of Thomas Jefferson*, ed. Koch and Peden, 261.

9. Ibid., 278–79. Since it is frequently asserted that the founding generation did not regard blacks as due the same natural rights as "all men," it is worth citing the wide variety of leading figures who opposed slavery and explicitly rejected this charge. (See McCoy, *The Last of the Fathers*, 261.) John Jay, for instance, wrote that fighting for independence from Britain and holding slaves was "inconsistent as well as unjust and perhaps impious" (Jay to Richard Price, September 27, 1785, in *The Founders' Constitution*, 538). During the Revolutionary War, Alexander Hamilton wrote that "the contempt we have been taught to entertain for the blacks, makes us fancy many things that are founded neither in reason nor experience," and concluded that "the dictates of humanity and true policy equally interest me in favor of this unfortunate class of men" (Hamilton to John Jay, March 14, 1779, in *The Papers of Alexander Hamilton*, ed. Syrett et al., 2:17–18). Hamilton's ideological opposite, Patrick Henry, shared his opposition to slavery. Writing in 1773, Henry asked, "Is it not amazing, that at a time, when ye. Rights of Humanity are defined & understood with precision, in a Country above all others fond of Liberty, that in such an Age, & such a Country we find Men . . . adopting a Principle as repugnant to humanity as it is inconsistent with the Bible and destructive to Liberty" (Henry to Robert Pleasants, January 18, 1773, in Robert Douthat Meade, *Patrick Henry: Patriot in the Making* [Philadelphia: J. B. Lippincott, 1957], 299–300).

10. *The Papers of Thomas Jefferson*, ed. Julian P. Boyd (Princeton: Princeton University Press, 1950–65), 2:471–72n. 473. See William Cohen, "Thomas Jefferson and the Problem of Slavery," *Journal of American History* 56 (December 1969): 509.

11. Cohen, "Thomas Jefferson and the Problem of Slavery," 525. Scholars have long wrestled with the difficult task of coming to terms with Jefferson's contradictions. However one resolves this tangle, it is important not to lose sight of a broader point: those contradictions reflect the deep imprint slavery made on American conceptions of liberty.

See Benjamin Schwarz, "What Jefferson Helps to Explain," *Atlantic Monthly*, March 1997, http://www.theatlantic.com/issues/97mar/jeffer/jeffer.htm.

12. This is the same point Lincoln later made in commenting on the reasoning in the *Dred Scott* decision that there is a contradiction between the claim that blacks have a natural right to freedom but do not have a right to be citizens of the United States: "I protest against that counterfeit logic which concludes that, because I do not want a black woman for a *slave*, I must necessarily want her for a *wife*. I need not have her for either, I can just leave her alone." Lincoln, "Speech at Springfield, Illinois," June 26, 1857, in *The Collected Works of Abraham Lincoln*, ed. Roy Basler (New Brunswick: Rutgers University Press, 1953), 2:405.

13. *The Life and Selected Writings of Thomas Jefferson*, ed. Koch and Peden, 257, 261–62.

14. Ibid., 256. The Jefferson Memorial omits the second clause in this sentence.

15. Tucker, *A Dissertation on Slavery*, 7–8 (emphasis in the original), 84–86 (emphasis in the original).

16. Ibid., 92.

17. Tucker to Jeremy Belknap, June 29, 1795, Massachusetts Historical Society Collections, 5th ser., 3:407–10, in *The Founders' Constitution*, 559.

18. Tucker, *A Dissertation on Slavery*, 48.

19. Such a situation raises the question of whether a civic freedom based on the distinction between natural and political rights can itself mediate between the plurality of individual rights. Storing shrewdly observed that while "only an invincible naivete can deny that Jefferson spoke truly," there is a more fundamental issue at work here, one he thought Jefferson knew as well. That issue is "the tendency, under the principles of the Declaration of Independence itself, for justice to be reduced to self-preservation, for self-preservation to be defined as self-interest, and for self-interest to be defined as what is convenient and achievable. . . . [A]t this deeper level the problem is not that [the Founders] betrayed their principles, the common charge; the problem lies rather in the principles themselves. The very principle of individual liberty for which the Founders worked so brilliantly and successfully contains within itself an uncomfortably large opening toward slavery" (Storing, "Slavery and the Moral Foundations of the American Republic," 142–44).

20. Jefferson to John Holmes, April 22, 1820, in *The Life and Selected Writings of Thomas Jefferson*, ed. Koch and Peden, 698.

21. "The Rejected Constitution of 1778," February 28, 1778, in Oscar Handlin and Mary Handlin, eds., *The Popular Sources of Political Authority* (Cambridge, MA: Belknap Press of Harvard University Press, 1966), 192.

22. "Return of Sutton, Massachusetts," May 18, 1778, in Handlin and Handlin, *The Popular Sources of Political Authority*, 231 (emphasis in the original).

23. Madison to Robert J. Evans, June 15, 1819, in *Writings*, ed. Hunt, 8:439.

24. See, for instance, James Madison, "Memorandum on an African Colony for Freed Slaves," ca. October 20, 1789, *The Papers of James Madison*, ed. William T. Hutchinson and William M. E. Rachal (Charlottesville: University of Virginia Press, 1979), 12:437–38; Madison, *Writings*, ed. Hunt, 8:439–47.

25. Madison, *Writings*, ed. Hunt, 8:440.

26. Schwarz, "What Jefferson Helps to Explain." For a subtle interpretation of Madison's treatment of slavery and colonization, see McCoy, *The Last of the Fathers*, chap. 7, especially 266, 267.

27. Tucker to Jeremy Belknap, June 29, 1795. See also Tucker, *A Dissertation on Slavery*, 82–84.

28. *The Founders' Constitution*, 1:555 (emphasis in the original).

29. All quotations in this section are from Tucker, *A Dissertation on Slavery*, 17–19, 86, 88, 89–96.

30. Jacobson, *Whiteness of a Different Color*, 23, 22, 26. In addition to colonial charters, state and federal laws, and literature, Jacobson relies on a psychoanalytic reading of the Founders' republicanism as a battle between "good" reason and "bad" passion. He draws on the work of Ronald Takaki, who argues that Americans' emphasis on homogeneity, virtue, and "fitness for self-government" revealed their own anxiety about whether they would be able to control themselves. In a fit of psychological repression, Takaki suggests, they projected these anxieties onto other races. This projection fed Americans' obsession with racial heterogeneity, individual freedom, and self-possession. Social exclusion was a product of a psychological need to suppress parts of the self that the Founders believed to be shameful. As slaves were denied freedom and free blacks and Indians were considered incapable of self-possession, "whiteness was tacitly but irretrievably written into republican ideology" (*Iron Cages*, 10, 11–12).

31. In effect, Jacobson takes the view that Chief Justice Roger Taney was right when he wrote in *Scott v. Sandford* that blacks at the time of the Founding "had for more than a century before been regarded as beings of an inferior order; and altogether unfit to associate with the white race, either in social or political relations; and so far inferior that they had no rights which the white man was bound to respect; and that the negro might justly and lawfully be reduced to slavery for his benefit." Taney also says explicitly that the Founders could not have meant to include blacks in the scope of "all men are created equal"; they would have been hypocrites. There were, of course, dissenting opinions in that case, such as Justice Benjamin Curtis's argument that free blacks were citizens in many states and that Taney was simply wrong in claiming that the "People" of the Constitution excluded blacks. There were also forceful counterinterpretations of the meaning of the Declaration and the Constitution at the time of that decision, notably those of Lincoln and Frederick Douglass discussed above. Most important, as we have seen, there were many Founders who understood themselves to be hypocrites, torn between what they considered the demands of justice to free the slaves and their own natural right to self-preservation. But Jacobson interprets Taney's opinion as the essential and complete truth about how the Founding generation saw slavery. Jacobson, *Whiteness of a Different Color*, 29–30.

32. As a factor in the Founders' decision to restrict citizenship, West justifies their simple dislike of different people as a legitimate, if not entirely elevated, concern. "From the point of view of the Declaration of Independence, this kind of preference for one's own, the love of one's own kind, is a permissible and understandable, although not particularly noble, basis for immigration and citizenship policy" (*Vindicating the Founders*, 170). This invocation of the Declaration as condoning any and all forms of partiality is rather peculiar, since the Declaration defends partiality solely in terms of a people defined by their political beliefs. West's faith in what he calls the "innocent love of one's own" sharply contrasts with the basic presuppositions shared by all the Founders that people will misuse power unless they have some interest in not doing so. He seems curiously confident that innocent love will not provide a large opening for those who want to disguise their prejudice and self-interest by claiming that certain character traits are

necessary in a democratic citizenry—or that it will not turn into murderous hatred of the other or the tyranny of a majority over a minority.

CHAPTER FOUR
AMERICANIZATION AND PLURALISM IN THE PROGRESSIVE ERA

1. Left-leaning Progressivism included a wide range of views. The social critic Horace Kallen offered the most pronounced defense of cultural pluralism. "Men may change their clothes, their politics, their wives, their religion, their philosophies, to a greater or lesser extent," he wrote. "[T]hey cannot change their grandfathers" (Kallen, *Culture and Democracy* [New York: Boni and Liveright, 1924], 122). Although most social reformers who worked with immigrants did not espouse Kallen's views, his analysis would later influence the rise of multiculturalism in the 1960s. In contrast to Kallen's defense of radical pluralism, the jurist Louis Brandeis emphasized the importance of immigrants undergoing a psychological and not merely legal transformation in their journey from alien to citizen. Brandeis believed that "to become Americanized the change wrought must be fundamental. However great his outward conformity, the immigrant is not Americanized unless his interests and affections have become deeply rooted here" (Brandeis, "True Americanism," in *Immigration and Americanization: Selected Readings*, ed. Philip Davis [Boston: Ginn, 1920], 639–40). See also Smith, *Civic Ideals*, 419–24; Gary Gerstle, "The Protean Character of American Liberalism," *American Historical Review* 99, no. 4 (October 1994): 1049–52; Rivka Shpak Lissak, *Pluralism and Progressives: Hull House and the New Immigrants, 1890–1919* (Chicago: University of Chicago Press, 1989), 147–56.

2. Gerstle, "The Protean Character," 1052.

3. Kettner, *The Development of American Citizenship*, 231, 264.

4. Schuck and Smith, *Citizenship without Consent*, 63–71; Kettner, *The Development of American Citizenship*, 287–333.

5. *Cherokee Nation v. Georgia*, 30 U.S. (5 Pet.) 1 (1831); *Worcester v. Georgia*, 31 U.S. (6 Pet.) 1 (1832). For an illuminating discussion of these cases, see Philip Bobbitt, *Constitutional Fate: Theory of the Constitution* (New York: Oxford University Press, 1982), 108–19.

6. *Dred Scott v. Sandford*, 60 U.S. (19 How.) 393 (1857).

7. Ueda, "Naturalization and Citizenship," 739.

8. Alexander Bickel, *The Morality of Consent* (New Haven: Yale University Press, 1975), 50–51; Schuck and Smith, *Citizenship without Consent*, 61–62, 86–88. The Expatriation Act was primarily a response to a conflict with Britain over the meaning of citizenship. Since Britain considered citizenship to be perpetual, it treated British citizens who had become naturalized citizens in America and fought against Britain as traitors. Britain also arrested naturalized Irish Americans for protesting British rule during the 1860s in Ireland.

9. Peter J. Spiro, "Questioning Barriers to Naturalization," *Georgetown Immigration Law Review* 13, no. 4 (summer 1999): 505. See also Spiro, "Dual Nationality and the Meaning of Citizenship."

10. States often prohibited the entry of criminals, paupers, migrants considered threats to public health, free blacks, and slaves who were being imported. In the 1850s, western states sought to restrict the entry of Chinese immigrants. Most of these regulations were not well enforced. For most immigrants this was a period of relatively easy entry. Neuman, *Strangers to the Constitution*, chap. 2.

11. Also excluded were lunatics, idiots, and persons likely to become public charges in 1882, and those with certain diseases, polygamists, and persons convicted of misdemeanors involving moral turpitude in 1891. Robert A. Devine, *American Immigration Policy, 1924–1952* (New York: Da Capo Press, 1972), 2; Archdeacon, *Becoming American*, 144–45.

12. Act of May 6, 1882, 22 Stat. 58; 8 U.S.C.

13. Smith, *Civic Ideals*, 359; Archdeacon, *Becoming American*, 145–59.

14. *In re Ah Yup* 1 F. Cas. 223 (C.C.D. Cal. 1878). Judge Sawyer pointed out that when Congress revised the law in 1870 to include naturalization for "aliens of African nativity, and . . . persons of African descent" it had not deleted the term "white." He concluded that Congress had therefore meant to make a single addition to those eligible for naturalization rather than revise the concept of white and its centrality in defining American citizenship.

15. *Yick Wo v. Hopkins*, 118 U.S. 356 (1886); *Wong Kim Ark v. United States*, 169 U.S. 649 (March 28, 1898).

16. In 1802, applicants for citizenship were required to file a "declaration of intent" to naturalize at least three years prior to doing so, a requirement reduced to two years in 1824. Until 1922, wives and minor children automatically received citizenship when their husbands or fathers were naturalized, although a small number of women did petition to be naturalized.

17. Steven Erie, *Rainbow's End: Irish-Americans and the Dilemmas of Urban Machine Politics, 1840–1985* (Berkeley: University of California Press, 1988), 51–53.

18. *Woodcock v. Bolster*, 35 Vt. 640–41 (1863). See also *Spragins v. Houghton* (Illinois, 1890); *Stewart v. Foster* (Pennsylvania, 1809); Jamin Raskin, "Legal Aliens, Local Citizens: The Historical, Constitutional and Theoretical Meanings of Alien Suffrage," *University of Pennsylvania Law Review* 141, no. 4 (April 1993): 1454, 1405–6.

19. Raskin, "Legal Aliens, Local Citizens," 1407.

20. In *In re Rodriguez*, the court determined that the 1836 Texas constitution accorded citizenship to all persons who were residents on independence, with the exception of blacks and Indians. Contrary to the logic of *Ah Yup*, history rather than race was deemed the defining factor, thus providing further indication of how the basis for citizenship could vary considerably. *In re Rodriguez*, 81 F. 337 (W.D. Tex. 1897).

21. *In re Halladjian*, 174 F. 834 (C.C.D. Mass. 1909). There is no such thing as a white or yellow race, the court said, adding that Europeans were themselves not unmixed. Indeed, the court denied that white even meant European. The "white" in the free white clause simply referred to inhabitants in 1790 and those not actually singled out for exclusion. Since Armenians had never been specifically excluded, they were eligible to be included.

22. *U.S. v. Balsara*, 180 F. 694 (2d C. 1910).

23. Quoted in Tyler G. Anbinder, *Nativism and Slavery: The Northern Know Nothings and the Politics of the 1850s* (New York: Oxford University Press, 1994).

24. Walzer, "What Does It Mean to Be an American?" 600. See also Dale Knobel, *Paddy and the Republic: Ethnicity and Nationality in Antebellum America* (Middletown, CT: Wesleyan University Press, 1986), chap. 2; Anbinder, *Nativism and Slavery*.

25. Bridges, *A City in the Republic*.

26. John Higham, "Integrating America: The Problem of Assimilation," in *Send These to Me: Immigrants in Urban America*, rev. ed. (Baltimore: Johns Hopkins University Press, 1984), 192.

27. Gleason, "American Identity and Americanization," 38–39.

28. Gerstle, "The Protean Character."

29. Ueda, "Naturalization and Citizenship," 743–44.

30. Woodrow Wilson, *A History of the American People* (New York: Harper and Brothers, 1902), 5:212–13.

31. The national committee of the IRL included the economist John Commons, the eugenicist Madison Grant, Lawrence Lowell, president of Harvard, and Franklin MacVeagh, secretary of treasury under Taft.

32. Prescott F. Hall, "The New Immigrants Threaten America's Racial Stock" (*North American Review*, 1912) in *Immigration: Opposing Viewpoints*, ed. Teresa O'Neill (San Diego: Greenhaven Press, 1992), 108–14.

33. *Reports of the Immigration Commission* (Washington, DC: GPO, 1911), 1:42–43, and vol. 5, *Dictionary of Races and Peoples*. See Robert Carlson, *The Americanization Syndrome: The Quest for Conformity* (London: Croom Helm, 1987), 77.

34. *Reports of the Immigration Commission*, 1:42–43, 14, 47. For a discussion of the economic and eugenic contributions to the Dillingham report, see Desmond King, *Making Americans: Immigration, Race, and the Origins of the Diverse Democracy* (Cambridge, MA: Harvard University Press, 2000), 73–76.

35. Americanizers focused their attention on immigrants from southern and eastern Europe; they largely ignored other immigrants, such as those from China or Mexico. In part, this exclusion resulted from these groups' concentration in the West, while Americanization was primarily an eastern and midwestern phenomenon. The exclusion of Chinese and Mexicans also resulted from the easy racial distinctions Americans made in their regard, which often precluded them from considering these groups as capable of being assimilated. Asians' status as "aliens ineligible for citizenship" in particular made assimilation for the Chinese a moot issue.

36. January 29, 1916, Records of the Immigration and Naturalization Service, Record Group 85, National Archives (hereafter cited as NA RG) entry 30, box 6, Sundry Educational Work of the Bureau of Naturalization, part 4. My analysis in chapters 4–6 draws on these and related primary records of the INS (then called the Bureau of Naturalization), the Department of Labor (RG 174), and the Bureau of Education (RG 12). There are a number of studies of the Americanization movement. Edward Hartmann's *Movement to Americanize the Immigrant* (New York: Columbia University Press, 1948), offers a helpful chronological survey. Desmond King's *Making Americans* is the most recent book to make use of these primary sources; I discuss King's analysis in chapters 6 and 8. The critical study of the Americanization movement to which all other studies are indebted is John Higham's *Strangers in the Land: Patterns of American Nativism, 1860–1925*, 2nd ed. (New Brunswick: Rutgers University Press, 1988); I draw on Higham's analysis throughout these chapters. Philip Gleason's 1980 essay "Americanization and American Identity" is another landmark study, a synthetic analysis to which I refer throughout this book. Other book-length studies of the Americanization movement include Robert Carlson's *Americanization Syndrome*, which treats the movement as an instance of an American tradition of conformity, and John J. Miller's *Unmaking of Americans: How Multiculturalism Has Undermined American's Assimilation Ethic* (New York: Free Press, 1998), which is far more appreciative of the movement and which I discuss in chapters 6 and 7. In a series of essays, John F. McClymer conducted careful analyses of the federal educational efforts: "The Federal Government and the Americanization Movement, 1915–1924," *Prologue* 10 (spring 1978): 23–41; "The

Americanization Movement and the Education of the Foreign-born Adult, 1914–1925," in *American Education and the European Immigrant: 1840–1940*, ed. Bernard Weiss (Urbana: University of Illinois Press, 1982). See also McClymer's book, *War and Welfare: Social Engineering in America, 1890–1925* (Westport, CT: Greenwood, 1980). Michael Kammen also made excellent use of the Americanization primary sources at the National Archives in his study of American popular constitutionalism in *A Machine That Would Go of Itself: The Constitution in American Culture* (New York: Vintage Books, 1987), 235–48.

37. Louis D. Brandeis, "Testimony before the United States Commission on Industrial Relations," *Senate Documents* (January 23, 1915), 64th Cong., 1st sess., vol. 26; Woodrow Wilson, *The New Freedom: A Call for the Emancipation of the Generous Energies of a People*, ed. William E. Leuchtenberg (Englewood Cliffs, NJ: Prentice-Hall, 1961), chaps. 8, 9, 12; Herbert Croly, *The Promise of American Life* (Boston: Northeastern University Press, 1989); Theodore Roosevelt, "The Strenuous Life" (speech before the Hamilton Club, Chicago, April 10, 1899), in *The Works of Theodore Roosevelt*, ed. Hermann Hagedorn (New York: Charles Scribner's Sons, 1926), 13:319–31.

38. For an exploration of what Jackson Lears calls a "crisis in cultural authority," see his *No Place of Grace: Antimodernism and the Transformation of American Culture, 1880–1920* (New York: Pantheon, 1981). On the implications of changes in patterns of production and consumption, see Warren Susman, *Culture as History: The Transformation of American Society in the Twentieth Century* (New York: Pantheon Books, 1973), especially his essay "Culture and Commitment," 184–210.

39. Walter Lippmann, *A Preface to Morals* (New York: Macmillan, 1929), 68. See also Henry Adams, *The Education of Henry Adams* (1907; reissued Boston: Houghton Mifflin, 1918), and *Mont-Saint-Michel and Chartres* (1904; reissued New York: Penguin Books, 1986).

40. The title of Nell Painter's survey of American history from 1877 to 1919 captures the feeling that these massive changes combined to create: a sense that Americans were "standing at Armageddon." Nell Irvin Painter, *Standing at Armageddon: The United States, 1877–1919* (New York: W. W. Norton, 1989).

41. Higham writes, "For a homogeneous people to have sprung from America's diversities, extensive interaction would have been required *between* the subordinate groups. . . . [T]he attention historians have given to spectacular incidents like the New York Draft Riots of 1863 has made us overlook the great extent to which ethnic groups in the nineteenth century kept out of one another's way" ("Integrating America," 185).

42. John Higham, "Another Look at Nativism," *Catholic Historical Review* 44 (July 1958): 147–58.

43. Gerstle, "The Protean Character," 1056n. 31.

44. John Dewey, *Reconstruction in Philosophy* (New York: Henry Holt, 1920); Dewey, *The Public and Its Problems* (New York: Henry Holt, 1927). See also Smith, *Civic Ideals*, 421.

45. John Dewey, "Interpretation of Savage Mind," in *John Dewey: The Middle Works, 1899–1924*, ed. Jo Ann Boydston (Carbondale: Southern Illinois Press, 1980), 2:39–52. See Lissak, *Pluralism and Progressives*, 151–53, 167–68.

46. John Dewey, "Nationalizing Education," in *John Dewey*, ed. Boydston, 10:204.

47. John Dewey, *Democracy and Education* (New York: Macmillan, 1916), 4. See also Dewey, "Nationalizing Education," 202–3; Dewey, "Nationalism and Its Fruits," in *Intelligence in the Modern World: John Dewey's Philosophy*, ed. Joseph Ratner (New York: Modern Library, 1939), 467–74.

48. Dewey, "Nationalizing Education," 202, 205.

49. Dewey, "Principle of Nationality," in *John Dewey*, ed. Boydston, 10:289. Reprinted from *Menorah Journal* 3 (1917): 203–8. See also Dewey, "Nationalizing Education," 202–15.

50. Alan Ryan, "Pragmatism, Social Identity, Patriotism, and Self-Criticism," *Social Research* 63, no. 4 (winter 1996): 12.

51. Dewey, *Reconstruction in Philosophy*, 202–04. See also Smith, *Civic Ideals*, 420–21.

52. Dewey, *Recontruction in Philosophy*, 205. See also Dewey, *The Public and Its Problems*, chap. 5 and 211–13.

53. All quotations in this section are from Randolph S. Bourne, "Trans-National America," *Atlantic Monthly* 18 (July 1916): 86–97. Reprinted in *War and the Intellectuals: Collected Essays, 1915–1919*, ed. Carl Resek (New York: Harper and Row, 1964), 109, 115, 112, 113, 117, 121, 118.

54. Walzer, "What Does It Mean to Be an 'American'?" 611.

55. David Hollinger, *Postethnic America: Beyond Multiculturalism* (New York: Basic Books, 1995), 94.

56. Bourne, "Trans-National America," 118, 119, 121.

57. Carlson, *The Americanization Syndrome*, 60–61.

58. John D. Buenker, "Sovereign Individuals and Organic Networks: Political Cultures in Conflict during the Progressive Era," *American Quarterly* 40 (1988): 196. See also Richard Hofstadter, *The Age of Reform: From Bryan to F.D.R.* (New York: Vintage Books, 1955), 9; Edward Banfield and James Q. Wilson, *City Politics* (New York: Vintage Books, 1963).

59. Bridges, *A City in the Republic*, 5. See also Erie, *Rainbow's End*; John D. Buenker, *Urban Liberalism and Progressive Reform* (New York: Charles Scribner's Sons, 1973). Jane Addams, "Why the Ward Boss Rules," *Outlook* 57 (April 2, 1898), reprinted in Jean Bethke Elshtain, *The Jane Addams Reader* (New York: Basic Books, 2002), 123.

60. Addams, "Why the Ward Boss Rules," 120, 124; Buenker, "Sovereign Individuals and Organic Networks," 195.

61. Carlson, *The Americanization Syndrome*, 63–65; Graham Taylor, quoted in McClymer, *War and Welfare*, 97.

62. Peter Skerry, "Citizenship Begins at Home," *The Responsive Community* 14, no. 1 (winter 2003/04): 26–37. See also Skerry, *Mexican-Americans: The Ambivalent Minority* (New York: Free Press, 1993), 27. Jane Addams, "Americanization," in American Sociological Society *Publications* 14 (1919): 206–14, reprinted in Elshtain, *The Jane Addams Reader*, 244; Jane Addams, "Immigration: A Field Neglected by the Scholar," *The Commons* 10, no. 1 (January 1905), reprinted in *Immigration and Americanization*, ed. Davis, 9.

63. Harry C. Boyte and Jennifer O'Donoghue, "The Jane Addams School for Democracy," *Blueprint*, spring 1999, http://www.ndol.org. On linking the private to the public and on bringing a more communal dimension to public life, see also Boyte, *Everyday Politics: Reconnecting Citizens and Public Life* (Philadelphia: University of Pennsylvania Press, 2004), chap. 6; and Jean Bethke Elshtain, *Jane Addams and the Dream of American Democracy* (New York: Basic Books, 2002), especially 157–58, 201–10.

64. "Relative to Further Restriction of Immigration," *Hearings before the Committee on Immigration and Naturalization*, U.S. HR, 62nd Cong., 2nd sess., part 1, 1912, 53.

65. Grace Abbott, *Immigrant and the Community* (New York: Century, 1917), 277.

66. Jane Addams, *Twenty Years at Hull House* (New York: MacMillan, 1910), especially chaps. 2, 4, 6; Addams, *Newer Ideals of Peace* (New York: Macmillan, 1907), chaps.

1, 8; Addams, introduction to *Democracy and Social Ethics* (Urbana: University of Illinois Press, 2002). See also Lissak, *Pluralism and Progressives*, 141–44.

67. John Dewey, "The School as Social Centre," *Proceedings and Addresses* of the National Education Association (1902), 373–83, reprinted in *John Dewey*, ed. Boydston, 2:91; Lissak, *Pluralism and Progressives*, 45; Addams, *Twenty Years at Hull House*, 365.

68. Allen Davis, *Spearheads for Reform: The Social Settlement and the Progressive Movement, 1890–1914* (New Brunswick: Rutgers University Press, 1967), 89. See also Daniel E. Weinberg, "The Foreign Language Information Service and the Foreign Born, 1918–1939: A Case Study of Cultural Assimilation Viewed as a Problem in Social Technology" (Ph.D. diss., University of Minnesota, 1973), 93. On Addams, see *Twenty Years at Hull House*, chap. 11; "Immigration," 17; Elshtain, *Jane Addams and the Dream of American Democracy*, 144–48.

69. Lissak, *Pluralism and Progressives*, 164–65.

70. John Dewey, "American Education and Culture," in *Intelligence in the Modern World*, ed. Ratner, 725.

71. Lissak, *Pluralism and Progressives*, 158, 162. Lissak identifies the high-Western culture elements that settlement house workers believed had formed an advanced American culture. But her contention that most social reformers, including Addams, sought primarily to homogenize immigrants is hard to reconcile with the reformers' programs and publications. "Addams' Victorian language of 'uplift' can sound condescending to modern ears," writes Harry Boyte. "But from another angle, compared to our era in which most poor and immigrant populations are seen as needy and deficient by professional service providers, what is remarkable is the underlying conviction that ordinary people—poor and working class people, without money, of varied backgrounds, with little social status—had talents to contribute to the public conversation" (*Everyday Politics*, chap. 6). See also Elshtain, *Jane Addams and the Dream of American Democracy*, 203, 302n. 36.

CHAPTER FIVE
NATIONALISM IN THE PROGRESSIVE ERA

1. *Report of the Commissioner of Naturalization* (Washington, DC: GPO, 1916), 459.

2. Quoted in Higham, *Strangers in the Land*, 241.

3. Roosevelt, "The Strenuous Life," 331.

4. Roosevelt, "National Life and Character" (August 1894, *The Sewanee Review*), *Works*, ed. Hagedorn, 13:15–17.

5. Croly, *The Promise of American Life*, 257.

6. Ibid., 453; See also Ryan, "Pragmatism, Social Identity, Patriotism, and Self-Criticism."

7. Thomas G. Dyer, *Theodore Roosevelt and the Idea of Race* (Baton Rouge: Louisiana State University Press, 1980), 33–44.

8. Theodore Roosevelt, *The Naval War of 1812* (1882), in *Works*, ed. Hagedorn, 6:23, 30; Roosevelt, *Gouverneur Morris* (1888), in *Works*, ed. Hagedorn, 7:324–25.

9. Theodore Roosevelt, *Thomas Hart Benton* (1887), in *Works*, ed. Hagedorn, 7:114.

10. Theodore Roosevelt, *The Winning of the West: An Account of the Exploration and Settlement of Our Country from the Alleghenies to the Pacific* (1890), in *Works*, ed. Hagedorn,

8:8; "National Life and Character," in *Works*, ed. Hagedorn, 13:212–13. See Gerstle, *American Crucible*, 22–24, 32–38, 62–65, 75–80.

11. Theodore Roosevelt, "The Japanese Question," *The Outlook* (1909), in *Works*, ed. Hagedorn, 16:288–94; Dyer, *Theodore Roosevelt and the Idea of Race*, 134–40.

12. Dyer, *Theodore Roosevelt and the Idea of Race*, 139. Part of Roosevelt's decision to exclude Japanese immigrants from entry issued from a compromise he engineered to limit racial exclusion at home. In 1906, the year prior to the Gentlemen's Agreement, the state of California had begun segregating Asian students in their public schools. Roosevelt promised California officials that he would limit Asian immigrants in return for an end to such segregation. In other words, national immigration laws restricting entry to Asians were enacted, in part, in the context of protecting Asians already living in the United States.

13. Theodore Roosevelt, "Americanism," address delivered before the Knights of Columbus, Carnegie Hall, New York, October 12, 1915, in *Works*, ed. Hagedorn, 18:13–15.

14. Higham, *Strangers in the Land*, 190.

15. Dyer, *Theodore Roosevelt and the Idea of Race*, 131–32.

16. Theodore Roosevelt, review of *National Life and Character*, by Charles H. Pearson, *Sewanee Review* (August 1894), in *Works*, ed. Hagedorn, 13:213; review of *The Law of Civilization and Decay*, by Brooks Adams, *The Forum* (January 1897), in *Works*, ed. Hagedorn, 13:250; see also Michael Lind, *The Next American Nation: The New Nationalism and the Fourth American Revolution* (New York: Free Press, 1995), 73.

17. Roosevelt, "Americanism," 392–93.

18. Ibid., 402.

19. Roosevelt, "True Americanism" (April 1894), *The Forum*, in *Works*, ed. Hagedorn, 13:22–24.

20. *Report to the President of the Commission on Naturalization*, 59th Cong., 1st sess., House of Representatives, Document No. 46 (Washington, DC: GPO, 1905), 11–15.

21. The commission consisted of Milton D. Purdy from the Department of Justice, Galliard Hunt from the Department of State, and Richard K. Campbell from the Department of Commerce and Labor.

22. The new Naturalization Division also standardized the naturalization process by issuing a single application form and certificate of naturalization, as well as making processing fees uniform. *Report to the President of the Commission on Naturalization* (1905). See also Louis DeSipio and Harry Pachon, *Making Americans, Remaking America: Immigration and Immigrant Policy* (Boulder, CO: Westview Press, 1998), 75–76. The naturalization process itself was further formalized after 1913, when the two parts of the Bureau of Immigration and Naturalization were established as separate entities under the Department of Labor, which had been split off from the Department of Commerce. The bureau oversaw a naturalization process that involved two steps. As soon as they established residency, male immigrants over the age of eighteen were eligible to file "First Papers" declaring their intention to seek naturalization. To petition for naturalization (called "Second Papers"), these immigrants had to have resided in the country continuously for five years and have held their First Papers for two years. After filing the Second Papers, the applicant had to wait ninety days and then appear before a court to be examined. Naturalization hearings were held in over two thousand state and federal courts. The Bureau of Naturalization's 62 examiners and 11 chief examiners represented the government at

their hearings. All declarations, petitions, and approvals of naturalization were sent to the bureau, which sought to ensure that only properly qualified applicants were approved for citizenship. In addition, many judges turned over to the bureau's examiners the task of actually examining candidates for citizenship. NA RG 85, INS, entry 30, box 6, Sundry Educational Work of the Bureau of Naturalization, part 8. See also R. E. Cole, "The Naturalization of Foreigners," in *Immigration and Americanization,* ed. Davis, 603.

23. *Report to the President of the Commission on Naturalization* (1905), 11.

24. Actions by which the government would presume citizens to have expatriated themselves included: naturalizing or taking an oath of allegiance to a foreign state; serving in another country's armed forces or performing the duties of any position in a foreign state for which only nationals of that state were eligible; and voting in another country's election. Special provisions were included to strip American women of their citizenship if they married foreigners and to revoke that of naturalized aliens if they took up extended residence in their native countries. Desertion during wartime and acts of treason were also identified as grounds for denationalization, and a provision was included that prevented citizens from expatriating themselves on American soil during wartime. 34 Stat. 1228; 8 U.S.C. 17.

25. The bureau also determined that the act included two educational requirements—speaking English and signing a form in one's own handwriting—that were easy enough to determine in court.

26. "Memorandum: The Matter of Obtaining Satisfactory Assurance That Applicants for Citizenship Are Attached to the Principles of the Constitution of the United States," February 11, 1915, NA RG 85, entry 30, box 6, Sundry Educational Work of the Bureau of Naturalization, part 3.

27. Earlier incidents of this reasoning had appeared in state courts. In 1889, a court in Utah had denied the naturalization petition of a native Hawaiian who could not identify the current U.S. president or demonstrate "sufficient intelligence to understand the principles of the government which may rest in part on his will." *In re Kanaka Nian,* 21 P. 993, 994 (Utah 1889). In 1894, the Eastern District of Pennsylvania held that naturalization should be denied when the applicant "was without such knowledge of the constitution as is essential to the rational assumption of an undertaking" of the required oath to support it, or had failed to demonstrate "at least some general comprehension of what the constitution is, and of the principles which it affirms." *In re Bodek,* 63 F. 813, 815 (E.D. Pa. 1894). In 1908, the U.S. Supreme Court denied citizenship to an applicant on the grounds that "a person cannot be attached to the principles of which he is entirely ignorant." *In re Meakins,* 164 Fed. 334 (1908).

28. Untitled Memorandum, NA RG 85, entry 30, box 6, Sundry Educational Work of the Bureau of Naturalization, part 8.

29. "Suggestions to Petitioners for Naturalization," May 7, 1909, NA RG 85, entry 30, box 1, 27671/9, 1–2.

30. Chief Examiner of Colorado to Commissioner of Naturalization, May 7, 1915, U.S. Government Participation in the Education and Mental Training of Aliens, part 1, NA RG 85, entry 30, box 1, 27671/25, 1–2.

31. "Qualifications for American Citizenship," NA RG 85, box 265, E18225. See also undated form letter from Assistant U.S. Attorney, San Francisco, NA RG 85, box 265, E18225.

32. Kammen, *A Machine That Would Go of Itself,* 237.

33. Chief Examiner of Colorado to Commissioner of Naturalization, May 7, 1915, 2.

34. Chief Examiner Cowley to Commissioner of Naturalization, June 5, 1915, NA RG 85, entry 30, box 6, 27671/25.

35. "On Becoming a Citizen," *Christian Science Monitor*, NA RG 85, entry 30, box 6, 27671/25. The chief examiner in St. Paul, Minnesota, enclosed this editorial in his report to the commissioner of naturalization, March 19, 1914.

36. "Qualifications for American Citizenship," 3.

37. Campbell to R. S. Coleman, chief examiner in St. Paul, October 28, 1914, NA RG 85, entry 30, box 6, 27671/25. See also Campbell to Post, "Memorandum for the Assistant Secretary," December 22, 1914, NA RG 85, entry 30, box 6, 27671/25.

38. Frank V. Thompson, *Schooling of the Immigrant* (1920; reprinted Montclair, NJ: Patterson Smith, 1917), 338, 339.

39. Campbell to Coleman, October 28, 1914.

40. "Memorandum for the Assistant Secretary," 3.

41. Thompson, *Schooling of the Immigrant*, 351.

42. "Memorandum: The Matter of Obtaining Satisfactory Assurance"; Thompson, *Schooling of the Immigrant*, 336

43. Chief Naturalization Examiner, Seattle, Washington, to Commissioner of Naturalization, November 14, 1923, NA RG 85, box 1, entry 30, 2.

44. In fiscal year 1915–16, 1,336 out of 105,838 applicants were "continued to ignorance of government"—i.e., put off until they could pass the test. By fiscal year 1917–18, 10,661 out of 163,631 were "continued for ignorance." *Report of the Commissioner of Naturalization* (Washington, DC: GPO, 1916), 434, 460; *Report of the Commissioner of Naturalization* (Washington, DC: GPO, 1918), 588. See also Crist to Campbell, December 23, 1914, NA RG 85, entry 30, box 6, 2–3.

45. Kammen, *A Machine That Would Go of Itself*, 237.

46. *Report of the Commissioner of Naturalization* (PO, 1916), 474.

47. Goodwin to Post, December 16, 1914, NA RG 85, entry 30, box 6, 27671/25.

48. Crist to Campbell, December 23, 1914, 2.

49. Ibid.

50. *Report of the Commissioner of Naturalization* (1916), 460.

51. Ibid., 462–63.

52. Ibid.

53. *Report of the Commissioner of Naturalization* (1916), 503–40. The secretary of labor worried that "approximately three quarters of our resident aliens retain foreign allegiance . . . and only 26 percent of those admitted to citizenship annually are the most desirable" (460).

54. Ibid., 467.

55. Ibid., 459.

56. In their annual reports, Campbell and Crist reported significant increases in the numbers of cities and towns providing classes for immigrants and in the number of aliens actually enrolled. By July 1916, the bureau claimed that 613 cities and towns had launched new programs, and over 1,000 by the time Campbell filed his report for 1916. In 1921, the bureau reported that 3,526 cities and towns offered courses. *Report of the Commissioner of Naturalization* (1916), 476; *Report of the Commissioner of Naturalization* (1921), 34. Subsequent estimates suggest that these figures were significantly overstated. McClymer, "The Americanization Movement and the Education of the Foreign

Born Adult," 102–4, 115. Margaret D. Moore, *Citizenship Training of Adult Immigrants in the United States* (Washington, DC: GPO, 1925).

57. According to the historian John McClymer, less than half of the students finished their courses. Yet attendance in many cases remained remarkably high. The Massachusetts Department of Education, for instance, characterized the many sacrifices immigrants made to attend naturalization courses as "both inspiring and pathetic." In Plymouth, a man rode ten miles to school after finishing work; in Shirley, Polish men went to class three nights a week and their wives attended the other two. See Charles Kelso, "Civic Education of Immigrants," NA RG 85, entry 30, box 6, 27871/25; Ueda, "Naturalization and Citizenship"; Thompson, *Schooling of the Immigrant*; McClymer, "The Americanization Movement and the Education of the Foreign Born Adult."

58. Raymond F. Crist, *Student's Textbook* (Washington, DC: GPO, 1918); Crist, *Teacher's Manual* (Washington, DC: GPO, 1918); U.S. Bureau of Naturalization, *Syllabus of the Naturalization Law* (Washington, DC: GPO, 1916).

59. "Memorandum: The Matter of Obtaining Satisfactory Assurance"; Los Angeles Chief Examiner Fred Jones to Bureau of Naturalization, April 2, 1915, NA RG 85, entry 30, box 6, 27671/25. Also see Thompson, *Schooling of the Immigrant*, 343–45.

60. Kelso, "Civic Education of Immigrants"; *Report of the Commissioner of Naturalization* (1916), 471, 462.

61. *Report of the Commissioner of Naturalization* (1916), 467–68.

62. Thompson, *Schooling of the Immigrant*, 357–58; Raymond F. Crist, report to the Commissioner of Naturalization, October 11, 1915, NA RG 85, entry 30, box 6, 5.

63. Fred Jones to Bureau of Naturalization, April 2, 1915; Bureau of Education, "Civic Education for Immigrants—Circular No. 1," NA RG 12, box 44.

64. "Address by Charles Kelso to Graduating Class," January 5, 1922, NA RG 85, entry 30, box 265, E18033-E17920. See also Kelso, "Civic Education of Immigrants."

65. Kammen, *A Machine That Would Go of Itself*, 238.

66. The rote nature of citizenship courses also reflected the influence of two streams of civic education at the time. These courses drew on a long tradition of legalism that emphasized the structure of government rather than how it functioned. They drew as well on the newly developed "community civics" approach, which focused extensively on local affairs. Neither approach regarded debate and deliberation on controversial issues as an important part of civic instruction. Thompson wrote of the community civics approach, "One would never suspect, in reading these texts, that there are affairs in government upon which honest men may differ" (*Schooling of the Immigrant*, 330–31).

67. "Extract from Examiner Tomlinson letter, Salem, Oregon, dated February 6, 1919," NA RG 85, entry 30, box 1, E14, 27675. "U.S. Textbook a Short Course in Citizenship," *Chicago Daily Tribune*, October 21, 1919, NA RG 85, entry 30, box 1, 27675. See also Chief Naturalization Examiner, Seattle, to Commissioner of Naturalization, November 14, 1923; Thompson, *Schooling of the Immigrant*, 348, 349.

68. William Sharlip and Albert A. Owens, *Adult Immigrant Education: Its Scope, Content, and Methods* (New York: Macmillan, 1925), 162–63. See also McClymer, "The Americanization Movement and the Education of the Foreign Born Adult"; *Evening Schools and Extension Work: Course of Study Manual, Pittsburgh Public Schools* (Pittsburgh: Board of Education, 1915), 26–27.

69. McClymer, "The Americanization Movement and the Education of the Foreign Born Adult," 109. See also Cole, "The Naturalization of Foreigners," 604.

70. Higham, *Strangers in the Land*, 239, 241–42.

71. Frances Kellor, *Out of Work: A Study of Employment Agencies, Their Treatment of the Unemployed, and Their Influence upon Homes and Business* (New York: Putnam, 1904).

72. D. Chauncey Brewer, the president, was a lawyer and active member of the Boston Chamber of Commerce. See Brewer, "A Patriotic Movement for the Assimilation of Immigrants," *Editorial Review* 3 (August 1910): 786–800. See Edward Hartmann, *The Movement to Americanize the Immigrant* (New York: Columbia University Press, 1948), 38–63.

73. Trumball to Claxton, April 1, 1919, NA RG 12, entry 6, box 11, Historical File 106: Child Health Organizations—Americanization War Work.

74. *Reports of the Immigration Commission*, 1:42–43.

75. Ibid.

76. Hartmann, *The Movement to Americanize the Immigrant*, 97–101; Higham, *Strangers in the Land*, 190, 241–42.

77. These funds were provided to the committee by its backers, including the railroad president Frank Trumball; the banker Felix Warburg; and the wives of prominent industrialists, such as Mrs. Vincent Astor and Mrs. Cornelius Vanderbilt. In a final report on the committee's work written in 1919, Trumball noted that $85,247.80 had been supplied to the bureau over the previous five years. "It is not too much to say," he noted, "that we think it has been largely responsible for the Americanization work undertaken" by the bureau during this period. The committee also provided workers to publicize the need for Americanization. Trumball to Claxton, April 1, 1919.

78. A formal "Memorandum of Understanding" between the secretary of the interior and the National Americanization Committee required that all policies "be discussed with duly authorized representatives of the National Americanization Committee." "Memorandum of Understanding between the Secretary of the Interior and the National Americanization Committee for the Extension of the Work of the Division of Immigrant Education in the Bureau of Education," May 2, 1919, NA RG 12, box 106.

79. Lane to B. F. Welty, May 15, 1918, NA RG 85, box 106. See also Frances Kellor, *Straight America: A Call to National Service* (New York: Macmillan, 1926), 101.

80. All quotations in this section are from Kellor, *Straight America*, 26, 44, 176, 182, 176, 32, 27–28, 31, 13.

81. "What Is Americanization," NA RG 12, Records of the Office of Education, Historical File, 1870–1950, box 12, entry 6.

82. Fred C. Butler, "Americanization: Its Purpose and Process," address to the Women's Federation of Wisconsin, Madison, 1919, NA RG 12, box 11, file 106, 4, 1, 9, 8, 10–12. Desmond King argues that Butler's faith in citizenship training contradicts his concern that Americanization not become too uniform and conformist. I read this issue more as the expression of a perennial tension between teaching broad principles while leaving room for disagreement over their application. King, *Making Americans*, 106.

83. Butler, "Americanization," 10, 11, 16, 17. Another essay that appears to have been written by Butler takes up the idea of "immigrant gifts," urging Americans to see that immigrants bring with them "something that we need and something that will add to the wealth of our common heritage. It may be an art, a custom, an ideal, a skill or perchance only a strong body—but there is a need here for whatever he brings." In this essay, Americanizers are admonished that "we do not want to destroy his customs, his

literature, his language. But we do want him to become an American" ("Making Americans," NA RG 12, box 11, file 106).

CHAPTER SIX
WORLD WAR I AND THE TURN TO COERCION

1. "Colonel Roosevelt's New Crusade," *Literary Digest* 52 (June 3, 1916): 1618; "Democratic Campaign Issues," *Literary Digest* 53 (July 1, 1916): 4. Higham, *Strangers in the Land*, 189–90, 198–99; McClymer, "The Americanization Movement and the Education of the Foreign Born Adult," 25.

2. *Annual Report of the Attorney General of the United States for 1920* (Washington, DC: GPO, 1920), 172–78. See David Bennett, *The Party of Fear: From Nativist Movements to the New Right in American History* (New York: Vintage Books, 1988), chap. 11.

3. *In re Halladjian*, 174 F. 834 (U.S.C.C. Mass. 1909).

4. *Terrace v. Thompson*, 274 F. 841 (1921).

5. *Ozawa v. United States*, 200 U.S. 1995 (1922).

6. *United States v. Bhagat Singh Thind*, 61 U.S.C. 616 (1923).

7. Jacobson, *Whiteness of a Different Color*, 236.

8. Speech given by Judge Bledsoe to petitioners in naturalization court, September 22, 1922, NA RG 85, entry 30, box 265, E18033-E17920, Los Angeles. "Self-government," he made clear, "means that the individuals who practice it and derive the benefits therefrom, have enough intelligence in the first place to know what do and what not to do, and in the second place have an idea of social obligation and intellectual self-restraint so that they will not seek to make the balance of the people suffer because of their own individual wants, desires, appetites, or aspirations. "

9. *In re Conner*, 279 Fed. 789 (1922), District Court for the District of Montana. See also three cases from the District Court for the Southern District of Texas: *In re Nagy*, 3 Fed. (2d) 77 (1924); *In re Raio*, 3 Fed. (2d) 78 (1924); *In re Philips*, 3 Fed. (2d) 79 (1924).

10. *United States v. Olsson*, 196 Fed. 562 (1912); *United States v. Swelgin*, 254 Fed. 884 (1918). In 1932 the Court ruled similarly on applicants for citizenship who advocated a constitutional amendment abolishing the departments of the federal government. *In re Saralieff*, 59 Fed. (2d) 436 (1932).

11. In 1919, a New York District Court cancelled a certificate of naturalization even though the applicant did not advocate the violent overthrow of the government. The court treated the applicant's "philosophical anarchism" as equally dangerous, since "it tends to create a spirit of unrest and dissatisfaction among our population, which is inimical to organized government and subversive of law and authority." *United States v. Stuppiello*, 260 Fed. 483 (1919).

12. *In re Roeper*, 274 Fed. 490 (1921). In 1921 an applicant who affirmed his conscientious reservations against killing, and who could not therefore serve in the military, was denied citizenship. In 1922, a Massachusetts court went further and indicated that attachment to the Constitution had to be demonstrated by active participation in support of it. Hence, it denied naturalization to an applicant who, as a resident alien, had not served in the military during the war. *In re Shanin*, 278 Fed. 739 (1922).

13. *United States v. Schwimmer*, 279 U.S. 644 (1929). See also *Macintosh v. United States*, 42 Fed. (2d) 845 (1930).

14. *Schurmann v. United States*, 264 Fed. 917 (1920), and 257 U.S. 621 (1922).

15. *Crane v. New York*, 239 U.S. 195 (1915); *Patsone v. Pennsylvania*, 232 U.S. 138 (1914).

16. *Frick v. Webb*, 263 U.S. 326 (1923).

17. See Kellor, *Straight America*, 38.

18. Slav and Magyar nationalities from Austria-Hungary were preponderate in eastern coal fields, constituted two-thirds of the workforce in the iron and steel industries and an equal proportion in the slaughterhouses, and labored in most of the munitions factories. When the United States declared war on Austria-Hungary in December 1917, its subjects became enemy aliens. (Higham, *Strangers in the Land*, 213.) Kansas, Nebraska, and South Dakota abandoned alien enfranchisement in 1918; Texas, Indiana, Mississippi, and Arkansas followed suit.

19. Leon E. Aylsworth, "The Passing of Alien Suffrage," *American Political Science Review* 25 (1931): 114, quoted in Raskin, "Legal Aliens, Local Citizens," 1416.

20. Higham, *Strangers in the Land*, 248.

21. Ibid., 237.

22. John Thomas Taylor to James Davis, November 17, 1921, NA RG 174, General Records of the Department of Labor 1907–42 (Chief Clerk's File), 163/127 Americanization, Sundry File, 1919–22, 162/219–163/127, box 164.

23. Undated National Council of Administration of the Veterans of Foreign Wars of the United States, "One Flag One Country, One Language," NA RG 174, Department of Labor Chief Clerk's Files, 163/127A–D, box 165.

24. Oregon required that foreign-language publications provide literal translations in English. Higham, *Strangers in the Land*, 260; Hartmann, *The Movement to Americanize the Immigrant*, 233–52.

25. Beall to Claxton, June 10, 1918, NA RG 12, file 106, box 7, entry 6.

26. Higham, *Strangers in the Land*, 207–8.

27. Quoted in Stephen Thernstrom, "Ethnic Groups in American History," in *Ethnic Relations in America*, ed. Lance Liebman (Englewood Cliffs, NJ: Prentice-Hall, 1982), 16.

28. Kellor, *Straight America*, 4, 39–40.

29. Kellor to Claxton, August 16, 1918, NA RG 12, file 106, box 7, entry 6.

30. Kellor succeeded in forging links among these concerns when the National Americanization Committee created the Immigration Committee of the U.S. Chamber of Commerce in 1917. The leadership of the two groups was virtually identical. National Americanization Committee, *A Call to National Service*, March 31, 1916.

31. Higham, *Strangers in the Land*, 249. Committee for Immigrants in America, *Memorandum to the Advisory Commission of the Council of National Defense Concerning a War Policy*, October 31, 1917 (quoted in Hartmann, *The Movement to Americanize the Immigrant*, 169–70). King, *Making Americans*, 110. The NAC and the Bureau of Education sought to carry out these and other proposals through an agency that had been recently established by Congress to integrate war-related projects: the Council on National Defense (CND). The council worked with state councils of defense whose mission was to coordinate the programs carried out by educational agencies (schools and teacher-training institutions), industrial agencies (chambers of commerce, Rotary Clubs), and a host of what they called cooperative agencies. These cooperative agencies were subdivided into official agencies (federal, state, county and municipal courts, bureaus, police, and so forth), racial and ethnic groups (newspapers, societies, employment agencies), social welfare organizations (charities, hospitals, libraries, Boy Scouts), religious organizations (churches,

YMCAs, religious charities), war and patriotic societies (Daughters of the American Revolution, Spanish War Veterans), and publicity agencies (newspapers, movies, and loan agencies). See "Organization Chart of Americanization in Pennsylvania," NA RG 12, Records of the Office of Education, Historical File, 1870–1950, file 106: Council of National Defense, box 12, entry 6. In the opening words to his pamphlet *What Americanization Means*, Herman L. Collins, the director of publicity and education for the Pennsylvania Council of National Defense, captured the urgent tone favored by this new effort: "It is proposed to knock 1,000,000 hyphens out of Pennsylvania" (NA RG 12, Records of the Office of Education, Records of the Office of the Commissioner, Historical File, 1870–1950, file 106: Council of National Defense, 1917–21, box 12, entry 6).

32. Kellor to Claxton, April 10, 1918: "English and civics are basic and essential but we cannot wait for them with the active anti-American influence at work." NA RG 12, file 106, box 7, entry 6.

33. Kellor to Claxton, March 1918 in NA RG 12, file 106, box 7, entry 6.

34. Kellor to Claxton, March 1918; Kellor to Claxton, April 17, 1918.

35. When analysts undertaking a Carnegie Foundation "Study of Americanization" suggested that this might confuse immigrants and thus deter naturalization, Crist suggested that only newly hired workers should be subject to this policy, and assured the analysts that "after two years of education as provided through text books issued by the Bureau of Naturalization, the employee would forget this coercive experience." "Memorandum of Conference between Messrs. R. F. Crist and M. C. Sturges, Bureau of Naturalization and C. C. Williamson, Adele McKinnie and A. T. Burns of the Study of Methods of Americanization," January 9, 1919, NA RG 174, box 165, 163/127-A.

36. James Davis to Samuel Shortridge, May 4, 1922, NA RG 174, Records of the Department of Labor, General Records, 1907–42, Chief Clerk's Files, box 165, 163/127-A.

37. Davis, *The Saturday Evening Post*, December 1, 1923, quoted in *The Foreign Language Press: America's Greatest Menace*, NA RG 12, box 12, entry 6, file 106, Council of National Defense, 1917–21.

38. NA RG 174, Records of the Department of Labor, General Records, 1907–42, Chief Clerk's Files, 163/127A–D, box 165, folder 163/127C, Americanization, Sundry Files, 1922–23.

39. "Copy of Resolutions Adopted by the Union of American Hebrew Congregations," January 26, 1923, NA RG 174, Records of the Department of Labor, General Records, 1907–42, Chief Clerk's Files, 163/127A–D, box 165, folder 163/127C, Americanization, Sundry Files, 1922–23.

40. William Rogers to Davis, June 20, 1922, NA RG 174, Department of Labor Chief Clerk's Files 163/127A–D, box 165.

41. Davis to Simon Wolf, March 25, 1923, NA RG 174, Records of the Department of Labor, General Records, 1907–42, Chief Clerk's Files, 163/127A–D, box 165, folder 163/127C, Americanization, Sundry Files, 1922–23.

42. Ibid.

43. Ibid.

44. Davis to Robert C. Deming, May 22, 1923, NA RG 174, Records of the Department of Labor, General Records, 1907–42, Chief Clerk's Files, 163/127A–D, box 165, folder 163/127C, Americanization, Sundry Files, 1922–23.

45. Dyer, *Theodore Roosevelt and the Idea of Race*, 168.

46. Lissak, *Pluralism and Progressives*, 178. On Taylor, see McClymer, *War and Welfare*, 126.

47. Addams, "Americanization," 247, 245, in Elshtain, *The Jane Addams Reader*.

48. One example was the Foreign Language Information Service (FLIS), which had begun in the Committee on Public Information as the Division of Work with the Foreign Born and had done much the same thing as Kellor's War Work Extension in the Bureau of Education. It had selected and created "loyal" foreign-language associations and, through them, spread patriotic information and ceremonies. As it expanded its work, the FLIS helped new arrivals learn English and prepare for naturalization as well as improve their living and working conditions. It maintained a strong "immigrant gifts" tradition, stressing that native and foreign born alike would have to undergo a process of mutual assimilation. By 1921, the organization's only source of support was the U.S. Department of Justice, then headed by Attorney General A. Mitchell Palmer. As a subsidiary of the Department of Justice, the FLIS had to support the government's position on such issues as deportation. When Secretary of Labor Davis initiated his program to register aliens, the service privately objected on the grounds that it threatened individual liberty, opened the possibility of government abuse, and worked contrary to American traditions and values. Publicly, the FLIS aided Davis in his registration efforts, defended the program in foreign-language publications, and reported to Davis the reactions of such. Daniel Weinberg, "The Ethnic Technician and the Foreign-Born: Another Look at Americanization Ideology and Goals," *Societas—A Review of Social History* 7 (1977): 209–27; McClymer, *War and Welfare*, 129–41.

49. Gerstle, "The Protean Character," 1054–55.

50. John Dewey, "Racial Prejudice and Friction," *Chinese Social and Political Science Review* 6 (1922): 13–14, quoted in Gerstle, "The Protean Character," 1058.

51. Randolph Bourne, "Twilight of Idols," *The Seven Arts* 2 (October 1917), in *War and the Intellectuals*, ed. Resek, 53–64; Bourne, "The State" (1919), in *War and the Intellectuals*, ed. Resek, 71; Bourne, "Trans-National American," 122.

52. Hollinger, *Postethnic America*, 94–95.

53. Roosevelt expanded the reach of the presidency by rooting executive power in direct appeals to the people rather than in formal constitutional authority. Those appeals enlarged the president's power while contravening limits on governmental authority. A similar dynamic was at work in Roosevelt's new nationalism. His form of nationalism was at odds with that of Washington and Lincoln, even though he claimed them as his heroes. He did not take to heart their concerns for a polity balanced between reason and reverence and dependent on moderate habits of character. Instead, as Charles Kesler observes, he revered them for "their greatness of soul, wholly apart from the ends or the understanding of justice to which they devoted their greatness." Kesler, "Teddy Roosevelt to the Rescue?" *The National Interest*, spring 1998, http://www.claremont.org; see also Croly, *The Promise of American Life*, 174. On Roosevelt's expansion of presidential authority, see Jeffrey Tulis, *The Rhetorical Presidency* (Princeton: Princeton University Press, 1985).

54. Some modern interpreters of Americanization see its turn toward coercion as a radical change from its prewar ideology and program. This view rightly honors the original inspiration behind the Progressives' effort to incorporate immigrants, but it too easily blames changes in the movement on the extreme circumstances created by the war. See Miller, *The Unmaking of Americans*; Geyer, *Americans No More*.

55. These scholars regard the movement as reflective of America's deeply illiberal traditions. In his recent analysis of the Americanization movement, the political scientist

Desmond King illustrates this viewpoint by situating the agencies and individuals involved in the context of increasingly dominant racialist, eugenicist, and restrictive modes of thinking. But he concentrates largely on the post-1918 period and has little to say about the dynamics of change within the movement. This lacuna fits well with his overall analysis, which emphasizes the powerful influence of nativist and racist thinking and programs in U.S. history. See also Carlson, *The Americanization Syndrome*; Perea, " 'Am I an American or Not?' "

56. See Higham, *Strangers in the Land*, 249, 259. On the Council on National Defense, see Director of CND to Claxton, January 24, 1918, NA RG 12, entry 6, box 7, file 106, Records of the Office of the Commissioner, Historical File 1870–1950.

57. *Meyer v. Nebraska*, 262 U.S. 390 (1923). The attempt to limit the influence of Catholic or parochial schools, the Court said in striking down an Oregon law requiring all children to attend public schools, was an unconstitutional effort to "standardize children" (*Pierce, Governor of Oregon et al. v. Society of Sisters*, 268 U.S. 510 [1925]). In a case involving a Hawaiian law regulating private, non-English-language schools, the Court found that the state could not regulate the parents' right to send their children to these schools, even though "such schools encouraged an understanding and love of foreign ancestral languages and cultures" (*Farrington, Governor of Hawaii, et al. v. Tokushige et al.*, 284 U.S. 298 [1926]). State courts also relaxed the ideological requirements for citizens, holding, as in a 1926 case in Michigan, that "[b]elief by an alien that changes should be made in the form of our government [does not] indicate lack of attachment to the principles of our Constitution. . . . The Constitution itself, providing as it does for its own amendment in any respect deemed desirable by the people . . . unanswerably refute[s] any notion of this sort" (*United States v. Rovin*, 12 Fed. [2d] 942 [1926]). Congress also ended the practice by which a female U.S. citizen lost her citizenship if she married a foreign male, and for the first time women, married or single, could apply for and be naturalized independently, ending a practice that automatically naturalized foreign-born women when they married an American citizen or when their husband naturalized (42 Stat. 1021; 8 U.S.C. 367 [1922]).

58. Quoted in McClymer, "The Americanization Movement," 110. Some immigrant groups accepted the Americanizers' assimilationist pressures and undertook positive steps in that direction. Even as the Catholic Church pressed for separate, parochial schools to protect members from Protestantism, it insisted on the use of English as the exclusive language in those schools. Jewish philanthropists created a range of programs to Americanize their co-religionists from eastern Europe. Many new immigrants also embraced the opportunity to leave behind the strictures of the old world and embrace the emancipatory possibilities America offered. The reaction of many immigrants, especially their leaders, to Americanization, was, however, decidedly negative, and this reaction quickened a countertrend that stressed pluralism rather than uniformity. Immigrant leaders pointed to immigrants' contributions to the war effort as all the evidence necessary of devotion, and they argued that compulsory methods of Americanization were counterproductive: "Under the present conditions," a Polish-language paper in Buffalo editorialized, "foreigners are likely to take out naturalization papers mostly in order to be left unmolested. This is a foolish movement which creates hypocrisy." Other papers pointed out that Americans themselves still had widely varying views on the meaning and culture of America and argued that there were significant aspects of American life to which no one, not even native-born Americans, should subscribe, "such as heedless materialism and mammon-worship." See Hartmann, *The Movement to Americanize the Immigrant*, 256, 258.

59. Even as the Americanization movement was losing energy in dealing with immigrants, Americanization as a matter of broad citizenship training expanded. Like their critics in the foreign-language press, some Americanizers were acutely conscious that many native-born citizens did not have even the rudimentary knowledge that was now expected of applicants for citizenship. They were sharply critical of those Kellor derided as "First Americans" and argued for a process of civic education and engagement for all Americans (*Report of the Commissioner of Naturalization* [1915], 467). In 1920, an exposition designed to promote Americanization treated as part of one larger issue "working out the great problems of bringing the immigrant into a closer community of interest with the native American," and helping "the Southern mountaineers in education and industry" (Statement by John A. Stewart, Chairman, Board of Governors, the American Society, for an Americanization Exposition to be held at the Grand Central Palace, May 29–June 12, 1920, 163/127 Americanization, Sundry File, 1919–22, NA RG 174, Records of the Department of Labor, General Records, 1907–42, Chief Clerk's File 162/219–163/127, box 164). In 1923 President Harding created the Federal Council of Citizenship Training to "develop better citizenship and higher standards of civic life." The council was aimed at "the Jew, the Gentile, the Catholic, the Protestant, the white and the black, and all other groups who are here, the class and the mass" ("An Opportunity for the Promotion of Better Citizenship," Federal Council of Citizenship Training Minutes, Lists of Members, Letters, folder 1, NA RG 85, E-30, Education and Americanization Files, Miscellaneous, box 422; "Problems Confronting the Federal Council of Citizenship Training," NA RG 85, E-30, Education and Americanization Files, Miscellaneous, box 423).

60. The ugly history of anti-Catholicism in America, to take a controversial example, does not mean that concerns about the influx of Catholics were necessarily unfounded. The story of Catholicism in the United States is the story both of an intolerant Protestant America and of Catholic skepticism toward religious pluralism and liberal democracy. As the historian Stephan Thernstrom pointed out about the nineteenth century, Protestant Americans' "conviction that Catholics were innately hostile to republican principles eventually proved mistaken, but it was not wildly implausible at the time" ("Ethnic Groups in American History," 8). For two explorations of Catholicism's misgivings about and contributions to American democracy, see George Weigel, "Catholicism and Democracy: The Other Twentieth-Century Revolution," in *Freedom and Its Discontents: Catholicism Confronts Modernity* (Washington, DC: Ethics and Public Policy Center, 1991), and Philip Gleason, "Pluralism, Democracy, and Catholicism in the Era of World War II," *Review of Politics* 49 no. 2 (spring 1987): 208–30.

61. Ueda, "Naturalization and Citizenship," 747.

62. Huntington, *Who Are We?* 135–36. See also Gerstle, *American Crucible*, 139.

63. Bourne, "Trans-National America," 111.

CHAPTER SEVEN
IMMIGRATION AND CITIZENSHIP AT CENTURY'S END

1. Nathan Glazer, in *Immigration and Citizenship in the 21st Century*, ed. Pickus, back cover.

2. Compare Julian Simon, *The Economic Consequences of Immigration* (Cambridge: Blackwell, 1989), to George J. Borjas, *Friends or Strangers: The Impact of Immigrants on*

the U.S. Economy (New York: Basic Books, 1990). Also see Thomas Muller, *Immigrants and the American City* (New York: New York University Press, 1993).

3. Nathan Glazer, *We Are All Multiculturalists Now* (Cambridge, MA: Harvard University Press, 1997), chap. 6.

4. Franklin D. Roosevelt, "Address on the State of the Union," January 11, 1944, *Congressional Record*, 78th Cong., 2nd Sess., vol. 90, pt. 1, 55–57. On the changes wrought by the New Deal, see Robert Dahl, "On Removing Certain Impediments to Democracy in the United States," in *The Moral Foundations of the American Republic*, ed. Robert Horwitz (Charlottesville: University Press of Virginia, 1977); Bruce Ackerman, "The Storrs Lectures: Discovering the Constitution," *Yale Law Journal* 93 (1984): 1013–72. For a more recent argument that some social programs that emerged from this period reinforced the exclusion of black Americans, see Robert Lieberman, *Shifting the Color Line: Race and the American Welfare State* (Cambridge, MA: Harvard University Press, 1998).

5. Gerstle, *American Crucible*, 129, chap. 5.

6. Martin Luther King Jr., *Where Do We Go from Here: Chaos or Community?* (1967), reprinted in *A Testament of Hope: The Essential Writings and Speeches of Martin Luther King Jr.*, ed. James M. Washington (New York: HarperCollins, 1986), 567.

7. Lyndon B. Johnson, "Inaugural Address," January 20, 1965, in *Public Papers of the Presidents of the United States: Lyndon B. Johnson, 1965* (Washington, DC: GPO, 1966), 1:73.

8. Reed Ueda, *Postwar Immigrant America: A Social History* (Boston: Bedford Books, 1994), 83.

9. For historical assessments of multiculturalism, see Gleason, "American Identity and Americanization," 47–54; Takaki, "Reflections on Racial Patterns in America," in *From Different Shores*, 26–37. On multiculturalism and the teaching of history, see Diane Ravitch and Arthur Schlesinger Jr., "Remaking New York's History Curriculum," *New York Times*, August 12, 1990, sec. E, p. 7. For philosophical and legal arguments over multiculturalism, see Iris Marion Young, "Polity and Group Difference: A Critique of the Ideal of Universal Citizenship," *Ethics* 99, no. 2 (January 1989): 250–74; Martha Minow, *Inclusion, Exclusion, and American Law* (Ithaca: Cornell University Press, 1990); Jeff Spinner, *The Boundaries of Citizenship: Race, Ethnicity, and Nationality in the Liberal State* (Baltimore: Johns Hopkins University Press, 1994). For critics of multiculturalism, see Glazer, *Affirmative Discrimination*; Morris Janowitz, *The Reconstruction of Patriotism: Education for Civil Consciousness* (Chicago: University of Chicago Press, 1983). On bilingual and bicultural education, see James Crawford, *Bilingual Education: History, Politics, Theory, and Practice* (Trenton, NJ: Crane, 1989), 104; Richard Rodriguez, *Hunger of Memory* (New York: Bantam, 1988), 11–40.

10. E. J. Dionne, *Why Americans Hate Politics* (New York: Simon and Schuster, 1991), 9.

11. Amitai Etzioni, *The Spirit of Community: Rights, Responsibilities and the Communitarian Agenda* (New York: Crown, 1993), 3. See also Mary Ann Glendon, *Rights Talk: The Impoverishment of Political Discourse* (New York: Free Press, 1991); Robert Putnam, *Bowling Alone: The Collapse and Revival of American Community* (New York: Simon and Schuster, 2000); Francis Fukuyama, *The Great Disruption: Human Nature and the Reconstitution of Social Order* (New York: Simon and Schuster, 1999).

12. See Saskia Sassen, *Losing Control? Sovereignty in an Age of Globalization* (New York: Columbia University Press, 1996); Hollinger, *Postethnic America*, chap. 6.

13. David Jacobson, *Rights across Borders: Immigration and the Decline of U.S. Citizenship* (Baltimore: Johns Hopkins University Press, 1996), chap. 4. For analysis and critiques of the growth of international rights codes and conventions, see J.H.H. Weiler, *The Constitution of Europe: "Do the New Clothes Have an Emperor?" And Other Essays on European Integration* (Cambridge: Cambridge University Press, 1999), chap. 2; Jeremy Rabkin, *Why Sovereignty Matters* (Washington, DC: AEI Press, 1998), 59–62, 104n. 5.

14. Jacobson, *Rights across Borders,* 89. To be sure, such a formulation underestimates how much control individual nation-states maintained over immigration and the treatment of aliens, but it did suggest the changed landscape within which policy was being forged. For cogent critiques of postnationalism in immigration and immigrant policy, see Christian Joppke, "Immigration Challenges the Nation-State," in *Challenge to the Nation-State: Immigration in Western Europe and the United States,* ed. Joppke (New York: Oxford University Press, 1988), 5–46; Gary Freeman, "The Decline of Sovereignty? Politics and Immigration Restriction in Liberal States," in *Challenge to the Nation-State,* ed. Joppke, 108; and Peter Schuck, "The Re-Evaluation of American Citizenship," *Georgetown Immigration Law Journal* 12, no. 1 (fall 1997): 1–34. For an early characterization of postnationalism, see Yasemin Soysal, *The Limits of Citizenship: Migrants and Postnational Membership in Europe* (Chicago: University of Chicago Press, 1994).

15. In a series of decisions traceable to *Graham v. Richardson* (1971), in which the Supreme Court struck down a state law denying welfare benefits to aliens, the Court deemed classifications based on citizenship "suspect" and placed aliens in the protected category of "discrete and insular minorities." Decisions such as *Plyler v. Doe* (1982), which required a state to provide free public education to the children of undocumented aliens, further established the importance of personhood and residency. For discussions of the implications of these decisions, see Peter H. Schuck, "Membership in the Liberal Polity: The Devaluation of American Citizenship," in *Immigration and the Politics of Citizenship in Europe and North America,* ed. William Rogers Brubaker (Lanham, MD: University Press of America, 1989), 51–65, and Schuck, "The Transformation of Immigration Law," *Columbia Law Review* 84, no. 1 (January 1984): 54–58. For a wide-ranging analysis of these trends in the United States and Europe, see James F. Hollifield, *Immigrants, Markets, and States: The Political Economy of Postwar Europe* (Cambridge, MA: Harvard University Press, 1992), especially chap. 8.

16. *Afroyim v. Rusk,* 387 U.S. 253 (1967).

17. *Perez v. Brownell,* 356 U.S. 44 (1958).

18. Martha Nussbaum, "Patriotism and Cosmopolitanism," *Boston Review* 19 (October/November 1994): 3; Commission on Global Governance, *Our Global Neighborhood: The Report of the Commission on Global Governance* (New York: Oxford University Press, 1995); Nina Glick Schiller, Linda Basch, and Cristina Blanc-Szanton, eds., *Towards a Transnational Perspective on Migration: Race, Class, Ethnicity and Nationalism Reconsidered* (New York: Annals of the New York Academy of Sciences, 1992); Nitza Bercovitch, *From Motherhood to Citizenship: Women's Rights and International Organizations* (Baltimore: Johns Hopkins University Press, 1999).

19. Immigration and Nationality Act of June 27, 1952.

20. Ibid.

21. On the unanticipated results of the 1965 legislation, see David M. Reimers, *Still the Golden Door: The Third World Comes to America* (New York: Columbia University Press, 1985), 74–76, 94–100. See also Frank D. Bean, Georges Vernez, and Charles B. Keeley,

Opening and Closing the Doors (Washington, DC: Urban Institute Press, 1989), xv. On immigration and interest groups, see Jacobson, *Rights across Borders*, chap. 3; and Daniel J. Tichenor, *Dividing Lines: The Politics of Immigration Control in America* (Princeton: Princeton University Press, 2002), chap. 8.

22. Jeffrey Passel and Karen Woodrow, *Immigration to the United States*, rev. ed. (Washington, DC: Bureau of the Census, 1989), 5–9; Reimers, *Still the Golden Door*, 201.

23. Robert C. Smith, "Transnational Migration, Assimilation, and Political Community," in *The City and the World: New York's Global Future*, ed. Margaret E. Crahan and Alberto Vourvoulias-Bush (New York: Council on Foreign Relations, 1997), 118–19; Roger Rouse, "Mexican Migration and the Social Space of Postmodernism," *Diaspora* 1, no. 1 (spring 1991): 14. See also David Rieff, *Los Angeles: Capital of the Third World* (New York: Simon and Schuster, 1991), 122.

24. Smith, "Transnational Migration, Assimilation, and Political Community," 110.

25. Stanley Renshon, *Dual Citizenship and American Identity* (Washington, DC: Center for Immigration Studies, 2001); Tony Smith, *Foreign Attachments: The Power of Ethnic Groups in the Making of American Foreign Policy* (Cambridge, MA: Harvard University Press, 2000). For an argument that the intense interest of minorities in their homelands may well have weakened claims to a more fervent multiculturalism in the United States, see Yossi Shain, *Marketing the American Creed Abroad: Diasporas in the U.S. and Their Homelands* (Cambridge: Cambridge University Press, 1999).

26. Ueda, "Naturalization and Citizenship," 747; David S. North, *The Long Gray Welcome: A Study of the American Naturalization Program* (Washington, DC: NALEO Education Fund, 1985); Robert R. Alvarez, "A Profile of the Citizenship Process among Hispanics in the United States," *International Migration Review* 21 (summer 1987): 327–47.

27. See Thomas C. Kohler, "Civic Virtue at Work: Unions as Seedbeds of the Civic Virtues," *Seedbeds of Virtue: Sources of Competence, Character, and Citizenship in American Society*, ed. Mary Ann Glendon and David Blankenhorn (Lanham, MD: Madison Books, 1995), 131–62.

28. Ronald J. Schmidt, "The Political Incorporation of Recent Immigrants: A Framework for Research and Analysis" (paper presented at the 1989 Annual Meeting of the American Political Science Association, Atlanta, August 31–September 3).

29. By supporting efforts to gerrymander districts on racial lines, white politicians could also respond to calls for increased minority representation without actually adding constituents whose needs might diverge from their own interests. (Skerry, *Mexican-Americans*, 336–41, chap. 9.) For alternative views of the Voting Rights Act, see Bruce Cain, "Voting Rights and Democratic Theory: Towards a Color-Blind Society?" and Luis R. Fraga, "Latino Political Incorporation and the Voting Rights Act," in *Controversies in Minority Voting: The Voting Rights Act in Perspective*, ed. Chandler Davidson and Bernard Grofman (Washington, DC: Brookings Institution, 1992), 261–77, 278–82.

30. Congress established Citizenship Day in 1950 as part of the Act to Dignify and Emphasize the Significance of Citizenship. The act set aside the third Sunday in May for public recognition of "all who, by coming of age or naturalization, have attained the status of citizenship, and that day shall be designated as 'I Am an American Day.'" The act required naturalization judges to "address the newly naturalized citizen upon the form and genius of our Government and the privileges and responsibilities of citizenship" (54 Stat. 178).

31. "Appendix I," January 1, 1936, File 25/127, reporting the results of an Immigration and Naturalization Service survey of naturalization procedures, in Marian Schisby,

Education Requirement for Naturalization (New York: National Council on Naturalization and Citizenship, 1936), 22. In a remarkable 1943 case (*Schneiderman v. United States*, 320 U.S. 119), the Court went so far as to question the idea that attachment to the Constitution necessarily means a commitment to shared values. The Justice Department contended that William Schneiderman—a Communist who believed in the abolition of private property without compensation, the establishment of a proletarian dictatorship with political rights denied to others, and the creation of an international union of soviet republics—could not be attached to the principles of the Constitution. In his majority opinion, Justice Murphy rejected this conclusion. Article V of the Constitution, he argued, indicates that there is no limit to what can be changed in the American system of government, with the sole exception noted in the text that no state can be deprived of equal representation. Murphy rejected the idea that naturalization is only for those whose political views coincided with those considered best by the Founders or by the majority today. He noted that the Fifth Amendment prohibits taking property without compensation, but pointed out that "throughout our history many sincere people whose attachment to the general constitutional scheme cannot be doubted have, for various and even divergent reasons, urged differing degrees of government ownership and control of our national resources." Slaves, he noted, were once considered property, yet their status was changed without compensating their owners. See Levinson, *Constitutional Faith*, chap. 4.

32. Kammen, *A Machine That Would Go of Itself*, 248.

33. Department of Justice Memo, August 14, 1946, NA RG 85, entry 33, 153/General Citizenship Education Program, 1945. See also Commissioner Miller, "The Attorney General's Advisory Committee on Citizenship," in the Immigration and Naturalization Service's *Monthly Review* 5, no. 5 (November 1947): 53.

34. Marian Smith, INS Historian, interview by the author, September 1, 2000. See also Geyer, *Americans No More*, 183–85.

35. Louis DeSipio, *Counting on the Latino Vote: Latinos as a New Electorate* (Charlottesville: University of Virginia Press, 1996), chap. 6; Fuchs, *American Kaleidoscope*, chap. 13.

36. See Lawrence Fuchs, "Immigration History and Immigration Policy: It Is Easier to See from a Distance," *Journal of American Ethnic History* 11 (spring 1992): 69, 71; Fuchs, *American Kaleidoscope*, 252–55; Frank D. Bean, Barry Edmonston, and Jeffrey S. Passel, *Undocumented Immigration to the United States: IRCA and the Experience of the Eighties* (Washington, DC: Urban Institute Press, 1990). For criticisms of IRCA as restrictive, see Roger Daniels, *Coming to America: A History of Immigration and Ethnicity in America* (New York: Harper Collins, 1990); and Alejandro Portes and Ruben G. Rumbaut, *Immigrant America: A Portrait* (Berkeley: University of California Press, 1990). I describe in greater depth the wrangling over the civic education component of IRCA in "'True Faith and Allegiance': Immigration and the Politics of Citizenship" (Ph.D. diss., Princeton University, 1995).

37. Wright offered a two-tiered process in which undocumented aliens would have a two-year grace period to meet the English and civics requirement or demonstrate that they are "satisfactorily pursuing a course of study" that enables them to achieve such knowledge. Applicants who passed the naturalization examination would automatically become permanent residents and, after five years, citizens. Applicants who completed the course of study would gain permanent residency status and be eligible for naturalization

after five years; if they did not complete the course they would lose their temporary legal status. The English/civics requirement was waived for applicants who were under the age of sixteen, over the age of sixty-five, over the age of fifty and had resided in the United States for at least twenty years, or physically unable to comply. These exemptions excused a significant portion of applicants. See *Immigration Law Report* 8, no. 1 (January 1989): 140.

38. *Congressional Record* (June 19, 1984), vol. 130, no. 84, 6066.

39. Ibid., 6068, 6075, 6071, 6068, 6073, 6066, 6067. Wright's amendment won over key proponents of enforcement and thus contributed to the narrow defeat of a proposal to abolish amnesty entirely (199–92). (The entire IRCA bill passed the House by a margin of only five votes, 216-211, in June 1984, but then it died in conference. In 1986, the House again passed IRCA, this time by a vote of 238 to 173, and President Reagan signed the bill into law on November 6.) Representatives who did not approve of the amnesty program at all saw in Wright's amendment an additional barrier to a successful legalization program. For those concerned about a loss of national sovereignty and related issues of fairness and respect for the law, the English/civics requirement promised to reassert a degree of control by creating a specific obligation. Wright's proposal also addressed the fear of a balkanization of cultures. By providing a more formal and involved process for the transformation from undocumented worker to applicant for naturalization, these programs reflected an assumption that legal residents ought to become citizens. See *Congressional Record* (June 19, 1984), H6074, and "Statement of Representative Peter Rodino Jr.," *U.S. Immigration Policy and the National Interest*, appendix B, 416.

40. For a list of these organizations, see U.S. Department of Justice, Immigration and Naturalization Service, *Directory of Voluntary Agencies* M-233 (Third Edition 1989 Y). A program recognized by the INS received up to five dollars an hour for every hour a student attended class. See *Interpreter Releases* 65 (March 21, 1988): 272–73.

41. Susan Gonzalez Baker, *The Cautious Welcome: The Legalization Programs of IRCA* (Washington, DC: Urban Institute Press, 1990), 172. Representative John Porter (R-Illinois) proposed that the United States adopt an "immersion" system similar to that offered by Israel, and he thought that even the United States' more extensive efforts for refugees were "close to cruelty" for those to whom "this country, its language, customs, history, government and systems [are] a complete mystery" (*Congressional Record* [June 19, 1984], 6076, 6076).

42. See "Stealing from Immigrants," *Los Angeles Times*, September 29, 1989, sec. 2, p. 6. Also see Baker, *The Cautious Welcome*, 176.

43. Gene Pyeatt, the INS deputy district director for legalization, acknowledged, "It'll be near impossible to use the federal text." Quoted in Michael Milstein, "School District Gets Jump in Producing Amnesty Material," *Los Angeles Times*, November 1988.

44. See the U.S. House of Representatives Judiciary Committee, "Immigration Control and Legalization Amendments Act of 1986," Report 99-682, 99th Cong., 2nd sess., July 16, 1986. Also see Baker, *The Cautious Welcome*, 25. For similar arguments advanced in the mid-1990s by activists campaigning for legal residence for Central Americans, see Susan Bibler Coutin, *Legalizing Moves: Salvadoran Immigrants Struggle for U.S. Residency* (Ann Arbor: University of Michigan Press, 2000), 149. According to Coutin, advocates in this period taught immigrants to link "U.S. immigration law to racism, xenophobia, discrimination, exploitation, injustice, and inequality" (100).

45. George Ramos, "Rights Group Urges Liberal Rules for 2nd Phase of Amnesty Program," *Los Angeles Times*, June 21, 1988, sec. 1, p. 15; "ESL/Civics: A Handbook for the

Planning and Implementation of English-Language and Civics Programs" (New York: American Council on Nationalities Services and the National Council of La Raza, 1988).

46. Ramos, "Rights Group Urges Liberal Rules"; interview by author at the Legalization Office of the Immigration and Naturalization Service, September 11, 1990, Washington, DC.

47. Bean, Vernez, and Keeley, *Opening and Closing the Doors*, 68. The programs also became simplified because the incentives shifted for the INS. Where once the INS sought to keep immigrants out, now they had to be equally concerned with helping them remain. Congressional proponents of legalization judged the agency by the number of successful applicants. States also had incentives to ensure that temporary residents qualified for permanent residency or citizenship, since this would add to their claims for increased resources and political representation. (Interviews by the author at the Immigration and Naturalization Service Outreach Office, September 11, 1990, Washington, DC; the Urban Institute, September 11, 1990, Washington, DC; and Health and Human Services Division of State Legalization Assistance, Office of Refugee Resettlement in the Family Support Administration, September 11, 1990, Washington, DC. See also Baker, *The Cautious Welcome*, 103.)

48. Stephanie Chavez, " 'Red-Eye' Citizenship Classes Attract Aliens," *Los Angeles Times*, May 26, 1988, sec. 1, p. 1; Pickus, " 'True Faith and Allegiance,' " chap. 4; Baker, *The Cautious Welcome*.

49. Baker, *The Cautious Welcome*, 19.

50. John J. Miller and William James Muldoon, "Citizenship for Granted" (Washington, DC: Center for Equal Opportunity Policy Brief, 1996); Doris Meissner, "Putting the 'N' Back into INS: Comments on the Immigration and Naturalization Service," *Virginia Journal of International Law* 35, no. 1 (fall 1994): 1–11; Louis DeSipio and Harry P. Pachon, "Making Americans," *Chicano-Latino Law Review* 12 (1992): 63.

51. T. Alexander Aleinikoff, "Citizens, Aliens, Membership and the Constitution," *Constitutional Commentary* 7, no. 1 (winter 1990): 9–34. See also Pickus, *Becoming American, America Becoming*, 10, 16; Linda S. Bosniak, "A National Solidarity? A Response to David Hollinger," and Joseph H. Carens, "Why Naturalization Should Be Easy: A Response to Noah Pickus," both in *Immigration and Citizenship in the 21st Century*, ed. Pickus, 101–5 and 141–46, respectively.

52. Bonnie Honig, "Immigrant America? How Foreignness 'Solves' Democracy's Problems," *Social Text* 16, no. 3 (fall 1998): 14.

53. Carens, "Why Naturalization Should Be Easy." Whereas most elites at the Founding and during the Progressive Era emphasized the creation of a people as a matter of politics, Carens and other rights advocates have stressed the recognition of persons as a matter of justice. In other work, Carens has advanced a complex model of citizenship that encompasses legal, psychological, and political dimensions and the relations among them. See *Culture, Citizenship, and Community: A Contextual Exploration of Justice as Evenhandedness* (New York: Oxford University Press, 2000), chap. 7.

54. Carens, "Why Naturalization Should Be Easy."

55. Gerald M. Rosberg, "Aliens and Equal Protection: Why Not the Right to Vote?" *Michigan Law Review* 75 (April–May 1977): 1092–1136.

56. Sanford Levinson, "Lawyers as Citizens: An Inquiry into National Loyalty and the Professional Identity of Lawyers," in *Diversity and Citizenship*, ed. Jacobsohn and Dunn, 27. "[T]he transnational lives of contemporary migrants," added the sociologists Nina Glick Schiller, Linda Basch, and Cristina Blanc-Szanton, "call into question the bounded

conceptualizations of race, class, ethnicity, and nationalism which pervade both social science and popular thinking" (*Towards a Transnational Perspective on Migration*, x).

57. Aleinikoff, "Citizens, Aliens, Membership and the Constitution," 28–30. "It is just wishful thinking to suggest that most Americans feel the kinds of obligations to other Americans that we usually associate with 'community,'" Aleinikoff asserted. A native-born U.S. citizen will not feel "any less an 'American' because a Honduran in the United States is entitled to similar benefits and opportunities, nor is the Honduran likely to feel any less Honduran."

58. Raskin, "Legal Aliens, Local Citizens," 1454 (quoting Cass Sunstein), 1457–61. Noncitizens have been able to vote in local elections and hold municipal office in Takoma Park, Maryland, since 1992. A number of other cities in Maryland allow noncitizen voting. Cambridge and Amherst, Massachusetts, have approved noncitizen voting, although this change requires state legislative approval as well. Chicago and New York have allowed noncitizen voting for school boards. The issue of noncitizen voting in city elections has recently roiled the waters in New York, Los Angeles, and Washington, DC.

59. Robert L. Bach et al., *Changing Relations: Newcomers and Established Residents in U.S. Communities* (New York: Ford Foundation, 1993), 58–59.

60. Honig, "Immigrant America?" 17–18.

61. Schuck, "Plural Citizenships." Schuck offers qualified support of dual citizenship although he does not subscribe to the rights position as a general matter.

62. Spiro, "Dual Nationality and the Meaning of Citizenship"; Schuck, "Plural Citizenships."

63. See Bill Ong Hing, *To Be an American: Cultural Pluralism and the Rhetoric of Assimilation* (New York: New York University Press, 1997).

64. Perea, "'Am I an American or Not?'"; Hing, *To Be an American*; Kevin R. Johnson, "The New Nativism: Something Old, Something New, Something Borrowed, Something Blue," in *Immigrants Out! The New Nativism and the Anti-Immigrant Impulse in the United States*, ed. Juan Perea (New York: New York University Press, 1997), 165–89.

65. Hiroshi Motomura, "Alienage Classifications in a Nation of Immigrants: Three Models of 'Permanent' Residence," in *Immigration and Citizenship in the 21st Century*, ed. Pickus, 204–6; Linda S. Bosniak, "Membership, Equality, and the Difference That Alienage Makes," *New York University Law Review* 69, no. 6 (December 1994): 1042–1149. Gary E. Rubin, *The Assault on Citizenship* (New York: NYANA Policy Series, 1998).

66. DeSipio and Pachon, "Making Americans," 62; Louis DeSipio, "Making Citizens or Good Citizens?" *Hispanic Journal of Behavioral Sciences* 18, no. 2 (May 1996): 197.

67. Louis DeSipio, *Counting on the Latino Vote: Latinos as a New Electorate* (Charlottesville: University of Virginia Press, 1996), 130–31.

68. Rodolfo O. de la Garza and Louis DeSipio, "Save the Baby, Change the Bathwater, and Scrub the Tub: Latino Electoral Participation after Seventeen Years of Voting Rights Act Coverage," *Texas Law Review* 71, no. 7 (June 1993): 1479–1539.

69. DeSipio, *Counting on the Latino Vote*, 181–83, 154–55. See also *First National Conference on Citizenship and the Hispanic Community, Proceedings* (Washington, DC: NALEO Education Fund, 1985). This approach received a significant boost in the late 1990s when, in response to legislative efforts to deny immigrants public benefits, the philanthropist George Soros established the Emma Lazarus Fund to provide $50 million for naturalization assistance and advocacy. These funds generated a significant increase

in naturalization applications, but there have been few major sources of support for these efforts after those funds ran out and the most stringent restrictions were modified.

70. Rubin, *The Assault on Citizenship*, 20.

71. Spiro, "Dual Nationality and the Meaning of Citizenship."

72. Michael Jones-Correa, "Why Immigrants Want Dual Citizenship (And We Should Too)," in *Immigration and Citizenship in the 21st Century*, ed. Pickus. See also Jones-Correa, *Between Two Nations: The Political Predicament of Latinos in New York City* (Ithaca: Cornell University Press, 1998), chap. 8.

73. Peter H. Schuck, "The Open Society: America Is Pro-immigration After All," *The New Republic*, April 13, 1998, 17.

74. Political leaders from rival parties, such as former Republican governor of Colorado Richard Lamm and former Democratic senator Eugene McCarthy, each wrote books articulating their worries (Richard Lamm and Gary Imhoff, *The Immigration Time Bomb: The Fragmentation of America* [New York: Truman Talley Books, 1985]; Eugene McCarthy, *A Colony of the World: The United States Today: America's Senior Statesman Warns His Countrymen* [New York: Hippocrene Books, 1992]). Nancy Wallace, who directed the Sierra Club's International Population Program, reflected the environmentalists' position when she argued that "any immigration legislation should be part of a national population policy moving toward stabilization as fast as possible" (quoted in Felicity Barringer, "A Land of Immigrants Gets Uneasy about Immigration," *New York Times*, November 14, 1990, 4). For two historians' assessments of the relation between environmentalism and nativism, see Bennett, *The Party of Fear*, chap. 10, and David Reimers, *Unwelcome Strangers: American Identity and the Turn against Immigration* (Baltimore: Johns Hopkins University Press, 1998), chap. 3.

75. See Reimers, *Unwelcome Strangers*, chap. 4.

76. See Espenshade and Calhoun, "Public Opinion toward Illegal Immigration and Undocumented Immigrants in Southern California," 8–10. See also Christine L. Day, "Ethnocentrism, Economic Competition, and Attitudes toward U.S. Immigration Policy" (paper presented at the Midwest Political Science Association, April 5–7, 1990); Edwin Harwood, "American Public Opinion and U.S. Immigration Policy," *The Annals* (AAPSS) 487 (September 1986): 202–12; Tarrance and Associates, *Research Report: California Immigration Survey* (April 1989), and *Research Report: Texas Immigration and Border Security Study* (May 1989); H. B. Moehring, "Symbol versus Substance in Legislative Activity: The Case of Illegal Immigration," *Public Choice* 57 (1988): 287–94.

77. Jack Citrin, Beth Reingold, and Donald Green, "American Identity and the Politics of Ethnic Change," *Journal of Politics* 52, no. 4 (November 1990): 1124–254. Those surveyed did not articulate the strongly Protestant worldview so prevalent in earlier periods of American history. It is also worth pointing out that if religious belief were a requirement for becoming an American, most immigrants would easily qualify. Consider, for instance, the number of Catholic emigres from Latin America. This analysis leaves the English language as the only "ascriptive" characteristic of American identity, one that can be learned.

78. Peter H. Schuck, "The Message of 187," *American Prospect* (spring 1995): 85–92.

79. Robert Reich, *The Work of Nations: Preparing Ourselves for 21st-Century Capitalism* (New York: Knopf, 1991); Mickey Kaus, *The End of Equality* (New York: Basic Books, 1992); Etzioni, *The Spirit of Community*; Glendon, *Rights Talk*; David Brooks, *Bobos in Paradise: The New Upper Class and How They Got There* (New York: Simon and Schuster,

2000), 260–64. For an overview of this revaluation and how it relates to immigration and citizenship policy, see Schuck, "The Re-Evaluation of American Citizenship."

80. Peter Brimelow, "Un-American Activities," *National Review*, June 16, 1997, 44. See also Brimelow, "Time to Rethink Immigration," *National Review*, June 22, 1992, 34; Brimelow, *Alien Nation: Common Sense about America's Immigration Disaster* (New York: Free Press, 1995); Lawrence Auster, "The Forbidden Topic: Link between Multiculturalism and Immigration," *National Review*, April 27, 1992, 42–44; John O'Sullivan, "America's Identity Crisis," *National Review*, November 21, 1994, 36; Jared Taylor, ed., *The Real American Dilemma: Race, Immigration, and the Future of America* (Oakton, VA: New Century Foundation, 1988); Chilton Williamson Jr., *The Immigration Mystique: America's False Conscience* (New York: Basic Books, 1996). On the organizations that represent some of these views, see Reimers, *Unwelcome Strangers*, chap. 6.

81. Quoted in Stephen L. Carter, "Nativism and Its Discontents," *New York Times*, March 8, 1992.

82. Auster, "The Forbidden Topic," 42.

83. Lawrence Auster, *The Path to National Suicide: An Essay on Immigration and Multiculturalism* (Monterey, VA: American Immigration Control Foundation, 1990), 45.

84. Brimelow, *Alien Nation*, 264–67; Lawrence Harrison, testimony given at U.S. Senate, Committee on the Judiciary, Subcommittee on Immigration, *Hearing on Naturalization Requirements and the Rights and Privileges of Citizenship*, October 22, 1996; Harrison, *Who Prospers: How Cultural Values Shape Economic and Political Success* (New York: Basic Books, 1992; Dan Stein, testimony given at *Hearing on Naturalization Requirements and the Rights and Privileges of Citizenship*, October 22, 1996; and Stein, "Oaths, Allegiance, and the Loss of Common Understanding" (paper delivered at the National Issues Forum, Brookings Institution, December 8, 1997).

85. Stein, "Oaths, Allegiance, and the Loss of Common Understanding," 14–16; Scott McConnell, "Americans No More?" *National Review*, December 31, 1997, 30–35.

86. Michael Barone, *The New Americans: How the Melting Pot Can Work Again* (Washington, DC: Regnery Publishing, 2001), 1. Most universal nationalists were generally supportive of generous admission policies. Some supported efforts to diversify the racial mix of immigrants on the grounds that concentrations of immigrants of a single nationality can hinder assimilation (Peter Salins, *Assimilation, American-Style* [New York: Basic Books, 1997], 213). Others were more cautious in terms of the volume and diversity of immigrants' cultural backgrounds, worrying that too many immigrants from too many cultures hinder the effectiveness and rapidity of assimilation efforts (Geyer, *Americans No More*).

87. Salins, *Assimilation, American-Style*, 55–59.

88. Ibid., 50, 51.

89. Miller, *The Unmaking of Americans*, chap. 4.

90. Miller, "The Naturalizers," 52; Miller, *The Unmaking of Americans*, 149; Geyer, *Americans No More*, chaps. 2–4. See also Salins, *Assimilation, American-Style*, 215; Lamar Smith, as quoted on *Morning Edition*, National Public Radio, March 25, 1997; and John Fonte, testimony given at U.S. Senate, Committee on the Judiciary, Subcommittee on Immigration, *Hearing on Naturalization Requirements and the Rights and Privileges of Citizenship*, October 22, 1996.

91. Geyer, *Americans No More*, 312–14. See also Geyer, "Mexican Leaders Encourage Split Loyalties," *American Enterprise*, December 2000, 23–25; Steve Chapman, "Two National Loyalties Are Not Better Than One," *Chicano Tribune*, April 19, 1998.

92. See Pickus, *Becoming American, America Becoming*, 25; John Fonte, "The Battle for American Allegiance," *American Legion Magazine*, December 2000.

CHAPTER EIGHT
A NEW CIVIC NATIONALISM

1. See introduction, n. 19. See also Peter Spiro, "The Citizenship Dilemma," *Stanford Law Review* 51 no. 3 (February 1999): 599.

2. For thoughtful discussion by two historians who share a commitment to civic nationalism but differ on how they read its history and contemporary implications, see Gary Gerstle, "Liberty, Coercion, and the Making of Americans," *Journal of American History* 84 (September 1997): 524–58, and Gerstle, "The Power of Nations," *Journal of American History* 84 (September 1997): 576–80; David Hollinger, "National Solidarity at the End of the Twentieth Century: Reflections on the United States and Liberal Nationalism," *Journal of American History* 84 (September 1997): 559–69.

3. T. Alexander Aleinikoff, "A Multicultural Nationalism?" *American Prospect* 9, no. 36 (January–February 1998): 80, 83.

4. Quoted in Mae M. Cheng, "Citizens of the World: New Americans Are Increasingly Keeping Dual Allegiances," *Newsday*, August 7, 2000, sec. A, p. 3; see also Aleinikoff, "Citizens, Aliens, Membership and the Constitution," 28; Aleinikoff, *Between Principles and Politics*, 25–40.

5. Hollinger, "Nationalism, Cosmopolitanism," 92–93.

6. Aleinikoff, "A Multicultural Nationalism?" 84.

7. Ibid.; Hollinger, "Nationalism, Cosmopolitanism," 94.

8. Lind, *The Next American Nation*, 260.

9. Ibid., 14. See also Hollinger, "Nationalism, Cosmopolitanism," 89.

10. William Kristol and David Brooks, "The McCain Insurrection," *The Weekly Standard* 5, no. 21 (February 14, 2000), http://www.weeklystandard.com.

11. William Kristol and David Brooks, "The Politics of Creative Destruction," *The Weekly Standard* 5, no. 25 (March 13, 2000), http://www.weeklystandard.com; William Kristol and David Brooks, "What Ails Conservatism," *Wall Street Journal*, September 15, 1997, sec. A, p. 22, cd. 4; David Brooks, "A Return to National Greatness: A Manifesto for a Lost Creed," *The Weekly Standard* 2, no. 4 (March 3, 1997): 16–21.

12. Brooks, "A Return to National Greatness." Kristol and Brooks acknowledge that their program is vague, calling it "silly to try to lay out some sort of 10-point program for American greatness." Their purpose is to get Americans "to think differently about politics," not to lay out a detailed policy agenda. "It almost doesn't matter what great tasks government sets for itself," notes Brooks, "as long as it does some tangible thing with energy and effectiveness."

13. John Fonte describes a more polarized set of positions. He distinguishes between left-leaning followers of Bourne, Dewey, Whitman, and the Italian Marxist thinker Antonio Gramsci, who look forward to the social transformation of America, and centrist or right-leaning adherents of Tocqueville, who celebrate America as an exceptional nation owing to its particular combination of individualism, religiosity, and patriotism. This distinction is helpful in drawing out important differences, but it points to a depth of disagreement that I am not convinced actually exists. Fonte, "Gramsci's Revenge:

Reconstructing American Democracy," *Academic Questions* 113, no. 2 (spring 2000): 49–62; Fonte, "Why There Is a Culture War: Gramsci and Tocqueville in America," *Policy Review* no. 104 (December 2000–January 2001): 15–31.

14. These tensions raise the critical issue of how American national identity might change. Will it come as a result of elite politics, of international courts and bureaucracies imposing a set of transnational rights? The growth of international human rights codes, which shift authority and legitimacy to the regional and global level, has already had the ironic effect of increasing the reach of these least democratic branches of government. This development has exacerbated significant worries about a democratic deficit in Europe and stoked critical public reaction, such as occurred notably following the 1992 pronouncement in the Maastricht Treaty that a European-wide citizenship had been established.

15. To be sure, there are strong reasons to be skeptical of claims to global governance and international justice. As the political scientist Jeremy Rabkin argues, these claims have too often served as covers for other nations, especially in Europe, to leverage their own preferred policies, and to criticize the United States as "undemocratic" because it maintains policies that are supported by the American public, though not by Europeans. Rabkin, "Is EU Policy Eroding the Sovereignty of Non-Member States?" *Chicago Journal of International Law* 1, no. 2 (2000): 273–90.

16. A movement toward greater integration in North America is nowhere near as developed as in Europe, and the trajectory of this movement will certainly differ. Still, integration is increasingly on the agenda as there are forces pressing Mexico, Canada, and the United States to conceive of issues (trade, environment, and immigration) in a regional rather than solely national way. Robert L. Earle and John D. Wirth, eds., *Identities in North America: The Search for Community* (Stanford: Stanford University Press, 1995); Robert D. Kaplan, *An Empire Wilderness: Travels into America's Future* (New York: Vintage Books, 1998); Anthony DePalma, *Here: A Biography of the New American Continent* (New York: Public Affairs, 2001).

17. Brooks, "A Return to National Greatness," 1997.

18. Peter Skerry, "What's Wrong with Group Rights?" unpublished paper on file with author.

19. John B. Judis and Michael Lind, "For a New Nationalism," *The New Republic*, March 27, 1995, 19–27.

20. Hollinger, "National Solidarity at the End of the Twentieth Century," 562. See also Gerstle, *American Crucible*, 129.

21. Hannah Arendt pointed to the limits of political responsibility when, in discussing the plight of refugees after World War II, she remarked that "the Rights of Man, supposedly inalienable, proved to be unenforceable" (Arendt, *The Origins of Totalitarianism*, 2nd ed. [New York: Harmount Press, 1962], 293). More recently, the legal scholar George Fletcher has noted that two of the most significant instances of aid across borders since the 1950s have occurred on the basis of national rather than universal commitments: Israel's rescue and absorption of Falashan Jews from Ethiopia and West Germany's reincorporation of East German citizens. (Fletcher, *Loyalty: An Essay on the Morality of Relationships* [New York: Oxford University Press, 1993], 9.)

22. There is, of course, much variation on these policies among the European countries. "While it would be unfair to characterize these comparatively generous provisions to non-citizens as explicit efforts to reduce naturalization rates," the sociologist Giuseppe Sciortino notes, "the development of such programs on the whole may be interpreted as

an indicator of the European tendency to resist the de-ethnicization of the definition of the citizenry" (Sciortino, personal correspondence with the author, November 2001). This suspicion is heightened by the absence of efforts to make more reasonable the rules for attaining citizenship. On the contrary, the granting of rights to "denizens" has often been accompanied by a strong resistance to altering citizenship rules, resistance that has often been justified on the grounds that immigrants do not desire to become citizens, that they are temporary sojourners who intend to return to their country of origin, and, paradoxically, that the formal status of citizenship does not matter much if social rights are provided. See Giuseppe Sciortino, "From the Social Construction of Homogeneity to the Social Construction of Difference" (paper presented at the seminar "Power and Democracy in Multicultural Societies," Rosendal, Norway, May 2001).

23. For a discussion of these issues in terms of broader questions of community and nationhood, see the exchanges among Seyla Benhabib, Michael Walzer, Richard Dagger, and Noah Pickus in Benhabib, "Dismantling the Leviathan: Citizen and State in a Global World," and Walzer, "Response," *The Responsive Community* 11 (spring 2001): 14–31; Dagger, "A Republican-Liberal's Perspective," and Pickus, "Citizenship and Commitment," *The Responsive Community* 11 (summer 2001): 90–82, 93–95; Benhabib, "Ungrounded Fears: American Intellectuals and the Spectre of European Harmonization—A Response to Michael Walzer and Noah M. J. Pickus," *The Responsive Community* 11 (fall 2001): 85–91. Benhabib suggests an intriguing analogy between Europe's current conflicts over immigration and naturalization and the tensions arising from the variations among individual U.S. states in their treatment of aliens from the Revolution to the Civil War. This analogy is helpful in reminding Americans of the struggle involved in forging common immigration and citizenship policies and a broader sense of national union. The unified policies and single national citizenship in the United States are, however, precisely what is at stake in Europe, where the outcome is by no means foreordained. The harmonization of European requirements necessary for the transition to citizenship is an important step in the direction of the United States and I join Benhabib in opposing onerous restrictions on naturalization and immigration procedures. But if some European nations want to choose differently in these areas, as well as on the broader question of union, we must not simply replace their citizens' capacity to determine who can become a member of their polity and on what terms with appeals to universal rights.

24. Boyte and O'Donoghue, "The Jane Addams School for Democracy."

25. For examples from the late 1980s and early 1990s, see, for instance, Jorge Bustamante, "Mexico-Bashing: A Case Where Words Can Hurt," *Los Angeles Times,* August 13, 1993. Rodolfo Acuna, "Where Are All the Liberals When the City Really Needs Them?" *Los Angeles Times,* December 27, 1991, sec. M, p. 6. See also Cornelius, "America in the Era of Limits," and Kevin R. Johnson, "Los Olvidados: Images of the Immigrant, Political Power of Noncitizens, and Immigration Law and Enforcement," *Brigham Young University Law Review* 1393, no. 4 (1993): 1150–52, 1162–74.

26. Coutin, *Legalizing Moves,* 178; George Sanchez, "Face the Nation: Race, Immigration, and the Rise of Nativism in Late Twentieth Century America," *International Migration Review* 31 (winter 1997): 1009–1030; Matthew Frye Jacobson, "The Newest Americans," review of *Unwelcome Strangers: American Identity and the Turn against Immigration,* by David M. Reimers, *Reviews in American History* 27, no. 2 (1999): 312–17.

27. Sanchez, "Face the Nation."

28. Coutin, *Legalizing Moves*, 161, 100, 154–55.

29. *League of United Latin American Citizens v. Wilson*, WL 141325 (C.D.Cal. 1998); *League of United Latin American Citizens v. Wilson*, 908 F. Supp. 755 (C.D.Cal. 1995). Roberto Suro calls Proposition 187 "a cry for help, not a workable plan of assistance." Suro, *Watching America's Door: The Immigration Backlash and the New Policy Debate* (New York: Twentieth Century Fund Press, 1996), 5.

30. Alan Wolfe, "Alien Nation," *The New Republic*, March 26, 2001, 30.

31. Hollinger, "National Solidarity at the End of the Twentieth Century," 562–63.

32. David Martin, "New Rules on Dual Nationality for a Democratizing Globe: Between Rejection and Embrace," *Georgetown Immigration Law Journal* 14 (fall 1999): 1–34.

33. After all, for most religions the ultimate allegiance must be to God's word, not human law. As a result, we often see conflicts such as whether religious believers must send their children to public schools when they find the schools' teachings inimical to their beliefs. See *Wisconsin v. Yoder* 406 U.S. 205 (1972); *Mozert v. Hawkins County Board of Education* (Tennessee, 1987).

34. See Hiroshi Motomura, "Whose Alien Nation?: Two Models of Constitutional Immigration Law," *Michigan Law Review* 94, no. 6 (May 1996): 1927–52.

35. See Peter Schuck, "Alien Rumination," *Yale Law Journal* 105, no. 7 (May 1996): 1963–2012.

36. See Etzioni, *The New Golden Rule*, 202.

37. For explorations of conflicts over alternative possibilities in these periods, see Smith, *Civic Ideals*; Dahl, "On Removing Certain Impediments to Democracy in the United States"; J. David Greenstone, "Political Culture and American Political Development: Liberty, Union and the Liberal Bipolarity," *Studies in American Political Development* 1 (1986): 1–49; Ackerman, "The Storrs Lectures."

38. See Jacobson, *Whiteness of a Different Color*; David Roediger, *The Wages of Whiteness: Race and the Making of the American Working Class* (London: Verso, 1991); Noel Ignatiev, *How the Irish Become White* (New York: Routledge, 1995). These historians have rightly emphasized the ways in which the exclusion of blacks from American nationhood has resulted from more than simply Americans' unwillingness to live up to their principles. But, as I argued in chapter 4, this school of thought tends to reduce the moral and political complexity of issues at the intersection of immigration, race, and citizenship. It also downplays the contribution of American ideals to the incorporation of racially diverse immigrants and limits analysis of the factors contributing to the status of black Americans today. See Nathan Glazer, "White Noise," *The New Republic*, October 21, 1998, 46.

39. Harry V. Jaffa, *Crisis of the House Divided* (Garden City, NY: Doubleday, 1959), 231.

40. Salins, *Assimilation, American-Style*, 50.

41. Walter Berns, *Making Patriots* (Chicago: University of Chicago Press, 2001). See also Wolfe, "On Loyalty"; Fletcher, *Loyalty*, 3–6.

42. John Fonte, "We Need a Patriotic Assimilation Policy," *American Outlook Today*, May 14, 2003.

43. Alan Wolfe, *Moral Freedom: The Impossible Idea That Defines the Way We Live Now* (New York: W. W. Norton, 2001), 24–25.

44. Huntington, *Who Are We?* 46–49, 357–66.

45. Hollinger, "National Solidarity at the End of the Twentieth Century," 564.

46. Two of the best recent historical treatments of Madison are Banning, *The Sacred Fire of Liberty*, and McCoy, *The Last of the Fathers*. Madison's reputation, while solid, has been eclipsed in recent years by the attention paid to his contemporaries, notably Thomas Jefferson, John Adams, and Alexander Hamilton. Michael Lind goes so far as to kick Madison out from the pantheon of heroes in his "Trans-American Nation," deriding him as "little Jimmy Madison" and characterizing him as "a relatively inconsequential figure" (Lind, *The Next American Nation*, 377). For attention to Jefferson, Adams, and Hamilton, see O'Brien, *The Long Affair*; Pauline Maier, *American Scripture: Making the Declaration of Independence* (New York: Knopf, 1997); Joseph Ellis, *Passionate Sage: The Character and Legacy of John Adams* (New York: W. W. Norton, 1993); David McCullough, *Johns Adams* (New York: Simon and Schuster, 2001); Karl-Friedrich Walling, *Republican Empire* (Lawrence: University Press of Kansas, 1999); and Richard Brookhiser, *Alexander Hamilton: American* (New York: Free Press, 1999).

47. This deliberative dimension of a Madisonian civic nationalism does not insist that we become a nation of constitutional scholars nor imply that everything must be subject to revision. It simply recognizes that a constitution will only do its job in securing rights and forging political unity if it is wrestled with and engaged by the citizens who embrace it as their most central document. On public deliberation, see Cass R. Sunstein, "Beyond the Republican Revival," *Yale Law Journal* 97 (1988): 1539–90. On limits to deliberation and constitutional change, see Walter F. Murphy, "An Ordering of Constitutional Values," *Southern California Law Review* 53 (1980): 750–57; Harris, *The Interpretable Constitution*, 164–208.

48. See Benhabib, "Dismantling the Leviathan," and "Ungrounded Fears."

49. This disconnection characterizes the work of a number of important legal theorists who have applied the Founders' republican emphasis on public deliberation to issues such as alien voting rights and dual citizenship. Raskin, "Legal Aliens, Local Citizens"; Neuman, *Strangers to the Constitution*, and "Justifying U.S. Naturalization Policies," *Virginia Journal of International Law* 35, no. 1 (fall 1994): 237–78; Spiro, "Dual Nationality and the Meaning of Citizenship."

50. Concerns have appropriately been raised about the "democratic deficit" in the development of the European Union—the process of negotiations among elites and the influence of courts and bureaucracies rather than the engagement of the European public. The comparative constitutional scholar J.H.H. Weiler describes a process in Europe that followed the biblical injunction "to do" (build institutions and practices) and then "to hearken" (to determine the ends to which those institutions and practices should be directed, including the question of a shared political identity). This approach inverts traditional social contract theory but is less at odds with Madison's own efforts to create a broader sense of peoplehood in support of a set of political structures that he and his compatriots had forged. On Europe, see Weiler, *The Constitution of Europe*, chap. 1. On Madison, see chapter 2 in this book and Pickus, " 'Hearken Not.' "

51. Hollinger, "Nationalism and Cosmopolitanism," 94.

52. Immigration analyst Susan Martin notes that, "restricting eligibility for safety net programs sends the message that immigrants are welcomed as workers, but not as full members of the community." Martin, "U.S. Immigration Policy: The Founding Myth Meets Contemporary Realities" (paper presented at the conference "Migrant Societies: Immigration in Postwar Germany and the United States," June 2000). But see Schuck, "The Open Society," on the extent to which many of the provisions restricting the rights of immigrants that surfaced in the 1990s were short-lived or have been scaled back.

53. Leiken, *Bearers of Global Jihad?* 137–43.

54. Alan Wolfe, *One Nation After All: What Middle-Class Americans Really Think about God, Country, Family, Racism, Welfare, Immigration, Homosexuality, Work, the Right, the Left, and Each Other* (New York: Penguin Books, 1998); Brooks, *Bobos in Paradise*, 256.

55. William A. Galston, review of *One Nation, After All*, by Alan Wolfe, *The Public Interest*, no. 133 (fall 1998): 116–20. There has been much speculation about the extent to which the September 11 terrorist attacks on the United States will stimulate a greater civic ethos and willingness to sacrifice. Many Americans certainly articulated a strong desire to "do something" for their country in response to the attacks. President Bush struggled to identify what Americans could actually do to channel their patriotic fervor. As Galston notes, this fervor offered an opportunity to reverse the decline in young Americans' interest in public affairs and in public service, but whether the nation could or would find ways to take advantage of it remained uncertain (Galston, "Can Patriotism Be Turned into Civic Engagement?" *Chronicle of Higher Education*, November 16, 2001).

56. Jordan's appointment as chair by President Clinton reflected the centrality of blacks to the American story, as well as her own skills and powerful evocation of the promise inherent in the nation's core. In 1973, as the House Judiciary Committee prepared to vote for Richard Nixon's impeachment, she declared that, despite feeling that blacks were originally left out of "We, the people," they had subsequently been included and thus her "faith in the Constitution is whole, it is complete, it is total." This moral authority gave special weight to the recommendations of the commission that legal immigration be reduced and that the nation undertake a renewed effort to Americanize immigrants.

57. U.S. Commission on Immigration Reform, *Becoming an American*, 28.

58. Ibid., 30–45.

59. For a summary of these views, see Pickus, *Becoming American, America Becoming*. See also Peter Skerry, "Do We Really Want Immigrants to Assimilate?" in *"What, Then, Is the American, This New Man?"* 37–43; Bosniak, "A National Solidarity?" 101–5; Perea, *Immigrants Out!*; and King, *Making Americans*, chap. 10. King concludes his exploration of the Americanization movement and its implications for today by suggesting that the story of America be told in a version that integrates "the values and preferences of previously excluded groups into the dominant political ethos of the United States in a way that recognizes that they are not isolated but, through interaction and shared experiences, have contributed to American political development. Assimilation, to be fair to previously excluded groups, necessitates a widening of the dominant values to complement the inculcation of the new entrants with prevailing values" (291). King's analysis is especially helpful in understanding the historical context from which claims to multiculturalism have arisen. It is difficult, though, to understand what he means by a "widening of the dominant values." Like the commission itself, there is a certain vagueness at the heart of this way of putting things. (Vagueness seems to be an occupational hazard for most of us who write about Americanization.) His conclusion that "diversity has been formed by inequalities as well by narratives based on success stories" is sensible enough, but what does it mean to "treat all groups' narratives coequally"? Like some of the Bourneian nationalists, it remains unclear what is to be included and how that process will effect the larger whole. Which preferences and values are to be included and on what basis? Are these preferences and values to be included simply on the basis that they are expressed by at least some members of these groups?

60. Kenneth L. Karst, *Belonging to America: Equal Citizenship and the Constitution* (New Haven: Yale University Press, 1989), ix.

61. Kwame Anthony Appiah, "Citizenship in Theory and Practice: A Response to Charles Kesler," in *Immigration and Citizenship*, ed. Pickus, 46.

62. Skerry, *Mexican-Americans*, 6.

EPILOGUE

1. "Mexico: Fox for Open Borders," *Migration News* 7, no. 9 (September 2000), http://www.migration.ucdavis.edu/mn/index.php; Jeff Faux, "Time for a New Deal with Mexico," *American Prospect* 11, no. 22 (October 23, 2000): 18–21; Robert S. Leiken, "With a Friend Like Fox," *Foreign Affairs* 80, no. 5 (September/October 2001): 91–104; "Migrants Don't Want Citizenship, Says Fox," *Los Angeles Times*, January 10, 2004.

2. Stewart J. Lawrence, "The Right Has Room to Woo Latinos," *Los Angeles Times*, February 11, 2001, sec. M, p. 5.

3. Gregory Rodriguez, "Latino Leadership Matures," *Los Angeles Times*, February 5, 1999, Sec. B, p. 9. See also Rodriguez, "Will 'Generation Mex' Politicians break from Their Elders?" *Los Angeles Times*, June 20, 1999, sec. M, p. 6.

4. Robert S. Leiken, personal correspondence with the author, August 2, 2000. See Leiken, *Melting Border: Mexico and Mexican Communities in the United States* (Washington, DC: Center for Equal Opportunity, 2000); Smith, "Transnational Migration, Assimilation, and Political Community."

5. Leiken, personal correspondence Leiken, *The Melting Border*. See also Rudolfo de la Garza and Louis DeSipio, "Interests and Passions: Mexican Americans' Attitudes toward Mexico and Issues Shaping U.S.-Mexico Relations," *International Migration Review* 32 (summer 1998): 401–22.

6. See Peter Skerry, "Immigrants and Trip-Wires: Dilemmas of Immigration Policy," unpublished paper on file with author. Also see Gary Freeman, "Modes of Immigration Politics in Liberal Democratic States," *International Migration Review* 29 (winter 1995): 881–902.

7. Paul Donnelly, "Make a Green Card the Real Payoff for Guest Workers," *Los Angeles Times*, February 12, 2001, sec. B, p. 7.

8. "The relevant principle here is not mutual aid but political justice," explains the political philosopher Michael Walzer. "As participants in our economy and subjects of our law, illegal aliens ought to be able to regard themselves as potential or future participants in politics as well. . . . [U]nless they have that choice, their other choices cannot be taken as so many signs of their acquiescence to the economy and law. . . . [I]f they do have that choice, the local economy and law are likely to look different" (*Spheres of Justice* [New York: Basic Books, 1987], 60–61). See also the exchange between Paul Donnelly and T. Alexander Aleinikoff: Donnelly, "The End of Ellis Island: Bush Abandons the American Immigrant Ideal while Democrats Dither," *The American Prospect*, April 4, 2001; Aleinikoff, "A Response: toward a New U.S.-Mexican Immigration Relationship— Logic and Legality," *The American Prospect*, April 26, 2001.

9. This approach has certain similarities with one advocated by Teddy Roosevelt. He condemned as pernicious a policy of what he called "let alone"; he believed that the federal government had to prevent resentment from developing among new arrivals by

actively incorporating them into American political life. Roosevelt proposed giving illiterate aliens chance to learn English and to work and deporting those who did not make sufficient progress. Such a measure is unduly harsh and unlikely to pass congressional or legal muster today. It is in the national interest to preserve a safety net of programs for immigrants. A more appropriate solution would be for the benefits provided to immigrants to change depending on their membership status.

10. The legal scholar Hiroshi Motomura compares this "transition" model to a "contract" model, in which immigrants accept certain conditions as part of a bargain, such as limits on welfare eligibility, and to an "affiliation" model that "recognizes a permanent approximation of citizenship." The transition model, by contrast, has both probationary and integrative dimensions that "are consistent and have a common basis: the idea that permanent residence is a transition to naturalization and citizenship." Motomura, "Alienage Classifications in a Nation of Immigrants," 206–18.

11. William Galston, "Political Knowledge, Political Engagement, and Civic Education," *Annual Review of Political Science* 4 (2001): 223–26.

12. Charles Merriam, *The Making of Citizens: A Comparative Study of Methods of Civic Training* (Chicago: University of Chicago Press, 1931), 301. See also Richard M. Merelman, "Symbols as Substance in National Civics Standards," *PS: Political Science & Politics* 29 (March 1996): 53–57. The constitutional scholar William F. Harris II used the phrase "citizen of the text" in his remarks at an Independence Hall naturalization ceremony, U.S. District Court, Philadelphia, July 2, 1990 (on file with author).

13. Fonte, "We Need a Patriotic Assimilation Policy."

14. Gary E. Rubin, personal correspondence with author, July 28, 1997. See also Rubin, *The War on Immigration: Why It's Hurting America* (New York: NYANA Policy Series, 1997).

15. Alan Wolfe, "The Return of the Melting Pot," *The New Republic*, December 31, 1990, 27–34. See also Wolfe, *Whose Keeper? Social Science and Moral Obligation* (Berkeley: University of California Press, 1989), 246–56.

16. Ueda, "Naturalization and Citizenship," 745.

17. Ueda, *Postwar Immigrant America*, 52.

18. Eduardo Aguirre, "Civic Integration—Citizenship after 9/11," November 13, 2003, Nixon Center, Washington, DC, http://uscis.gov/graphics/aboutus/congress/testimonies/2003/EA111303.pdf; Thomas Modzelesky, "U.S. Citizenship Policy after September 11," *Nixon Center Program Brief* 9, no. 26, 2003 (see especially the summary of comments made by Alfonso Aguilar, chief of the Office of Citizenship).

19. See Manhattan Institute for Policy Research and the National Immigration Forum, "New Americans Citizenship Initiative," May 2003, memo on file with the author; Modzelesky, "U.S. Citizenship Policy"; Matthew Spalding, "Strengthen Citizenship in INS Reform," *Heritage Foundation Executive Memorandum*, no. 809, April 8, 2002; Tamar Jacoby, "How to Turn More Immigrants into Americans," *New York Sun*, July 3, 2002, http://www.manhattan-institute.org/html/_nys-how_to_turn.htm.

20. DeSipio, "Making Citizens or Good Citizens?" 201–11, 197–99; de la Garza and DeSipio, "Save the Baby, Change the Bathwater, and Scrub the Tub."

21. Elshtain, *Jane Addams and the Dream of Democracy*, 203. Although Elshtain is describing Addams's view of the city in this passage, she applies this characterization especially to the "immigrant city"; it is a description that encompasses much of Kellor's views as well.

22. Amitai Etzioni, "On Ending Nationalism," *International Politics and Society* 2 (2001): 149. On social capital, see Putnam, *Bowling Alone*; Fukuyama, *The Great Disruption*; Theda

Skocpol, "Associations without Members," *The American Prospect* 10, no. 45 (July 1, 1999). On the limits of social capital, see Mark Warren, *Dry Bones Rattling: Community Building to Revitalize American Democracy* (Princeton: Princeton University Press, 2001).

23. Peter Skerry's article "Citizenship Begins at Home" is the clearest expression of the argument that immigrants need structures and strategies to become fully integrated into American society and public life. The example of the Resurrection Project and the quote from the pastor come from this article. On the St. Paul example, see Boyte and O'Donoghue, "The Jane Addams School for Democracy," and Boyte, *Everyday Politics*, chap. 6. Boyte's work also addresses immigrants' needs for more than material benefits— "I was often struck by how many older Hmong women voice the desire to 'learn how to act in public' in the United States," he writes—and he focuses as well on the mutual process of education about public engagement that the Addams School fosters between immigrants and native-born citizens.

24. See Noah Pickus and Suzanne Shanahan, "The Changing Boundaries of Membership," unpublished essay on file with author. See also Robert O. Keohane, "Globalization and Changes in Sovereignty," discussion paper prepared for the John F. Kennedy School's "Visions of Governance for the Twenty-First Century" project, June 10, 1997, on file with author.

25. Christopher Lasch, *The Revolt of the Elite and the Betrayal of Democracy* (New York: W. W. Norton, 1995), 6.

26. Mark Fritz, "Pledging Multiple Allegiances," *Los Angeles Times*, April 6, 1998, 1.

27. Sandel, *Democracy's Discontent*, 330–33.

28. See Albert O. Hirschman, *Exit, Voice, and Loyalty* (Cambridge, MA: Harvard University Press, 1970); Martin, "New Rules on Dual Nationality for a Democratizing Globe."

29. Fritz, "Pledging Multiple Allegiances."

30. Martin, "New Rules on Dual Nationality for a Democratizing Globe." Martin also suggests, and I agree, that the possibility of a dual citizenship should be maintained only so long as continued ties to the home country remain vital. "Respecting the complexity of loyalty and identity requires no greater acceptance of plural nationalities than such notions of loyalty and identity can sustain," Martin writes. "The immigrant generation can certainly be expected to feel those contradictory pulls, and so may its children, raised around a heart where accounts of the old country were frequently shared, perhaps in that country's tongue. But as generational distance increases, multiple formal nationalities will usually lose any claim to reflect real identification. Any new global rules should reflect this reality and avoid the perpetuation of nationality after genuine links have been broken."

31. Frances Stead Sellers, "A Citizen on Paper Has No Weight," *Washington Post*, January 19, 2003, sec. B, p. 1. Sellers was prompted to register to vote, she says, because of Yaser Esam Hamdi, the American-born Taliban fighter and Saudi citizen who was "trying to reap the benefits of American citizenship without having shouldered any of its responsibilities."

32. For the complexities involved in swearing allegiance to the Constitution, see Levinson, *Constitutional Faith*, chap. 4. For the commission's language, see U.S. Commission on Immigration Reform, *Becoming an American*, 51, and for several alternative versions of a revised oath, see Pickus, *Becoming American, America Becoming*, 31–32. See

also testimony of Lawrence Fuchs, U.S. Senate Committee on the Judiciary Subcommittee on Immigration, October 22, 1996; Schuck, "Plural Citizenships," 176–81, 190; Spiro, "Dual Nationality and the Meaning of Citizenship," 1479–80; David Martin, "The Civic Republican Ideal for Citizenship and for Our Common Life," *Virginia Journal of International Law* 35, no. 1 (fall 1994): 302. One version of the oath that circulated internally at the Bureau of Immigration and Citizenship Services made plural the object of allegiance. It required allegiance to "the United States, its Constitution, and its laws" (Miller, "Swearing Oaths").

Index

Note: Parenthetical page numbers indicate discussions of legal cases identified in notes.

DATE DUE

3-28-09			
			Printed in USA

HIGHSMITH #45230